PYRRHO, HIS ANTECEDENTS, AND HIS LEGACY

Pyrrho, his Antecedents, and his Legacy

RICHARD BETT

OXFORD

UNIVERSITY PRESS

OXFORD
UNIVERSITY PRESS

Great Clarendon Street, Oxford OX2 6DP

Oxford University Press is a department of the University of Oxford.
It furthers the University's objective of excellence in research, scholarship,
and education by publishing worldwide in

Oxford New York

Athens Auckland Bangkok Bogotá Buenos Aires Calcutta
Cape Town Chennai Dar es Salaam Delhi Florence Hong Kong Istanbul
Karachi Kuala Lumpur Madrid Melbourne Mexico City Mumbai
Nairobi Paris São Paulo Singapore Taipei Tokyo Toronto Warsaw

and associated companies in Berlin Ibadan

Oxford is a registered trade mark of Oxford University Press
in the UK and in certain other countries

Published in the United States
by Oxford University Press Inc., New York

British Library Cataloguing in Publication Data

Data available

Library of Congress Cataloging-in-Publication Data
Bett, Richard Arnot Home.
Pyrrho, his antecedents, and his legacy/Richard Bett.
p. cm.
Includes bibliographical references and indexes.
1. Pyrrhon, of Elis.   2. Skeptics (Greek philosophy)   I. Title.
B613.B48 2000   186′.1—dc21   00-025843
ISBN 0–19–825065–7

1 3 5 7 9 10 8 6 4 2

Typeset in Times by
Cambrian Typesetters, Frimley, Surrey
Printed in Great Britain
on acid-free paper by
T. J. International Ltd.
Padstow, Cornwall

PREFACE

Pyrrhonism is not a single philosophical outlook; the Pyrrhonian tradition encompassed (at least) three distinct outlooks during its long and discontinuous history. Because of this variety, a complicated story needs to be told about the transitions between one phase of the tradition and the next—a story that, while paying attention to the differences between the phases, also explains how Pyrrhonism could none the less have seemed to its participants to be a unitary tradition. And because the earliest phase of Pyrrhonism—the position of Pyrrho himself—is significantly different from what has generally been thought of as *the* Pyrrhonist outlook—namely, the sceptical outlook of Sextus Empiricus' *Outlines of Pyrrhonism*—a new story also needs to be told about the origins and antecedents of the tradition; it is not hard to identify elements in early Greek philosophy that can broadly be called sceptical, but the prehistory of Pyrrhonism has little or nothing to do with these.

These are the main conclusions argued for in this book. I am aware that they are controversial; my arguments will certainly not put an end to disagreements in this area. I will be satisfied if the book changes some minds, and if it leads, more generally, to a rethinking of standard views about Pyrrhonism and its place in Greek philosophy.

The book in its present form was written, in the intervals between other responsibilities, during 1996, 1997, and 1998. But the project of which it is the culmination goes back much further than that. Its starting point was a paper about Pyrrho and his predecessors that I presented to the Princeton Classical Philosophy Colloquium in December 1991. The reactions to that paper convinced me of two things: first, that I had got hold of a topic of considerable interest, and, secondly, that my current ideas on this topic were hopelessly inadequate. That paper was never published (though it has occasionally been referred to in print by members of the colloquium audience). But the rethinking that followed it led to several sizeable articles a couple of years later; and by that point I felt myself ready to start putting my ideas into the form of a book.

As it happened, the fulfilment of this project was delayed for another couple of years by an invitation to write a different book: a translation of, introduction to, and commentary on Sextus Empiricus' *Against the Ethicists* for the Clarendon Later Ancient Philosophers series. However, the work on that volume helped to solidify my ideas for the present volume in ways that I could not have anticipated. I came to the conclusion that the version of Pyrrhonism represented in *Against the Ethicists* (and in a few other scanty sources) was different from, and earlier than, the version to be found in most of Sextus. Moreover, though I did not pursue this line of thought in the commentary, this earlier Pyrrhonism promised to provide the crucial missing link between the ideas of Pyrrho himself and the later Pyrrhonism to which Sextus mostly adheres. So by the time I had finished the Sextus volume, my conception of the shape of this book's argument was much clearer than it had been. Indeed, for this reason the Sextus volume—which is appearing in paperback at around the same time as this book first appears—can be thought of as in a certain sense a companion to this one. In my own mind, in any case, this book is a natural sequel to the Sextus volume; and I began work on it in earnest almost as soon as the previous one was out of my hands.

I have many people to thank. First, I thank the audience at the 1991 Princeton colloquium (an especially high-powered audience, I might add, since the colloquium that year coincided with a memorial service for the recently deceased Gregory Vlastos) for pushing me to rethink my fledgling ideas. In particular, I thank Julia Annas, who was my commentator on that occasion. She more than anyone else gave me a sense of what a decent treatment of the subject might look like—and how far that initial paper was from filling the bill. In addition, her support and encouragement of my work—despite continuing and fundamental disagreements, which will undoubtedly extend to the present volume—have made an important difference at several other points in the intervening years; her dealings with me have been a truly inspiring model of constructive scholarly engagement.

More recently, I have presented parts of this material at several other meetings: at a conference on scepticism in Helsinki in 1996, at the Society for Ancient Greek Philosophy in 1997, at a conference on ancient epistemology in Chicago in the spring of 1998, and at Harvard, in conjunction with the Boston Area Colloquium in Ancient Philosophy, in the autumn of 1998. I thank the audiences at all these venues; invariably I learned a great deal from their questions and comments. I would like to single out James Allen and Eric Lewis, who served as commentators at Chicago and Harvard respectively, as well as Erik Curiel, Mary Louise Gill, Emidio Spinelli, and Nicholas White. I wish to emphasize, however, that my debts on these occasions extended well beyond the individuals just named.

I spent the academic year of 1994/5 at the Center for Hellenic Studies in Washington, DC. I was working at the time on Sextus' *Against the Ethicists*. However, for the reasons explained above, that work was also enormously beneficial in the development of my ideas for this book. I am therefore happy to repeat my gratitude to the Center (already on record in the preface to the Sextus volume), and especially to its then and current Directors, Deborah Boedeker and Kurt Raaflaub.

Tad Brennan wrote extensive and characteristically hard-hitting comments on an early version of Chapters 1 and 2, which proved extremely helpful. He forced me to modify my position in several places, and to clarify or expand upon it in many others. I am sure that he will not be happy with the result; I am equally sure that the book is much better because of his intervention, and I thank him for that. (A version of some of these comments, directed against one of my earlier articles (Bett 1994*a*), was subsequently published as 'Pyrrho on the Criterion', *Ancient Philosophy*, 18 (1998), 417–34, to which parts of Chapter 1 can be regarded as a reply.) More recently, the comments of two other anonymous readers of the entire manuscript, one for Oxford University Press and the other for Princeton University Press, prompted improvements on numerous points of detail.

Finally, I must record my debt to Fernanda Decleva Caizzi, whose pioneering work on Pyrrho and early Pyrrhonism has been absolutely essential to all subsequent study. I refer to her work in footnotes—sometimes in agreement, sometimes in disagreement—probably more than to that of any other scholar. I am pretty sure that this project would not even have begun in the absence of her edition of the fragments and testimonia relating to Pyrrho, to say nothing of her many important articles. So far, our acquaintance has been limited to an occasional exchange of offprints. But I none the less feel that I owe her as much as anyone else I have named.

This book makes use of material from several already published (or in some cases, as of the time of writing, soon to be published) articles. In some cases this material has been substantially reworked, while in others it reappears here with little alteration. I am grateful for permissions; the details are as follows.

Parts of Chapter 1 (especially Sects. 1–4) are a reworking of material from 'Aristocles on Timon on Pyrrho: The Text, its Logic and its Credibility', *Oxford Studies in Ancient Philosophy*, 12 (1994), 137–81, ed. C. C. W. Taylor. By permission of Oxford University Press.

Sections 5 and 6 of Chapter 2 are a reworking of material from 'What did Pyrrho Think about "The Nature of the Divine and the Good"?', *Phronesis*, 39 (1994), 303–37. By permission of Van Gorcum, then the publisher of the journal.

Much of Chapter 4 (especially Sects. 1–3, 6) is a reworking of material from 'What does Pyrrhonism have to do with Pyrrho?', in J. Sihvola (ed.), *Ancient Scepticism and the Sceptical Tradition* (Acta Philosophica Fennica, 64, Helsinki: The Philosophical Society of Finland, 2000). By permission of the Philosophical Society of Finland.

Parts of Chapter 3 (especially Sects. 2, 3, 5, 7, 8) draw on material from 'On the Pre-History of Pyrrhonism', *Proceedings of the Boston Area Colloquium in Ancient Philosophy*, 15 (1999), to be published by Brill.

Part of Chapter 3, Section 2, draws on material from 'Reactions to Aristotle in the Greek Sceptical Traditions', *Méthexis: International Journal for Ancient Philosophy*, 12 (1999). By permission of the editorial committee of the journal.

This book takes no account of Maria Chiesara's edition of the fragments of Aristocles in the Oxford monographs series. I have been told, and I would anyway have guessed, that this edition contains much that would have been highly pertinent to my analysis, especially in Chapter 1, of the passage of Aristocles dealing with Pyrrho. But as of the time of writing, this volume has not yet appeared in print, and I have not seen the typescript. I was also unable to take account of Ramón Román Alcalá, *El escepticismo antiguo: Posibilidad del conocimento y búsqueda de la felicidad* (Córdoba: Universidad de Córdoba, Serie Monografia 213), most of which focuses on Pyrrho and his antecedents. I first became aware of the existence of this volume from a notice in *Phronesis* in 1997. But it proved extremely difficult to get my hands on a copy in the United States; an interlibrary loan request failed to yield a result until very recently, by which time my manuscript was complete and about to be sent off. I hope, however, that Alcalá's book will also help to stimulate interest in the questions with which we are both concerned.

R.B.

July 1999

CONTENTS

ABBREVIATIONS

DC   F. Decleva Caizzi, *Pirrone: Testimonianze* (Naples: Bibliopolis, 1981). References are sometimes to texts, sometimes to the editor's discussion. In the former case, the number of the text is cited, preceded by T (e.g. T3); in the latter case citations are by page number.

DK   H. Diels and W. Kranz, *Die Fragmente der Vorsokratiker* (6th edn.; Berlin: Weidmann, 1951).

LS   A. Long and D. Sedley, *The Hellenistic Philosophers* (Cambridge: Cambridge University Press, 1987). Citations are by volume and page number when the reference is to the editors' discussion, by section number plus letter (e.g. 1F) when the reference is to a specific text.

LSJ   H. Liddell, R. Scott, and H. Jones, *Greek–English Lexicon* (9th edn; Oxford: Clarendon Press, 1968).

Abbreviations for ancient authors, and the titles of ancient works, are given in the *index locorum*.

Introduction

1. Pyrrho, Pyrrhonism, and the current state of scholarship

Very little is known about the life of Pyrrho of Elis. He is generally thought
to have lived from around 365–360 BC until around 275–270 BC.[1] We are told
by Diogenes Laertius (9.61) that he studied with a certain 'Bryson son of
Stilpo'; but it is very doubtful that much credence should be placed in, or that
much information can be derived from, this report.[2] We are also told by
Diogenes that he learned from Anaxarchus of Abdera, and accompanied him
to India with Alexander's expedition; and this is more credible. The first point
is confirmed by the Peripatetic Aristocles (in Eusebius, *Praep. evang.*
XIV.18.27), in a passage that will be a major focus of attention for much of
this book. In addition, a range of authors place Anaxarchus with Alexander;[3]
besides Diogenes, Sextus Empiricus (*M* 1. 281–2) and Plutarch (*Alex. fort.
virt.* 331e) both report an association between Pyrrho and Alexander; and
Diogenes recounts two anecdotes connecting Anaxarchus and Pyrrho (9.63),
independently of his initial mention of their association. According to
Diogenes, Pyrrho acquired his philosophy as a result of meeting some 'naked
wise men' (*gumnosophistai*) while on his Indian travels; we shall discuss the
plausibility of this later—as well as the nature of his philosophical links with
Anaxarchus and with a number of other figures (Chapter 3). He wrote nothing, except perhaps a poem honouring Alexander.[4] On returning to Greece,

---

[1] For the evidence see von Fritz (1963).

[2] If we assume that Stilpo is the Megarian of that name, the text as it stands is extremely
difficult to credit; Pyrrho and Stilpo were rough contemporaries, so it is scarcely possible that a
son of Stilpo could have taught Pyrrho. For this reason Nietzsche (and independently Röper)
proposed altering the text to 'Bryson or Stilpo' (*Brusōnos ē Stilpōnos* for *Brusōnos tou
Stilpōnos*); but Stilpo himself is still, for chronological reasons, implausible as a teacher of
Pyrrho. The Suda (s.v. Pyrrho) also names a certain Bryson as teacher of Pyrrho (DC T1B, cf.
T2). But the evidence on Bryson is confusing, and may have conflated two or more people of
the same name; in any case, we know virtually nothing about him (or them). For a survey of the
literature on Bryson, see Giannantoni (1990: iv, Note 10). Finally, the report may well be simply
the product of later authors anxious to construct 'successions' of philosophers among whom
they perceived common ground; for this view see LS ii. 1–2, Hankinson (1995: 58–9), and for
more on the topic see below, Ch. 3, Sect. 9.

[3] See the texts collected in DK 72.

[4] Sextus mentions this poem, and says that Pyrrho was rewarded for it with ten thousand
gold pieces (*M* 1.282); Plutarch also mentions the gold pieces (*Alex. fort. virt.* 331e), though
without saying why he received them. According to Diogenes Laertius (1.16, 9.102) and
Aristocles (in Eusebius, *Praep. evang.* XIV.18.2), there were no writings by Pyrrho. But two of

however, he appears to have attracted numerous followers; the most notable is Timon of Phlius, on whom more below, but the sources mention several other names. He also appears to have achieved some celebrity in his native city. Pausanias (6.24,5) reports seeing a statue of him in the marketplace; perhaps less reliably, Diogenes (9.64) says that he was made high priest, and that in honour of him philosophers were made exempt from taxation.[5]

Pyrrho was adopted as a philosophical figurehead by a group of sceptics who lived several centuries later than himself. No plausible evidence suggests that his ideas or way of life continued to attract a following after Timon and other immediate disciples.[6] But in the first century BC a new philosophical movement, claiming inspiration from Pyrrho, was started by a certain Aenesidemus of Cnossos; and it is to this Pyrrhonist tradition that Sextus Empiricus, of whom we have voluminous surviving works, later belonged. The scepticism of this later Pyrrhonist tradition has received much scholarly attention, particularly in recent years. But the views of Pyrrho himself have received much less attention. Pyrrho has typically been assigned a chapter in general studies of ancient scepticism;[7] and in the last two decades of the twentieth century a small body of articles and at least one book were devoted specifically to Pyrrho, as distinct from later Pyrrhonism.[8] What is missing, however, is a study that treats in a thorough fashion *both* the philosophy of Pyrrho himself *and* the nature of the connections between Pyrrho and other philosophers—the later Pyrrhonists who took him as a figurehead, and also those earlier philosophers from whom he himself might have taken inspiration—and that treats these issues in close connection with one another. The aim of the present work is to provide such a study. The result, I hope, will be a comprehensive picture of a subject that is at present poorly understood: the origins and development of the Pyrrhonist tradition.[9]

these three texts say that Pyrrho 'left nothing in writing' (rather than simply that he wrote nothing at all), which would be consistent with his having written a poem that never made it back from Alexander's travels. In any case, it is clearly philosophical writings with which these authors are concerned; and here the verdict is unanimous.

[5] On this text, see further Ch. 2 n. 13.

[6] Diogenes (9.115–16) lists a succession of philosophers stretching from Pyrrho to Sextus and beyond. But not all the authorities he mentions are said to agree on this. In any case, the list is highly suspect; see Glucker (1978: 351–4), Decleva Caizzi (1992a: 177–9). On the possibility of Pyrrho's influence on the early sceptical Academy of Arcesilaus, see the beginning of Ch. 4, Sect. 1.

[7] See e.g. Brochard (1923); Stough (1969); Hankinson (1995).

[8] The book is Conche (1994).

[9] I shall use the terms 'Pyrrhonism', 'Pyrrhonist tradition', etc. to refer generically to the entire discontinuous tradition encompassing Pyrrho himself, together with his immediate followers, as well as Aenesidemus and those after him, including Sextus, who claimed inspiration from Pyrrho. I shall use 'later Pyrrhonism' to refer specifically to Aenesidemus and the movement he started; and I shall occasionally use 'early Pyrrhonism' to refer to Pyrrho and his immediate followers only. (We shall also see in Ch. 4 that later Pyrrhonism itself includes two

2. *Themes and layout*

It is usually supposed that Pyrrhonism takes roughly the following form. The Pyrrhonist—that is, the sceptic—assembles opposing arguments on as wide a range of topics as possible. On placing the arguments, on any given topic, in confrontation with one another, he discovers that they have the feature of *isostheneia*, 'equal strength'; the arguments on one side, he finds, incline him towards acceptance no more and no less than those on the other side. This *isostheneia* also has a counterpart in the 'unresolvable disagreement' (*anepikritos diaphōnia*) that he takes to exist, on any topic you care to name, among philosophers—and perhaps among ordinary people as well. Faced with this unresolvable disagreement, and with his own perception of the 'equal strength' of the arguments, the sceptic finds himself suspending judgement about the real nature of the objects under discussion. If this approach is applied sufficiently broadly—and the sceptic certainly professes to apply it across the board—the result is an entirely general suspension of judgement (*epochē*) about the real nature of things. This suspension of judgement does not prevent things striking the sceptic in certain ways rather than their opposites; honey tastes to him sweet, for example, rather than bitter—at least, if he is not suffering some disease that affects his taste buds, or any other unusual physiological or psychological state. But though he will register the fact that honey tastes to him that way, and will allow this fact to shape his behaviour, he will not take it as in any way indicative of honey's real nature; on that question the existence of equally powerful opposing arguments has driven him to withdraw from any position. Yet this global suspension of judgement about the nature of things itself has an important practical effect; it results in *ataraxia*, 'freedom from worry'—the very goal that philosophers, whether sceptical or not, were generally presumed to be seeking. Most philosophers think that they can attain this tranquil state by discovering the truth about things. But the sceptic sees that it is precisely that ambition that produces turmoil, and that *ataraxia* is to be attained, on the contrary, by relinquishing any such pretensions.

This conception of Pyrrhonism is certainly not false. It, or something like it (for naturally there is room for dispute about some of the details), is the outlook characteristic of the final phase of the Pyrrhonian tradition, the phase represented by Sextus Empiricus' *Outlines of Pyrrhonism*. But was Pyrrhonism always of this form—even as early as Pyrrho himself? Traditionally, the answer has tended to be 'yes'; Pyrrho's own views have been seen as an incipient version of the views expressed in *Outlines of*

distinct and chronologically separable outlooks, which I shall refer to as the 'initial' and the 'terminal' phases of later Pyrrhonism.)

Pyrrhonism—not as fully worked out, perhaps, and not as sensitive to possible objections, but none the less a recognizable specimen of the same outlook. As we shall see, however, a strong case can be made for the conclusion that Pyrrho's own outlook was significantly different from this—so different, in fact, that the term 'sceptic', in the usage of later Pyrrhonism, would not even have been applicable to Pyrrho. Rather than suspending judgement because of the 'equal strength' of incompatible views and perspectives, it looks as if Pyrrho declared reality to be inherently indeterminate, and recommended that we describe the way things are by a form of speech that captures that very indeterminacy. In Sextus' own terms, Pyrrho would thus qualify as a 'dogmatist' rather than as a sceptic.

If this is correct, however, new questions clearly arise. The obvious question is why, if Pyrrho's outlook was substantially different from that of later Pyrrhonists, they were tempted to see in him a forerunner or inspiration. But a second and less obvious question also presents itself if one looks *backwards* from Pyrrho instead of forwards. Scholars have sometimes tried to identify precursors of scepticism among the Presocratics, or more generally among philosophers prior to Pyrrho. However, this search has typically been conducted with later Pyrrhonism, and the traditional view of Pyrrho's relation to the later movement, in mind; the aim has been to detect elements in early Greek philosophy that might be thought to foreshadow Pyrrhonism, where 'Pyrrhonism' is understood primarily as the view familiar to us from Sextus.[10] This may well be of some intrinsic interest. On the other hand, if Pyrrho's outlook was not the same as that of Sextus, this enterprise can no longer be thought to contribute to an understanding of the philosophical antecedents of *Pyrrho*. The early Greek philosophers thus identified may in some sense be viewed as 'precursors' of the later Pyrrhonian sceptics— though not in a sense that is alive to the actual, historical development of the Pyrrhonist tradition; but their relation, if any, to Pyrrho will need to be rethought. Equally, if Pyrrho's ideas differed from those of the later Pyrrhonists, there may be *other* previous philosophers, not previously considered in this context, by whom Pyrrho can plausibly be thought to have been affected. Thus, if we rewrite our account of Pyrrho, our account of the likely influences upon him must also be rewritten, just as much as our account of how he could have been taken as an inspiration by the later Pyrrhonists. Though I am not by any means the first to propose an understanding of Pyrrho that distinguishes him sharply from the later movement that took his name, very little work has been done on either of those tasks.

---

[10] See e.g. Brochard (1923), whose chapters on sceptical elements in pre-Pyrrhonian philosophy are mostly concerned with the kinds of epistemological difficulties that drive much of later Pyrrhonism. And the same is largely true of Hankinson (1995: ch. 3 ('Precursors')), even though he himself is at least partially sympathetic to a non-standard reading of Pyrrho.

Yet, as I suggested, we do not properly grasp Pyrrho's philosophical significance—or even, in the broadest sense, the place of Pyrrhonism as a whole in Greek philosophy—unless we treat in conjunction the question of what his ideas and attitudes were, and the question of how those ideas and attitudes are connected with other philosophical movements before and after him.

Chapter 1 will examine Pyrrho's most general philosophical ideas, and particularly what I shall call the 'indeterminacy thesis'—that is, the thesis mentioned above, that reality is inherently indeterminate—drawing attention to the ways in which these ideas contrast with later Pyrrhonism. Chapter 2 will consider Pyrrho's practical attitudes—the subject with which most of the surviving evidence on Pyrrho has to do—in the light of the conclusions just reached. We shall consider the credibility of, and the motivations behind, the accounts that portray him variously as prudent, as eccentric, and as a lunatic. We shall also consider the question of his reliance on 'appearances' as a guide to how to act; the question of his views, if any, about what a much-discussed fragment of Timon calls 'the nature of the divine and the good'; and the question of Cicero's portrayal of Pyrrho as a severe and forbidding moralist. Again, comparisons and contrasts with later Pyrrhonism will be noted and explored.

Chapter 3 will address the question of Pyrrho's precursors, and the possible influences upon him. A variety of earlier thinkers will be considered for their connections, if any, with Pyrrho. It will be suggested that Presocratic worries about the possibility of knowledge, which have usually been seen as central to the pre-history of Greek scepticism, are of little relevance when it comes to identifying the antecedents of Pyrrho. Far more important are those earlier philosophers who either discuss or advocate views according to which, in some sense, the world around us is indeterminate—most prominently, Plato and the Eleatics. Besides Greek influences, the question of the possible influence of Eastern thought on Pyrrho—as suggested by Diogenes' report about the origin of Pyrrho's philosophy—will be considered.

The fourth and final chapter will address the subsequent phases of Pyrrhonism, and how they can be understood, despite the differences already alluded to, as successors of the ideas of Pyrrho. Though there is plainly at least some common ground, and though the ancient sources nowhere suggest that an exact fit between Pyrrho and the later Pyrrhonists needs to be sought, this issue may be much better understood, I shall argue, if we realize that later Pyrrhonism itself is not monolithic. There is the view expressed in *Outlines of Pyrrhonism*, and in some of the other surviving books of Sextus; there is also the earlier view of Aenesidemus, the originator of later Pyrrhonism. This latter view is known to us in outline from the meagre evidence relating specifically to Aenesidemus; but it, or something closely related to it, is also represented by a book of Sextus himself—namely, *Against the Ethicists*. This view is noticeably distinct from that of *Outlines of Pyrrhonism*. It is also distinct from that of Pyrrho. None the less, it is far easier to see how Pyrrho's ideas might have served as a forerunner to those of Aenesidemus than to see how they might have served as a forerunner to *Outlines of Pyrrhonism*. If I am right, of course, we are now faced with the further question of how the transition might have occurred from the phase represented by Aenesidemus to that represented by *Outlines of Pyrrhonism*. But this too, I shall argue, turns out to be quite comprehensible—much more so, again, than a direct transition from Pyrrho to *Outlines of Pyrrhonism* would have been. Aenesidemus thus represents an intermediate phase in the Pyrrhonist tradition, recognition of which allows us to make sense of developments in that tradition. It would be surprising if Pyrrhonism had not undergone significant changes over some five centuries; the important thing is to recognize the nature of the changes, while still taking into account the degree of continuity implied by the abiding use of the label 'Pyrrhonian' itself.

3. *The evidence and how to approach it*

How is one to determine the views of an ancient philosopher who wrote nothing? Pyrrho is certainly not the only Greek thinker for whom this question arises. But the question is always a difficult one, and it always needs to be answered with careful attention to the details of each individual case. Issues having to do with the credibility of the evidence on Pyrrho will occupy us at many points. Here I consider in a general and preliminary way the nature of our evidence, how it should be handled, and the status of whatever claims we may be prepared to make on its basis.

   Much of what we hear about Pyrrho comes directly or indirectly from his disciple[11] Timon, who wrote numerous poems and prose works. These themselves survive only in fragments and second-hand reports; and many of the fragments are not about the ideas and demeanour of Pyrrho, but are satirical thumbnail sketches of other philosophers. Nevertheless, a considerable body of evidence about Pyrrho is to be derived from Timon (and even the satirical sketches may sometimes be helpful in this regard, in as much as they may

---

[11] A passage of Sextus (*M* 1.53) refers to Timon as the *prophētēs* of Pyrrho's words. *Prophētēs* has generally been taken in the neutral sense 'interpreter' or 'expounder'. But David Blank has recently argued (in Blank 1998: commentary *ad loc.*) that the term is pejorative—and that Sextus has taken it over from the critics of Timon to whom he responds in this passage. Originally it refers to priests or priestesses who interpret and expound the will of the gods, as expressed either in oracles or (as, for example, in Teiresias' case) in a variety of other ways; as applied to philosophers, according to Blank, it retains this original sense 'prophet', but with an ironic or demeaning tone added. In any case, with or without the demeaning tone, 'prophet' fits well the dual role of expositor and devotee of Pyrrho's ideas that Timon was generally thought to have occupied.

suggest what intellectual or other traits Timon understood Pyrrho to have disvalued or, occasionally, valued). Virtually the only other identifiable near-contemporary source is Antigonus of Carystus, a biographer of the mid-third century BC, who is cited frequently in Diogenes' life of Pyrrho, and is also mentioned by Aristocles (in Eusebius, *Praep. evang.* XIV.18.26). Opinions have varied as to the extent to which Diogenes, in this account, is relying on him even when he does not specifically cite him;[12] but clearly he is the source of much, if not most, of the biographical material that has come down to us. Beyond this, a few snippets of information about Pyrrho are ascribed to other early authorities, such as his own follower Philo of Athens (DL 9.67) or Eratosthenes (DL 9.66)—though these too may have been transmitted to us via the medium of Antigonus or Timon. And then there are a number of remarks about him by much later authors who do not name their sources (if any) at all; for this reason alone, it is far from obvious to what extent we should trust them.

If we want, then, to try to reconstruct the ideas and attitudes of Pyrrho, it is above all Timon and Antigonus who would seem to deserve our attention. But now, how are we to tell whether either of these two is portraying Pyrrho accurately? One view of the matter is that the historical Pyrrho, 'Pyrrho as he really was', is simply not accessible to us given that he did not write anything; all we have are the various 'images' of Pyrrho developed by others during and immediately after his lifetime.[13] One might compare the situation with that of Socrates. In recent years there has been a notable decline in confidence about our ability to recover the historical Socrates—beyond, perhaps, a few quirks of behaviour and appearance, and some very general aspects of his philosophical orientation—from the exclusively second-hand evidence at our disposal. Many of us might *prefer* to think of Socrates as having been more like the figure portrayed by Plato than the figure portrayed by Xenophon (let alone Aristophanes); but it is now widely held that there is no non-circular way of arguing for this conclusion. Is our situation with respect to Pyrrho something similar to this?

The answer, I suggest, is that the situation is different in at least two important ways. First, whereas it may be impossible to tell whether Plato's portrait of Socrates is more or less accurate than Xenophon's—or whether both are departures, and equally so, from historical reality—there are clear reasons for

---

[12] Wilamowitz-Moellendorff (1881) thought that almost all the biographical material in the life of Pyrrho, and much of the biographical material in sources other than Diogenes, derived from Antigonus; for a more sceptical view see Long (1978). Long in turn maintains that 'In all probability Antigonus of Carystus and other biographers of Pyrrho drew largely upon the writings of Timon' (p. 70). This may well be true in some instances. However, the parallels between the biographical material on Pyrrho and the fragments of Timon, on which Long relies for this claim, are not always as close as he suggests; I return to this issue in Ch. 2.

[13] For this view, see Ferrari (1981: esp. 339–43); also Ferrari (1968).

treating the evidence of Timon more seriously than that of Antigonus. Secondly, whereas neither Plato nor Xenophon ever simply *summarizes* the philosophy of Socrates, there are reasons for thinking that, in at least one central case, Timon does intend to give us a precise and systematic exposition of the main points of Pyrrho's philosophy. Taken together, these two points suggest an approach to the evidence that allows us to proceed responsibly, yet also promises some results.

First, then, Antigonus' evidence needs to be treated with suspicion. For one thing, he almost certainly lived too late ever to have met Pyrrho.[14] In addition, there is no reason to believe that Antigonus was particularly attuned to philosophical subtleties;[15] even assuming that Pyrrho did behave in roughly the ways Antigonus reports, Antigonus may very well have been insensitive to, and may therefore have failed to convey, whatever philosophical point or basis originally underlay these activities. And finally, it is far from clear that Antigonus was even particularly interested in the accuracy of his account. His lives of philosophers, which Diogenes mentions in numerous other places besides the lives of Pyrrho and Timon, belong to a genre of philosophical biography going back at least to Aristotle's pupil Aristoxenus, in which malicious gossip is often just as important as genuine information concerning activities and doctrines.[16] Moreover, Antigonus was also the author of a work, which has survived, called *historiōn paradoxōn sunagōgē*, 'Collection of Incredible Observations', belonging to the genre sometimes known as 'paradoxography', of which the pseudo-Aristotelian *On Marvellous Things Heard* is probably the example best known to philosophers.[17] Clearly, then, he had a penchant for tall tales, and it is very possible that many of his anecdotes about Pyrrho are pure fabrications.

On at least the first two of these three counts, Timon is to be preferred to Antigonus, and obviously so. Unlike Antigonus, Timon knew Pyrrho personally and was a devoted follower. And we have fragments or reports suggesting that Timon took part in complex philosophical controversies of the

[14] According to Diogenes, he also wrote a life of Timon, mentioning Timon's death at the age of nearly 90 (9.112); this surely makes him too young to have had any personal contact with Pyrrho.

[15] The numerous references to Antigonus of Carystus' lives of philosophers in Diogenes (2.136, 143, 3.66, 4.17, 22, 5.67, 7.12, 9.62, 110, 111, 112) almost all have to do with biographical details; the closest we come to philosophical matters is when Antigonus is reported as saying that Menedemus of Eretria wrote nothing, and so never fixed on any particular doctrine (2.136). (The Antigonus whom Diogenes mentions as having proclaimed himself the pupil of Menedemus (2.141) is not Antigonus of Carystus, but the Macedonian king Antigonus Gonatas.) References to him in Athenaeus are similar, mostly having to do with various philosophers' culinary or sexual preferences (44e, 162e–f, 345c–d, 419e–f, 547d, 563e, 565d–e, 603e, 607e–f).

[16] Fragments of Aristoxenus' lives of Pythagoras, Archytas, Socrates, and Plato are collected in Wehrli (1967–78: ii). The remarks on Socrates and Plato, in particular, are largely scurrilous.

[17] Antigonus' work and other examples of the genre are collected in Giannini (1966).

day—on the divisibility of time and on the legitimacy of proceeding by way of hypotheses—quite independently of his role as advocate for Pyrrho (Sextus, *M* 3.1–2, 6.66, 10.197);[18] unlike in the case of Antigonus, there is no good reason to question Timon's ability even to *comprehend* what Pyrrho said and did. But now, what of the third point? Should we assume that Timon's primary purpose is to report the ideas of Pyrrho in the most historically accurate fashion possible? Or is he engaged in some other enterprise in which, again, accuracy is not the main aim? After all, Timon's *Silloi* (*Lampoons*), from which the majority of our fragments derive, is full of malicious slander about philosophers other than Pyrrho; equally, we may assume that Timon is interested, in the *Silloi* and no doubt in other works of which we know very little, in boosting Pyrrho's reputation to the maximum possible extent. Why, then, should Timon's hyper-complimentary portrait of Pyrrho, coupled with his slander of most other philosophers, be given any more credence than the gossip of Antigonus?

But the cases are not precisely analogous—and this takes us to the other main issue mentioned a few paragraphs back. It is true that most of Timon's fragments derive from works belonging to poetic genres in which it cannot be assumed that literal accuracy is a major goal.[19] But there is at least one crucial case that can plausibly be considered an exception to this rule. Aristocles gives us a summary of an account by Timon of Pyrrho's central ideas, which will be at the centre of our attention in the first chapter. Now, this certainly looks like straightforward doxography. A systematic set of ideas is expounded; and, as Aristocles presents it, this set of ideas is offered by Timon, the person better placed to know than anyone else, as a survey of what Pyrrho thought.[20] If this is indeed the status of the passage, then we are clearly better off with this evidence than with anything offered us by Antigonus—or even, perhaps, than with anything offered us about Socrates by either Plato or Xenophon. Plato and Xenophon never simply say 'Here in a nutshell is Socrates' philosophy' (in fact, with the possible exception of the letters, Plato never simply *says* anything at all in his own person, about Socrates or anyone else); if they had done so, those passages would not have been liable to the same kinds of suspicions as attach to the texts that we in fact have.

There is, however, a complication. It is sometimes suggested that Aristocles'

---

[18] For discussion of this evidence, see Decleva Caizzi (1984*b*); LS ii. 17; and see further below Ch. 3 n. 135.

[19] Besides the *Silloi*, we have a few fragments from another poem in elegiac couplets, *Indalmoi* (*Images*); but we know virtually nothing of its subject matter or general character—on this point see Bett (1994*c*: 329–32). Diogenes, on the authority of Antigonus, says that he also wrote epics and dramatic works, as well as *kinaidoi*, 'obscene poems' (9.110); but nothing of these, if they existed, has survived.

[20] This, at least, is the generally accepted view. It has recently been argued, however, that only one part of the passage fits this description, and that the rest consists of developments of Pyrrho's ideas by Timon himself. I argue against this, and in favour of the standard view, in Ch. 1, Sect. 1.

summary draws on Timon's prose work *Pytho*,[21] and this may well be true; there is at any rate no other obvious candidate among the titles of Timon's works known to us. We are told by Diogenes that in this work Timon gave a lengthy and thorough account (*diasaphei, diexeisin*) of Pyrrho's 'disposition' (*diathesin* (9.67)); and Aristocles himself subsequently refers to it, in criticizing Pyrrho and Timon, in terms that make clear that he too takes it to contain an exposition of Pyrrho's philosophical outlook (*Praep. evang.* XIV.18.14–15). But Aristocles also tells us that *Pytho* was a *dialogue*, and this may reignite suspicion. If *Pytho* was Aristocles' source, then Timon did not, after all, simply tell us what Pyrrho thought, but instead *depicted* Pyrrho in discussion; and, if so, we might conclude that Aristocles is simply naïve in treating Timon's account as a historically accurate account of Pyrrho's philosophy.

But this difficulty is not as serious as it might sound. Let us agree to suppose that Aristocles' summary is based on the dialogue *Pytho*—a hypothesis that has some plausibility, though not any definite evidence in its favour. Now, this dialogue was unlike anything in Plato, and almost anything in Xenophon. It had just two characters, and the other character besides Pyrrho was Timon himself. Timon depicted Pyrrho as expounding his philosophy, and himself as learning from Pyrrho; this is clear, again, from the terms in which Aristocles couches his comments and criticisms. This does not, of course, make *Pytho* any more likely to be a record of an actual conversation than the dialogues of Plato or Xenophon (including the many at which Xenophon claims to have been personally present). However, it *would* be hard to see the point of the exercise unless the *ideas* Timon puts in Pyrrho's mouth were ideas that he took Pyrrho actually to have held; it would be very odd to have 'Pyrrho' expounding ideas that were in fact Timon's own, deliberately projected onto Pyrrho, given that Timon himself is also a character in the discussion, presented as the *recipient* of these ideas. In the one passage of Xenophon where he himself actually appears speaking to Socrates (*Mem.* 1.3.8–13)—a frank discussion of the perils of sexual attraction—the sentiments Socrates is made to express are clearly sentiments that he, Xenophon, regards as a model, and a model that he took to be exemplified in the real person Socrates. One of the reasons why it is tempting to suppose that Plato often purposely puts into Socrates' mouth ideas that are in fact his own, perhaps originally inspired by ideas of the historical Socrates but going far beyond them, is that Plato himself never appears in the dialogues as an interlocutor; if he had done so, our ideas about the historicity of his portrait of Socrates—or, at least, our ideas about his *intentions* in this regard—would no doubt be rather different.

There is, then, good reason to suppose that one central text, whether or not it is based a portion of the dialogue *Pytho*, gives us Pyrrho's ideas as Timon

---

[21] This is conjectured by Ferrari (1968); Long (1978: 83 n. 6); DC 220; LS ii. 6.

understood them, and not any kind of *intentional* misrepresentation such as Plato and, to a lesser extent, Xenophon may be suspected of committing in the case of Socrates.[22] This of course leaves open the possibility that Timon may have misunderstood Pyrrho, or that he may *unconsciously* have projected onto Pyrrho ideas that were in fact his own developments of things Pyrrho said. On the other hand, as noted earlier, he enjoyed a close and extended acquaintance with Pyrrho, and he was not devoid of philosophical acumen; so there is no specific basis for suspicion here.[23] Still, it is important to keep in mind that what we have, even in this case, is Pyrrho *as Timon understood him*, and not the very words of Pyrrho himself. But even so, it is clear that 'Pyrrho as Timon understood him' is inherently a great deal more trustworthy than the anecdotes of Antigonus. Most scholars place Aristocles' summary of Timon at the centre of their interpretation of Pyrrho; though there will be more to say, at the beginning of Chapter 1, about the credibility of this text, the considerations just offered already make clear that they are right to do so.

This text, then, gives us a certain core of ideas around which it is best to proceed, in trying to reconstruct Pyrrho's philosophy. I therefore begin, in the first chapter, with a close analysis of it. Only *after* this is in place is it appropriate to take into account the remainder of the evidence concerning Pyrrho; and the latter evidence always needs to be evaluated in relation to this central core. We have already mentioned difficulties with the biographical evidence from Antigonus. But the more 'literary' aspects of Timon's portrait of Pyrrho—the verse fragments from the *Silloi* and the *Indalmoi*, in which Pyrrho is elevated to superhuman status—are doubtless also somewhat fictional. Whatever the exact context in which these poems were written, the point is plainly to defend and to glorify Pyrrho, and to denigrate other philosophers by comparison, in the face of actual or potential attacks from other movements.[24] In the service of that end, and given the highly charged

[22] I say that Xenophon does this to a lesser extent because the *Memorabilia* do not consist purely of dialogues; they are also full of extended remarks by Xenophon as author, in which he tells us something about Socrates' personality, ideas, or behaviour. Xenophon may indulge in some idealization in these passages; but even if so, I take it that he is giving us an idealized version of Socrates as he remembers him. (Again, though, Xenophon never offers a concise account of what he takes to be the central points in Socrates' philosophy, as Timon here purports to do for Pyrrho's philosophy.)

[23] Pyrrho and Timon appear to have been somewhat different in temperament; most obviously, Pyrrho seems, from Timon's own portrait of him, to have been uninterested in argument or controversy (philosophical or otherwise), whereas Timon seems to have relished it. But I see no reason to believe that this difference in itself created an obstacle to Timon's *comprehension* of Pyrrho's ideas—even if it may have stood in the way of Timon's own *attainment* of the tranquillity he so strikingly attributes to Pyrrho.

[24] This point is made by Frede (1973: 806). But Frede seems to conclude that Timon's evidence as a whole is suspect, even though he earlier *distinguished* Aristocles' summary from the other evidence from Timon, suggesting—more or less as I have just done—that the former is more trustworthy, as a source of information about Pyrrho, than the latter.

polemical tone, exaggeration of Pyrrho's accomplishments, and attribution to him of attitudes and ideas that, in Timon's own view, show him in the best possible light, but which extend beyond anything he actually said, would not be unexpected. Even here, though, there is an obvious connection with Pyrrho himself; and for this reason it makes sense to prefer the evidence of Timon as a whole over that of Antigonus, and to judge the latter, where possible, against the former. Timon's portrait of Pyrrho is presumably constructed in the light of ideals that he had learned, or took himself to have learned, from Pyrrho; it thus represents the kind of outlook or demeanour that Timon, following Pyrrho, thinks one should strive for. To the extent that elements in this portrait can be plausibly linked to elements in Aristocles' summary (and, as I shall argue, this can generally be done), we have all the more reason to take them seriously. None the less, it has to be admitted that we may not be able fully to disentangle those elements that genuinely belonged to Pyrrho himself from those elaborated by Timon on the basis of hints suggested to him by Pyrrho. (For this reason I shall sometimes speak generically of 'early Pyrrhonism' rather than simply of Pyrrho.)

To conclude, there is reason for some limited optimism about our prospects for recovering the philosophy of Pyrrho. But clearly, all the evidence has to be handled carefully, and with an eye to its sources and to the motivations of its authors. And, even if we do so, there is clearly no prospect of our being able to *establish* the correctness of any comprehensive interpretation of Pyrrho's philosophy. Probably such a goal is out of reach for any ancient philosopher, or even for most modern ones; but the paucity and the varied quality of the evidence relating to Pyrrho make it particularly obvious, in this case, that certainty is not to be attained. Considering the merits of different interpretations is, rather, a matter of assessing competing probabilities. My aim, therefore, is necessarily more modest: to persuade the reader that my own interpretation is more probable than the alternatives.

In the first instance, this has to be done by looking at the evidence concerning Pyrrho himself; and this task will occupy the first two chapters. However, the business of interpreting Pyrrho's philosophy should not be considered to end there—as if the rest of the book was devoted to a quite distinct set of topics. For another way to assess the merits of an interpretation of some philosopher, besides comparing it with the direct evidence available, is to see how well it succeeds in making sense of the subject's position in the history of philosophy. For this reason, then, Chapters 3 and 4, in which I consider, respectively, Pyrrho's antecedents and the later Pyrrhonist movement, should be considered *part* of the case for my interpretation of Pyrrho's philosophy, and not merely as an adjunct to it. I shall approach these topics by asking what is the most plausible account of the influences on Pyrrho, and of his own influence on the later Pyrrhonists, *if* the interpretation offered in Chapters 1 and 2 is accepted. However, if the accounts I develop of these matters are themselves historically and philosophically satisfying, then this very fact may be taken as further support for the interpretation of Pyrrho's philosophy with which they start; or, at the very least, it may serve to rebut the possible objection that Pyrrho *cannot* have thought what I claim that he thought, because that would make no sense given his antecedents or (more likely) given his legacy. The whole volume should be seen, then, as a kind of exercise in reflective equilibrium. The totality of the considerations bearing upon our understanding of Pyrrho need to be evaluated against one another; the better they all fit together with one another, the more the entire resulting picture is recommended. Again, this is certainly not proof, but it is the best outcome available in the circumstances. And again, *this* is not something for which we need to apologize; for the situation is no different in kind in the case of a great many ancient philosophers. The nature of the evidence makes the task difficult and hazardous—which is why we need to cast our net as widely as possible. However, given the importance of Pyrrho as an emblem for a whole movement—a movement with far-reaching effects in the history of philosophy—the attempt to make sense of him, even given the difficulties, is surely worthwhile.

Pyrrho the Non-Sceptic

Was Pyrrho a sceptic according to the later Pyrrhonist mould? It must be admitted that some evidence seems to support this verdict; some texts do speak of Pyrrho and Sextus in the same breath, and a number do attribute to Pyrrho himself very much the same kind of outlook as we find in later Pyrrhonism. On the other hand, none of these texts predates the revival of Pyrrho by Aenesidemus; thus it is at least possible that this interpretation of Pyrrho results from anachronistically reading back onto Pyrrho himself ideas that in fact appeared only much later. If we want, then, to determine what was the philosophy of Pyrrho himself, and not simply assume that it was the same as that of the later Pyrrhonists, we need to try to restrict ourselves to evidence that is free from any such contamination. In this first chapter I argue that this can indeed be done, and that this untainted evidence, derived from Timon, suggests that Pyrrho's own position was by no means the same as the later Pyrrhonism familiar to us from Sextus' *Outlines of Pyrrhonism*. Again, in the nature of the case, we cannot hope for certainty on this matter; but I try to show that the probabilities are strongly on the side of this conclusion. And if this is correct, I contend, then the evidence that runs together Pyrrho and the later Pyrrhonists is indeed liable to the charge of anachronism, and should carry no weight. What this chapter amounts to, then, is the case for a non-sceptical Pyrrho.

1. The Aristocles passage and its importance

We will be occupied for much of the time with just one text, the centrality of which has already been emphasized in the Introduction. This is a short extract from book VIII of the *Peri philosophias* (*On Philosophy*) by the Peripatetic Aristocles of Messene, and it is the only text to offer anything like a general summary of Pyrrho's philosophy. This work survives only in fragments; passages on Pyrrhonism and on numerous other philosophies are quoted, for his own anti-pagan purposes, by Eusebius, the fourth-century bishop of Caesarea, in his *Praeparatio evangelica*. Aristocles himself appears to have lived in the late first century BC, or perhaps in the early first century AD; he speaks of Aenesidemus as having 'yesterday and the day before' (*echthes kai prōēn* (XIV.18.29)) revived the thought of Pyrrho—which had previously been unnoticed since the time of Pyrrho himself—and Aenesidemus may with fair reliability be dated in the first half of the first century BC.[1] In any case, Aenesidemus is the only Pyrrhonist, other than Pyrrho and Timon themselves, of whom Aristocles shows any cognizance; he appears to know nothing of the extended *tradition* of Pyrrhonian scepticism in which Sextus situates himself. Even more important for our purposes, the passage dealing specifically with the thought of Pyrrho (XIV.18.1–5) gives the strong impression of being uncontaminated by any later phase of Pyrrhonism, either that of Aenesidemus or that of Sextus. For one thing, Aristocles is very explicit that he is reproducing a passage from the writings of Timon (and we shall return to this point in a moment); for another, as commentators have noticed, several of the important terms in the passage are unparalleled in the works of Sextus—or, we might add, in the surviving evidence on Aenesidemus—but were in currency prior to Timon's day.[2] Since it is quite clearly the single most important text for anyone hoping to reconstruct the thought of Pyrrho,[3] the passage has been minutely examined by many scholars; I shall try to avoid scholarly wrangling as much as possible, but the passage cannot be seriously discussed without engaging in this at least to some extent.[4]

For convenience, I begin with a translation of the whole passage. However, it must be noted immediately that, even in the act of translating, one is forced to take a stand on numerous controversial issues. These matters will be discussed below; but the reader should be aware from the start that the English version that follows is not a neutral rendering of what the text says— there can be no such thing.

---

[1] 'Yesterday and the day before' clearly means 'recently'; but there is room for disagreement about how broad a time span that might be thought to allow. However, it seems impossible (*pace* Decleva Caizzi 1992*a*: 177 n. 5) that Aristocles should have lived as late as the second century AD, as traditionally thought on the basis of his supposed identification as the teacher of Alexander of Aphrodisias. See Moraux (1984: 83–92). On the dating of Aenesidemus, see further Ch. 4 n. 3 and accompanying text.

[2] *astathmētos, aklinēs*, and *akradantos* do not appear in Sextus, nor in the chapter of Photius' *Bibliotheca* (169b18–171a4) summarizing the views of Aenesidemus (with which we shall be occupied in Ch. 4). But the first two are attested in the late fifth and early fourth centuries respectively; *akradantos* itself is not attested before Timon, but the verb *kradainein*, from which it derives, is found in Homer and Xenophanes. See LS ii. 6; DC 224, 228.

[3] Luibhéid (1995) faults Conche (1994) for failing to justify his decision to focus heavily on the Aristocles passage. But the justification is very simple: no other text comes close to this one in the detail and specificity of its account of Pyrrho's central ideas, or in its promise of authenticity. Conche's own 'nihilistic' interpretation of the Aristocles passage, however, leaves much to be desired; for a brief but sufficient refutation, see Görler (1994: 740).

[4] A much fuller engagement with the secondary literature occurs in Bett (1994*a*). Here I confine myself mainly to references to works that have appeared, and to significant and persistent doubts that have been expressed to me orally, since that article was written.

It is necessary above all to consider our own knowledge; for if it is our nature to know nothing, there is no need to enquire any further into other things. There were some among the ancients, too, who made this statement, whom Aristotle has argued against. Pyrrho of Elis was also a powerful advocate of such a position. He himself has left nothing in writing; his pupil Timon, however, says that the person who is to be happy must look to these three points: first, what are things like by nature? second, in what way ought we to be disposed towards them? and finally, what will be the result for those who are so disposed? He [Timon] says that he [Pyrrho] reveals that things are equally indifferent and unstable and indeterminate; for this reason neither our sensations nor our opinions tell the truth or lie. For this reason, then, we should not trust them, but should be without opinions and without inclinations and without wavering, saying about each single thing that it no more is than is not or both is and is not or neither is nor is not. Timon says that the result for those who are so disposed will be first speechlessness, but then freedom from worry; and Aenesidemus says pleasure. These, then, are the main points of what they say.

The passage purports, then—or so it would seem—to be a summary of an account by Timon, Pyrrho's most devoted disciple, of Pyrrho's most general philosophical attitudes. As was observed in the Introduction, we do not know from which work of Timon this account derives. But in his subsequent critical discussion of Pyrrho, and also of Aenesidemus, Aristocles quotes four times from Timon's satirical verses, the *Silloi* (XIV.18.17, 19, 28); he also refers to the *Silloi*, and to Timon's prose work *Pytho* (XIV.18.14), in terms that make clear that he has first-hand acquaintance with these works.[5] In addition, as was suggested a moment ago, in our passage itself Aristocles refers specifically to the writings of Timon—contrasting Timon with Pyrrho himself, who wrote nothing—and uses the words 'Timon says' or 'he says' three times in the course of a very few sentences; it is clear, then, that he has access to Timon's own words on the subject, and that he is taking pains to reproduce Timon's account accurately. Moreover, in numerous other cases, where we can check Aristocles' reports on philosophical doctrines against their originals, he reveals himself as careful and reliable, even when, as in the present instance, he is himself strongly opposed to the doctrines in question. Or at least, he is reliable in those instances where he may be presumed to have had access to texts systematically expounding these doctrines, as is again the case here.[6] Aristocles does not claim to be *quoting* Timon;[7] but all the indications are that his account of what Timon said deserves to be taken seriously.

A further question, which has recently been raised by Jacques Brunschwig,[8] is whether *Timon* is reliable as a source for *Pyrrho's* views.

---

[5] For details on this, see Bett (1994*a*: 173).

[6] On Aristocles' reliability in general, see Bett (1994*a*: sect. VI). See also below, n. 54.

[7] Indeed, in at least two cases he is pretty clearly *not* doing so. His use of the term 'tell the truth' (*alētheuein*) in connection with sensations and opinions, and his assertion that we should not 'trust' (*pisteuein*) them (XIV.18.3), is similar to his own use of these terms in connection with other philosophers (XIV.17.1–2, XIV.20.1).　　　　　[8] Brunschwig (1994*a*).

Now, as I emphasized in the Introduction, Timon was both intimately acquainted with Pyrrho and philosophically astute—so that we might expect his understanding of Pyrrho's ideas to be beyond reproach. Still, it is, of course, not impossible for followers, even intelligent and devoted ones, to misunderstand or misrepresent those whom they are following. But what specific reason is there for thinking that the present passage does not accurately represent the ideas of Pyrrho? Brunschwig's answer is that, while, as we have already noted, Aristocles several times uses the words 'Timon [or "he", referring to Timon] says', there is only one place in the passage where we are actually told that a certain position was maintained by Pyrrho. Now, Brunschwig infers that this is the only position, among those mentioned in the passage, that Timon explicitly attributed to Pyrrho, and that 'the rest of the text, either in part or wholly, contains things that were at least *not explicitly* attributed to Pyrrho by Timon' (1994*a*:194). He goes on to develop an interpretation according to which important parts of the passage represent a distinctive twist imposed by Timon himself on Pyrrho's ideas—even though Timon 'probably takes it to be quite faithfully true to his master's thought' (1994*a*: 203).

However, the inference with which he begins is not compelling. It is perfectly possible that Timon was throughout explicit about the fact that he was summarizing the views of Pyrrho, but that *Aristocles* did not trouble to mention this more than once. Aristocles tells us that Pyrrho was a powerful proponent of the view that 'it is our nature to know nothing'; he then adds 'but he himself left nothing in writing, but his pupil Timon says that . . .'—and there follows the summary of what Timon said. The most natural way of reading this is as saying that we do not have Pyrrho's actual words, but that we do have what is the next best thing—the next best thing, that is, for the purpose of supporting the claim that *Pyrrho* held that 'it is our nature to know nothing'—namely, Timon's account of Pyrrho's words. It is true that we are not specifically told that Timon's account was an account *of the views of Pyrrho*. But it is hard to see what else would be the point of introducing Timon into the discussion at this juncture,[9] or why, if this was not the case, Aristocles should have opened the discussion by putting Pyrrho at the centre of attention. If, on the other hand, Aristocles thought (as he could quite sensibly have thought) that he had made it sufficiently clear that he is offering a summary of an account, by Timon, of the views of Pyrrho, then he would have had no

[9] Brunschwig seems to maintain that the purpose of the passage is to summarize what had been said by the Pyrrhonian sceptics in general, on the basis of what he took Timon to have said (1994*a*: 193). But this introduction to the passage says nothing about a *group* of Pyrrhonians; it simply refers to Pyrrho, observes that first-hand knowledge of his words is impossible, and then refers to Timon as a (presumably less than ideal, but still quite acceptable) substitute. A substitute in what capacity? The obvious answer would seem to be 'a substitute as a source for ascertaining what Pyrrho thought'. It is true that Aenesidemus is also mentioned at the very end of the passage (xiv.18.4). But this is clearly an isolated reference, and in no way impugns the suggestion that what is otherwise going on is that Aristocles is reporting what Timon said about Pyrrho.

reason constantly to say 'Timon said that Pyrrho said' rather than simply 'Timon said'. If the passage turned out to be best understood as separable into two parts, the contributions of Pyrrho and the contributions of Timon, then we would have to revise this verdict; but otherwise we may take it that we are throughout being offered the views of Pyrrho as recorded by Timon. And in fact, as we shall see, the passage is naturally understood as offering a single, coherent, and continuous argument.[10]

So it seems legitimate to view the passage as a reliable report of Timon's account of Pyrrho's philosophy;[11] and there is at least no obvious reason for suspecting that Timon's understanding or representation of that philosophy is defective. We cannot, of course, prove in advance that the words that appear in Aristocles' text accurately summarize Pyrrho's position; the only way to arrive at a verdict on that question is to try to determine what position the passage attributes to him, and how much sense it makes, historically and philosophically, that he should have held such a position—a task with which we shall be occupied, in one way or another, throughout the book. But plainly, if we are to have any hope of understanding the philosophy of Pyrrho, this passage is where we must begin. Now, what does the passage tell us? We are told that the person who is to be happy (*ton mellonta eudaimonēsein*) must address three connected questions: (*a*) what is the nature of things, (*b*) how should we be disposed towards these things, and (*c*) what will be the result for those who are so disposed? The answer to (*c*) is explicitly made to depend on the answer to (*b*), and the answer to (*b*), in turn, may be assumed to depend on the answer to (*a*); how we should be disposed towards things depends on the nature of those things. The rest of the passage then tells us what Pyrrho's answers were to each of the three questions, and it is clear that these answers are indeed connected in the manner we were led to expect. But what, precisely, are the answers in each case? Here matters become much more complicated. I shall proceed slowly through the passage in order.

2. *The nature of things*

In answer to the first question, Pyrrho is said to 'reveal' (*apophainein*) that things are equally (*ep'isēs*) *adiaphora* and *astathmēta* and *anepikrita*. I will

---

[10] Brunschwig holds otherwise. I have contested his view that Pyrrho's and Timon's contributions are distinguishable within the passage (and also discussed in more detail the matters treated in this paragraph) in sect. III of Bett (1996); see also Barnes (1996), and below, n. 31.

[11] As we saw in the Introduction, it does not matter whether Aristocles' source is the dialogue *Pytho* or some other work, now unknown to us, in which Timon simply laid out the essentials of Pyrrho's philosophy in his own voice. Either way, there is no reason to doubt that Timon did intend to tell us what the essentials of that philosophy were, and no reason to suspect that Aristocles is misled on this score.

return later to the question of the significance of the term 'equally'—into which many recent scholars have read a great deal. There is an immediate and crucial issue concerning the translation of the three epithets. *Adiaphora* is usually translated, here and elsewhere, by 'indifferent'; but in this case, is Pyrrho speaking of a property possessed by 'things' intrinsically—their lack of differentiating features—or is he speaking of *our inability*, for whatever reasons, to make differentiations among things? If the latter is correct, the translation 'undifferentiable' would be more precise; and the Greek word certainly does sometimes admit of this translation. Similarly, *astathmēta*—derived from *stathmos*, 'balance'—could mean 'unstable' or 'unbalanced', describing an intrinsic property of things,[12] without reference to our abilities or inabilities. Alternatively, it could mean 'not subject to being placed on a balance', and hence 'unmeasurable'; but 'things are unmeasurable' would naturally be taken as equivalent to 'we are incapable of measuring things', which would again place the focus on our cognitive deficiencies and away from the intrinsic features of the things themselves. And the third epithet, *anepikrita*—derived from *epikrisis*, 'arbitration' or 'determination'—is subject to a similar ambiguity as well. The point may be that things are 'indeterminable' by us, without any implications as to the thing's intrinsic character; or it may be that things in themselves lack any determinate character, that they are *in themselves such as* not to admit of any determination, by ourselves or by any other beings—even, say, by divine beings who can see everything as it really is.[13] In the latter case 'indeterminate' might be a more suitable translation than 'indeterminable'. The group of three epithets, then, may be read on the one hand as drawing attention to something about things in themselves, or on the other hand as drawing attention to something about our grasp of, or cognitive access to, things. I shall call these two readings the 'metaphysical' and the 'epistemological' readings respectively.

One might object that the opposition between these two readings is a false one. A statement to the effect that things are in themselves without any definite character immediately *entails* a statement to the effect that no definite character is apprehensible in them. Conversely, to say that no definite character is apprehensible in the things is also to say that the things themselves are, in their *intrinsic nature*, such as to resist apprehension of any definite character in them. The 'metaphysical' and the 'epistemological' claims cannot be disentangled from one another.

This line of thinking, though ultimately mistaken, forces us to clarify something that was treated too hastily a moment ago. Let us suppose that, in

---

[12] This seems to be its usual meaning in fifth- and fourth-century texts; see LSJ and DC 224.

[13] The fact that *anepikrita* looks 'subjective' in view of its etymology does not, then, settle anything—*pace* Stopper (1983: 292); even a subjective-looking word may be used to make an 'objective' point (and *anepikrita* has no prior usages that might help us to judge this matter).

accordance with what I called the 'epistemological' reading, the translations 'undifferentiable', 'unmeasurable', and 'indeterminable' are adopted. Now, if things are being described by these epithets, we need to be clear *by whom* they are being said to be 'undifferentiable', 'unmeasurable', and 'indeterminable'. In particular, are we speaking of them as being 'undifferentiable', 'unmeasurable', and 'indeterminable' by human beings; or as being 'undifferentiable', 'unmeasurable', and 'indeterminable' by any beings whatever, including omniscient divine beings? In the latter case, it would be quite correct to say that the 'epistemological' and the 'metaphysical' readings amount to the same thing; there is indeed no difference between speaking of what is 'indeterminable' *from the god's-eye view* and speaking of what is in itself 'indeterminate'. In introducing the 'epistemological' reading, however, I spoke of things as being 'undifferentiable', etc., *by us humans*—for the obvious reason that the passage goes on to speak of *our* sensations and opinions, what *our* attitude towards them should be, what *we* should say about things, and so on. Clearly it is *our* cognitive access to things that the statement is talking about—supposing that cognitive access is in fact the central issue—and not the cognitive access of omniscient beings. And once this is made fully explicit, then it is clear that the two readings do after all differ significantly. The claim that things in themselves lack any definite character does certainly *entail* that no definite character is apprehensible in them *by us*; and this point will be of some importance later in the chapter. But, except on the crudest kind of verificationism, the two claims are not by any means *equivalent*; the first claim is about things, irrespective of any cognitive relation in which we may stand to them, and the second is about that very cognitive relation. And, on the other side, it is true that 'things are undifferentiable, unmeasurable and indeterminable by us' trivially entails 'things are (intrinsically) such as to resist our differentiating, measuring or determining them'. But the latter claim is by no means equivalent to saying that things *in themselves have no* fixed and definite character— which is the burden of Pyrrho's statement on the 'metaphysical' reading. A thing might very well possess the feature 'being such that human beings cannot apprehend any definite character in them', but possess many other definite characteristics as well—characteristics that were, of course, beyond our ability, for any of a variety of reasons, to discern. So, except in the special case of those relational features of things having to do, precisely, with their cognitive accessibility to us—which is *not* what, on the 'metaphysical' reading, Pyrrho is primarily talking about—it is one thing to speak about the nature of things, and it is another thing to speak about our ability or inability to *grasp* the nature of things. There is, then, a difference between what I called the 'metaphysical' and the 'epistemological' readings of Pyrrho's answer to the first question (and I shall now drop the quotation marks around these terms). Moreover, as we shall see, it is of great importance for our interpretation of the whole passage which of these two readings we adopt.

It might be thought that the metaphysical reading is favoured by the fact that Pyrrho is here supposed to be answering the question 'What is the nature of things?' On the metaphysical reading he is indeed giving us substantial information about the nature of things, whereas on the epistemological reading the information we get about the nature of things goes no further than the unhelpful 'things are of such a nature that we cannot determine what they are like'. But this is by no means conclusive. The latter statement does tell us something, even if not very much, about the nature of things; and in any case, it would be a quite appropriate form of answer to the question 'What is the nature of things?' to reply that their nature is not accessible to us. It is true that Pyrrho is said to 'reveal' or 'declare' (*apophainein*) that things are a certain way, which certainly seems to imply that some *specification* of the nature of things is forthcoming, rather than an acknowledgement that no such specification is possible (beyond the minimal 'things are by nature such that no (further) specification of their nature is possible'). However, if the evidence in favour of the epistemological reading is strong enough, this point will carry little weight. Furthermore, if one approaches this passage with the Pyrrhonism of Sextus in mind, one will surely be inclined to prefer the epistemological reading. Though Pyrrho is not, even on this reading, giving us the *same* as the Pyrrhonism of Sextus—for, as we have seen, the modalized claim that we *cannot* apprehend the features of things does entail at least one point about things in themselves, namely that they are such as to resist our apprehending them[14]—he is clearly a great deal *closer* to Sextus' outlook

---

[14] On this reading Pyrrho would be subject to the same kind of criticism as Sextus levels at the Cyrenaics (*PH* 1.215): they are not sceptics, because, unlike himself, they *assert* that things have an inapprehensible *nature*. By contrast, Sextus himself—at least, when he is being careful—avoids modal epistemological claims, and the accompanying entailments having to do with the nature of things, and confines himself instead to claims about what has been experienced 'up to now' (*mechri nun* or *achri nun*).

It might be suggested that even this degree of contrast between Sextus and Pyrrho is unnecessary. As is well known, adjectives in Greek bearing the suffix *-tos* often admit of two different translations, one with modal force and one without; so why should *astathmēta* and *anepikrita* not be translated 'unmeasured' and 'undetermined' rather than 'unmeasurable' and 'undeterminable'? (And, if this is allowed, perhaps we can render *adiaphora*, too, by 'undifferentiated' rather than 'undifferentiable'.) If so, not even the minimal claim that things are of such a nature as to resist our apprehending (anything else about) their natures needs to be attributed to Pyrrho. But the trouble with this is that the three epithets are offered, precisely, as a *characterization* of 'things' (*ta pragmata*), in answer to the question 'What is the nature of things?' On the epistemological reading, the reply may be treated as *equivalent* to a claim about our cognitive access; but the actual form of the reply is '*Things are* . . .'. So the amount of information the statement conveys about the nature of things may be minimal, but it cannot very well be non-existent. It is for this reason, I take it, that the proponents of the epistemological reading uniformly use adjectives with the '-able' or '-ible' suffix in their translations. See Stough (1969: 17–18); Stopper (1983: 292); Annas and Barnes (1985: 11); Long (1986: 80–1); Annas (1993: 203); and Pellegrin (1997: 23–5) (though Pellegrin also to some extent follows Brunschwig (1994*a*) in separating the contributions of Pyrrho and Timon).

than he would be on the metaphysical one; the epistemological reading sounds like a naïve, early version of what later became the outlook of Sextus, whereas the metaphysical reading sounds like a quite different view.

The only way to settle the question is to see which reading better fits the logic of the passage. And in this connection the clause that follows is vital; the passage continues by saying that 'for this reason neither our sensations nor our opinions tell the truth or lie' (*dia touto mēte tas aisthēseis hēmōn mēte tas doxas alētheuein ē pseudesthai*). In this case, unlike the case we have just been discussing, the translation is unproblematic. Now, this clause is presented as an *inference* from the preceding claim about the nature of things; the question, therefore, is what understanding of the preceding claim makes the inference a comprehensible and, hopefully, a legitimate one. On the epistemological reading, we would be being told that the nature of things is undiscoverable, and that 'for this reason neither our sensations nor our opinions tell the truth or lie'. But this makes no sense at all. If the nature of things is undiscoverable, then it will *also* be undiscoverable whether our sensations and opinions are true or false or neither; in order to pronounce on the truth-value of our sensations and opinions, one needs to be in a position to say what the objects of those sensations and opinions are actually like.[15] Yet Pyrrho *is* pronouncing on the truth-value of our sensations and opinions—he is asserting that they are neither true nor false—and this would be flatly inconsistent with the claim that the nature of things is undiscoverable. Of course, if the claim was that we are *unable to tell* whether our sensations or opinions are true or false, the inference would be easy and natural. But that is not what the text says; it says that our sensations and opinions *are neither* true *nor* false.[16]

---

[15] To forestall a possible misunderstanding: I am not making the second-order point that the undiscoverability of the truth-value of our sensations and opinions would itself have to be an *instance* of the undiscoverability of the nature of things; that might or might not be the case, depending on how the thesis was understood. My point is much simpler. In claiming that the nature of things is undiscoverable, one is necessarily renouncing any pretensions to being able to judge the truth-value of sensations and opinions having to do with those things; one cannot claim that the nature of things is undiscoverable and *also* commit oneself as to the truth-value of sensations and opinions, since the latter commitment presupposes that one *has* 'discovered' something about the real character of the objects with which those sensations and opinions deal. (It might be wondered whether sensations and opinions in general have to do with anything so grandiose as 'the nature of things'. I shall have a good deal to say in later chapters on the question what exactly is meant by the claim that things are a certain way 'by nature'. But for now, we need not worry about such matters. However exactly the argument is supposed to work, it is clear that Pyrrho has a certain view about how things are—either that things are indeterminate or that they are undiscoverable—that he takes to have an immediate consequence for the status of our sensations and opinions; he must, then, conceive of sensations and opinions as purporting to tell us about how things are—and at some level it is hard to disagree.)

[16] This claim has not ceased to be controversial since I first proposed it in Bett (1994*a*). As noted above, the Greek words admit of only one possible rendering into English. However, it is objected that I am relying on a *particular understanding* of the sentence in question, and that other possible understandings yield different interpretations of the inference. This matter is too

Compare this with the metaphysical reading. Here we are told that the nature of things is inherently indeterminate, and 'that for this reason neither our sensations nor our opinions tell the truth or lie'. And this time the logic is perspicuous. In order for a certain sensation or opinion to be either true or false, there must be some definite *state of affairs* that the sensation or opinion either correctly or incorrectly represents. But if reality is inherently indeterminate, there are *no* definite states of affairs;[17] nothing is determinately either the case or not the case. Hence our sensations and opinions, each of which does have a certain definite content[18]—or, in other words, does represent certain definite states of affairs as obtaining—are neither true nor false. They are not true, since the sensation that the tomato is red, or the opinion that the earth is spherical, could be true only if certain definite states of affairs (the tomato's being red or the earth's being spherical) actually obtained—which is precisely what the indeterminacy thesis denies. But they are not false either, since that too would require that there be some definite state of affairs, a state of affairs *contrary* to the one represented by the sensation or opinion—such as the tomato's being *not* red (but, say, green), or the earth's being *not* spherical (but, say, cylindrical).[19]

It might be objected that Pyrrho after all is, and cannot avoid, making some definite assertions—namely, the *assertion that* reality is indeterminate, that

cumbersome to address either in the main text or in a footnote, but too important to omit; I address it in the Appendix to this chapter.

[17] Or, at least, no definite states of affairs having to do with particular things in the world. The global claim that reality is indeterminate is, of course, presented as itself determinately true, as is the claim that our sensations and opinions are neither true nor false, and the rest of the claims in this passage. On this, see the next paragraph in the main text.

[18] It may be objected that this is not true of all sensations. But, since the claim about the truth-value of our sensations and opinions is offered as an immediate inference from the claim about the nature of things, I assume that the 'sensations' Pyrrho has in mind here are those that purport, precisely, to *tell* us something about the nature of things—namely, the everyday sense perceptions of someone in an ordinary state of consciousness. And these *are* 'definite' at least to the extent (which is enough for the purposes of Pyrrho's argument) that they have a content that can be expressed by means of definite declarative sentences such as 'the tomato is red, round, squishy, etc.'.

[19] One might protest that Pyrrho *ought* to say that our sensations and opinions are false; for surely we are bound to say that reality is other than the way our sensations and opinions present it as being. But if reality is indeterminate, the conclusion does not follow from the premiss. In order for the sensation or opinion that x is F to be false, it must be the case that $- (x$ is $F)$. But, if reality is indeterminate, the state of affairs designated by '$- (x$ is $F)$', just like the state of affairs designated by 'x is F', neither obtains nor does not obtain. Reality may be other than as portrayed by the proposition 'x is F', but *not* in such a way that the negation of that proposition is true. It seems to me that Hankinson (1995: 62), though sympathetic to this type of reading, makes excessively heavy weather of this point; there is no need to invoke the suggestion that 'Pyrrho takes falseness to mean absolute falseness'—an everyday conception of falseness will work for him perfectly well. (We will, however, eventually need to consider in more detail what Pyrrho is committed to, in claiming that reality is indeterminate, and here similar issues will arise once more; I take up this matter in Ch. 3.)

our sensations and opinions are neither true nor false, and the other assertions that form the passage itself. Hence either Pyrrho's position is self-refuting, if the metaphysical interpretation is correct, or he is forced to claim a special, privileged status for a certain class of assertions—a status that he gives no hint of claiming for them, and which it is hard to see how he plausibly could claim for them. Either way, it may be said, the metaphysical interpretation is severely compromised.[20] In fact, however, it is not difficult to see how these assertions can be understood as exempt from their own scope. First, the 'things' (*pragmata*) whose nature is here said to be indeterminate may easily be taken to be particular objects and states of affairs in the world around us; in this standard, everyday use of the term *pragmata*, there is no reason to take the indeterminacy thesis as self-applicable, or as applicable to any of the other assertions that form the passage itself. Then again, these assertions are clearly not the content of any sensations, and so are not, on that account, to be inferred to be neither true nor false. And nor, finally, need they be understood as the content of any opinions. For there is a well-established usage of the term 'opinion' (*doxa*) in Greek philosophy, associated especially with Parmenides and Plato, according to which it refers to certain types of opinions *about* the ordinary objects and states of affairs normally designated by the term *pragmata*, 'things'. In Plato the reference is typically to everyday, non-theoretical opinions such as 'that temple is beautiful' or 'this suitcase is heavy';[21] and this may be part of what Parmenides means by *doxa* as well. But at least part of what Parmenides has in mind is cosmological speculation that attempts systematically to *explain* the workings of these ordinary objects and states of affairs; the cosmology in the poem itself constitutes the *doxa* section—this much is clear—and previous cosmologists are also arguably among the 'mortals who know nothing' stigmatized in the first part of the poem for their devotion to *doxa*.[22] *Doxai*, then, are those opinions that take the familiar world as it appears to us in ordinary experience as fully real, as a source of truth, or, at the very least, as open to rational explanation—whereas in fact, in the view of the exponents of this usage, it is a *mistake* to accord this degree of respect to this familiar world, since true reality, and the true deliverances of reason, are something quite *other* than either ordinary people or cosmologists suppose. Now, if Pyrrho is following this usage, he may quite legitimately say that the statements constituting the passage itself are *not* mere 'opinions'; on the contrary, these statements tell us the genuine *truth*—

[20] For this objection, see Annas (1993: 203–4 n. 11)—who regards it as decisive—and Hankinson (1995: 62)—who thinks that it probably never occurred to Pyrrho, but suggests two possible ways of answering it.

[21] The *locus classicus* for this usage is the end of *Republic* V (476d–480a); see also, e.g., *Timaeus* 28a, c, 51d–e.

[22] For a comprehensive recent treatment of Parmenides' conception of and attitude to *doxa*, with plentiful references to other views, see Curd (1998: esp. chs. 1, 3).

as neither everyday opinions nor cosmology could ever do, since they mistakenly trust ordinary experience and take reality to be determinate.[23]

There is thus no need to accuse Pyrrho either of self-refutation or of arbitrarily exempting his assertions from their own scope. So far, then, it looks as if the metaphysical interpretation makes sense of the train of thought, while the epistemological interpretation makes nonsense of it. But I have not yet mentioned a complication. Some have argued that the text should be changed at this point;[24] the change, they urge, is both necessary in itself and decisive in favour of the epistemological reading. The suggested change is from 'for this reason [*dia touto*] neither our sensations nor our opinions, etc.' to 'on account of the fact that [*dia to*] neither our sensations nor our opinions, etc.'. The effect, obviously, is to reverse the order of the inferences; the assertion about the nature of things now becomes a *consequence* of the assertion about the status of our sensations and opinions, not a reason for it. Now, this textual change is admittedly small, and the corruption would be quite understandable, given that 'for this reason' (*dia touto*) does occur in the next sentence. On the other hand, there is no disagreement among the manuscripts at this point, nor any other paleographic reason to suspect that the text is in disarray. Why, then, is it supposed to be necessary to change the text, and why is this supposed to be helpful to the epistemological interpretation?

Two linguistic reasons are given for the change. First, the clause beginning 'for this reason'—if that is how it begins—contains no particle, and this is thought to be problematic; Greek has a great number of these small connecting words (often untranslatable, but often rendered by words such as 'for', 'however', 'then', etc.), and in normal cases every sentence contains one. But if the text read 'on account of the fact that', there would be no need for a particle, since there would not be a separate main clause. Secondly, the form of the negatives *mēte . . . mēte*, 'neither . . . nor' is thought to be incorrect Greek with 'for this reason', but correct Greek with 'on account of the fact that'; in the former case one would have infinitives in indirect discourse, in which case the correct form of the negatives would be *oute . . . oute*, whereas in the latter case one would have infinitives with the definite article, in which case *mēte . . . mēte* would be correct. Neither of these arguments, though, is persuasive. In sentences beginning with demonstrative phrases like 'for this

[23] Note that the thesis that reality is indeterminate is not itself a piece of cosmology; it is not a rational explanation of the workings of the cosmos, but a way of rejecting the possibility of any such explanation. In this respect it resembles the assertions in the *Republic*, the *Timaeus*, and elsewhere to the effect that sensible things are not full-grade beings, and hence are the objects of (mere) *doxa*—assertions that are not *themselves* instances of *doxa*. (We shall return to the Platonic parallel in Ch. 3.)

[24] The emendation was originally proposed, without explanation, in Zeller (1909: 501). It is adopted and defended by Stopper (1983: 292–3), and by Annas (1993: 203); see also Annas and Barnes (1994: p. x).

reason', referring back to the previous sentence, it is by no means unheard of to dispense with any particle; the demonstrative phrase itself serves as the connective.[25] And the rule that infinitives in indirect discourse use negatives of the form *ou* rather than of the form *mē* is subject to exceptions (among which the present case might be argued to belong) even in the classical period,[26] and later appears to be more or less abandoned.[27]

[25] Brunschwig (1994a: n. 19) (relying on correspondence or conversation with Fernanda Decleva Caizzi) furnishes several other philosophical examples of *dia touto* without particle; see Plutarch, *De animae procreatione in Timaeo* 1018b; Plotinus 5.1.7.20, 6.7.16.20; Simplicius, *In De caelo* 563.7; Philoponus, *De aeternitate mundi* 278.28, 439.14. But, with the possible exception of the first, these are all much later than Aristocles, and a sceptic might easily dismiss them. However, the case can be made without recourse to contentious examples. According to Denniston (1950: pp. xliii–xliv), 'a backward-pointing pronoun or demonstrative adverb, usually at or near the opening of the sentence . . . diminishes the necessity for a connecting particle'; this is mentioned as one of three standard types of case where asyndeton is unobjectionable. See also Smyth (1956: 484–5). Among his examples, Denniston cites a passage of Xenophon's *Anabasis* (1.2), and we can follow his lead. Xenophon is an example of standard, unpretentious classical Greek if anyone is; the following is a (relatively limited) selection of cases in the *Anabasis* where a sentence begins with some form of *houtos* (sometimes with a preposition) without any particle included: 1.2.5, 1.2.6, 1.2.19, 1.2.24, 1.3.7, 1.3.13, 1.3.16 (*meta touton*), 1.3.20, 1.4.5, 1.4.9 (*meta tauta*), 1.4.16, 1.5.5 (*en toutois*), 1.5.17, 1.6.1, 1.6.2, 1.6.3, 1.6.9 (*pros tauta*), 1.7.6, 1.9.26, II.1.3, II.1.4, II.1.5, II.1.11 (*pros tauta*), II.1.12 (*meta touton*), II.2.3 (*meta tauta*), II.2.5, II.2.12, II.3.6, II.3.21 (*pros tauta*), II.3.28, II.4.1 (*meta tauta*), II.4.18, II.4.27, II.5.1 (*meta tauta*), II.5.24, II.5.37 (*meta tauta*), II.5.39 (*pros tauta*), II.5.40 (*epi toutois*), II.5.42 (*pros tauta*), II.6.4 (*ek toutou*). I hope this is enough to dispel the idea that there is anything particularly unexpected about Aristocles' use of *dia touto* without particle.

[26] See Smyth (1956: 617–18). In Smyth's words, 'Verbs of *saying* and *thinking* take *mē* in emphatic declarations'; also, '*mē* is often used with verbs and other expressions of asseveration and belief . . . The use of *mē* indicates strong assurance, confidence, and resolve.' Though I have not seen any examples from the fifth or fourth centuries, it seems at least arguable that the verb 'reveal' (*apophainō*) falls under one of these headings. (According to Brunschwig (1994a), the infinitives actually follow the verb *phēmi* ('say'), and not, as most commentators have assumed, the verb *apophainō*; if this is correct, the linguistic acceptability of the received text is still clearer—see the following note.)

[27] See Gildersleeve (1880); Birke (1897); Green (1902). As these works amply document— the second and third, in particular, consist largely of lists of references—there is a gradually increasing willingness (even if the situation varies somewhat from author to author) to use *mē* with infinitives in indirect discourse, both within and beyond the class of cases where this was permitted in classical times. See also Jannaris (1897: 430–1); Schwyzer (1950: 590–9). In particular, Diodorus Siculus, who is either contemporary with or earlier than Aristocles, five times uses *mē* with infinitives following the *same* verb *apophainō* as occurs in the Aristocles passage (though always in the middle rather than the active form): 3.18.5 (where the specific form of the negative is *mēte . . . mēte*, as in the case that interests us), 3.62.2, 12.14.2, 17.68.4, 19.34.2. According to Green (1902: 473), he also uses *mē* in 'general *oratio obliqua*' (that is, *oratio obliqua* 'without any special introductory word') forty-nine times in the first five books. Given this state of affairs, there is clearly *no* particular expectation that an author in Aristocles' time (even on the earliest possible view of when that was) will use *oute* in this context rather than *mēte*. (The appeal to other authors is needed because the fragments of Aristocles himself are too exiguous for us to decide the question on the basis of his own usage. *Mē* occurs with infinitive after *legō* and *phēmi* at *Praep. evang.* XI.3.8 and, in the Pyrrhonist chapter itself, XIV.18.7, 8, 9, 15; but this would not be especially surprising in the classical period, either—see again Smyth (1956: 617–18).)

There is, then, no strong linguistic reason for changing the text. What logical reason might be adduced for doing so? The thought seems to have been that with the text as it stands in the manuscripts, the inference from the claim about the nature of things to the one about sensations and opinions is unintelligible, and that the emendation renders the thought coherent—and the epistemological interpretation correct. Again, the opposite is in fact the case. First, I have already indicated how, on the metaphysical interpretation, and with the manuscript reading, the inference is quite intelligible. Secondly, the epistemological interpretation is no more successful with the emendation than without it. According to this interpretation, we are now being told that the nature of things is undiscoverable *because* our sensations and opinions are neither true nor false. But this is nonsense. Again, the assertion that our sensations and opinions are neither true nor false presupposes that the nature of things *has* been discovered; in order to pronounce upon the truth-value of sensations and opinions, one must take oneself to have some grasp of the nature of their objects. Again, of course, if the claim were that we are *incapable of discerning* the truth-value of our sensations and opinions, then the inference, with the emended text, would be easy and natural, and the epistemological interpretation secure; but again, that is not what the text says.[28] But now, if we abandon the epistemological interpretation, the motivation for the emendation disappears. Clearly, on the metaphysical interpretation, it makes far more sense for the inference to go in the direction provided by the manuscripts, with the thesis about the nature of things being the basis for the claim about the truth-value of our sensations and opinions, not a consequence of it. As just noted, the claim about the truth-value of our sensations and opinions clearly presupposes a view about the nature of things; specifically, it presupposes the very view about the nature of things that is actually offered in the passage—the view that things are indeterminate in their natures—or something very close to it. It could hardly serve, therefore, as a *justification* for this latter view. Of course, we are not told what was the basis of Pyrrho's view that reality is indeterminate (Aristocles is, after all, giving us only the *kephalaia*, the basic points, of his philosophy), and that will eventually have to be considered. But at least in the text as it stands, and without any emendations, the metaphysical interpretation makes good sense of the argument; on the other hand, both the emendation and the epistemological interpretation, whether separately or in conjunction, render the argument mysterious.

One more issue needs to be considered before we can move on. I have so far ignored the word 'equally' (*ep'isēs*) in the statement about the nature of things; Pyrrho does not say simply that things are indifferent, etc., but that they are *equally* indifferent, etc. It has recently been suggested that this term

---

[28] For a response to the objections that have been made against this claim, see again the Appendix to this chapter.

'equally' is to be connected with the notion of the 'equipollence' (*isostheneia*) of conflicting claims, which is central to the later Pyrrhonism of Sextus;[29] if so, of course, then the metaphysical interpretation, according to which Pyrrho is confidently asserting a dogmatic and unopposed thesis, would be ruled out. But, first, there is no general reason for assuming that occurrences of the term 'equally' in Pyrrho, or in any other author, must be connected with the 'equipollence' of Sextus. *Ep'isēs* in Greek, just like 'equally' in English, is a common everyday term; only if the use of the term by Pyrrho is specifically reminiscent of Sextus' equipollence will we be justified in assuming some philosophical connection here.[30] And, in fact, Pyrrho's use of the term appears to be very distant from Sextus' notion of equipollence. Nothing at all is said in this context about conflicting claims or appearances—that is, the kinds of items between which, according to Sextus, equipollence is to be brought about; it is *things*, not *claims about* things, that are said to be 'equally indifferent'. And, even if the point were about claims rather than about things, it is not easy to see how 'equally indifferent' can mean 'equally trustworthy', 'equally persuasive', or the like—as it would need to in order for anything resembling Sextus' notion of equipollence to be at issue here.

What, then, is the significance of 'equally'? There are at least two possible answers, both of them philosophically insignificant. The point might be that all three of the epithets used to describe 'things' apply to those things 'equally' well—that is, that things are *every bit as* indifferent as they are unstable and indeterminate. Or it might be that every thing is every bit as indifferent (and perhaps, also, every bit as unstable and indeterminate) as every other thing—that is, that the epithet 'indifferent' (and perhaps the others as well) apply 'equally' well to *all* the items in the category of 'things'. In either case—and I do not think we need to try to choose between them— 'equally' functions simply to add emphasis; it is as if Pyrrho had said 'things are (and I really mean this) indifferent and unstable and indeterminate'.

So far, then, the evidence suggests that Pyrrho does mean to assert a metaphysical thesis—things are in their own nature utterly indefinite—and that he infers from this a consequence having to do with our sensations and opinions. If this is correct, to say that things are 'indifferent' presumably means that they are not, in their real natures, any different from one another—no doubt because they do not *have* any real natures of a sort that would permit such differentiation;[31] to say that they are 'unstable' must mean that they do not

---

[29] See Annas (1993: 203 n. 8), and Annas and Barnes (1994: p. x) also Decleva Caizzi (DC 223) (who none the less adopts a version of the metaphysical interpretation).

[30] For the same reason, attempts to connect Pyrrho with other philosophers, such as Parmenides or the Stoic Aristo of Chios, on the basis of the term *ep'isēs* are also flawed; for criticisms of several such proposals, see Bett (1994a: sect. II).

[31] This is what *adiaphora* means in Aristotle; see e.g. *An. post.* 97^{b}7, *Rhet.* 1373^{a}33. Some have attempted instead to connect Pyrrho's usage of *adiaphora* with the ethical usage of the

have any *fixed* natures; and to say that they are 'indeterminate' must mean that they do not have any *definite* natures. Clearly all those features are closely related, and for convenience I shall speak from now on, as I sometimes have already, simply of the 'indeterminacy thesis'. Many questions might, of course, be raised about this thesis; and, to repeat, I shall return to examine further its nature and its motivations in later chapters. But for now, enough has been said in order for the analysis of the passage to go forward.

3. How we should be disposed towards things

The first question, then, has now been answered, and an implication drawn from this answer. This implication in turn serves as the starting point for the answer to the second question, the question what our attitude towards things should be. Timon continues that, because our sensations and opinions are neither true nor false, 'we should not trust them', and then describes the attitude we should take by means of another sequence of three epithets;[32] we should be 'without opinions [*adoxastous*] and without inclinations [*aklineis*] and without wavering [*akradantous*]'. We should be 'without opinions',

Stoics (where the term refers to those things that are neither good nor bad), and particularly of the unorthodox Stoic Aristo, whom Cicero links with Pyrrho in numerous passages—and also to devise ethical interpretations of the other two epithets. See Ausland (1989); Brunschwig (1994a). But these proposals face the insuperable difficulty that a consequence clearly *not* confined to ethics—that is, the consequence having to do with the truth-value of our sensations and opinions—is immediately inferred from the claim about things. Against Ausland's proposal, see Bett (1994a: n. 49). Brunschwig's proposal, by contrast, is that it is *Timon* who has added the consequence concerning sensations and opinions to Pyrrho's doctrine about things, which was originally solely ethical. But, if *adiaphora* has this original ethical sense in *this passage*, then again, the consequence concerning sensations and opinions is a complete *non sequitur*, and positing a distinction between Pyrrho's and Timon's contributions does nothing to mitigate this. If, on the other hand, Timon has *already* (that is, prior to embarking on his account of Pyrrho's philosophy) transformed the sense of *adiaphora* in such a way that it can plausibly be thought to yield the consequence concerning sensations and opinions, then the passage actually provides *no* evidence for the alleged earlier ethical sense. It is not entirely clear, in the end, which of these alternatives Brunschwig wants to adopt, but neither will do the job he needs. For further discussion of this matter, see Bett (1996: sect. III). One other interpreter who inclines towards a purely ethical reading of the passage is Hankinson. He suggests (Hankinson 1995: 66–7) that the term 'sensations' may refer only to evaluative perceptions, such as 'that cake looks good to eat' or 'the bed looks comfortable'. But this is a forced reading of the Greek word *aisthēsis*, here translated 'sensation'; at least in the absence of clear indications to the contrary, *aisthēsis* in philosophical Greek is naturally taken to refer to sense perceptions in general. (By the same token, *doxa*, translated 'opinion', would not be understood to be confined to ethical opinions unless this was specified by the context.)

[32] It has often been observed that the passage contains several groups of three terms or phrases. Contrary to some scholars, I do not see that this has any particular significance for the interpretation of the passage; see Bett (1994a: nn. 50, 84).

clearly, because any opinions we might have would be neither true nor false. If they were true, that would be no problem; and if they were simply false, we could simply switch to a contrary set of opinions; but since they are neither true nor false (but purport to be true), we can avoid misconception only by avoiding opinions entirely. In keeping with this, we should be 'without inclination' in that we should not incline one way or the other—neither towards accepting certain sensations or opinions as true nor towards rejecting them as false. And we should be 'without wavering' in the sense that we should steadfastly persist in our mistrust of sensations and opinions; we should not oscillate between one opinion or another, or between having opinions and not having them. The attitude recommended, then, is easily understood as a corollary of what was previously said.

The description of our attitude is now expanded to include an account of what we should *say*; we should say 'about each single thing that it no more is than is not or both is and is not or neither is nor is not'. I begin with the first part of this, that it should be said of each thing 'that it no more is than is not'. As is well known, the words 'is' and 'is not' (or the words *esti* and *ouk esti*) admit of a multiplicity of usages in Greek philosophy. On one common philosophical usage, 'is' and 'is not' are understood as if a predicate is to follow, but without any particular predicate being specified; 'is' is read as 'is something-or-other', and the reader is to imagine any arbitrary predicate being inserted. In contemporary terminology, this usage of 'is' and 'is not' would be rendered by 'is F' and 'is not F', where F is any arbitrary predicate. Now, it is plausible to suppose that this is at least among the usages intended here. For the form of words that we are being told to employ is one that is supposed to express our lack of trust in sensations and opinions. A great many sensations and opinions are to the effect that some object is of some particular character; their linguistic expression, then, is schematically of the form 'x is F' ('the tomato is green', 'the suitcase is heavy', and so on). And to say of each thing that it 'no more is F than is not F', whatever exactly it amounts to, is surely an expression of some kind of lack of commitment to or trust in sentences of the form 'x is F'. So we may take it that we are being told—perhaps among other things[33]—to assert of each thing that it no more is F than it is not F. Now, what is the significance of 'no more'?

In *Outlines of Pyrrhonism* (1.188–91), Sextus tells us that 'no more' has a special use in scepticism. To say that something is no more F than not F is either to say that one does not know whether it is F or not F, or it is to pose a question of the form 'Why [suppose that the object is] F rather than not F?' Either way, the phrase is used to express suspension of judgement as to whether the object is F or not F. We should not simply assume, however, that

---

[33] As we will see, it is likely that this is not the only usage of *esti* that Timon wants us to have in mind.

Pyrrho intends the term 'no more' in the same way as Sextus. For, first, Sextus' construal of 'no more' is a redefinition, and a peculiar one at that. To say '*x* is no more *F* than not *F*' would *not*, in ordinary parlance, be taken to express suspension of judgement as to whether *x* was *F* or not *F*; rather, it would be taken (and the point is the same in the original Greek as in translation) as *asserting* that *x* was *to no greater extent F* than not *F*, or that the claims '*x* is *F*' and '*x* is not *F*' were true to the same degree. Indeed, Sextus concedes this. He says (1.191) that the phrase 'displays the character of assent and denial'—that is, that '*x* is no more *F* than not *F*' sounds as if it is making a definite assertion; but he then goes on to say that the sceptics use it differently. Secondly, the words *ou mallon* or *ouden mallon*, 'not more' or 'no more', in the normal and expected usage just referred to, are (as one might also expect) standard and common Greek vocabulary; there are all kinds of reasons, in everyday non-philosophical speech, to say that something is 'no more' one way than another way. Hence the fact that Pyrrho uses the term 'no more' gives us no reason to suppose that he intends to make a point similar to one that Sextus might have made using the same term.

This point has generally been overlooked, or even denied, because of a remark attributed by Diogenes Laertius to Timon (9.76). In the course of his own explanation of the phrase 'no more', Diogenes remarks that 'the phrase means, as Timon says in the *Pytho*, determining nothing and withholding assent'; and it has been assumed that this entitles us to infer that the usage of 'no more' by Pyrrho and Timon themselves is essentially the same as Sextus' usage in *Outlines of Pyrrhonism*. But this is not so. Of course, to suspend judgement as to whether *x* is *F* or not *F*, as Sextus proposes to do with the sentence '*x* is no more *F* than not *F*', clearly would qualify as 'determining nothing and withholding assent'. But other attitudes might also satisfy that description. In particular, to offer the definite assertion that *x* is to no greater extent *F* than it is not *F*—which is what '*x* is no more *F* than not *F*' would naturally be taken to mean—could very well count as a case of 'determining nothing and withholding assent'; one is making no determination for, or one is withholding assent from, the alternative '*F*' as against the alternative 'not-*F*'. Indeed, it is worth noting that, according to Diogenes' account, which the reference to Timon is supposed to supplement, the sceptical usage of 'no more' is the same as that illustrated by the everyday, non-philosophical sentence 'Scylla no more existed than the Chimaera' (9.75). In this sentence there is clearly no question of a suspension of judgement as to which of the two existed; the point is to *assert* that neither existed to any greater extent than did the other.[34] I conclude that

---

[34] Diogenes says that this is a case of using 'no more' negatively; the point is that neither Scylla nor the Chimaera existed at all. As we will see shortly, Pyrrho cannot intend his 'no more' statement to have comparable negative implications. However, as we shall see in Ch. 4, this does

Diogenes' reference to, and probable quotation[35] from, Timon gives us no compelling reason to read occurrences of 'no more' in early Pyrrhonism as conforming to the usage laid down in *Outlines of Pyrrhonism*; for all that Timon or Diogenes says, '*x* is no more *F* than not *F*' can perfectly well be used in the normal way, as an assertion to the effect that *x* is to no greater extent *F* than it is not *F*.

What Pyrrho does mean here must, therefore, be settled by looking at the context. When he says that 'we should say about each single thing that it no more is [*F*] than is not [*F*]', is it plausible to take him as suspending judgement about whether some given thing is *F* or not *F*? Or is it more plausible to take him as asserting that the thing is to no greater extent *F* than it is not *F*? If our reading of the passage so far has been on the right lines, the notion of suspension of judgement seems to have no place here. According to the answer to the first question, things are indeterminate in their real natures; Pyrrho is prepared to assert this, and to draw from it a consequence concerning the truth or falsehood of our sensations and opinions. But, if one is prepared to assert that things are in their real nature indeterminate, one has no reason to *suspend judgement* about whether some given thing is *F* or not *F*. On the contrary, if one takes oneself to be able to assert the indeterminacy thesis, and therefore to assert that our sensations and opinions are neither true nor false, one will also take oneself to be in a position to offer a specific *assertion* in answer to the question 'is the thing *F* or not *F*?'; the answer will be 'it is not determinately *F*, nor is it determinately not *F*; there is no definite state of affairs such that either the predicate *F* or the predicate not-*F* applies—or, for that matter, fails to apply'.

Unlike the reading of 'no more' as expressing suspension of judgement, the other reading is entirely compatible with this. To say, as Pyrrho does say according to this other reading, that *x* is to no greater extent *F* than it is not *F* is to say that *F*-ness and not-*F*-ness are on a par with respect to *x*; both predicates apply to *x* to precisely the same extent (which may be 100 per cent, or

seem to fit rather better with Aenesidemus' usage of 'no more', as well as that of Sextus in *Against the Ethicists*. Still, this subtle difference in the further implications of various sentences containing 'no more' is insignificant compared with the question whether Pyrrho must be assumed to mean 'no more' in the redefined sense in which it expresses *suspension of judgement* as between the two alternatives; my current point is that neither Diogenes' reference to Timon, nor the context in which it is embedded, forces us to assume any such thing—'no more' may very well mean simply 'no more', and the Scylla and Chimaera example suggests that this is precisely what it does mean.

[35] What makes this probable is the word *aprosthetein*, translated 'withholding assent', which is not part of the standard vocabulary of later Pyrrhonism—in fact, it occurs nowhere else in extant Greek literature; it is probably Timon's own coinage. Decleva Caizzi (DC 234–5) suggests that *aprosthetein* is not in fact equivalent to the later Pyrrhonist *epechein*, 'suspending judgement'; if this is correct, the case for interpreting the passage in a manner distinct from what *Outlines of Pyrrhonism* would lead one to expect is further supported.

not at all, or something else again).[36] Now if, as the indeterminacy thesis entails, neither predicate either applies or fails to apply to *x*, both predicates are indeed on a par with respect to *x*; the degrees to which, and the ways in which, the predicates *F* and not-*F* apply to *x* are exactly the same. So if we read 'no more' as meaning simply 'to no greater extent than'—as ordinary usage would lead us to expect—then Pyrrho's statement that 'each single thing' 'no more is than is not' is telling us something that follows easily and naturally from previous considerations; if, on the other hand, we read 'no more' as expressing suspension of judgement, Pyrrho's statement appears confused and unmotivated. It seems best, therefore, to read him as following ordinary usage.

I turn now to the further alternatives 'both is and is not' and 'neither is nor is not'. The crucial question to ask about these is what is their relation to the portion of the statement already discussed. One possibility is that they are two additional, self-sufficient formulations of what we should say 'about each single thing', each either equivalent to, or in some other way an alternative to, 'no more is than is not'; that is, that we are supposed to say 'about each single thing that it

(1) no more is than is not, or [that it]
(2) both is and is not, or [that it]
(3) neither is nor is not'.

But another possibility is that 'both is and is not' and 'neither is nor is not' are each on a par with 'is' and 'is not' separately, the whole comprising a *single* 'no more' statement covering four alternatives; that is, that we should say 'about each single thing that it no more

(1) is, than
(2) is not, or
(3) both is and is not, or
(4) neither is nor is not'.

Syntactically, both readings are perfectly possible. It is also possible to find parallels for both readings in other authors, parallels that may well be argued to be relevant to the interpretation of the present passage. In characterizing those who would deny the Law of Non-Contradiction in *Metaphysics* IV, Aristotle employs a form of words that sounds reminiscent of what, on the *first* reading, Pyrrho claims that we should say (1008ª30–4). On the other hand, Aulus Gellius (11.5.4) refers to Pyrrho as using the words 'this is no

---

[36] It has been observed in both ancient and modern times that 'no more *F* than not *F*' may, given appropriate background conditions, imply 'both *F* and not *F*'', or it may imply 'neither *F* nor not *F*' (or it may not imply either of these); see again DL 9.75 and n. 34, also DeLacy (1958: 60); Woodruff (1988: 146–7). A particularly clear example of the 'positive' usage, where 'no more *F* than not *F*' implies 'both *F* and not *F*'(and where, again, suspension of judgement is simply not at issue) occurs at Plutarch, *Adversus Coloten* 1109a–c.

more this way than that way or neither way', which sounds more like the
second reading of the present passage than the first;[37] and some Buddhist
thinkers—possibly related to the Naked Philosophers with whom Pyrrho
came into contact in India—are said to have used arguments exploring sets of
four possibilities of the form 'x is F', 'x is not F', 'x is both F and not F', and
'x is neither F nor not F', which again would be more closely analogous to
the second reading than to the first.[38] The only way to settle which of the two
readings is preferable, then, is to see which makes better sense of the passage
itself.

On the first reading, Pyrrho is saying that we should be prepared to *assert*,
at least as one possibility among others, that some given thing is both F and
not F—or, again, that it is neither F nor not F. But it is difficult to see how he
could think we should be willing to assert these things, seeing that he has just
told us that our sensations and opinions are neither true nor false and that we
should not trust them. If we are prepared to assert that each thing is both F
and not F, then we are conceding that the opinion that it is F, and the opinion
that it is not F (and the opinion that it is both), are *true*, not neither true nor
false. Indeed, we are being far *more* trusting of our sensations and opinions
than any normal person would be; we are in danger of implying, as on some
readings Protagoras did with his Man the Measure thesis, that *all* sensations
and opinions are true. On the other hand, if we are prepared to assert that each
thing is neither F nor not F, we are conceding that a vast number of opinions
are *false*. The first reading, then, seems to be very far from giving us a form
of speech that is consonant with our being 'without opinions and without
inclinations and without wavering'.[39]

The second reading, on the other hand, gives us a form of speech that does
indeed leave us 'without opinions', and so on. On this reading we are supposed
to say about each thing that the possibility that it is F, the possibility that it is

[37] It properly parallels the second reading provided that one takes 'this way' and 'that way'
as standing for contraries ('red' and 'not red', for example). This is certainly possible, but not
necessary; one might also take 'this way' and 'that way' to stand for two distinct predicates
('red' and 'blue', for example). In the latter case the sentence would not be a genuine parallel
for either reading—though (with 'no more' again being understood in its natural usage) it would
still be a readily intelligible consequence of the indeterminacy thesis.

[38] We shall return to the question of these parallels in discussing Pyrrho's antecedents—see
Ch. 3.

[39] This point seems to be neglected by Hankinson (1995: 62–4), who adopts a version of the
first reading where 'both is and is not' and 'neither is nor is not' are 'different ways of interpreting ["no more is than is not"], rather than genuine alternatives to it'. 'Both is and is not' is
said to be correct if predication is interpreted 'weakly'—that is, where 'x is F' is taken to mean
that 'x has some F-ness about it', rather than that x is F without qualification—and 'neither is
nor is not' is said to be correct if predication is interpreted strongly—such that 'x is F' does
mean that x is exclusively or unrestrictedly F. The problem with this is that, whichever of the
two is correct, and whichever understanding of predication is assumed, some obvious and sizeable set of sensations or opinions will thereby be allowed to be true or to be false.

not *F*, the possibility that it is both, and the possibility that it is neither, *each* obtains 'no more' than any of the others. And the *only* way in which this could be so is if none of these four possibilities is either true or false. As we saw, the 'no more' locution itself is consistent with the items compared being true, or being false; all that 'no more' entails is that the truth-value of all the items is identical. But, in the present case, one could not coherently *affirm* all four possibilities. For either the first two possibilities, 'is' and 'is not', are directly in conflict with one another; or, if we suppose that they might both be affirmed simultaneously, but in different respects, this would still conflict with the affirmation of the fourth possibility, 'neither is nor is not'. Nor, by the same reasoning, could one *deny* all four possibilities; either the denial of 'is' would conflict with the denial of 'is not', or the denial of 'neither is nor is not' would conflict with the denial of 'is' and 'is not' together.[40] But now, if one cannot either affirm or deny these possibilities, yet one is supposed to say that they all hold to an equal degree, the burden of one's assertion must be, precisely, that none of them is either true or false; the status 'neither true nor false', unlike the others considered, is one that could coherently attach to all four possibilities equally.

In fact, I suggest that this is *why* the further alternatives 'both is and is not' and 'neither is nor is not' are introduced. 'No more is than is not', by itself, admits of the two possibilities 'is *F*' and 'is not *F*' both being true or both being false, and hence does not sufficiently reflect the utter indefiniteness of things. The addition of the other two alternatives, each of them in turn holding true 'no more' than the first two, rules out these eventualities,[41] and really does exclude us from saying anything definite about anything. If the question is whether some given object is F, the answer, according to the form of speech we are being told to adopt, is not that it is *F*, nor that it is not *F*, nor that it is both *F* and not *F*, nor that it is neither; none of these would be correct. Yet none of them would be incorrect, either; the negation of these possible answers would be no more appropriate than their assertion. So there is

---

[40] This assumes, of course, that the Law of Non-Contradiction holds. We shall see later (Ch. 3, Sect. 2) that there is no good reason to suppose that Pyrrho denied the Law of Non-Contradiction. But, as far the present point is concerned, we would still reach the same conclusion even if we imagined that the Law of Non-Contradiction was suspended. In this case all four of 'is', 'is not', 'both is and is not', and 'neither is nor is not' *could* in principle be jointly true, or jointly false. But then, again, the result would be that all sorts of sensations and opinions would be true or false or both; and this would be very odd, given that Pyrrho has just insisted that our sensations and opinions 'neither tell the truth nor lie'—in other words, that they have a distinct and special status that is neither truth nor falsehood. On this point see further Ch. 3 n. 26 and accompanying text.

[41] As should be clear by now, it is actually the alternative 'neither is nor is not' that does the work here; 'both is and is not' is not strictly speaking necessary. The passage of Aulus Gellius mentioned above (11 5 4) in fact omits the alternative 'both is and is not'; if Pyrrho's form of words in that passage does indeed parallel the 'no more' locution in the Aristocles passage (see above, n. 37), this one difference between the two possibly indicates a recognition of that point.

absolutely nothing that we can say about the object—or at least, absolutely
nothing definite; all we can say is that it is no more F than not F or both or
neither.[42] On the second reading, then—and on these grounds the second
seems far preferable to the first—we are being told to adopt a form of speech
that precisely captures the indeterminacy thesis introduced earlier in the
passage, and which remains entirely consistent with the inference immediately drawn from that thesis, that our sensations and opinions are neither true
nor false.[43]

We have been assuming so far that 'is' and 'is not' are to be interpreted as
'is F' and 'is not F'—the predicative use of *esti*, with any arbitrary predicate
to be supplied, that is common in Greek philosophy. The sense that this has
allowed us to make of the passage is a good indication that this is at least *one*
possible reading. But it is quite possible that other uses of 'is' are also
intended, in particular the existential use (which is also common at least in
later Greek philosophy), and also, if among the 'things' included under 'each
single thing' are states of affairs, the 'veridical' use, where to say that something *esti*, 'is', is to say that it *is so*, or *is the case*. In any of these usages, to
say that something 'is', or that it 'is not', would be to allow that reality was
not wholly indeterminate, or that some sensations or opinions might be true
or might be false. If our speech is truly to remain consistent with the indeterminacy thesis, we have to maintain, for whatever usage of 'is' may be at issue,
that any given thing no more is than is not or both is and is not or neither is
nor is not, where this expresses the fact that all four possibilities obtain to an

---

[42] I assume that the form of speech here recommended is supposed to be used in those cases
where it is the characterization of *how things are in their true natures* that is at issue—not that
this is the only kind of remark we are *ever* allowed to make. There may be other ways of speaking about things that do not purport to capture their true natures (for example, speaking about
how they appear to us), and that are therefore not ruled out by Pyrrho's prescription concerning
what we should say. We shall return to this point in the next chapter.

[43] Note that we need not take this form of speech to be self-applicable; that is, we need not
take it that the utterly indefinite state of affairs referred to in this form of speech itself obtains
'no more' than its negation (or both or neither). As with the 'things' (*pragmata*) spoken of in the
indeterminacy thesis, it is plausible to suppose that by 'each single thing' Pyrrho means to refer
to each of the objects of everyday experience. The form of speech we are being offered is one
that is supposed to reflect the fact that our sensations and opinions are neither true nor false; it
is thus likely that the 'things' about which we are supposed to adopt this utterly indefinite form
of speech are the things that are the content of those sensations and opinions. (Recall that 'opinion' can be understood in an Eleatic/Platonic fashion, as referring specifically to opinions that
take on trust the world of ordinary experience.) Of course, the indeterminacy thesis casts doubt
on the very notion of distinct individual 'things'. But if the intended usages of 'is' are broader
than the predicative usage assumed so far (see the next paragraph), this point is again taken
account of by the utterly indefinite form of speech here recommended; 'each single thing' no
more exists than does not exist, etc. If the 'things' in question are the items given to us in ordinary experience—an experience that we have just been told not to trust—it is only to be
expected that their status should be called into question; and the recommended form of speech
allows for this, since it itself calls into question, at least implicitly, whether the phrase 'each
single thing' has any genuine referents.

equal degree—and where this, in turn, is true because none of them either obtains or does not obtain.

4. The results for those who are so disposed

I conclude my analysis of the passage with a brief look at the answer to the third question, the question what will be the result for those who adopt the attitude just described. The result according to Timon is said to be *aphasia* and *ataraxia*. We are also told that Aenesidemus said that the result (presumably, that is, the result of adopting whatever comparable attitude he recommended) is pleasure; but this is not, of course, part of Timon's account of Pyrrho, and for our current purposes may be left aside.[44] *Ataraxia*, 'freedom from worry', is familiar from later Pyrrhonism, as well as from Epicureanism; though the route to freedom from worry may or may not be the same for Pyrrho as for Sextus, there is at least no doubt about the meaning of the word. With *aphasia* things are a little different. Sextus devotes a chapter to *aphasia* (*PH* 1.192–3) in the section of book I of *Outlines of Pyrrhonism* on the sceptical 'formulae', or stock expressions (such as 'no more', discussed above), and there it is clear that the term refers to an attitude of 'non-assertion', closely related to suspension of judgement; to be in a state of *aphasia* is to refrain from commitment to any claims, positive or negative, about the nature of things. On the other hand, the usual and literal meaning of the word is 'speechlessness'. It might be thought that, since we have just been told *what we should say* about things, *aphasia* cannot be used here in its literal sense 'speechlessness'. However, since *aphasia* is not itself the attitude expressed by statements of the type we have been told to use concerning 'each single thing', but is the *result* of adopting that attitude, this does not follow. If there is any attitude of 'non-assertion' in the passage, it is surely that very attitude captured by the special form of words that we have been told to adopt. As we saw, this form of words clearly amounts to a certain kind of withdrawal from definite claims (and this much is true *however* we understand the term 'no more'); it may not be the very same type of non-assertion as Sextus is talking about—we will come back to this point in a moment—but it is clearly non-assertion of some sort. But now, it would be odd to say that non-assertion is the *result* of adopting this form of words, if non-assertion was what adopting the form of words itself consisted

---

44 Some scholars have supposed that Timon originally listed some third effect of adopting the recommended attitude, and that Aristocles has for some reason replaced this with the reference to Aenesidemus. But the supposition is quite unfounded; on this see Bett (1994a: n. 84), and, on the significance of the reference to Aenesidemus, pp. 173–5.

in. And this suggests that literal 'speechlessness' is after all what Timon has in mind by *aphasia*.[45] The wholly unopinionated attitude that is being proposed, and the wholly indefinite form of speech that accompanies it, are indeed astonishing, and could easily be expected to reduce to a stunned silence someone who first assumes them.

This last point is worth following a little further. Timon does say that *aphasia* is the *first* effect of adopting the attitude specified in answering the second question. He does not say that it is a continuing or final effect. In fact, the Greek *prōton men aphasian, epeita d'ataraxian* suggests, or at least can very easily be read as suggesting, that *aphasia* is *only* an initial effect—the effect is first *aphasia but then* (instead) *ataraxia*. The implied contrast between these two effects suggests, further, that *aphasia*, as opposed to *ataraxia*, is something disturbing, which is then superseded by the lack of disturbance termed *ataraxia*. According to the Greek lexicon—and consultation of the passages there cited[46] bears this out—*aphasia* frequently refers to a speechlessness brought on by 'fear or perplexity'; and this fits the present passage very nicely. The indeterminacy thesis is indeed very surprising, and so is the attitude recommended for those who accept it; until one gets used to it, it might well leave one tongue-tied from intellectual vertigo. But once one does get used to it, one finds that shock and speechlessness are replaced by peace of mind.[47] Or, at least, this is the claim; we shall need to consider later *why* it

---

[45] It is worth emphasizing that the case for this reading is quite independent of my broader metaphysical reading of the passage. Whether or not my interpretation is right—and, in particular, whether or not the *ou mallon* statement expresses indeterminacy or suspension of judgement—the *ou mallon* statement constitutes a certain kind of non-assertion; and *this* is why it is better not to understand *aphasia* itself as meaning 'non-assertion'. I have been accused of implausibly rendering *aphasia* as 'speechlessness' as part of a misguided project of assembling every possible scrap of evidence, no matter how flimsy, for the indeterminacy thesis. But, quite apart from the fact that there is nothing inherently implausible or flimsy about translating a word according to its normal usage, this translation has nothing whatever to do with my case for the indeterminacy thesis.

[46] Euripides, *Helen*, 549; *Iphigenia at Aulis* 837; Aristophanes, *Thesmophoriazusae* 904; Plato, *Laws* 636e5; *Philebus* 21d4.

[47] The meaning of the term *aphasia* in this passage has been discussed recently in Brunschwig (1997: sect. I). Brunschwig's analysis is in accord with my own on many points, and especially in taking the word in its original sense 'not speaking', rather than in Sextus' more technical sense. Brunschwig (1997: 304–5), none the less criticizes my suggestion (as argued for in Bett 1994a: sect. IV) that a *contrast* is intended between *aphasia* and *ataraxia*. He maintains that (1) the text does not require us to understand a contrast—it is possible that *ataraxia* is supposed to be superimposed on *aphasia* rather than replacing it; (2) since the answer to the third question is supposed to give the results of a procedure followed by those who were seeking *happiness*, one would expect the effects described here to be beneficial rather than troubling; and (3) *aphasia* need not denote a *total* silence, but might refer instead to an exceptional reticence (such as Pyrrho is elsewhere said to practice (see Ch. 2, n. 31))—just as other terms with alpha privative need not, according to Aristotle (*Met.* 1022^{b}32–1023^{a}4), denote total privation. On the first point, I agree that the *prōton men . . . epeita de* formulation does not force my interpretation; but it does clearly permit it. On the second point, I do not see why the fact that the

should be supposed that freedom from worry is the ultimate effect of adopting the recommended attitude—and also how far this may square with the reason Sextus gives for its being the effect of his own sceptical procedure. I return to these questions in the next chapter.

5. Contrasts with later Pyrrhonism, and an alleged conflict with Aristocles

I have argued for a reading of the Aristocles passage that makes Pyrrho's position look substantially different from the later Pyrrhonist outlook expounded in *Outlines of Pyrrhonism*; and it may be helpful at this point to summarize just what these differences are. As noted just above, the alleged end point, *ataraxia*, is the same in both cases.[48] And it is also true that this end point is achieved, in both cases, through a certain type of withdrawal from the holding of opinions. But the character of this withdrawal differs a good deal from the one to the other. Most centrally, Pyrrho does not adopt the later Pyrrhonist attitude of *epochē*, suspension of judgement. On the contrary, he holds a metaphysical position—reality is inherently indeterminate; his prescription that we should avoid opinions is based precisely on his adherence to this metaphysical position, which, as I have suggested, he may be understood to regard as itself *more* than mere opinion. He also tells us to employ a form of words reflecting the utter indefiniteness of things. And again, this is not a matter of our being told to *refrain* from any attempt to describe how things are—as the *epochē* of later Pyrrhonism would lead us to expect. Rather, we are being told that we *should* describe how things are—namely, by using this complicated formula reflecting utter indefiniteness. In doing so, we are, as mentioned earlier, in a sense adopting a form of 'non-assertion'; we are making no definite claims about things, in the sense that we are attributing no definite characteristics to things. But this is not by any means the same as Sextus' posture of 'non-assertion', where one does not commit oneself in any way

goal is happiness is a difficulty for my reading; the *eventual* result certainly is something that can qualify as happiness, and there is nothing in the passage to rule out the possibility that troublesome states of mind may need to be endured *before* that ultimate goal can be achieved. And on the third point, though *aphasia need* not perhaps denote a condition in which one says nothing at all (as opposed to saying very little), this is surely its usual sense. However, I accept that Brunschwig's alternative suggestion cannot be excluded. This minor uncertainty does not, as far as I can see, have implications for any other aspect of Pyrrho's thought.

[48] We shall see in the next chapter that there seem to be some differences in the finer details of what *ataraxia* consists in for the two thinkers; but this need not occupy us at present.

on the question how things are in their true natures. Pyrrho's recommended form of speech does involve a commitment concerning the real natures of things; it attributes no definite characteristics to things precisely because it expresses a commitment to the thesis that, in their real natures, things *have* no definite characteristics.

Hence, besides there being no suspension of judgement, there is also none of the balancing of conflicting claims, the undecidability or 'equal strength' (*isostheneia*) of opposing positions, which in *Outlines of Pyrrhonism* is crucial to generating suspension of judgement. Pyrrho is quite prepared to make a certain type of claim about how things are—namely, that they are utterly indefinite. And the effect of this is to invalidate all the other, more normal claims that we might be inclined to make about things—claims that qualify, in his usage, as 'opinions'. These claims are invalidated not in the sense that we become unable to discover whether or not they are correct, but in that they *are* discovered to be neither correct not incorrect; their truth-value is not unknown, but known to be something other than the value 'true'.

If I have been right, then, it looks as if epistemological difficulties play little or no part in Pyrrho's general scheme. The account does have what are, in a loose sense, epistemological consequences; because of the indeterminacy thesis, we are told that we should not trust our sensations and opinions. But, as just noted, this is not because of any difficulties we might have in determining their accuracy; Pyrrho claims to have settled that question—they are *not* accurate, for they are neither true nor false. Questions about our ability to know things do not seem to worry him at all; what drives his account is, rather, the *conviction* that things are in reality very different from how we ordinarily take them to be.

Now, I have developed this interpretation of Pyrrho solely on the basis of an examination of the actual words in which Aristocles summarizes Timon's account. As I emphasized at the outset, this is undoubtedly the place to *start*, if one is trying to reconstruct Pyrrho's philosophy. But equally clearly, one cannot *end* there; one also has to consider the relation between Aristocles' summary of Timon and other relevant evidence. And it may be objected at this point that much of the other evidence bearing on the question of Pyrrho's thought creates severe difficulties for the understanding of Pyrrho that I have proposed. An obvious place to begin, in assessing this issue, is the text that is literally the closest to Aristocles' summary of Timon—that is, his own introduction to this summary; it will immediately be claimed that Aristocles here makes clear that, in his view at least, the passage does have to do with epistemological concerns and not metaphysical ones. The opening of the passage, to recall, is as follows:

It is necessary above all to consider our own knowledge; for if it is our nature to know nothing, there is no need to enquire any further into other things. There were some among the ancients, too, who made this statement, whom Aristotle has argued against. Pyrrho of Elis was also a powerful advocate of such a position.

What are we to make of these remarks?[49]

The first thing to say about them is that they very probably serve as the introduction not just to the discussion of Pyrrho, but to a much longer discussion of a number of philosophies that might be thought, in one way or another, to impugn our knowledge of things. Eusebius reproduces five passages on this theme from book VIII of Aristocles' *Peri philosophias* (*Praep. evang.* XIV.17–21); there are chapters on the Eleatics and those who supposedly shared their views, on the Cyrenaics, on Protagoras, and on the Epicureans, in addition to the chapter on the Pyrrhonists, which itself contains discussion of Aenesidemus as well as Pyrrho and Timon. It is clear from internal evidence that Eusebius does not give these excerpts in the original order;[50] and it seems highly likely that the chapter on Pyrrho and others, with its general opening remarks, originally introduced the entire sequence, even though it does not occur first in Eusebius. As befits his Aristotelian affiliation, Aristocles is opposed to all these philosophies; this is implied by the reference to Aristotle in the passage just quoted, but also by the following statement, with which the entire sequence appears to have closed.[51] 'Indeed we make bold to say that those who employ both sensations and reason for the knowledge of things are philosophizing correctly' (XIV.17.9). Both these faculties are necessary, and, with both of them, knowledge of the world around us is indeed possible; anyone who places credence in just one of them, dismissing the other, or who denies the possibility of knowledge in general, must be vehemently opposed.

Now, as we have seen, Pyrrho did say that sensations and opinions were not to be trusted. This by itself, then, qualifies him as a target for Aristocles' criticism—in the same way that the Eleatics' suspicion of the senses qualifies them for inclusion and criticism (XIV.17), even though they too came to this suspicion through a metaphysical thesis concerning what truly is, rather than through primarily epistemological considerations. However, this does not entirely close the issue; for Aristocles specifically singles out Pyrrho as among those who said that it is our nature to know nothing. Why should he do this if, as I have claimed, epistemological difficulties are not the main focus of Pyrrho's attention according to the summary?

Part of the answer is that, although the chapter on the Pyrrhonians begins with a summary of the views of Pyrrho in particular, it also makes numerous references to Aenesidemus; and we know from elsewhere that the impos-

---

[49] Cf. XIV.18.8, 9, where Pyrrho and Timon are said to hold that 'everything is unknowable' (*panta agnōsta*).

[50] On this, and on the order of the chapters in Aristocles' text, see Moraux (1984: 124–7).

[51] On this point, again see Moraux (1984: 124–7).

sibility of our achieving 'apprehension' (*katalēpsis*) of things was for Aenesidemus a major concern.[52] In addition, though some of Aristocles' later criticisms refer specifically to the details of his summary of Pyrrho's views— as when he challenges the claim that things are 'equally indifferent' (XIV.18.6)—it is clear at several points that he regards the views of Pyrrho and of Aenesidemus as amounting to essentially the same thing.[53] One such case is the incidental reference to Aenesidemus in the passage on which we have concentrated; Aristocles says that Aenesidemus took the effect of adopting the attitude previously discussed to be pleasure—as if that attitude itself, so far attributed only to Pyrrho, could just as readily be attributed to Aenesidemus. Later (XIV.18.16) he speaks in the same breath of Timon's work *Silloi* and 'the lengthy expositions of Aenesidemus'; and at the end of the chapter he asserts that, though the ideas of Pyrrho and Timon were long forgotten, recently 'a certain Aenesidemus began to revive this babble' (XIV.18.29). And, since Aenesidemus is, for Aristocles, by far the more recent figure—without whom, he implies, he would not have had to bother with this particular mode of thinking at all—it is entirely possible that his impression of Aenesidemus would have coloured his attitude towards the Pyrrhonian tradition as a whole. Thus, since Aenesidemus was indeed concerned about the 'inapprehensibility' (*akatalēpsia*) of things, it is not surprising that Aristocles should have emphasized this concern when speaking of Pyrrho and Timon as well.

Aristocles may be a careful and reliable reporter of other people's views— as I noted earlier, the evidence seems to bear out this verdict[54]—but his reactions to the views he summarizes may of course be shaped by his own perspective and his own agenda. This is no doubt the case here; he assimilates Pyrrho to Aenesidemus, because Aenesidemus is much more vivid to him. In addition—and this is really the more important point—he concentrates on the

---

[52] See esp. Photius' summary of Aenesidemus' *Pyrrhonian Discourses*—169b20, 25–6, 28–9, 170b11–12, 170b25–6, etc. We shall return to this issue in Ch. 4.

[53] This is true even though his objections to the claim that things are 'equally indifferent' seem to presuppose the interpretation of 'equally indifferent' according to which it purports to specify the nature of things—an activity from which Aenesidemus, with his much greater epistemological caution, would have rigorously refrained; more on this in the next section.

[54] For a review of the evidence on Aristocles' credibility, see Bett (1994a: sect. VI). Note also that there is no difficulty in distinguishing between his summary of Pyrrho's views and his own reactions to them. As we have seen, he repeatedly makes clear that in the summary he is closely following Timon; he also makes clear exactly where the summary begins (the first 'Timon says' (XIV.18.2)) and where it ends ('These, then, are the main points of what they say; let us examine whether they speak correctly'—XIV.18.5). There is, then, nothing arbitrary about favouring the evidence of the summary over the evidence of Aristocles' own verdicts on Pyrrho and Timon (as I am in effect doing); the summary tells us—to all appearances reliably—what Timon himself said, while the rest of the passage has to do with the *uses* to which Aristocles himself, a philosopher with quite distinct goals of his own, wishes to put that summary—and it is easy to see which is which.

epistemological implications of both thinkers' views because epistemology is what *his* book (or this part of it, at least) was all about. From this point of view, the difference between Pyrrho and Aenesidemus would surely have seemed unimportant to him. Pyrrho's view, as Aristocles' own summary presents it, is just as inimical to what he takes to be the right epistemological view as is the view of Aenesidemus; and, given his interest, in this part of *Peri philosophias*, in insisting on the right epistemological view as against various rival views, it is not surprising that he would speak of Pyrrho's view as, first and foremost, a specimen of the view that we can have no knowledge.

It is not as if this is simply false, on the reading of Pyrrho that I am proposing. On the contrary, there is a sense in which it is quite true—and we touched on this much earlier—that Pyrrho's view, even on the metaphysical interpretation, entails that we know nothing. We have no knowledge, that is, of things as they are presented to us through our sensations—of the relatively stable, distinct and determinate material objects that we ordinarily, and Aristocles after philosophical reflection, take to make up the real world. We can have no knowledge of these objects, because, given the indeterminacy thesis, things are in reality *not* like this at all—in fact, it is not clear that we can even speak of some definitely denumerable set of 'things'—and this is why our sensations are not to be trusted. So the world containing the things of which Aristocles thinks we can have knowledge is indeed a world of which Pyrrho would say—if the question was put to him in this way—that we know nothing; for, in the nature of things, there is *no* such world. To judge from Aristocles' own summary of his views, Pyrrho would probably not have chosen to frame the issue in this way. But that is the issue that Aristocles, for his own purposes, chooses to address.

For these reasons, then, we need not see Aristocles' introduction to the passage as derailing the conclusion that epistemology was not a particular interest of Pyrrho; it is, at this stage in his work, a particular interest of Aristocles, and that affects the focus of what he has to say about Pyrrho. Pyrrho's views, as Aristocles himself reports them, certainly do pose a *threat* to our knowledge, and this is what Aristocles wants to talk about; moreover, he is especially eager to talk about it given that there is a much more overt threat to knowledge in the writings of his near-contemporary Aenesidemus, who claims to be a follower of Pyrrho. But the fact that he introduces Pyrrho as holding that we know nothing[55] does not show that the central features of

---

[55] What of the words '*it is our nature* [*pephukamen*] to know nothing', which seem to direct the focus towards our cognitive shortcomings, and away from any consideration of the nature of things? I do not think that this phrase can be taken as evidence for the outlook of Pyrrho in particular. It is not initially introduced with Pyrrho, or indeed any particular thinker, in mind; Aristocles says that an examination of our own knowledge must precede all other enquiries, and that, if this pessimistic view about our knowledge is correct, then enquiry in general is at an end. The pessimistic view is not connected with Pyrrho until a few lines later; Aristocles first

Pyrrho's philosophy were epistemological in character, or that Aristocles thought they were; all it shows is that this is the aspect of Pyrrho's philosophy about which Aristocles happens to care in this context.

6. Other evidence (1): echoes or confusions?

In this section and the next I consider other texts concerning Pyrrho that touch on issues akin to those raised by the Aristocles passage. To repeat, one of the reasons why the metaphysical interpretation of that passage—versions of which have been proposed by a number of scholars[56]—remains controversial is the perception that this is too difficult to square even with other evidence relating to Pyrrho himself (let alone the later Pyrrhonist tradition). But this, I shall suggest, is not so. A few other texts actually appear to echo the evidence of the Aristocles passage, read metaphysically (and these are the concern of the present section); several other texts are at least compatible with it; and those that are not compatible, of which there are admittedly a number, are easily explicable as the result of a projection back onto Pyrrho of ideas that in fact belong to some later phase of the Pyrrhonist tradition. As we saw, no such suspicion attaches to the Aristocles passage itself; whatever questions may be raised about its credibility, it is at least not to be faulted for anachronism, since Aristocles gives every appearance of basing his report directly and closely on the words of Timon. Moreover, the Aristocles passage is by far the most detailed and specific of any report on Pyrrho's philosophy. For both reasons, these other conflicting texts may be taken to undermine neither the authority of the Aristocles passage, nor the metaphysical interpretation of that passage; if the metaphysical interpretation makes the best sense of the passage, then that is how we should understand the philosophy that Timon recorded from Pyrrho, and these other texts pose no obstacle to that understanding.

First, then, the evidence that might be thought to support the metaphysical interpretation. We may begin by noting that Aristocles himself, despite his primary concentration on the epistemological implications of Pyrrho's views,

---

connects it vaguely with 'some of the ancients'. Then, when he does connect it with Pyrrho, he says that Pyrrho strongly maintained 'such things' (*toiauta*), which certainly suggests that Pyrrho held *some* epistemological view that puts a stop to further enquiry—as he does, according to my reading of the subsequent summary—but which leaves open the possibility that this view may not have been best captured by *precisely* the words 'it is our nature to know nothing'. Finally, as already noted (above, n. 49), when he does attribute a pessimistic epistemological view to Pyrrho and Timon specifically, it is with the words *panta agnōsta*, 'everything is unknowable', which, at least on the surface, is a claim about the things rather than about our cognitive powers.

[56] See e.g. DC 218–34; Sedley (1983*a*: 14); LS i. 16–17; Sakezles (1993: 77–95).

appears to read Pyrrho's claim that things are 'equally indifferent' in the metaphysical way. His sarcastic response (XIV.18.6) is that, if things really are 'equally indifferent', then Pyrrho and Timon themselves will not be any different from the ordinary run of humanity; and this response has point only if Pyrrho's words are understood as saying that *there are no intrinsic differences* between things, rather than that we are unable to differentiate between them. However, since he is being sarcastic, and since he is in general very unsympathetic to all varieties of Pyrrhonism, this point is of no great value; Aristocles might easily be accused of distorting the meaning of the passage for polemical purposes.

There is also a line of Timon quoted by Sextus, coupled with Sextus' introduction to it. In *Against the Ethicists* (*M* 11.140), Sextus says that the only way to release the dogmatist from his troubled existence is 'if we show to the person who is disturbed on account of his avoidance of the bad or his pursuit of the good, that there is not anything either good or bad by nature, "But these things are judged by mind on the part of humans", to quote Timon'.[57] The burden of this text is not that we must suspend judgement about the goodness or badness of things, but that *nothing is* good or bad by nature; and this is a view whose truth we are said to be in a position to *show* to the dogmatists.[58] Now, we are not specifically told that this view was held by Timon. However, the context of the quotation at least implies that he held some such view; Sextus certainly makes it sound as if Timon's words 'these things' refer to good and bad, and the 'but' suggests that what preceded the quoted line was some deflationary comment about the non-reality of good and bad. It is also true that there is no mention of Pyrrho here; and it cannot simply be assumed that anything Timon says, even without mentioning Pyrrho, is also part of what Pyrrho believed, or even part of what Timon took Pyrrho to believe. However, it is at least clear that the view in question fits better with the metaphysical interpretation of the Aristocles passage than with the epistemological one.

But the most substantial text giving the impression of being in tune with the Aristocles passage, read metaphysically, occurs near the beginning of Diogenes Laertius' life of Pyrrho (9.61). Diogenes tells us that Pyrrho 'said that nothing is either fine or ignoble or just or unjust; and similarly in all cases that nothing is the case in reality [*mēden einai tēi alētheiai*], but that human beings do everything by convention and habit; for each thing is no more this than that'. One would certainly not gather from these words that Pyrrho suspended judgement, or adopted any other distinctively epistemological attitude; instead, the passage

---

57 'By mind' (*noōi*) is sometimes emended to 'by convention' (*nomōi*). This is possible but not necessary; see Bett (1997: commentary *ad loc*).

58 On the consistency of this with Sextus' own strategy in *Against the Ethicists*, see Bett (1997: introduction and commentary, *passim*); also below, Ch. 4, Sect. 3.

appears to represent him as maintaining a thesis about the nature of things, a thesis according to which, as in the Aristocles passage, things have no definite characteristics.[59] Again, as in the Aristocles passage, the words 'no more', which appear in the final clause, invite a straightforward and literal interpretation, rather than the special redefinition given them in *Outlines of Pyrrhonism*; 'each thing is no more this than that' has to be understood as a corollary of the previous claims of indefiniteness, and hence it must mean 'each thing possesses any given quality to no greater extent than it possesses the opposite quality'.[60] Nor is it possible to understand the passage as providing just one half of a *pair* of opposing positions that *together* were designed to induce suspension of judgement. First, there is no indication in the text of any position opposing this one. But more important, Diogenes immediately continues 'he was consistent [with the position just stated] in his life' (9.62), and goes on to describe Pyrrho's alleged refusal to trust his senses. Whether or not there is any truth to this story—and we will return to this matter in the next chapter—it is clear that Diogenes takes Pyrrho's philosophical position to be adequately summed up in the passage just discussed; Pyrrho commits himself to the view that 'nothing is the case in reality', and *so*, it is alleged, he places no credence in the definite states of affairs presented to him by his senses. These remarks about the practical effect of his philosophy also indicate, incidentally, that Diogenes, or his source, does not intend the preceding passage to be understood as solely ethical in focus.[61] It is true that the specific examples of opposite qualities neither of which is possessed by anything are ethical qualities. But this does not show that the generalization 'similarly in all cases nothing is the case in reality' is to be understood as restricted to ethical qualities; and the fact that the practical consequence of the position is supposed to be total mistrust of the senses suggests, on the contrary, that the position is understood by Diogenes or his source as applying also to sensory qualities—in other words, as having the same kind of range as the indeterminacy thesis has in the Aristocles passage.

Does this passage of Diogenes then provide positive *support* for the metaphysical reading of the Aristocles passage? Unfortunately, there is a complication. The passage is immediately preceded by a remark, attributed to the otherwise unknown Ascanius of Abdera, about Pyrrho 'introducing the form [of philosophy] consisting of inapprehensibility and suspension of judgement'. Clearly Ascanius thinks that Pyrrho was the first adherent of the kind

---

[59] I shall return in the next chapter to the possible significance of the remark about 'convention and habit'.

[60] There is nothing here corresponding to Aristocles' additional components 'both is and is not' or 'neither is nor is not'. Although, as I argued above, these do serve a purpose within the logic of the Aristocles passage, their omission is easily explicable as an effect of Diogenes' frequently terse and telegraphic style of writing.

[61] *Contra* Ausland (1989: 371–2); Brunschwig (1994*a*, 208); and cf. above, n. 31.

of philosophy we find in the later Pyrrhonists—not just that he was a figure-head for that later tradition, but that he himself espoused the same outlook,[62] even if he did not perhaps use the very same *terms* 'inapprehensibility' and 'suspension of judgement'.[63] And, if this is so, it may be said, the passage that follows does nothing at all to support a metaphysical interpretation of Pyrrho's philosophy; all it shows is that Ascanius confused 'Pyrrho *would not assert that anything* is either fine or ignoble or just or unjust', or something of the kind—in other words, a genuinely suspensive remark—with the meta-physical-sounding 'Pyrrho *said that nothing* is either fine or ignoble or just or unjust'.

That there is some confusion here is undeniable. The metaphysical-sound-ing remarks do not properly *illustrate* the claim that Pyrrho was the first prac-titioner of suspension of judgement, as they purport to do. However, it does not follow that the culprit is Ascanius, or that the metaphysical-sounding remarks are necessarily to be discounted. First, it is not at all clear that these latter remarks are to be attributed to Ascanius. The passage reads 'Hence he [Pyrrho] seems to have philosophized most nobly, introducing the form [of philosophy] consisting of inapprehensibility and suspension of judgement, as Ascanius of Abdera says; for he [Pyrrho] said that nothing is either fine or ignoble or just or unjust', and so on. The only point clearly to be attributed to Ascanius is that Pyrrho 'introduced' inapprehensibility and suspension of judgement; it is entirely possible that what follows derives from a *different* source—that Ascanius held the common later view (on which more in the next section) that Pyrrho and the later Pyrrhonists espoused the same philos-ophy, but that the following lines accurately reflect an earlier phase of the tradition in which this assimilation had not taken place. If so, of course, we must suppose that Diogenes himself is confused, since he has juxtaposed these points in an inconsistent and misleading way. But, as every reader of Diogenes knows, he is very far from being immune to confusions of this kind; there would be nothing surprising here.

Besides, not all of the metaphysical-sounding passage can be explained away as easily as was suggested. The words 'similarly in all cases that noth-ing is the case in reality, but that human beings do everything by convention and habit' are not readily understood as due to a confusion between 'did not say that anything . . .' and 'said that nothing . . .'. The second part of this,

---

[62] For this usage of *eisagein*, 'introduce', to refer to the introduction of an idea into philo-sophical currency, compare Aristotle, *NE* 1096[a]13 on Plato's 'introduction' of the Forms. Contrast Eusebius (*Praep. evang.* XIV.17.10 (=DC T25B)), who speaks of 'Pyrrho, from whom the school of those called Sceptics originated'. This places Pyrrho as the *starting point* of the philosophy of *epochē*, without necessarily being an adherent of it himself; but the word *eisagein* cannot be read as weakly as this.

[63] This may be the point of the curious periphrasis 'the *form* [*eidos*] consisting of inappre-hensibility and suspension of judgement' (on this, see DC 136).

about 'convention and habit', clearly represents something Pyrrho *did* say, not something he *refrained* from saying; but if this is true of the second part, it must be true of the first part also. Now, one can always postulate that these words are the result of some deeper confusion by Diogenes or his source; such hypotheses can never be conclusively ruled out. But it is not clear why this route should be thought preferable to the other one, which takes the meta-physical-sounding remarks at face value (and as chiming with the Aristocles passage), and then supposes that Diogenes (or his source) has confused the issue by throwing in the reference to Ascanius and suspension of judge-ment.[64]

It must, though, be admitted that none of the texts we have been looking at provides clear corroborating evidence for the metaphysical understanding of the Aristocles passage. What we can say, however, is that these texts certainly provide no *obstacle* to the metaphysical understanding of the Aristocles passage; indeed, *if* the metaphysical understanding is accepted as the most plausible reading of that passage, then these texts fit nicely with the view of Pyrrho's philosophy that it suggests. And that is all that this part of my argument is designed to show. Since the Aristocles passage is the only one purporting to give a general summary of Pyrrho's philosophical views, it is not surprising if no other text gives positive support to one particular reading of it. What I am trying to establish here is simply that no other text creates any serious *difficulties* for the reading of it for which I have argued.

7. Other evidence (2): the inconclusive and the anachronistic

Other evidence relating to Pyrrho is at least compatible with that reading— though here, unlike in the cases considered so far, one would not even be

---

[64] A couple of other texts seem to derive from the same doxographical tradition as the passage of Diogenes we have been considering. The Suda under 'Pyrrho' (=DC T1B) says that Pyrrho 'thought that nothing was by nature ignoble or fine, but by habit and convention'. And in book I of his *Refutation of All Heresies*, Hippolytus tells us (23.2) that, according to Pyrrho, 'nothing is true, either of intelligible things or of sensible things', and also (23.3) that the followers of Pyrrho say 'that fire is no more fire than anything else'. (This passage occurs as DC T82.) But these texts are clearly of no help in settling how we should interpret the Diogenes passage. For one thing, the Hippolytus text contains the same apparent contradiction as occurs in Diogenes, saying that Pyrrho 'first introduced the inapprehensibility of everything' (1.23.1); see also the remark in the Suda under *epochē* (=DC T1C), which is clearly copying either Diogenes or his source on the same point. But, in any case, the Suda is much more sketchy on these matters than Diogenes, and Hippolytus is even more confused than Diogenes; he refers to Pyrrho as the originator of the sceptical Academy—but then also speaks as if the Academics and Pyrrhonians are two separate groups. (He also attributes to Pyrrho (1.23.2) the Heraclitean view that 'reality is in flux and changeable and never stays in the same state'; on this, see further Ch. 3 n. 38.)

tempted to try showing that it actively supports it. I mentioned earlier the passage of Aulus Gellius (11.5.4) that might be taken to throw light on the Aristocles passage's usage of 'no more'. Pyrrho, says Aulus Gellius— almost certainly relying on Favorinus, a contemporary of Plutarch who associated himself with Academic scepticism—used the expression 'this thing is no more this way than that way or neither way'; to give an added impression of authenticity, the quotation is in the original Greek. Now, I said earlier that the Aristocles passage, in the part where we are told what we should say 'about each single thing', appears to be in agreement with the expression quoted by Gellius in that it treats 'neither is nor is not' (as well as 'both is and is not', not mentioned by Gellius) as a disjunct on a par with each of the two initial alternatives 'is' and 'is not'. In both authors, that is, we are to say of the thing that it is no more (i) F than (ii) not F or (iii) neither F nor not F.[65] But as to the sense of 'no more' (*ou mallon*) itself— whether it expresses suspension of judgement as between the various alter- natives, or whether it is used to *assert* that none of the alternatives holds to any greater extent than any other—the Gellius passage offers little help. I have insisted that, in the Aristocles passage, 'no more' is to be understood in the latter, linguistically more straightforward way. But Gellius certainly appears to treat the expression he quotes as if it is to be used to express suspension of judgement. He cites it as an expression that the Pyrrhonists recommend as a way of avoiding rash and precipitate judgement, given that the truth about things is inapprehensible (*inprensibilem*). However, the fact, if it is one, that the Pyrrhonists of Gellius' or Favorinus' day used the expression in this way—a fact that, given Sextus' slightly later usage, would not be at all surprising—does not, of course, show that this was how it was originally meant by Pyrrho himself; and, since Gellius quotes only the single sentence, we have no idea of the context in which it originally occurred. Whatever use the expression was later put to, it is perfectly possi- ble that 'no more' originally meant what it said, just as it does in the Aristocles passage; Gellius' quotation does not constitute evidence one way or the other on this question.

Similarly, Aristocles himself, in the critical portion of his chapter on the Pyrrhonists, quotes Timon as saying 'Why "yes" and why "no"?' (XIV.18.7). This is clearly reminiscent of Sextus' explanation of his 'no more' formula as doing duty for a question; 'P no more than not P' is equivalent to 'Why P rather than not P?' (*PH* 1.189). But it does not follow that the early Pyrrhonists used these words with precisely the same intention as Sextus had

---

[65] See again n. 37; my claim here applies on one reading of the Gellius passage, but another reading is possible in which the parallel is far less close. The uncertainty as between these two readings does not, however, affect my main point here, concerning the sense of *ou mallon*. On Gellius' omission of the alternative 'both is and is not', see again n. 41.

in using his 'no more' formula. 'Why "yes" and why "no"?' need not express suspension of judgement as to whether some proposition is really true or false; it could just as well be taken to express a *conviction* that the proposition in question is *neither* true nor false—precisely the type of conviction that the Aristocles passage represents as an immediate consequence of the indeterminacy thesis. ('Why *P*?' might be inviting the answer 'there is no reason to assume *P*', or it might be inviting the definite conclusion that *P* is not the case.) In fact, the context in which Aristocles quotes Timon implies that this is so. Aristocles says that, if everything is 'equally indifferent', so that one should not hold opinions, then there is no difference between differing and not differing, or between holding opinions and not holding them; the quotation is then supposed to indicate that Timon is committed to this consequence, a consequence regarded by Aristocles as a *reductio*. Aristocles, then, seems to understand 'Why "yes" and why "no"?' as accepting an intrinsic lack of differences among things—including an indeterminacy as to whether, in some particular case, one has an instance of 'differing' or 'not differing', or 'holding opinions' or 'not holding opinions'—and not as expressing suspension of judgement between opposing alternatives.[66] Again, Aristocles' highly polemical tone makes it unwise for us to regard him as supplying decisive evidence for what Timon meant here. Still, this is clearly *one* possible way of understanding Timon's words.

Later in his critique, Aristocles quotes some lines from Timon praising Pyrrho for his freedom from 'opinion and pointless laying-down-of-the-law' (*doxēs te kai eikaiēs nomothēkēs* XIV.18.19 (=DC T58)).[67] Pyrrho's rejection of opinions we have already discussed. But what of 'laying-down of the law'? If this refers to confident assertions about how things are—and this is supported by Epicurus' use of the very similar term *nomothesia* to refer to assertions about the physical world that go beyond the available evidence (*Ep. Pyth. apud* DL 10.87)—then it might be objected that Pyrrho himself, according to the metaphysical reading of the Aristocles passage, 'lays down the law' about the nature of things, in asserting the indeterminacy thesis. However, it is *pointless* laying down the law from which Pyrrho is said to be free; his own assertion of the indeterminacy thesis would presumably not qualify for this epithet. Besides, 'laying-down of the law' could well refer in this context to

---

[66] Aristocles also attributes to Timon the words 'and even why "why"?' (*kai auto to dia ti dia ti*). I think Decleva Caizzi (DC 234) is right in suggesting that these are more likely to be an additional flourish by Aristocles than anything actually said by Timon himself. Their second-order or self-reflexive character is highly consonant with the concerns introduced by Aristocles' critique; and the other evidence suggests that an explicit focus on such second-order concerns played no part in early Pyrrhonism.

[67] Also for not being weighed down by *patheōn*—perhaps 'passions', but perhaps more generally 'affections', including sensory experience; this text will be discussed in more detail in Ch. 2.

attempts to attribute some *fixed and definite character* to things; and this is precisely what the indeterminacy thesis does not do.[68]

A scholium on a passage of Lucian,[69] where Pyrrho is put on trial by Painting[70] and fails to appear (because, it is claimed, 'he thinks that nothing is a true criterion'),[71] says that Pyrrho 'had the aim of doing away with all existing things' (*eiche skopon panta anairein ta onta*). Now, *anairein*, 'do away with', is a term occurring frequently in both Diogenes Laertius and Sextus to characterize the sceptic's activity; what exactly this activity amounts to in a later Pyrrhonist context will receive some consideration in Chapter 4. For now, however, we may note that, whatever the similarities or differences may be between Pyrrho and later Pyrrhonism, there is a sense in which it is clearly true that Pyrrho, as we have reconstructed his philosophy so far, 'does away with all existing things'; since, according to the indeterminacy thesis, reality has no definite character, there are not, in the nature of things, any of the stable objects that we normally take to compose the world around us. Again, Diogenes reports that 'Aenesidemus in the first book of his *Pyrrhonian Discourses* says that Pyrrho determines nothing dogmatically because of contradiction, but follows appearances' (9.106). The talk of following appearances will be a topic for the next chapter. But the talk of 'determining nothing' is again typical of later Pyrrhonism; 'I determine nothing' is one of the stock sceptical expressions discussed in *Outlines of Pyrrhonism* (1.197), and Photius' summary of Aenesidemus' own ideas makes clear that he also employed it (*Bibl.* 170a11–12). Yet there is again a sense in which it is quite correct to say that Pyrrho 'determines nothing'; he does not attribute a determinate character to anything—in fact he maintains that nothing has any determinate character.[72] This is certainly not what Sextus

---

[68] A similar verdict applies to Pausanias' remark (6.24,5) that Pyrrho was a man who 'arrived at firm agreement on no argument' (*es bebaion homologian epi oudeni logōi katastantos*). Pausanias says this in the course of mentioning that there is a statue of Pyrrho in the market-place at Elis. Decleva Caizzi (DC 163) argues persuasively that the terminology here is pre-Hellenistic, and that Pausanias has read these words off the base of the statue itself. This does not, of course, automatically make the remark reliable; inscriptions on monuments are not generally known for their philosophical acuteness. However, it is worth noting that there is one sense in which 'arriving at firm agreement on no argument' is perfectly compatible with the indeterminacy thesis (even if other ways of reading these words may seem more congenial to the scepticism of *Outlines of Pyrrhonism*). If one thinks that reality is inherently indefinite, then arguments claiming to show that things really are some particular and definite way will not inspire 'firm agreement'; agreement to such arguments cannot be 'firm' because the things that are the subject matter of the arguments are themselves not 'firm'.

[69] *Bis. acc.* 25. This scholium occurs as DC T5.

[70] For desertion (cf. *Bis. acc.* 13). DL 9.61 tells us that Pyrrho was originally a painter; the scholiast, who repeats this information, apparently has access to the same biographical tradition.

[71] We shall return to this point in a moment.

[72] If he 'determines nothing', then it is *a fortiori* true that he 'determines nothing dogmatically'. The word 'dogmatically' (*dogmatikōs*) is a technical term from an era much later than

means by 'I determine nothing', but it is just as legitimate a way to understand the words themselves. Now, is it also correct, according to the interpretation developed here, to say that Pyrrho determines nothing 'because of contradiction'—that is, presumably, because of the presence of contradictory theories or impressions about how things are? The answer is that the Aristocles passage, and the other texts we have consulted so far, offer no information on this question; as already noted, the Aristocles passage does not say *why* Pyrrho adopted the indeterminacy thesis, merely that he did so. This is, of course, a topic we will eventually need to consider; and I shall argue in Chapter 3 that it is in fact highly probable that considerations having to do with 'contradiction' did motivate the thesis. But, at any rate, the reference to contradiction does not itself contradict anything in Aristocles' account of Pyrrho's philosophy.

In considering this last text, I have bent over backwards to take seriously evidence that might be thought to conflict with my interpretation of Pyrrho's central ideas. It is entirely possible that the apparent conflict can be explained away much more easily, as the simple product of anachronism. First, it is by no means impossible that Aenesidemus, whose work *Pyrrhonist Discourses* was (at least primarily) an account of his own philosophy, not of Pyrrho's, distorted Pyrrho's ideas so as to make them accord more closely with his own. If so, then 'determines nothing dogmatically because of contradiction' could be read through the spectacles of later Pyrrhonism, as describing some variety of suspension of judgement;[73] but this would not tell us anything directly about Pyrrho's own views. Secondly, it is quite possible that Diogenes is being inaccurate here. The much more detailed summary of book I of Aenesidemus' *Pyrrhonist Discourses* in Photius' *Bibliotheca* (169b36–170b3) attributes to the Pyrrhonists—that is, the *later* Pyrrhonists, of whom Aenesidemus himself was the leader—a view in which determining nothing,

---

Pyrrho (unlike the word 'determine' (*horizein*), which was in ordinary usage well before his lifetime). Hence there is certainly some anachronism in applying it to him; and this may incline us to suspect that DL's evidence is not wholly reliable—a suspicion for which there are other grounds (see below). However, if we continue to assume that the report does properly apply to Pyrrho, it is not impossible to reconcile it with the Aristocles passage. If the right attitude, here referred to as 'determining nothing', is to refrain from attributing any definite character to things—because they *have no* definite character—then the philosophers later labelled 'dogmatists' (namely, those who do offer specific 'determinations' of the nature of things), will indeed be subject to criticism, and it may be worth indicating that Pyrrho himself is immune from such criticism; cf. above on the term 'laying-down of the law'. It might be objected that Pyrrho's own indeterminacy thesis is itself, by the standards of later Pyrrhonism, a piece of 'dogmatism'. But that is not the point here. If 'determines nothing' here means 'attributes no determinate character to things', then the indeterminacy thesis itself does not count as a case of 'determining' something—and hence not as a case of 'determining' something 'dogmatically'.

73 I shall argue later (Ch. 4) that suspension of judgement in Aenesidemus is not precisely the same as suspension of judgement in *Outlines of Pyrrhonism*. In neither case, however, does the Pyrrho of the Aristocles passage qualify as suspending judgement.

freedom from dogmatism, and attention to contradictions in our experience of things all figure prominently. Diogenes' words 'determines nothing dogmatically because of contradiction' might very aptly be used to encapsulate this view. But, in Photius' summary, the view is never attributed to Pyrrho, only to the Pyrrhonists. The text does represent (169b26–7) a Pyrrhonist as 'one who philosophizes in the manner of Pyrrho'; but this need not suggest a following of Pyrrho on every detail of his philosophy: it might indicate only a general similarity of outlook and approach. The attribution of these ideas to Pyrrho, on the authority of Aenesidemus, could easily have resulted from a not especially careful reading of Aenesidemus by Diogenes himself or his source.

We have now shaded into the topic of the contamination of the record on Pyrrho by elements from the later Pyrrhonist tradition. A number of texts ascribe to Pyrrho ideas or attitudes that clearly are incompatible with the picture we have derived from the Aristocles passage—unlike anything considered so far. But in every case this can very naturally be explained by contamination of this sort; for the texts in question are all from a time subsequent to the revival of Pyrrhonism, and are by authors who may be expected to have been far more familiar with the revived Pyrrhonism than with the thought of Pyrrho himself. Whatever we are to say about the passage of Diogenes just discussed, some passages from Diogenes' life of Pyrrho evidently do belong in this category. Diogenes tells us (9.62) that 'Aenesidemus says that he [Pyrrho] philosophized according to the principle of suspension of judgement [*kata ton tēs epochēs logon*], but that he did not do everything without foresight'. Diogenes reports Aenesidemus' claim as a counterweight to those who alleged that Pyrrho's philosophy led him, Pyrrho, to ignore altogether what his senses told him—so that his friends had to rescue him from the edges of cliffs, from under the wheels of wagons, and so on; unlike these people, Aenesidemus maintained that Pyrrho's philosophy did *not* lead him to behave like a lunatic. Again, we will return to the question of Pyrrho's behaviour in the next chapter. But, for now, we can observe that the suggestion that Pyrrho practised suspension of judgement, like the previous case, could easily be the result either of Aenesidemus' assimilation of Pyrrho's views to his own,[74] or of Diogenes' careless paraphrasing of what Aenesidemus said. The precise details of Pyrrho's philosophy are not, in any case, the main point here; the point is that Pyrrho's philosophy, *whatever* exactly it consisted of, did not (as often alleged) make him unable to act in a sane fashion. Again, Diogenes asserts that all the followers of Pyrrho were called Pyrrhonians after the name of their teacher—and he names Timon and a couple of others whom Pyrrho is supposed personally to have taught—but also 'aporetics, sceptics, and even ephectics and zetetics from their doctrine (so to speak)' (9.69). Since only one

---

74 Aenesidemus' relation to Pyrrho receives more detailed consideration in Ch. 4, Sect. 4.

of these terms is attested prior to the period of Pyrrho and his immediate followers,[75] this claim is extremely unlikely to be literally true; but we know very well from Sextus (*PH* 1.7) that the later Pyrrhonians did call themselves by these names. Despite the valuable evidence about the differing phases of Pyrrhonism that his life of Pyrrho contains, it is clear that Diogenes himself is not sensitive to developments in the history of Pyrrhonism; and the present passage is plausibly to be accounted for as a telescoping of this history by him or his source.

Galen, too, occasionally speaks of Pyrrho, and represents him as a sceptic according to a later Pyrrhonist model;[76] but, again, there is no reason to take this seriously.[77] The Pyrrhonists were certainly of some concern to Galen; he takes their view to be a live possibility in his own day, and to be subversive, not surprisingly, of his own epistemology and medical methodology.[78] But the question whether Pyrrho's ideas were identical with those of the later Pyrrhonists is of no concern to him whatever; and, since the later Pyrrhonists did, after all, call themselves followers of Pyrrho, it could have seemed to him perfectly natural to talk occasionally of Pyrrho rather than of the Pyrrhonians, while really having in mind the Pyrrhonians all the time. Similarly Plutarch (*Table-Talk* 652b), in criticizing Epicurus for the allegedly sceptical consequences of his views, says that these views 'bring us through Protagoras straight to Pyrrho'; expanding upon this supposed consequence, he then introduces material clearly reminiscent of Aenesidemus' sixth Mode,[79] on mixtures. Once more, we need not conclude that this material derives, in this form, from Pyrrho himself; 'brings us . . . to Pyrrho' is just Plutarch's way of saying 'has damaging sceptical consequences'. Pyrrho also appears in a few

---

[75] *Zētētikos* is found in Plato (*Meno* 81e; *Rep.* 528c); the earliest author in whom any of the others is attested is Philodemus (*skeptikos*)—except for a medical use of *ephektikos* in the sense 'able to hold in check' (used in connection with various bodily excretions), which dates back to the third century BC. For the details, see LSJ. On the use of *skeptikos* in Philodemus and Philo of Alexandria, see Tarrant (1985: 23–6).

[76] *Subfig. emp.* 82,22–8 Deichgräber (which forms part of DC T67), *PHP* 5.4.12. The first of these passages, however, may contain some more reliable biographical information (to which we shall return in the next chapter); it says that Pyrrho was a man of few words (on this see also *Subfig. emp.* 84,31–85, 3 Deichgräber (=DC T68)), and cites Timon on his general demeanour. Later I shall be distinguishing between two forms of later Pyrrhonism: Aenesidemus' version and the version that appears in *Outlines of Pyrrhonism*. For our current purposes it does not matter which of these two Galen attributes to Pyrrho; for what it is worth, however, the second text seems to fit slightly better with the version found in *Outlines of Pyrrhonism*, while the first is indeterminate as between the two versions. On Galen's reactions to scepticism, see DeLacy (1991).

[77] The same may be said of the pseudo-Galenic *On the History of Philosophy*, ch. 7, p. 604 Diels (=DC T27), where Pyrrho is referred to as 'aporetic', even excessively so.

[78] e.g. *De libris propr.* 19.40K; *Diff. puls.* 8.711K; *Praenot.* 14.628K.

[79] Sixth, that is, in Sextus' and Diogenes' orderings (*PH* 1.124–8; DL 9.84–5).

passages of Lucian; he is referred to as a sceptic,[80] as a practitioner of suspension of judgement,[81] and, as we saw, as denying that there is any criterion.[82] But there is even less reason to take this as historically accurate. The point is to poke fun at scepticism, and, because the later Pyrrhonians portrayed themselves as followers of Pyrrho, Pyrrho's was no doubt the name most widely associated with scepticism; this is why Lucian chooses to depict him rather than any other sceptic—the precise details of Pyrrho's philosophy have nothing to do with it.

Finally, there is a passage referring to Pyrrho in the anonymous Commentary on Plato's *Theaetetus* (60.48–61.46 (=LS 71D)). The author contrasts Theaetetus' use of 'as it now appears' (151e2), praised by Socrates as indicating a willingness to state his beliefs, with that of the Pyrrhonians, for whom the restriction to 'what now appears' is precisely a way of *not* asserting any definite doctrines. The passage continues with a more detailed explanation of how, 'according to the man'—that is, according to Pyrrho— nothing other than what appears can serve as a criterion, and what appears is no guide to what is, because arguments and impressions on opposite sides are equal. The date of the anonymous commentator is not completely clear; but he certainly dates from a period subsequent to Aenesidemus' revival of Pyrrhonism.[83] Moreover, his account of these ideas is full of terminology from debates that flourished after Pyrrho's time—'criterion', 'convincing impression' (*pithanē phantasia*), 'apprehensive impression' (*kataleptikē phantasia*), and 'dogmatize' (*dogmatizein*); Pyrrho himself cannot have said anything closely resembling what is here attributed to him. However, this is no cause for concern. Like the other authors just examined, the anonymous author is clearly using 'Pyrrho' as a shorthand for 'the (later) Pyrrhonians'. He introduces the ideas he wishes to discuss as Pyrrhonian, and continues with the suggestion that these are the ideas of Pyrrho—as if there is no difference between the two. But, again, this is perfectly understandable, given that the Pyrrhonians represented themselves as followers of Pyrrho; only someone deeply concerned with the history of sceptical ideas—as the anonymous commentator is not—would have troubled to enquire whether the ideas of Pyrrho were really quite the same as those of the later thinkers who adopted his name.

It is possible that some of the later Pyrrhonians themselves had some scruples here. Sextus is extremely cautious about the term 'Pyrrhonian'; all he says about it is (*PH* 1.7) that the sceptics call themselves Pyrrhonian 'from

---

[80] *Vit. auct.* 27 (=DC T78) (and see also the scholium to this passage, which appears as DC T79).

[81] *Icaromen.* 25 (=DC T77).   [82] *Bis. acc.* 25 (=DC T76).

[83] See Tarrant (1983); Bastianini and Sedley (1995: 254–6). Both place the work in the late first century BC (though for different reasons); traditionally it was dated considerably later than this.

the fact that Pyrrho seems to us to have approached scepticism in a more bodily fashion and more manifestly than those before him'. And the little-known Theodosius, in a work called *Sceptical Summaries* (*skeptika kephalaia*), is said actually to have denied that the sceptics should call themselves Pyrrhonians, in part because of the difficulty of knowing what Pyrrho actually thought (DL 9.70). Of course, this may merely reflect the sceptics' paranoia about committing themselves to any positive assertions.[84] But Sextus, at least, is elsewhere quite happy to attribute views to other philosophers—indeed, he constantly does so—without any qualms about whether these philosophers really held them. So it may be, rather, that his caution in this case has to do with a specific uncertainty about how far Pyrrho's own ideas actually did resemble those of later Pyrrhonism. In *Against the Grammarians* (*M* 1.305–6) he does allude in passing to Pyrrho as a practitioner of suspension of judgement. But the issue at hand is the interpretation of a simile applied to Pyrrho by Timon, in some lines to which we shall return in the next chapter; the question of the degree of resemblance between Pyrrho's views and later Pyrrhonism is not the focus of attention, and the passage does not provide clear evidence that Sextus had a firm view on the matter.[85]

Whatever the truth of this, the conclusion that emerges is that those ancient authors who do represent Pyrrho's thought as if it was a form of the philosophy adhered to by later Pyrrhonists may safely be disregarded.[86] The

---

[84] It has been plausibly argued that Sextus in *PH* 1.7 is actually responding to the suggestion of Theodosius; see DC 200–4; Barnes (1992: 4285). Sextus' caution can thus be explained as stemming from the concern to maintain a proper sceptical distance from any precise claims about what Pyrrho actually thought—claims to which Theodosius implies that the adoption of the label Pyrrhonism commits one. See, however, the following note.

[85] Suppose that Sextus had been aware of credible texts summarizing the ideas of Pyrrho in terms that made quite clear their affinity with later Pyrrhonism; would he have hesitated to make use of these texts in justifying the label Pyrrhonism in response to Theodosius' challenge? Given his usual practice, it seems unlikely. See further Decleva Caizzi (1981: 125–6). For what it is worth, at least one other person is supposed to have denied that Pyrrho was a sceptic; according to Diogenes, 'Numenius alone said that he actually dogmatized' (DL 9.68). However, it is very unclear who this Numenius was, or whether any weight can be attached to this testimony. If the reference is to the neo-Pythagorean of that name, Diogenes' report would seem to be in conflict with Numenius' characterization of Pyrrho and Timon as sceptics (Eusebius, *Praep. evang.* XIV.6.4–6 (=LS 68F)); see also Stopper (1983: 270).

[86] I have not mentioned a few texts that actually refer to 'Pyrrho and Sextus' or 'Sextus and Pyrrho' (or in some cases 'Sextuses and Pyrrhos', collectively indicating the adherents of a certain style of thought), as if these names were simply interchangeable. But here the conclusion just stated is still more clearly true. None of the authors who speak in this way is earlier than the fourth century AD, and some are as late as the eleventh or twelfth; none shows any knowledge of, or interest in, the details of the development of Pyrrhonism, and none needs to be taken seriously as historical evidence concerning Pyrrhonism. See DC T89, T90, T91, T93, T94, with Decleva Caizzi's comments (DC 283–4); the texts are Gregory of Nazanzius, *Or.* XXI. 12, 393; *Carm.* II.1, 12, 304 (fourth century); Agathias, *Historiae* II.29 (sixth century); John of Sicily, *In Hermog. De ideis* p. 397 (Rabe) (eleventh century); Georgius Cedrenus, *Compend. histor.* 1.283 (eleventh or twelfth century).

Aristocles passage carries far greater authority than any of these; it gives every indication of being modelled closely on a passage of Timon in which Pyrrho's central ideas were expounded, and it is much more informative than any other single text relating to Pyrrho. These conflicting texts, on the other hand, give no indication of being based on any early source; and it is quite understandable how a later Pyrrhonist type of outlook could have been foisted on Pyrrho by these authors whether or not this was historically accurate. So, if the Aristocles passage shows us a non-sceptical Pyrrho, there is nothing in the rest of the evidence on Pyrrho that should cause us to doubt this. I have argued that this is indeed the most plausible way of understanding the logic of the passage itself; my argument is in no way undermined by the evidence considered in this section. We could be deterred from concluding that Pyrrho held the indeterminacy thesis, and drew from it the inferences I found in the Aristocles passage, only if (1) my interpretation of the passage was faulty, (2) there was some reason to distrust Aristocles as a reporter of Timon's account, (3) there was some reason to distrust Timon as a reporter of Pyrrho's ideas (or to doubt that simply *reporting* Pyrrho's ideas was what he was doing in the passage that Aristocles summarized), or (4) my interpretation rendered the history of Pyrrhonism incomprehensible. Concerning the first three of these alternatives, I have now done all I can. I do not pretend to have excluded them beyond all possible doubt; but I do claim that no adequate reason has so far been given for accepting them. As for the fourth, that is a topic for later chapters. I shall argue that the metaphysical interpretation of the Aristocles passage is in fact at least as plausible historically as the epistemological one; the indeterminacy thesis is a clear relative of other ideas that were being aired in the period immediately preceding Pyrrho, and the development of the Pyrrhonist tradition itself makes at least as much sense on the assumption that Pyrrho held the indeterminacy thesis as on the assumption that he did not.

8. Pyrrho as pragmatist?

We may continue to suppose, then, at least for now, that Timon depicted Pyrrho as espousing a metaphysical thesis to the effect that things are in their real nature indeterminate. But, clearly, this bare statement leaves a good many things unclear. In particular, it is not clear exactly what the indeterminacy thesis amounts to. What does it mean to say that things are indeterminate, and what does the claim commit one to? And what is the precise import of the qualification 'in their real nature'? Then again, it is not clear why Pyrrho, or anyone, might be motivated to *accept* the indeterminacy thesis. As we have noted, Aristocles himself does not tell us why Pyrrho adopted it. But it would obviously be helpful to our understanding of Pyrrho's philosophy if we were able to make some progress in sorting this out.

These questions will become particularly pressing when the question of Pyrrho's antecedents arises in Chapter 3, and we shall return to them then. However, it is worth taking care of one issue in this area before we proceed any further. It has recently been suggested that Pyrrho adopted the indeterminacy thesis as a 'pragmatic hypothesis'.[87] He could not, it is argued, consistently have claimed to *know* the truth of the thesis, or to have some objectively acceptable justification of it; rather, he did not assume or affirm it to be objectively true at all, but adopted it for the sake of the beneficial consequences of believing it—that is, for the *ataraxia* it brings.

Attractive though it may sound, there are various difficulties with this suggestion. The indeterminacy thesis is presented as the answer to the question 'what is the nature of things?', which is normally the equivalent, or one equivalent, in ancient Greek philosophy of asking 'what is the objective truth about things?' Then again, the immediate consequence of the thesis is that our sensations and opinions are neither true nor false. In ancient Greek philosophy, 'true' and 'false' regularly mean 'true [and "false"] *of* an objective reality';[88] when Pyrrho says that our sensations and opinions are neither true nor false, he would surely be expected to mean that *things in themselves* neither are nor are not as our sensations and opinions represent them as being. It is true that Pyrrho says that the question 'what is the nature of things?' is one of the questions that must be answered by anyone who is to be happy. But this does *not* mean that the question 'what is the nature of things?' is itself to be understood as equivalent to the question 'what view of the nature of things would you be happiest believing?'[89] The sequence of three questions offered in the Aristocles passage suggests, rather, that Pyrrho, like many other Greek philosophers, thinks that it is only by achieving a *correct* view of the nature of things—by seeing things as they really are—that happiness can be attained. His motivation for engaging in philosophy, like that of the Epicureans, may indeed be the attainment of *ataraxia*; but it does not follow that either Pyrrho or the Epicureans sought simply to adopt those philosophical beliefs that it is most comfortable to believe, without caring about their truth. The Epicureans think, on the contrary, that *ataraxia* is achieved by exposing various damaging illusions, and substituting the true account of the nature of things; if I am right that Pyrrho, too, had what he regarded as a true account of the nature of things—namely, that they are indeterminate—his attitude towards this

---

[87] By Sakezles (1993). I should emphasize that, despite my disagreement here, Sakezles' treatment of the Aristocles passage is on many points in agreement with my own—most notably, of course, on the idea that Pyrrho does put forward a thesis to the effect that reality is indeterminate.

[88] For discussion of this point, see Burnyeat (1982).

[89] As Sakezles (1993: 90), seems to imply.

account would be likely to be something similar. Finally, as I argued earlier, there is no difficulty in the notion that Pyrrho thought that the indeterminacy thesis could be known or justified; for we need not suppose that the indeterminacy thesis itself qualifies as the content of either a sensation or an opinion—and it is only sensations and opinions that he tells us not to trust.

What, then, was the justification for the thesis? I shall argue later that it may most plausibly be thought to have arisen from reflection on the opposite ways in which things strike people at different times or in different circumstances. Reflection on such oppositions was commonplace in Greek philosophy since well before Pyrrho's time; it is relatively easy to reconstruct how such reflections could have motivated the indeterminacy thesis; and, if this was the starting point of the thesis, this also makes it more understandable how the later Pyrrhonists could have seen in him a forerunner—and more specifically, how Aenesidemus' philosophy could be viewed as specially related to Pyrrho's. Before we get to these matters, however, we need to fill out the account that has been developed of Pyrrho's philosophy so far, connecting it with the evidence having to do with his practical attitudes, demeanour, and way of life. This will be the task of the next chapter.

APPENDIX

On the meaning of *alētheuein* and *pseudesthai*

In the main text of this chapter, I translate *mēte tas aisthēseis hēmōn mēte tas doxas alētheuein ē pseudesthai*, a crucial clause in the Aristocles passage, by 'neither our sensations nor our opinions tell the truth or lie'. I proceed on the assumption that this means that any given sensation, or any given opinion, is neither true nor false; and this is the crux of my argument in favour of the metaphysical reading of the passage and against the epistemological one. If Pyrrho is prepared to make a commitment—even this very unusual commitment—as to the truth-value of sensations and opinions, he must think that he is aware of how things actually are; so he cannot be insisting, as the epistemological interpretation would have it, that such awareness is not available to us. Others, however, have different ideas about the interpretation of this crucial clause. While the clause is regularly translated in essentially the same fashion as I have done[90]—and it is not clear how one could do otherwise—it is sometimes held that these words allow of different understandings from the one I am presupposing.

One suggestion is that 'neither our sensations nor our opinions are true or false' is really *equivalent* to 'we cannot determine whether our judgements about things are true or false'.[91] But it is very hard to see how this can be so—at least, if we assume that Pyrrho and Timon were clear about what they meant to say. Not only are the two statements not equivalent; they are actually incompatible with one another. Whatever its exact implications, the first statement does at least give a *definite answer* to the question 'What is the truth-value of our sensations and opinions?', whereas the whole point of the second statement is to say that we are not in a position to give *any* definite answer.

Another view is that the clause is to be understood as meaning that our sensations and opinions 'are neither constant truth-tellers nor constant liars', and that this lack of constancy makes them unreliable;[92] the effect of this would be that we would be unable to determine, in the case of any *given* sensation or opinion, whether it was true or false, which would again give support to the epistemological interpretation of the passage. But nothing in the text warrants the addition of the word 'constant'. If Pyrrho had wanted to say that our sensations and opinions are not *constant* truth-tellers or *constant* liars, he could have said *bebaiōs alētheuein ē pseudesthai*, or something of

---

[90] With the partial exception of Stopper (1983) (see below, n. 93), this is true of all the adherents of the epistemological interpretation listed at the end of Ch. 1 n. 14.

[91] The words 'we cannot determine whether our judgements about things are true or false' are taken from the explanation of the passage in Annas (1993: 203); but others have proposed the same view to me in discussion.

[92] See Stopper (1983: 292–3), followed by Brunschwig (1994a: 198). If I seem to treat this possibility at tedious and excessive length, it is because I have found this to be the alternative to my own proposal that is most widely assumed to be correct (or at least, an equally serious contender).

the kind, instead of the simple *alētheuein ē pseudesthai*. Of course, *alētheuein* can be used to *refer* to a constant practice of telling the truth, if the context makes clear that repeated activity over time, rather than some single performance, is at issue—just as, in English, if I say to a child who has just lied to me 'You really should tell the truth', it is understood that I am talking about telling the truth *in general, and from now on*. (See e.g. Xenophon, *Cyropaideia* 1.6.33, Aristotle, *NE* 1139^{b}15, and, for this usage in Aristocles himself, Eusebius, *Praep. evang.* XIV.17.2, XIV.20.10.) No doubt an analogous point also holds for *pseudesthai*. But this is not at all to say that *alētheuein*, here or anywhere else, *means* 'constantly tell the truth', or that *pseudesthai* means 'constantly lie'; they just mean 'tell the truth' and 'lie' respectively.[93] Hence there is no reason to take 'neither our sensations nor our opinions tell the truth or lie' to mean 'neither our sensations nor our opinions *constantly* tell the truth or *constantly* lie (though they may do either one of these things on individual occasions, and unfortunately we are not in a position to tell when they are doing the one and when the other)'. On the contrary, the statement is a simple, and quite general, denial that our sensations or opinions tell the truth or lie. If one insists on bringing a notion of 'constancy' into the passage, one might express the point as follows: our sensations and opinions *constantly fail either to tell the truth or to lie*. (If the generality of the context sometimes allows 'tell the truth' to be used to refer to *constancy in telling the truth*, then a similar generality ought to allow the *denial* that someone or something tells the truth to be used to refer to *constancy in failing to tell the truth*—not to a *failure to maintain constancy* in telling the truth.) But this is clearly no help to the epistemological interpretation, since it is again a *definite assertion* as to the truth-value of sensations and opinions.

What can be meant, then, by 'neither our sensations nor our opinions tell the truth or lie'? Once these other renderings have been dismissed, I do not see any alternative to the reading with which I began. Pyrrho is denying that our sensations or opinions tell the truth or that they lie; what else can this mean than that any given sensation, or any given opinion, is neither true nor false? It may be said that, since the entire passage on Pyrrho is admittedly only a summary of the key points (*kephalaia* (XIV.18.5)), one may very well expect that the full meaning needs to be arrived at by imaginative expansion, and not by restricting oneself to the actual words.[94] What one would *not* expect, however, is that the full meaning should be arrived at by an expansion containing elements *incompatible* with the actual words in the text, as is the case with both of the above suggestions. Again, 'neither our sensations nor our opinions tell the truth or lie', read at face value, *gives* a verdict on the truth-value of sensations and opinions; any sentence that constitutes a *withholding* of all such verdicts cannot, then, be what the quoted words, in their proper expanded form, really mean. And in any case, as we have seen, the words have a perfectly intelligible meaning *without* any

---

[93] For the same reason, it is dubious for Stopper to use 'are neither truthful nor liars' in his initial translation of the clause; 'be truthful' and 'be a liar' differ from 'tell the truth' and 'lie' precisely in that the former, since they refer to dispositions rather than to acts, have an implication of constancy or reliability built into their content, whereas the latter do not. ('Be faithless' does occur as one possible meaning of *pseudesthai* in LSJ. But in the one text they cite as an example (Hesiod, *Works and Days* 283), the word has the standard sense 'lie'.)

[94] This point was made to me by Eric Brown.

expansion (even though a full examination of their *implications* might very well be a lengthy process—which Timon might, for all we know, have embarked upon in the longer account of which Aristocles is giving a summary). One may, of course, maintain that Aristocles, or Timon, or even Pyrrho himself, really *meant* to say 'we cannot determine whether our sensations or opinions are true or false', but said something else owing to haste or confusion. Conjectures of this sort can never be proved wrong. But, equally, there is no reason to accept them if, as I attempt to show in this chapter, the text makes good sense as it stands.

2

Putting it into Practice

Much of this chapter will be occupied with the numerous colourful anecdotes about Pyrrho's activities, most of them recorded in Diogenes' life of Pyrrho. How seriously should we take these stories? One obvious way to approach this question—which has, however, received very little attention—is to consider the relation between the stories and the crucial passage of Aristocles discussed in the previous chapter. As I have insisted, it is there, if anywhere, that we find a reliable account of the central core of Pyrrho's philosophy; so we need to examine whether or not there is some plausible connection between the stories and the philosophy expounded there. Also important will be a set of utterances of Timon having to do primarily with Pyrrho's practical attitudes. These need to be investigated both for their relations with the ideas contained in the Aristocles passage, and for their connections, if any, with the anecdotes in Diogenes and elsewhere. A further issue will be what Pyrrho might have had to say on the question how someone who accepts the indeterminacy thesis, and who claims not to trust sensations and opinions, can consistently make any choices or decisions at all. Is Pyrrho's policy on this matter the same as that of the later Pyrrhonists—namely, that they rely on appearances? Again, we are here dependent above all on the evidence of Timon. Finally, it will be necessary to examine some troublesome texts suggesting that Pyrrho held strong and definite ethical views—views that, at least at first sight, seem quite incompatible with the indeterminacy thesis. The similarities and the differences between Pyrrho's position on these various matters and that of Sextus' *Outlines of Pyrrhonism* will be alluded to periodically, but will be summed up more systematically in the chapter's final section.

1. Pyrrho's behaviour: a first look at the biographical material

Perhaps the best-known anecdote about Pyrrho is the one from Antigonus of Carystus, reported in Diogenes (9.62), which has him taking no precautions whatever in the face of precipices, oncoming wagons, and dangerous dogs, 'and generally putting no trust in his senses', and needing to be rescued from disaster by the friends who followed him around.[1] Other activities reported by Antigonus are less obviously foolhardy, but still verge on the lunatic. Pyrrho is supposed to have been 'always in the same state' (DL 9.63); thus, Antigonus tells us, he would continue speaking even if his interlocutor left in the middle of his speech,[2] and he passed by when his teacher Anaxarchus was lying in a ditch, just as if no one was there—and was subsequently praised by Anaxarchus for his 'indifference and lack of affection' (*to adiaphoron kai astorgon*).

Antigonus adds that he would often leave home with no warning, and wander around with whomever he felt like. A little earlier in the same passage, we are told that he would withdraw from human companionship altogether, and in particular from his own household. Both stories appear to illustrate a total disregard of the conventions prescribing social interactions with the members of one's own family and social class. A similar disregard for convention is suggested by some stories from Eratosthenes' *On Wealth and Poverty* (DL 9.66). Pyrrho would sometimes personally take poultry and pigs to sell at the market;[3] he also performed housework 'indifferently' and also personally[4] washed a pig 'through indifference'—that is, heedless of those social differences governing who should or should not do such work, and also, at least in the second case, of the disgusting character of the job. A less dramatic illustration of this indifference comes in a story in Athenaeus (419d–e), but deriving from Hegesander, a gossip writer from the second century BC; Pyrrho goes to a sumptuous dinner with a friend, and says that he will not see him again if he is received in this fashion, because what is important is good company rather than a display of unnecessary luxury. Here, as in some of the other anecdotes, Pyrrho's behaviour is reminiscent of that of the Cynics; we shall come back to this point in the next chapter.

Other accounts point to an indifference to one's circumstances that goes beyond mere disregard of convention. Diogenes says (9.67), this time without naming his source, that Pyrrho did not even frown when subjected to the

---

[1] A similar refusal to accept even the existence of other people, or other aspects of his environment, is suggested by several stories from Quintilian (*Inst. or.* 12.2, 24) and from Lucian (*Bis. acc.* 25 (=DC T76); *Vit. auct.* 27 (=DC T78)), in which Pyrrho is represented as incapable of taking part in a trial because of his non-acceptance of certain basic facts, such as that there are judges in front of him. As Decleva Caizzi suggests (DC 276, 278), such stories may be presumed to have been inspired by elements in the biographical tradition such as this one.

[2] Slightly later (9.64) we are also told that he was once discovered talking to himself, and explained that he was 'training to be good'. The precise point of this is not clear. But it is at any rate much easier to see that it might have a point; talking to oneself as part of some self-improvement regime would seem to make much more sense than saying to an empty room what one had started out saying to other people.

[3] Note the stress implied by *hote kai autos pherōn*, 'sometimes actually taking [the animals to market] himself'.

[4] Again, the word *autos* is included.

horrors of ancient surgery;[5] and a passage of Cicero seems to support the idea that he was exceptionally unaffected by pain, and probably by other sensations—or, at any rate, that he promoted the *ideal* of being thus unaffected. Cicero says (*Acad.* 2.130) that, according to Pyrrho, the wise man would not even notice (*sentire*) the things labelled by the orthodox Stoics as indifferents—that is, everything other than virtue and vice—and that this state of insensitivity was called *apatheia*. Prominent among the things classified as indifferents by the Stoics are pain and pleasure; part of what is entailed, then, by Cicero's report is that Pyrrho held that the wise man will not even feel pain (or, for that matter, pleasure). Now, the report cannot very well be a literal reproduction of anything that Pyrrho actually said. One would not expect Pyrrho to have *any* articulated view applying specifically to that category of items called 'indifferent' by the Stoics (and 'the wise man' (*sapientem*) is also Stoic terminology); Zeno of Citium, the original Stoic, cannot even have invented this category until late in Pyrrho's life,[6] and, in any case, Pyrrho was not known for his interventions in debates about the doctrines of other philosophers (more on this later). The report presumably derives, then, from someone *else's* reflections on what Pyrrho would have said about those items labelled 'indifferents' by the Stoics. But such reflections would none the less be quite natural if we assume that among the attitudes or reactions Pyrrho was reported to have expressed were *both* heedlessness to those things that social norms induce us to care about—an attitude exemplified, as we have seen, in numerous surviving anecdotes—*and* heedlessness to physical pain (and pleasure); it would not take any great stretch of imagination to summarize these two sets of attitudes collectively as an extraordinary lack of attention to what the Stoics called 'indifferents'.

Finally, there are two pairs of texts describing not only Pyrrho's behaviour in various circumstances, but also his own expressed views about how one *ought* to behave. First, Pyrrho is said to have remained calm in a ship at sea during a storm, pointing to a pig cheerfully munching its food, and citing it as a model for the wise man to emulate.[7] The story is attributed to Posidonius by Diogenes (9.68); it also occurs in Plutarch (*Prof. virt.* 82e–f) without any named attribution. The ideal to be strived for is referred to as *ataraxia* in Diogenes' version and as *apatheia* in Plutarch's version.

---

[5] Tertullian (*Apol.* L 14 (=DC T73)) also lists Pyrrho among those pagan philosophers advocating 'tolerance of pain and death'.

[6] The evidence concerning the date of Zeno's birth is obscure and conflicting; see Dorandi (1991: ch. 5). However, it seems clear enough that he was considerably younger than Pyrrho.

[7] This story also brings to mind a pair of remarks attributed to Pyrrho by Stobaeus (4.53, 28 ff.), to the effect that it makes no difference whether one lives or dies. This, of course, would be the ultimate expression of an 'indifferent' attitude. However, very little weight can be put on this passage; Stobaeus gives no indication as to where he got his information, and the same pair of remarks, with virtually identical wording, is attributed by Diogenes to Thales (1.35).

Secondly, two incidents are reported in which Pyrrho failed to maintain his calm; Diogenes and Aristocles both report them (DL 9.66; *Praep. evang.* XIV.18.26), and Aristocles attributes them to Antigonus. There was an incident involving his sister, a friend, and a sacrifice, in which he got angry; and there was an occasion when he was chased by a dog and became scared.[8] The details of the first incident are obscure, but at the centre of it is clearly Pyrrho's exceptional lapse from his ideal, referred to as *apatheia* in Aristocles' version and as *adiaphoria* in Diogenes'; Pyrrho is also given a defence of, or at any rate a comment on, this lapse, but its significance is not easy to assess.[9] To the second incident, however, is appended (in both versions) an admission by Pyrrho to the effect that it is difficult to 'strip off humanity' (*ekdunai ton anthrōpon*). The implication, clearly, is that one's ultimate aim should be to do precisely this, and, in the version that appears in Diogenes, the remark is amplified as follows: 'but one should strive as far as possible against things [*ta pragmata*], first by deeds, but if not that, at any rate by reasoning [*tōi ge logōi*].' This last point seems to be echoed in Plutarch's version of the story about the pig on the ship, where Pyrrho is represented as saying that *apatheia* is to be attained 'by reasoning and philosophy' (*ek logou kai philosophias*).

Two central questions arise concerning these numerous stories. First, how far, if at all, should we believe them? Secondly, what, if anything, do they have to do with the philosophical outlook discussed in the previous chapter? Neither question has received the scrutiny it deserves. The stories have tended either to be accepted or to be rejected as a group, without serious consideration of the merits of the case;[10] and, as I observed at the outset, very little has

---

[8] Diogenes also tells us of one of his followers, the otherwise unknown Eurylochus, who got so angry with his cook that he chased him with a spit (and the meat still on it), and who was so troubled by the difficulty of his students' questions that he jumped into the river Alpheus (9.68–9); this type of behaviour is referred to as a 'lapse' or 'defeat' (*elassōma*).

[9] The comment has something to do with the appropriateness or inappropriateness of displaying *apatheia* or *adiaphoria* where a woman is concerned; but in the longer version reported by Aristocles, both the text and the sense are disputed. An extensive analysis of this story, and of the differences between the two versions of it—particularly with regard to Pyrrho's comment about his burst of anger—is given by Brunschwig (1992). Brunschwig convincingly concludes that the fuller version given by Aristocles is closer to the original, and that Diogenes has shortened and simplified the story because he did not understand what he read in Antigonus. In Diogenes' version, Pyrrho's comment is a piece of simple misogyny; but in Aristocles' version it is capable of being read in a much more subtle way, as a multi-layered ironic snub to his friend. Even in the latter case, however, it does not appear to express a general philosophical moral; its significance seems to be internal to the incident to which it is a reaction. Brunschwig sees the differences between the two versions as telling us something about the evolution of ancient interpretations of Pyrrho and Pyrrhonism; but he admits (p. 145) that the incident does not help us in our own attempts at interpreting Pyrrho.

[10] Thus Stopper (1983: 269–70) rejects the stories *en bloc*, without distinguishing between those deriving from Antigonus and those deriving from other sources, and largely on the basis of some brief and highly questionable remarks about the nature of biography. Others who have been equally hasty in accepting the stories include Reale (1981) and Conche (1994).

been said about the relation between the stories and the ideas summarized in the Aristocles passage. A comprehensive picture of Pyrrho's philosophy requires sustained attention to both questions; and it requires us to treat them in close conjunction with one another. For, to repeat, it seems clear that one of the best methods for assessing the stories is to consider whether, and how, the kinds of behaviour described in the stories might be understandable as a practical expression of the central tenets of Pyrrho's philosophy.

The story in which Pyrrho needs to be rescued by his friends from the edges of cliffs, from under the wheels of wagons, and so on has an obvious connection with the position reported in the Aristocles passage; the latter passage says that one should not trust one's senses, and the story is designed to illustrate precisely this mistrust. But there are several reasons why this story should not be taken at face value. It might seem scarcely necessary to say this. However, several scholars have accepted the story as serious biographical information;[11] so it is worth spelling out, at least briefly, just how hard this is to accept. First, as was explained in the Introduction, Antigonus' evidence must always be treated with caution. It may be true that he received information about Pyrrho directly from people who had been his followers[12]—the chronology is certainly compatible with this; but it is also likely that a story's colourful nature was a matter of greater interest to him than its veracity. Secondly, it is inherently difficult to believe that someone who had a philosophical following, and who was honoured by his city with a statue in the centre of town (Pausanias 6.24,5) and perhaps even a priesthood (DL 9.64),[13] was a lunatic, a menace to himself and others. Thirdly, and most importantly, if Pyrrho's behaviour, in these scenarios, was supposed to be motivated by his philosophical outlook, then that outlook would be quite obviously self-refuting. Pyrrho may place no trust in his senses, but he can get away with this only because others, who are not so foolish, protect him from the consequences. His acting consistently with his theory—if that is what he is doing—is dependent upon others *not* doing so, and this shows precisely

[11] See Reale (1981: 292–5); Conche (1994: 135–6); more tentatively DC 152–5.

[12] As suggested by von Fritz (1963: 89).

[13] Diogenes here appears to cite Nausiphanes as his source; the remark about Pyrrho's being honoured with the priesthood is syntactically the second of a pair of indirect statements (accusative and infinitive) governed by *elege*, 'he said', where 'he' is Nausiphanes. The same passage indicates that Nausiphanes had personal contact with Pyrrho; so, if the syntax is not misleading, this may be regarded as one of the most reliable anecdotes in Diogenes. Unfortunately, however, we cannot be very confident about this. The remark has no thematic connection with what immediately precedes it, and may very well have been carelessly inserted here by Diogenes or his source, having been originally quite unconnected with Nausiphanes; there is a long sequence of indirect statements using the accusative and infinitive construction in the previous section, where it is Antigonus who is the narrator. Still, there is no obvious reason to disbelieve the report. (On the subject of honours, Diogenes also claims, citing Diocles, that the Athenians honoured Pyrrho for killing Kotus the Thracian (9.65); this, by contrast, is totally unreliable—see DC 163–4.)

that the senses *do* have to be trusted. It has been suggested that, rather than actually living this way—to this extent, it is admitted, Antigonus is mislead-ing—Pyrrho was performing a kind of pantomime, intended as a dramatic illustration of his philosophy. But it is quite unclear what this performance could plausibly be taken to symbolize—other than that, again, the philosophy is practically unsustainable, which is hardly the moral Pyrrho would be seek-ing.[14]

It is not hard to explain the origin of Antigonus' stories of Pyrrho's poten-tially suicidal behaviour. As a number of scholars have pointed out, these stories have much in common with Aristotle's discussion, in *Metaphysics* IV, of how those who profess to deny the Law of Non-Contradiction are bound to betray, by their actions, that they do not really do so; it is not, Aristotle says, as if it is all the same to these people whether they walk to Megara or walk over a cliff.[15] The stories suggesting that Pyrrho constantly needed to be rescued from mortal danger are best understood as an instance of the same type of criticism; both suggest that action is impossible in the absence of defi-nite beliefs. Antigonus has simply presented what should be (and no doubt originally was) a hostile hypothetical account of what someone who held Pyrrho's position *would* have to do, in order to live consistently with that position, as an actual account of what Pyrrho did do.[16] Thus, although

---

[14] Conche, the author of this suggestion (see above, n. 11), argues that it symbolizes the universality of appearance; everything is appearance, there is no such thing as reality, and the performance illustrates this dramatically by suggesting that the distinction between (e.g.) a precipice and a non-precipice is mere appearance—a moral that is then generalized to every-thing else. But, if this was the point, it would seem to backfire disastrously. Again, the fact that Pyrrho needed to be rescued would most naturally suggest, on the contrary, that precipices, wagons, etc. are *more* than mere appearances; bystanders would be given precisely the opposite message to the one Conche thinks was intended, and it would surely be obvious in advance that this would be so. Conche suggests (1994: 136) that the *particular* appearance that a precipice was in front of him would of course be one to which Pyrrho would in real life pay attention, but that the moral of the performance has to do with appearance in general, not with particular appearances. But I fail to see how Pyrrho, or anyone, could imagine that this distinction might be conveyed by means of the performances described (and if the distinction had to be explained afterwards, then the performances would again be plainly irrelevant, and even an obstacle, to the lesson they are alleged to illustrate).

[15] See esp. 1008^{b}12–20. The parallel is noted by Long (1981: 94–7); LS ii. 2; DC 152–5; Reale (1981: 292–3); Conche (1994: 76).

[16] Decleva Caizzi (DC 154–5, 167) and Reale (1981: 294–5) both compare these stories with the story of Pyrrho's being scared by the dog, and his accompanying remark that it is difficult to 'strip oneself of humanity'. But the point of the latter story may be quite different. It need not be that Pyrrho thought that the *right* reaction would have been to let the dog attack him (and perhaps have his friends rescue him). Rather, the 'human' reaction from which he failed to 'strip' himself might simply have been fright, and the panicky actions that accompany fright—such as climbing a tree, as Aristocles' version of the story has him do; it would have been prefer-able, though difficult, to have retained his *ataraxia* even in these circumstances. *Ataraxia* in this case would have been quite compatible with (in fact, it would probably depend on) avoiding the dog's attack, though in some less panicky way.

Aristocles does say that Pyrrho told us not to trust the senses, we should not infer that he expressed this mistrust by behaving in the manner Antigonus suggests. Of course, if we reject Antigonus' testimony on this point, but continue to accept what Aristocles tells us, this makes it incumbent on us to find some other, more plausible account of what Pyrrho's mistrust of the senses amounts to. We shall come back to this issue later in the chapter.

To dismiss the most outlandish of the anecdotes concerning Pyrrho is not, however, to dismiss all of them. The evidence from Antigonus may be less than obviously reliable. But, firstly, not all the stories derive from Antigonus. Even if we suppose that Antigonus lies behind the unattributed stories as well as those specifically ascribed to him—in other words, even if he is the main source for the whole biographical section in Diogenes—there still remain the stories attributed to Eratosthenes and to Posidonius.[17] Eratosthenes lived in the third century BC, at least as early as Antigonus; and, unlike Antigonus, he was a serious thinker and scholar. He also spent time in Athens studying with Aristo,[18] and this almost certainly coincided with the period in which Timon was in Athens (DL 9.110). It is at least tempting to speculate that he got his information from Timon personally.[19] Posidonius was substantially later (*c.*135–*c.*50 BC), but his story, too, is presumably independent of Antigonus; if Diogenes or his source had found the same story in Antigonus, on whom he is clearly relying for much of the time, it would be hard to see why he would cite Posidonius rather than Antigonus himself. It must be admitted, though, that Posidonius' reliability as a historian of philosophy is not easy to assess.[20] Secondly, however, quite apart from the inherent trustworthiness, or otherwise, of these various sources, the majority of the stories add up to a consistent picture, a picture of someone who was in numerous respects highly indifferent to, or unaffected by, the world around him. We may reject as embellishment or fabrication the lunatic fringe among these stories, but nothing in what has been said so far gives us reason to dismiss all of them out of hand. The question of their credibility needs further consideration.

I shall approach this issue in a somewhat roundabout way. I shall begin, in the next section, by addressing the question of the relation between the stories and our other main source of evidence concerning Pyrrho's attitude and demeanour—namely, that offered by the verse fragments of Timon. As was

---

[17] Also Nausiphanes (see above, n. 13).   [18] On this, see Ioppolo (1980*b*: 23–4).

[19] Wilamowitz-Moellendorff (1881: 28–9) maintains that Eratosthenes' anecdotes are transmitted to Diogenes through Antigonus. This is by no means obviously correct; but even if we agree, it is not clear that this reduces the stories' credibility (as Decleva Caizzi (DC 164) observes).

[20] Kidd (1988–9) contains just seven passages, including the present one, under the heading 'History of Philosophy' (F285–F291). At least a pair of these (F285, F286) does not initially inspire confidence; Posidonius is said to have held that a Sidonian named Mochus was the originator of the atomic theory. But see Kidd's commentary (pp. 972–4), for some possible bases Posidonius may have had for this view.

suggested in the Introduction, these fragments themselves are not necessarily to be taken as giving us the literal truth about Pyrrho; they present a certain image of Pyrrho, and this image may well be partly the product of embellishment and exaggeration. Still, comparison between the fragments and the stories does allow us to see that the two are (1) generally consistent with one another, yet (2) not so close to one another as to invite the suspicion that the stories are simply invented on the basis of hints in the fragments; and these are both encouraging results. I shall then return, in the following section, to the relations between these two sets of evidence, taken together, and the evidence furnished by the Aristocles passage.

2. Pyrrho's practical attitudes: the anecdotes and the fragments of Timon

Several fragments from Timon depict Pyrrho's calm and unperturbed attitude, and contrast it with the agitated attitudes of other philosophers, or of other people in general. First, we have four lines preserved by Aristocles. In the course of his criticism of the views presented in the passage with which we were occupied in the previous chapter, Aristocles tells us that Timon uttered the following lines about Pyrrho (*Praep. evang.* XIV.18.19):

A. But such he was—I saw him, the man without vanity and unbroken
    By all the things by which both the unknown and the celebrated among
        mortals are overpowered,
    Empty hosts of people, weighed down on this side and that
    By affections, opinion, and pointless laying-down of the law.[21]

Secondly, Diogenes Laertius quotes the following lines from Timon's *Silloi* (9.64–5):

B. Pyrrho, old man, how and whence did you find a way out
    From servitude to opinions and empty-mindedness of sophists,
    And loosened the bonds of every deception and persuasion?
    You were not concerned to enquire what winds
    Hold sway over Greece, from where everything comes and into what it
        passes.

---

[21] I follow the text printed in DC (T58); Long and Sedley (LS 2B) print *homōs* instead of *brotōn* in the second line. The MSS are not in agreement at this point (and there are other divergences besides this one); Timon is clearly using Hesiod, *Works and Days* 3, as a model, which reads *brotoi andres homōs aphatoi te phatoi te*, but neither reading is clearly preferable on that basis. However, the reading *brotōn* seems to me to involve marginally less editorial interference. See the apparatus criticus in DC (*ad loc.*), and Decleva Caizzi's discussion of textual matters in the commentary (DC 244); also the app. crit. in Heiland (1925: 65). In any case, no substantial matter of interpretation turns on this issue.

In addition, a composite fragment of seven lines can be assembled from three different places in Diogenes and Sextus; according to Diogenes (9.65), they come from Timon's *Indalmoi* (*Images*).

C.   This, Pyrrho, my heart longs to hear
     However you, a man, conduct yourself with the greatest ease and tranquillity
     Always heedless and uniformly unmoved
     Paying no attention to the whirls of sweet-voiced wisdom.
     You alone lead humans in the manner of the god
     Who revolves back and forth around the whole earth
     Showing the flaming circle of his well-turned sphere.[22]

And a single line quoted in Sextus (*M* 11.141)—

D.   When I perceived him, then, in windless calm—

almost certainly referred in its original context to Pyrrho's extraordinary tranquillity.[23] Finally, Timon gives us a briefer but similar portrait of Pyrrho's follower Philo of Athens, quoted by Diogenes (9.69):

E.   Or the man at leisure by himself,[24] talking to himself, away from humanity,
     Not busying himself with opinion and contests, Philo.

The parallels with elements in the stories mentioned before are numerous. Pyrrho's 'windless calm' in fragment D recalls the calm he maintained even during high winds at sea, in Posidonius' story; in Diogenes' version even the same word for 'calm' occurs (*galēnos*). Then again, fragments A and C suggest that Pyrrho's freedom from disturbance reaches a level unique among human beings. In passage C Pyrrho is actually accorded godlike status. This passage also suggests that humans are constitutionally liable to disturbances; the first sentence seems to express amazement that Pyrrho, though only a man, manages to be so trouble-free. Such language recalls Pyrrho's expressed aim, in one incident, of 'stripping off humanity'—in a context in which he

---

[22] ll. 1, 2, and 5 are quoted by DL; the second half of l. 2 to the end of l. 4 by Sextus, *M* 11.1; and ll. 5–7 by Sextus, *M* 1.305. I follow the text of DC (T61) and LS (2D). On DC's own conjecture *diageis*, 'conduct yourself', in l. 2 (accepted by LS), see commentary *ad loc. Dinois*, 'whirls', for the MSS reading *deilois*, was originally proposed by Nauck; see DC 254 for other suggestions. Jacques Brunschwig proposes to retain *deilois*; see Brunschwig (1994b: 213). However, his translation 'wretchedness' seems difficult to accept; and no other understanding of the word in this context seems to yield sense. Again, these issues do not make a serious difference to the interpretation of the fragment.

[23] The same is probably true of a half-line quoted just before: 'For calm extended everywhere.' Sextus reveals nothing of the context of these lines, or even the name of the poem from which they derive; for discussion, see Bett (1997: commentary *ad loc.*).

[24] I follow Meineke's generally accepted emendation *autoscholon*. The word might also be understood to mean 'schooling himself'; this translation is favoured in particular by di Marco (1989: 224–5). However, di Marco's argument against the other reading seems to me insufficient—'at leisure by himself' is not simply equivalent to 'away from humanity'; DC 197 suggests that both meanings are intended, and this seems more probable.

himself succumbed, unusually, to all-too-human disturbances. More generally, of course, his unperturbed attitude in the fragments of Timon is thoroughly consistent with his unperturbed attitude in the stories. This
unperturbedness is characterized, more specifically, as an exceptional stability; Pyrrho is 'uniformly unmoved', and, unlike other people, he is not
'weighed down on this side and that'. And this recalls Antigonus' comment
(DL 9.63) that he was 'always in the same state'. The solitude Antigonus
ascribes to him in the same passage also recalls Philo's solitude in the last
fragment from Timon; in addition, these passages apparently agree in attributing to Philo and Pyrrho a tendency to talk to themselves.[25]

  Again, we should not simply take on trust what Timon tells us in these
fragments. But, even aside from the issue of Timon's truthfulness, it may be
argued that these parallels between the fragments and the stories tell against
the reliability of the stories. The parallels, it may be said, indicate that the
stories are simply fabrications based on hints in Timon; Timon gives a general
description (truthful or not) of Pyrrho's attitudes, and other authors then
invent specific incidents in which these attitudes—or frequently, a distorted
parody of them—are exemplified.[26] Now, in some cases this may indeed be
correct. I have already argued that the stories of Pyrrho 'putting no trust in his
senses' should be explained in this sort of way; Timon tells us, according to
the Aristocles passage, that in Pyrrho's view the senses should not be trusted,
and Antigonus (or whoever first invented these stories) devises incidents in
which Pyrrho literally takes no notice of what his eyes tell him. The same may
well be true of Antigonus' examples of Pyrrho's remaining 'always in the
same state'; 'always in the same state' is here interpreted to mean not just
'always staying on an even keel psychologically'—a condition clearly attributed to Pyrrho in fragments A–D above—but 'always continuing the same
activities, regardless of whether or not circumstances change'.[27]

  However, this line of thought is most plausible in those cases where we
have independent reason to be suspicious of the stories—those cases, that is,
where Pyrrho's behaviour seems dysfunctional or insane. In other cases, the
relation between the biographical material and elements in Timon's portrait of

---

[25] Again there is a verbal parallel; Pyrrho is found 'talking to himself' (*hautōi lalōn*
(9.64)), and Philo is described as 'self-talker' (*autolalētēn*). Moreover, if 'schooling himself' is
indeed part of what is meant by *autoscholon* (see above, n. 24), there is a further parallel in Pyrrho's
explanation that he is 'training to be good'. On 'training to be good', see further n. 67 below.

[26] Long (1978: 69–70) seems largely to adopt this view (cf. above, Introduction, n. 12).

[27] The story of Pyrrho's 'calm' in the storm, paired with Timon's description of Pyrrho as 'in
windless calm', perhaps constitutes another case of the same kind. The additional element of
Pyrrho's use of the pig as an exemplar might seem to count against this. But it is not hard to
imagine someone hostile to Pyrrho's ideal inventing this element with the following thought in
mind: someone who maintains his calm even in circumstances in which it makes no sense to do
so has a mental life no better than that of a dumb animal such as a pig, and might as well be
thought of as taking such animals as a model to emulate.

Pyrrho is less straightforward than this. Most of the time, it is not a matter of an idea or phrase being lifted from Timon, read in a perversely literal way, and then extrapolated into an anecdote. Even in the case of some of the parallels cited a couple of paragraphs back, the relation between Timon and the biographical material is much more oblique. The ideal of 'stripping off humanity', in particular, is not directly present in Timon. Timon's use of the word 'a man', read with careful attention to its wider implications, can be seen to resonate with this ideal; but it is not easy to imagine an irresponsible gossip-monger inventing the ideal out of this hint from Timon—for this would presuppose a sensitivity to textual evidence quite out of character with the activity he would *ex hypothesi* be engaging in. Again, some of the parallels involve two different people— Pyrrho, on the one hand, and his follower Philo, on the other; however much one might expect the two to have had shared goals and practices, one would not expect a pseudo-biographer to invent Pyrrho's biography on the basis of remarks in Timon about someone else.[28] Furthermore, many of the stories have to do, as we saw, with Pyrrho's radical unconventionality, and with his almost complete immunity to the kinds of affective responses to which most of us are subject. But, with the exception of fragment E—which is about Philo, not Pyrrho—these aspects of the biographical material are no more than gestured at in the surviving fragments of Timon; it would be an overstatement for us to speak here of 'parallels' at all. The stories are entirely consistent with the fragments, but the fragments themselves do not provide nearly enough to serve as a basis on which the stories could have been dreamed up. I shall return to this point after examining in a little more detail the picture of Pyrrho (and Philo) suggested by the fragments of Timon.

The main message is that the source of other people's trouble is their holding of opinions and their engaging in theoretical enquiry; Pyrrho achieves his extraordinary degree of tranquillity through not holding any opinions and refraining from all theorizing. As noted in the previous chapter, it is very possible that 'pointless laying-down of the law' (*eikaiēs nomothēkēs*), in passage A, refers to baseless theorizing; Epicurus uses the closely related word *nomothesia* to refer to arbitrary postulates in physics (*Ep. Pyth. apud* DL 10.87). But, in any case, passage B makes clear that theorizing is what Pyrrho avoided,[29] and that he is thereby free from the 'servitude to opinions'

---

[28] One might reply that, if Timon portrayed Philo as talking to himself, he may very well have done the same for Pyrrho, and *this* may be the source of the anecdote. But, if so, the anecdote is not to be dismissed as an *invention* based on something in Timon; it is, rather, an accurate *reproduction* of what Timon said, and as such deserves whatever level of credence we decide to give to Timon's verse fragments.

[29] In addition, Timon himself seems to express opposition to theorizing about grammar, in a pair of (somewhat obscure) lines quoted by Sextus in *Against the Grammarians* (*M* 1.53). At any rate, this is how Sextus interprets Timon in this passage, and his seems to be as plausible a reading of the lines as any; see Blank (1998; commentary *ad loc*).

(*latreiēs doxōn*) to which other philosophers are subject.[30] Similarly, passage C traces Pyrrho's tranquillity to his lack of concern for 'sweet-voiced wisdom' (*hēdulogou sophiēs*)—or rather, it may be assumed, for what passes for wisdom in other philosophical circles. As for opinions more generally, passages A and B both cite them as responsible for the failure of other people to attain anything like Pyrrho's tranquillity. Again, fragment E describes Philo as 'not busying himself with opinion and contests' (DL 9.69)—where the 'contests' in question are surely verbal contests with other philosophers. And this may perhaps also be the point of another line from Timon, quoted by Aristocles (*Praep. evang.* XIV.18.17): 'Indeed, no other mortal would compete with Pyrrho.'[31]

Passage A also lists 'affections' (*patheōn*) among the sources of disturbance. This no doubt refers, at least in part, to emotions or passions, the kinds of states called *pathē* by the Stoics; but it may also refer, more generally, to any kind of psychological 'affection', including sensory experience. Two

---

[30] Diogenes tells us, on the authority of Timon, that Pyrrho's follower Eurylochus was 'most hostile to sophists' (9.69). As in the other cases recounted by Diogenes (see above, n. 8), Eurylochus seems to be introduced as an example of someone who had learned from Pyrrho, but who had not learned enough. One should set oneself against the modes of thought represented by theorizers (I take it that the term 'sophist' has this wide scope in the current context, rather than the more specialized usage made prominent by Plato); but it does not follow that one should be 'most hostile' towards them, and there is no hint that Pyrrho himself adopted any such attitude—for this, of course, would merely reintroduce disturbance at another point. (It might be added that Timon himself seems to invite similar difficulties through his obvious failure to avoid 'contests'; see just below in the main text, and cf. Introduction, n. 23.)

[31] This interpretation is mentioned, though not fully endorsed, by Decleva Caizzi (DC 242–3). However, the other interpretation, according to which Timon is simply saying that no one is on the same level as Pyrrho (in which case 'could compete with' would be a better translation of *ouk an . . . erisseien* than 'would compete with'), seems preferable. First, it is clearly what Aristocles understands the line to mean. And, secondly, if the point was that Pyrrho did not trouble to engage in contentious discussion with other philosophers, one would expect 'Pyrrho would compete with no other mortal', not 'No other mortal would compete with Pyrrho'.

The picture of Pyrrho as a philosophical non-combatant appears to be contradicted by a sentence in Diogenes, which says that Pyrrho had a high reputation as a speaker and debater (9.64), and at least implies that debating was a regular activity of his. But the remainder of the evidence is so uniformly in opposition to this picture that the remark should probably be dismissed. (Brunschwig (1997: 299) reads *exōdikos legein kai pros erōtēsin* in this sentence as meaning 'speaking in continuous discourse even in response to questions', and takes it as another example of Pyrrho's bizarre habits of speech, like his habit of talking to himself. But this does not account for the claim that Pyrrho 'was looked down upon by no one' for his speaking abilities; flouting the rules of philosophical exchange would cause ridicule, not admiration. On this phrase, see also LS ii. 3.) It is true that Pyrrho's speaking and debating skills are cited as the reason for Nausiphanes' admiration for him. But this too is suspect; for immediately afterwards Nausiphanes is cited as saying that one should follow Pyrrho in respect of his disposition (*diatheseōs*) and *not* in respect of his words (*logōn*). On the specific issue of how much Pyrrho spoke, Galen cites the empiricist Menodotus as praising Pyrrho, on the contrary, for being a man of few words—apparently as a result of philosophical considerations (*Subfig. emp.* 84,31–85,3 Deichgräber; cf. 82,22–83,2).

other terms in this passage are also ambiguous. I suggested that 'laying-down of the law' may well refer primarily to physical theorizing. But it may also refer more straightforwardly to legislation, or to the promulgating of unwritten codes of conduct; if so, the point will be that Pyrrho was uninterested in promoting or following the generally approved forms of behaviour. Similarly *doxēs*, which I translated as 'opinion' in both passage A and in the lines about Philo, may also have the sense 'glory', and it is very possible that both senses are intended;[32] if so, this will again be something that the subjects of the fragments will be said to have no interest in attaining.

We are now better able to see the limited degree of correspondence between Timon's portrait of Pyrrho in the verse fragments and the one offered by the biographical material. As noted earlier, the anecdotes in Diogenes and elsewhere emphasize Pyrrho's lack of concern for social norms, and his lack of susceptibility to various kinds of powerful (but common) emotional reactions. We can now see that these elements are not entirely absent from Timon's account, but that they play a decidedly minor role there. The dominant theme in Timon's fragments is that Pyrrho was free from disturbance because of his freedom from opinions and from theorizing; and these points seem to have little direct connection with anything in the anecdotes.

The position, then, is this. In a few cases it seems to make the most sense to read a certain story as an irresponsible invention based on a suggestive phrase in Timon. But for the most part the stories, on the one hand, and the verse fragments of Timon, on the other, amount to distinct—though not inconsistent—accounts. Various hints in Timon point in the same direction as the bulk of the stories; but these hints do not go nearly far enough to have served in themselves as a starting point for the kinds of 'irresponsible inventions' just mentioned. Now, these points taken together seem to suggest that both the fragments of Timon and the bulk of the stories have some claim to be accepted, at least in the general picture they suggest of Pyrrho's attitude and behaviour. The stories do not look as if they are simply parasitic on Timon's writings; yet, if we are indeed dealing with two independent accounts, then their evident consistency, together with the overlap between them (limited though it may be), is a point in their favour. If, then, we treat the fragments of Timon and the biographical material as complementary sources of evidence, the composite picture this evidence adds up to is of a man who achieved exceptional tranquillity *both* through refraining from opinions and from theorizing, *and* through not caring about social norms or many of the other things—danger, pain, and the like—that affect most of us deeply. The sources of his tranquillity will thus be both theoretical and practical, with Timon's fragments tending to stress the theoretical aspect and the biographical material the practical aspect. The theoretical and practical attitudes or

[32] On this point, see DC 197, 245.

states in question are variously referred to in the sources as *adiaphoria*, 'indifference', *apatheia*, 'freedom from affections', and *ataraxia*, 'freedom from disturbance'.

It may be replied that this is all far too optimistic. We have only a few fragments of Timon on the subject of Pyrrho's practical attitudes. There is no reason to assume that what we have is representative of the entire works from which they derive; it is, therefore, perfectly possible that other lost portions of these poems were much more obvious prototypes for the majority of the stories than are the fragments that we have. So we cannot conclude that the stories are largely independent of Timon; they may, after all, be nothing more than fabrications taking suggestive turns of phrase in Timon's verses as their starting point. This will leave us, then, with just the few surviving pieces of Timon's portrait of Pyrrho. Moreover, if we want to treat these fragments as a reliable source of evidence about Pyrrho, then we will have to assume that Timon's portrait is not substantially a product of his own creativity and exaggeration. But this, too, is surely a hazardous assumption.

It may be impossible to refute this line of thought in its entirety. What we can do, however, to strengthen the case for treating both Timon's verse fragments and the biographical material with some degree of seriousness, is to consider how the composite picture they suggest might be related to the ideas expounded in the Aristocles passage. If the connections can be reconstructed without much difficulty—or, better still, if they are obvious on their face—then this increases the likelihood that the verse fragments and the biographical material give us an authentic picture of Pyrrho, or at least of his ideals and aspirations; to the extent that the kinds of things Pyrrho is described as saying and doing in these other sources can be seen as natural extensions of the ideas that the Aristocles passage ascribes to him, it becomes plausible to suppose that he did indeed behave in something like the way they suggest. Exploring these connections and their significance, then, is the task of the next section.

3. Connections with the Aristocles passage

In the case of what I called the dominant theme in the fragments of Timon, the link is obvious enough. Timon repeatedly says that Pyrrho is tranquil because he lacks opinions and avoids theoretical enquiry, and that other people are troubled because they have opinions and/or because they engage in theoretical enquiry. This is entirely consistent with the Aristocles passage, where we are told that we should be 'without opinions' (*adoxastous*), and that *ataraxia* will be the result of this stance. Recall that 'opinions', in this context, may be taken to refer, in Platonic or Parmenidean fashion, to those opinions that take as real—or, at the very least, as rationally explicable—the ordinary objects and states of affairs revealed to us by the senses; these may include both the everyday opinions of ordinary people, and the theories of cosmologists. Pyrrho's own thesis, as reported in the Aristocles passage—that reality is inherently indeterminate—is not an opinion in this sense; it is not an everyday opinion, nor is it an attempt to render the ordinary world rationally explicable.[33] By the same token, Pyrrho's own thesis is very different from the kind of theorizing that these fragments of Timon refer to as an obstacle to tranquillity. The theorizing to be avoided is the kind that seeks to discover 'what winds hold sway over Greece, from where everything comes and into what it passes'—in other words, precisely the kind that seeks a rational explanation for the processes occurring in the world around us.[34] Again, in declaring that reality is indeterminate, Pyrrho is turning his back on this kind of theorizing. Indeed, if 'pointless laying-down of the law', in the first fragment of Timon, does also refer, as suggested, to theorizing about the world around us, the term is apt; from Pyrrho's standpoint, the problem with cosmology and related enterprises is that they attempt to impose a fixity upon that which is inherently lacking in fixity. Finally, if *pathē*, 'affections', in the same fragment, refers to sensory experience, there is another clear connection with the Aristocles passage; for that passage groups 'sensations and opinions' together as what one should not trust, because they are neither true nor false.

Suppose, on the other hand, that we take *pathē* as referring to passions; as we observed, it is highly probable that this is at least part of what is intended by the term. If so, another dimension is introduced to Pyrrho's *ataraxia*, and to the troubles of other people, and the question of the connection with the Aristocles passage becomes more complicated. Recall, too, that this further dimension is also represented, and far more prominently, outside the fragments of Timon; Pyrrho's lack of susceptibility to various forms of emotional disturbance was one major component of the biographical material. That passions are disturbing is an unsurprising thought to encounter in Greek philosophy. That it is both possible and desirable to be without them altogether is a thought to be found most prominently in Stoic philosophy; but less extreme views recommending a moderating or even a minimizing of the passions are widespread. However, the Aristocles passage says nothing about passions.

Nor does it say anything about social expectations and conventions. Pyrrho's disregard of these, I suggested, is probably implied by two other ambiguous terms in Timon's fragment A: *doxēs*, translated 'glory' rather than

---

[33] On the latter point, see again Ch. 1 n. 23.

[34] The theorizing referred to by Timon is thus a *subset* of 'opinions', in the usage I have attributed to the Aristocles passage. And this fits nicely with Timon's own usage of 'opinion' in fragment B; those thinkers who sought to discover 'what winds hold sway over Greece', etc., are said to be in a state of 'servitude to opinions' (*latreiēs doxōn*). (In fragments A and E, however, 'opinion' may easily refer to everyday opinions as well.)

'opinion', and 'laying-down of the law', understood literally as referring to
the enactment of laws and other social norms, rather than to theorizing about
the cosmos. But, again, the same characteristic figures in a much more obvious way elsewhere; Pyrrho's disregard of convention is clearly another major
dimension of the biographical material.

Connections, if any, between *these* aspects of Pyrrho's attitude—the
aspects stressed particularly by the biographical material—and the Aristocles
passage are, therefore, a matter for interpretation. However, it is not too hard,
in either case, to construct a plausible connection. The connections that I shall
suggest, in the two cases, turn out to be related to one another, and also related
to the more general issue discussed just before, that of the avoidance of opinions.

What connection can be devised between the Aristocles passage and
Pyrrho's avoidance of emotional disturbances? It is reasonable to suppose—
the Stoics, for one, clearly did suppose—that a passion arises as a result of,
or as part and parcel of, one's *caring* tremendously about whatever is the
object of that passion; if it matters to one a great deal that one achieve a
certain goal, or that a certain outcome occur (for example, that one make it
safely through a storm at sea, with one's cargo intact), then very strong feelings are liable to attend success or failure, the occurrence or the non-occurrence of the outcome in question—or even the contemplation of these
outcomes beforehand. If, on the other hand, one does not regard the achievement of any particular goals, or the occurrence of any particular outcomes, as
of any great importance, then one will not have any emotional investment in
what happens. Now, both the biographical material and the evidence from
Timon suggest that Pyrrho enjoyed, or would in consistency have viewed as
ideal, just such a state of emotional indifference.[35] And it is at this point that
a connection can be posited with the views expressed in the Aristocles
passage.

If one thinks, as according to that passage Pyrrho does, that reality is inherently indefinite—if one takes things in themselves not to possess any determinate features—then one will think, in particular, that no object or state of
affairs is, in reality, either good or bad;[36] hence it will not be of any great

---

[35] In the case of the storm at sea, he is represented as maintaining this attitude, but not without effort. In Diogenes' version of the story he does remain calm, but we are also told that the
example of the pig was a means by which he 'strengthened his soul' (*anerrōse tēn psuchēn*
(9.68)); in Plutarch's version, he remarks that this calmness is only to be achieved 'by reason
and philosophy'.

[36] At this point, of course, the Stoics will disagree; for them it is crucial that virtue is by
nature good and vice by nature bad. These beliefs do not, however, engender *pathē* because
pathē, as they define the term, are essentially *misguided* beliefs concerning what is really worth
caring about. It is also true that the Stoics allow for distinctions of value even among the things
which they label indifferent; as we will see later in the chapter, it is for this reason that Cicero
several times distinguishes the orthodox Stoics from another group including both unorthodox

importance to one how things in the world turn out, and hence one will not be subject to the disruptive influence of powerful emotional reactions to events.[37] One will be, in Timon's own words, 'non-avoiding and non-choosing' (*aphugēs kai anairetos*). Sextus quotes these words in a context suggesting that it was intended to express the ideal attitude of indifference (*M* 11.164).[38] The point will then be not that one should be absolutely inactive— Sextus' purpose in this section is to show, precisely, that the sceptic is not liable to this charge, and one can hardly suppose that Timon would have wanted to invite it, either—but that one should not have any serious *stake* in what happens; one neither 'chooses' nor 'avoids' certain outcomes in the sense that one does not permit their occurrence or non-occurrence to *matter* to one. This is quite compatible with (calmly) seeking those things that generally give pleasure, avoiding those things that generally give pain, and so on. But it is not compatible with being devastated if one fails to attain, or to avoid, the things in question—or with being overjoyed if one succeeds. Those reactions would make sense only if one thought that these outcomes really were, in the nature of things, worth choosing or worth avoiding.

Similarly, if one thinks that nothing is in itself either good or bad, intrinsically either worth having or worth avoiding, one may be expected not to attach any great importance to conventions that prescribe what should and should not be done, or to achieving good repute in society's eyes. So if 'laying-down of the law' does refer to legislation or the devising of other types of norms, it would again be quite understandable that Pyrrho should not exercise himself with such activities, and that he should regard other people

Stoics and Pyrrho. My point in mentioning the Stoics was simply this: they understand the passions as due to people caring excessively about things that are not really worth caring about, and it makes sense to see Pyrrho as thinking along similar lines.

[37] Why *should* one be any less emotionally invested in things, if one decides that they are not *in reality* good or bad, or possessed of any other kind of value or disvalue? Surely, one might say, the important question is how much value one places in them oneself, not how much value they may possess in the nature of things. But that seems to be a distinctively modern reaction. At any rate, the assumption is widespread in the ancient world that the things that really warrant our care and concern are the things that are really, or by nature, good or valuable—and that everything else is, or should be, of incomparably lesser weight in our decisions. Both Plato and Aristotle clearly subscribe to versions of this assumption; but the most striking case is, again, the Stoics. On the Stoic view it makes sense (usually) to pursue health and avoid sickness, or to pursue pleasure and avoid pain; yet the outcome of these pursuits and avoidances, which have to do with things that are neither good nor bad, is quite unimportant compared with the question whether or not one is approaching the world in a virtuous frame of mind. Finally, within the Pyrrhonist tradition itself, Sextus consistently links the dogmatists' torments with their benighted belief that there are things in the world that are by nature good or bad; the sceptic lacks all such beliefs, and *therefore* is free from emotional turmoil (*PH* 1.25–30, 3.235–8; *M* 11.110–67). However it may seem to us, then, the line of thinking I am attributing to Pyrrho would have been commonplace in the ancient context. On the parallel between Pyrrho and Sextus in this area, see further Sect. 7.

[38] On this, see Bett (1997; commentary *ad loc.*).

who do engage in such activities and attach great importance to them as creating unnecessary troubles for themselves. It is also easy to see why Pyrrho would be unconcerned with achieving glory—if that is part of what is conveyed by *doxēs*—and why he would regard the dedicated pursuit of glory as conducive to disturbance. By the same token, it is understandable that he would be quite happy to engage in such activities as washing pigs and doing housework. Other people of Pyrrho's station would be expected to scorn such activities as inherently repugnant and also, especially, as not befitting *them*; but Pyrrho's 'indifference'—his thinking that reality is indefinite, as applied to the specific area of value predicates—rules out his taking seriously any such attitudes about what is 'fitting' for whom, or about what activities are worth doing or worth avoiding.[39]

All the main aspects of the practical attitudes and behaviour attributed to Pyrrho—his avoidance of opinions and theorizing, but also his lack of susceptibility to passions and his disregard of convention—can, then, be understood as connected with the general philosophical outlook summarized in the Aristocles passage; they can be connected not just in a general way with his aspirations to *ataraxia*, as reported in that passage, but also more specifically with what I argued to be his central thesis, the thesis that reality is indefinite. And this seems to lend further support to the tentative verdict put forward at the end of the last section, concerning the credibility of the biographical material and the verse fragments of Timon. I shall return to this point in a moment. But, first, there is one more important point needing discussion, having to do with the practical effects of the indeterminacy thesis and of its immediate corollaries.

This issue, indeed, already arose in the previous chapter, but the texts under discussion in that chapter were inadequate to resolve it. Ceasing to theorize, and ceasing to trust one's sensations and opinions, are plainly what the Aristocles passage recommends; hence there was no difficulty connecting the ideas in that passage with those in fragments A–E of Timon. But why should it be supposed that adopting *this* stance should result in *ataraxia*—or that the opposite would lead to disturbances? It was not difficult to see why avoidance of the passions and disregard of convention might be thought to yield *ataraxia*; the crucial point was the abandonment of any opinions specifically to the effect that things were in reality *good* or *bad*, and hence the shed-

---

[39] One might, of course, refuse to 'take such attitudes seriously' in the sense of lacking any commitment to the idea that any particular ways of behaving are good or bad in the nature of things, and yet still *act* conventionally; one's style of behaviour could be due purely to habit and training, and not to any beliefs or ideologies. Along these lines, Sextus regards laws and customs as one of the major determinants of behaviour for the sceptic (see *PH* 1.17, 23–4, 231, 237; *M* 9.49, 11.166); and Pyrrho could have adopted a similar posture as an expression of his indeterminacy thesis—instead of ignoring and even flouting convention, as the evidence suggests that he did. I return to this discrepancy between Sextus and Pyrrho in Sect. 7.

ding of the unwarranted levels of concern inevitably associated with those opinions. But how is the abandonment of opinions, of theories, or of trust in one's sensations *in general*—even when good and bad and other evaluative predicates are not at issue—meant to yield *ataraxia*? There seems to be an unexplained gap here. Indeed, the supposition that *ataraxia* would be the result might well seem quite unintuitive; it might well be thought, on the contrary, that to cease trusting these familiar sources of information would be to invite anxiety and insecurity.[40] Yet the Aristocles passage appears to say nothing at all about the question; it tells us that, in Pyrrho's view, adopting the 'unopinionated' attitude he recommends will lead to *ataraxia*, but it gives no direct indication as to why this should be so. Is it possible that the evidence on which we have been focusing in this chapter may shed some light upon this question?

It appears from fragments A and C of Timon, taken together, that Pyrrho enjoys a *stability* of temperament that is utterly denied to those who put their trust in opinions and theorizing. According to passage C, Pyrrho is 'uniformly unmoved' (*akinētōs kata t'auta*) because of his lack of attention to the 'wisdom' by which others are seduced; the language recalls, probably intentionally, the terms in which Parmenides describes the changelessness of What Is.[41] By contrast, those who are subject to opinions are, according to passage A, 'weighed down *on this side and that*' (*barunomen'entha kai entha*). Lacking, so to speak, the ballast that Pyrrho's attitude, as described in the Aristocles passage, provides him, they are 'empty' (*koupha*); hence their opinions are liable to sway them uncontrollably from side to side.[42] The same

---

[40] Analogous questions have often been raised about the scepticism of Sextus; Sextus does have an answer to the question (*PH* 1.27–30, 3.235–8; *M* 11.110–67), though there is room for considerable debate about how successful it is. It is noteworthy that Sextus, too, couches his explicit remarks on the benefits of scepticism almost entirely in terms of the sceptic's avoidance of beliefs to the effect that things are by nature good or bad. Again, I return to this issue at the end of the chapter. For further discussion of Sextus' position on this matter, and references to other treatments, see Bett (1997: commentary on chs. IV and V; on the relevance of *non*-ethical beliefs, and the sceptic's avoidance of them, to *ataraxia* in Sextus, see esp. pp. 131–2); I also touch on this matter in Sect. 7 below.

[41] As is pointed out by Reale (1981: 310–11). For the parallel in Parmenides, see DK 28B8, ll. 26, 29. Note also that Parmenides compares What Is to a 'well-rounded sphere' (*eukuklou sphairēs* (28B8, l. 43)); the 'flaming circle' of the 'well-turned sphere' (*eutornou sphairēs purikautora kuklon*), in the comparison between Pyrrho and the Sun-God, seems to be reminiscent of this. If, as is likely, the parallels with Parmenides are not mere coincidence, the point they make is a complex one. Pyrrho himself achieves a degree of stability comparable to that enjoyed by What Is in Parmenides; yet this is precisely through his recognition that nothing like that degree of stability is to be encountered in any external objects or states of affairs—either in the world of ordinary experience (here Parmenides would agree), or in any other realm to which reason might be thought (as by Parmenides) to have access.

[42] Decleva Caizzi (DC 244–5) regards the juxtaposition of 'empty' and 'weighed down' as an oxymoron. But I think the point is, rather, that these people, being in themselves 'empty', are unduly vulnerable to whatever 'weights' are imposed upon them by opinions and the like.

kind of thing is suggested by the term 'whirls', used in connection with 'wisdom' in passage C.[43] And this picture seems to be supported by another piece of purportedly early evidence. Diogenes cites Pyrrho's follower Philo (though without telling us the source of his information) as saying that Pyrrho frequently referred admiringly to Homer (9.67).[44] The parts of Homer that he is said especially to have admired are those having to do with the shortness and precariousness of human life—a single line and another pair of lines on this subject are cited as favourites of his—but also, more generally, those dealing with 'the instability and vain zealousness and childishness of human beings' (*to abebaion kai kenospoudon hama kai paidariōdes tōn anthrōpōn*). Now, why should opinions and theorizing produce temperamental instability? Here, finally, a connection with the Aristocles passage becomes apparent. If reality is indeterminate—if things, as the Aristocles passage tells us, are in their own nature 'unstable' (*astathmēta*)—then one can hardly expect that any opinions or theories about them should attain stability. Since there is nothing firm for these opinions or theories to get a grip on, they are bound to be fleeting and changeable, and therefore unsatisfactory; in putting one's faith in them, one is bound to be 'weighed down on this side and that'—that is, buffeted from one set of opinions and theories to another—and this process itself is bound to be experienced as, in another sense, weighing one down—that is, as oppressive and debilitating.[45] The only way to avoid this state, and thereby to attain *ataraxia*, is to avoid opinions and theories altogether; and this is what Pyrrho, with his understanding of the nature of reality, is uniquely able to achieve.

Let me now tie together the threads of this rather tortuous discussion. We began by supposing that the verse fragments of Timon were to be treated with caution, and the biographical material from Antigonus and others even more so. The portrait of Pyrrho in the former could be largely Timon's own creation, but it would at least be a creation that in some sense expressed Timon's devotion to Pyrrho himself; in Antigonus' case, however, not even this degree of closeness to the original could be assumed. What we saw in the last section was that, with a few exceptions, the stories from the biographical material were not naturally read as inventions based on points suggested by Timon's words, but also that the relations between the two sets of sources—their compatibility, as well as the occasional points of contact between them—seemed to suggest that neither was simply an *invention* at all. However, it was acknowledged that, given the paucity of the surviving evidence, this argument was somewhat flimsy. The biographical material

---

[43] If the emendation *dinois* is correct; see again n. 22.

[44] Also to Democritus; we shall return to this point in the next chapter. On Pyrrho's reading of Homer, see also Sextus, *M* 1.272, 281.

[45] Compare the Homeric use of *barunetai* to refer to physical exhaustion (*Il.* 19.165).

might represent a creative extrapolation from parts of Timon's work that have been lost; and that would leave us with no more than the verse fragments of Timon to rely on, as well as an unanswered question about their credibility.

What we have now seen is that the main message of the verse fragments of Timon—Pyrrho's avoidance of opinions and theorizing, and the exceptional stability or tranquillity that results—is quite plainly connected with the Aristocles passage; in fact, the portrait of Pyrrho (and the portrait of Philo) contained in these fragments is really just a filling-out, with a little specific detail, of what it would be like to succeed in doing what, according to the Aristocles passage, Pyrrho recommended. And the main message of the biographical material, of which there are a few hints in the verse fragments of Timon as well—that is, Pyrrho's lack of susceptibility to emotional disturbance and his disregard of convention—can also be interpreted, without any great effort, as connected with the ideas in the Aristocles passage. So, if the Aristocles passage is as credible a source of evidence as I have argued, and if the content of the passage is what I have argued it to be, then we now have rather better reasons for putting some faith in these other sources. The verse fragments of Timon emerge as no less believable, at least in their picture of the ideal towards which Pyrrho strived, than the Aristocles passage itself. We cannot hope to settle how far Pyrrho really succeeded in freeing himself from opinions and theorizing. But, given the nature of the links with the Aristocles passage, it seems fair to conclude that Timon is at least showing us the condition towards which he understood Pyrrho himself to have aspired; this is fiction of a kind, but fiction that is an unadulterated expression of the philosophy Timon understood Pyrrho to have espoused. And this conclusion is further supported by the fact that, as we just saw, the verse fragments of Timon actually seem to help in elucidating a point about the Aristocles passage itself—the question why avoidance of opinions should produce tranquillity.

The credentials of the biographical material are less secure than this; a determined critic could still maintain that it is largely pure invention, perhaps picking up on suggestions or turns of phrase from the lost portions of Timon. But there is at any rate no clear reason in *favour* of such a proposal; and the specific ways in which this material (again, with some exceptions) complements the evidence from Timon—both the verse fragments and the Aristocles passage itself—encourage the conclusion that it, too, tells us something true about Pyrrho. Again, exactly how eccentric, or how unperturbed, Pyrrho really was we cannot hope to settle. But we are not being excessively credulous if we take the majority of the anecdotes to represent a type towards which Pyrrho aspired, and which he achieved to a sufficient degree to attract considerable notice.

We may, then, accept the terms *adiaphoria*, 'indifference', *apatheia*, 'freedom from affections', and *ataraxia*, 'freedom from disturbance', all reported

in the sources, as jointly describing Pyrrho's ideal. These terms may not all
have been used by Pyrrho or even by Timon, and the last two certainly had
homes in the vocabulary of other philosophical schools or movements. But
there is no good reason to deny their applicability to Pyrrho's case.[46] Nor,
even with all due caution, is there good reason to deny that the concrete
significance of these terms, as applied to Pyrrho's philosophy, is roughly that
suggested by the verse fragments of Timon together with the bulk of the
biographical material.

4. Deciding what to do: the role of appearances

We began with a reference to Antigonus' stories depicting Pyrrho as a lunatic
who ignored cliffs, oncoming wagons, and the like. Clearly setting himself
against any such account of Pyrrho's practical stance, Aenesidemus said,
according to Diogenes, that, 'while he philosophized according to the method
of suspension of judgement, he did not, however, do everything without foresight' (9.62).[47] If this simply means that Pyrrho did not wander into the paths
of oncoming wagons, and so on, we can accept the point. However, it is possible that Aenesidemus is exaggerating the normality of Pyrrho's behaviour. As
we saw, a sizeable portion of the evidence (to which we are now giving our
qualified assent) suggests that Pyrrho did act in a radically eccentric and
unconventional manner. To judge from Sextus, at any rate, this could well
have been embarrassing to the later Pyrrhonist tradition; Sextus several times
tells us that the sceptic acts in accordance with the laws and customs of the
society in which he lives (*PH* 1.24, 237, cf. 3.2; *M* 11.166). So Aenesidemus'
verdict on Pyrrho's behaviour may be assimilating Pyrrho to the later tradition to a misleading extent.

Aenesidemus also tells us that Pyrrho followed appearances; according to
Diogenes (9.106), this claim appeared in the first book of his *Pyrrhonist
Discourses*. Should this too be viewed with suspicion? One may well wonder,
again, whether Aenesidemus has simply attributed to Pyrrho a procedure that
he himself considered important, whether or not Pyrrho had actually adopted
it. The Anonymous Commentator on the *Theaetetus* also says that Pyrrho

---

[46] On this point see LS ii. 12.

[47] The point here is not that Pyrrho did not apply his philosophy to everyday life—that his
suspension of judgement was 'merely philosophical', as the scepticism of modern philosophers
is often said to be. (On the attribution of suspension of judgement to Pyrrho, see Ch. 1, Sect. 7).
Rather, it is that the practical consequence of Pyrrho's philosophy was not, as some critics might
maintain, that he was unable to act with foresight. It is universally assumed in the ancient
world—and the present text is no exception—that one's philosophy has to be applied to everyday life; on this see Bett (1993).

relied, both in philosophical discussion and in everyday life, on what appears (61.10–15, 40–6); but as we saw in the previous chapter, this passage is thoroughly contaminated with later philosophical concepts, and it would not be surprising if this were another example. Galen, too, tells us that in everyday life Pyrrho followed what is evident (*sequens evidentia* (*Subfig. emp.* 82,26 Deichgräber)); but we saw similar reasons for suspicion about Galen's evidence, and these are reinforced in the present case by the fact that Pyrrho is introduced as 'Pyrrho the sceptic' (*piron sketicus* (82,23 Deichgräber)). This issue is clearly an important one. To the ancients, a philosophy concerning which it was not clear whether, or how, it could be put into practice was *eo ipso* a defective philosophy;[48] we may assume that the early Pyrrhonists had something to say about how a life was to be lived consistently with their general philosophical outlook. Either the sources just quoted are right— Pyrrho did claim to live by following appearances—in which case we have a significant area of overlap between Pyrrho and the later Pyrrhonists; or we need to try to find some other way in which Pyrrho might be thought to have regulated his behaviour. And in either case the answer that we give needs to be shown to be consistent with the general outlook expounded in the Aristocles passage.

The Aristocles passage itself is silent on this question, as one might expect; we have seen throughout this chapter that it is not helpful on issues having to do with the modes of behaviour the follower of Pyrrho is to engage in. It tells us to adopt a certain peculiar form of speech expressing our mistrust of sensations and opinions; but it gives no explicit indication as to how, if at all, this recommendation is to be connected with our everyday practice. There are, however, three other texts from Timon bearing on the question of early Pyrrhonism's attitude towards appearances; it is clearly upon these that our main attention must be directed.

First, we are told that Timon said, in his book *Pytho*, that he had not 'gone beyond *sunētheia*'; I leave open for the moment the question of the translation of *sunētheia*. Next, there is a line from Timon's *Images* (*Indalmoi*): 'But the appearance is powerful everywhere, wherever it comes.'[49] Then there is a quotation from another work by Timon, the otherwise unknown *On the Senses* (*Peri aisthēseōn*): 'That honey is sweet I do not posit, but that it

---

[48] It is arguable that the ancients were right about this; it is also arguable that the contrast between ancient and modern philosophy in this respect is not as stark or as clear as has sometimes been suggested. Again, see Bett (1993). On the central importance, in ancient philosophy, of articulating a certain way of life, see also Hadot (1995).

[49] Long and Sedley (LS 1H) translate *elthēi* by 'goes', and write (ii. 8), 'It is odd to write of "the appearance" as going anywhere'; they therefore supply 'one' (i.e. 'someone') as the subject. But this is unnecessary as well as syntactically awkward; *elthēi* may be taken in the sense 'comes' or 'arrives', and the point will be that whatever appearances confront us are powerful.

appears so I agree.' All three pieces of evidence occur (in this order) in the same passage of Diogenes (9.105); the line from the *Indalmoi* is also quoted (though the work is not named) in Sextus (*M* 7.30) and in Galen (*De dignosc. puls.* 8.781 K).[50]

Both the direct quotations from Timon seem to invite us to read them in just the manner suggested by Aenesidemus' claim; they look as if they are indeed offering appearances as what Sextus will later call a 'practical criterion' (*PH* 1.21)—that is, a means for deciding what to do. If so, later Pyrrhonism will in this respect be unchanged from early Pyrrhonism. However, although this is how the quotations have usually been understood,[51] there have been some dissenting voices. The most plausible alternative is this: the quotation from the *Indalmoi* is not recommending that one shape one's behaviour in the light of the appearances—on the contrary, it is bemoaning the fact that the appearances have such power to hoodwink people. If reality is indeterminate, the appearances do not present reality as it is; yet they have the power to convince almost everyone to think otherwise[52] (with the result that people are, as Timon elsewhere says, 'weighed down . . . by passions, opinion and pointless laying down of the law'). Similarly, the quotation from *On the Senses* is simply making the point that things *appear* to us as having determinate qualities, such as sweetness, but that this may be accepted without in any way committing one to their having such qualities in reality; it is not telling us anything at all about how to direct our behaviour.[53]

Taken by themselves, the two quotations do admit of this more restricted reading. However, the contexts of the quotations, and comparisons with certain other texts, tell in favour of the standard reading. As I said, Diogenes quotes both remarks together; and this is in the context of replies offered by Pyrrhonists to the objection that Pyrrhonism makes life impossible. The Pyrrhonists are represented as saying (9.104–5) that this objection fails, because they have not denied the existence of sense experience, or the fact that things appear a certain way; they merely refrain from claiming that things really are the way they appear. The point is clearly that the ability to talk

[50] With *alla* altered to *ei ge* to suit the construction of Galen's sentence. Decleva Caizzi (DC T63C) prints this passage as if Galen quotes only half the line; in fact, save for this one alteration (which does not, however, disrupt the metre), the whole line is intact.

[51] See e.g. LS i. 17–18.

[52] See DC 262–4. Decleva Caizzi connects this with her interpretation of Antigonus' stories about Pyrrho's literal disregard of the evidence of the senses, stories that she takes seriously (see above, n. 11). However, one could adopt this reading of the line from the *Indalmoi* even while rejecting those stories as a fabrication, as I have done; the point could simply be that the power of the appearances typically prevents people from accepting or even countenancing the indeterminacy thesis.

[53] See Decleva Caizzi (1984*b*: 94–5). This quotation does not appear in Decleva Caizzi's collection of texts relating to Pyrrho, because the work *On the Senses* is in her view more plausibly regarded as a philosophical contribution by Timon himself than as an account of the ideas or activities of Pyrrho. I shall return to this point at the end of this section.

about, and base one's choices on, the way things appear is what allows the
Pyrrhonist, contrary to the objection, to live quite satisfactorily. And the
quotations from Timon are introduced in corroboration of this point. Now, it
might be answered that Diogenes is not to be relied on in this matter; he or
his source may quote Timon as if he is espousing the appearances as a practical criterion, but we should not necessarily believe this. But the line from the
Indalmoi is also quoted, as mentioned above, by Sextus and Galen. Sextus is
specifically talking about the sceptic's practical criterion, and explicitly offers
this interpretation of Timon's line. And Galen's point in quoting it is also
essentially the same—even though the context is somewhat less straightforward. Galen is attacking the refusal of the Empiricists to recognize the dilating of the arteries (8.776 ff. K). He takes himself to have forced them into a
position in which 'It will not be possible to say "Perhaps the artery is dilated,
yet it does not appear so", but [they will have to say] on the contrary "Perhaps
it is not dilated, however it appears so" ' (and thus they will have to recognize
the dilating of the arteries, at least as something that *appears* to occur). He
then adds, 'For this is the consequence for those who posit only the appearance, and not the judgement additional to it, if indeed "The appearance is
powerful everywhere, wherever it comes", as Timon says.' Here again, then,
the line is clearly represented as offering a basis on which practical judgements can be made; whatever may be the case in reality, one accepts that
things appear in certain guises, and this in turn shapes one's reactions to the
world—including, presumably, one's medical practice. All three authors,
then, adopt the same interpretation of the line, and there is no indication that
any one of them is dependent for this interpretation on any of the others; the
contexts are quite different from one another.[54] To suppose that three authors
have independently made the same misinterpretation of the line seems more
than a little strained.[55]

The quotation from *On the Senses* appears only in Diogenes. Again,
however, there is reason to think that he is not deceived in his understanding
of the comment about honey. Sextus uses the very same example (*PH* 1.20);
he does not quote or mention Timon, but his words can very well be thought
of as a paraphrase of Timon's words, and give the strong impression of having
been inspired by them.[56] Unlike the Diogenes passage, this one is not expli-

---

[54] The subject matter in the Sextus and Diogenes passages is clearly related. But there are no
verbal parallels that might lead us to suppose that the passage in Diogenes is drawing upon the
passage in Sextus.

[55] Decleva Caizzi (DC 264) regards the opening 'but' as supporting her interpretation, since
it suggests that the state of affairs referred to concerning 'the appearance' is one to be deplored.
I see no reason to accept this; 'but' shows that this state of affairs was contrasted with something else mentioned in the previous lines, but we have no idea what that other thing was.

[56] Note especially Sextus' assertion that 'we agree' (*sunchōroumen*) that honey appears to
sweeten, which sounds like an echo of Timon's 'I agree' (*homologō*).

citly directed to explaining the Pyrrhonist's practical criterion; but that does become the focus in the following chapter (1.21–4), with which the present one is closely connected. Sextus here emphasizes (1.19–20) that, contrary to certain unnamed critics, the sceptics do not 'do away with' (*anairousi*) or 'overturn' (*anatrepomen*) the appearances; that is, they agree that things appear to us in certain ways, merely questioning whether they really are as they appear—and the sweet appearance of honey is cited as an example. The following chapter begins (1.21) by picking up this point. 'That we pay attention to the appearances', Sextus says, 'is clear from what we say about the criterion'; and the use of appearances as a guide to action then becomes explicit. At least part of what it means, then, to accept the appearances, rather than 'doing away with' or 'overturning' them, is to make use of them in deciding what to do. Of course, even if Sextus (or his immediate source) is drawing on Timon, that does not *prove* that Timon used the example to make the same point as that for which Sextus uses it. But if Diogenes understands Timon as recommending that we live by following the appearances; if Sextus uses Timon's words with the same point in mind; and if Sextus and Diogenes are, as again they surely are, independent of one another; then we need some substantial grounds for refusing to accept that this was indeed Timon's original point—and there are none. One should note, finally, that the example of honey and sweetness has on its face an air of practical applicability. This is precisely the kind of example one *would* come up with if one was thinking of the kinds of appearances by which choices were to be guided; the fact that honey generally appears sweet governs whether or not one spreads it on one's bread, or uses it in various recipes. Aristotle had already used the judgement that some things are sweet and others not sweet as an example of the kind of judgement all of us reveal in our actions—even those who claim to deny the Law of Non-Contradiction (*Met.* 1008^{b}20). If Timon's words were intended merely as an answer to the objection 'The world certainly does not *seem* indeterminate, as you claim it is', then the example of honey would be no more suitable than a great many others (for example, 'The sky appears blue', which has no obvious practical implications). But the example acquires a particular point if the objection is of the form 'How can you make *choices* in a world that you take to be utterly indeterminate? For example, how can you decide whether to spread honey on your bread or nail-polish?'[57]

---

[57] Decleva Caizzi (DC 263) claims that arguments from the impossibility of choice and action are Hellenistic, and that it is therefore anachronistic to see Timon as responding to them. But Aristotle uses such arguments in *Met.* IV, interspersed with more abstract philosophical considerations (see esp. 1008^{b}12–19, 1010^{b}1 ff.). Again, Antigonus' stories about Pyrrho's lunatic behaviour, read in the way I argued to be the most plausible, are an example of this kind of argument. Finally, Pyrrho's position would naturally invite such arguments; it is of a kind such that objections of the form 'If that is what you think, how can you act?' are inherently likely to arise, whether or not they were regularly bandied about among philosophers at the time.

It is no doubt true that Pyrrho and Timon would have thought of most people as being *taken in by* the appearances of things. Things appear to us, on given occasions, in determinate ways, and most people assume that they are in reality as they appear; Pyrrho resists this assumption, since he holds that reality is in fact indeterminate, and it is in *this* sense that he mistrusts the senses. However, it is quite compatible with this to shape one's behaviour to the determinate ways in which things appear on given occasions, and this is what the two quotations from Timon are best understood as recommending. Now, what of Timon's other obscure claim, as reported by Diogenes—that 'he has not gone beyond *sunētheia*'? This occurs in the same context as the quotations, and seems to be understood by Diogenes as saying something similar to them—that sceptical views do not render one unable to lead one's life; it is presented as a consequence of, or as an expression of the same point of view as, the preceding discussion (*hothen*, 'hence'), in which the Pyrrhonists' acceptance of the fact that things appear to us in certain ways, and the availability of this as a basis for living one's life, is the main point. Again, we cannot be sure that Diogenes, or his source, has understood Timon's point correctly; but if there is a reading of the claim according to which Timon does mean what Diogenes thinks he means, then (other things being equal) this is the reading to be preferred.

Sunētheia can mean various things. Among the meanings that might be thought relevant, the most common is perhaps 'custom'. However, although this meaning occurs in some translations of the passage,[58] it does not seem suitable here. As we saw, much of the biographical information about Pyrrho—evidence that we found no good reason to dismiss *en masse*— suggests that he was not at all inclined to act in customary ways. Besides, this would certainly require us to attribute a misunderstanding to Diogenes; the objection to which Diogenes presents Timon's remark as a response is not that the sceptics reject *conventional* behaviour, but that they reject life as a whole. Another possible meaning is 'standard linguistic usage'. However, it is again very unclear how a claim not to have departed from standard usage could be thought relevant to the objection to which it is supposed to be a reply.[59] A third possible meaning is 'ordinary experience'; and it is note-

---

[58] Hicks' Loeb translation has 'has not gone outside what is customary'; Long and Sedley (LS 1H) have 'has not departed from normal practice'.

[59] Decleva Caizzi (DC 236–41) favours this understanding on the ground that the previous sentence places emphasis on what 'we say' (*legomen, eipōmen*) in certain circumstances. But there is no particular reason to think that Diogenes is presenting Timon's remark as a response to the considerations offered in the previous sentence alone; it could just as well be presented as a response to the entire paragraph so far—that is, to the sceptics' willingness to recognize that things appear to us in various ways. (Decleva Caizzi (DC 237) draws attention to the *kai gar* introducing the previous sentence, pointing out that this indicates a new section of argument. But it does not follow that a later remark, presented as a consequence of previous considerations, could not be meant as a consequence of a whole *sequence* of such considerations,

worthy that this usage tends to occur particularly in contexts where an actual or potential sceptical *undermining* of ordinary experience is at issue. Diogenes tells us that Chrysippus studied in the Academy with Arcesilaus and Lacydes, and that this caused him to argue both for and against *sunētheia* (7.183–4); he also lists, in the catalogue of Chrysippus' works, six books against*sunētheia* and seven books in its favour (7.198). That *sunētheia* here means 'common experience', and especially sensory experience, is confirmed by a passage of Plutarch (*Sto. rep.* 1036c–1037c), where the books against *sunētheia* are said to contradict the Stoics' doctrine of 'apprehensive impressions'. Plutarch talks of Chrysippus' arguments as discrediting the senses (1036c); he also quotes from a work of Chrysippus called *On Ways of Life* (*Peri biōn*), where Chrysippus talks of people 'apprehending in accordance with *sunētheia* both sensible things and other things that proceed from the senses' (1036e). Cicero also refers to the same arguments of Chrysippus (*Acad.* 2.75, 87), calling them arguments against the senses, but also arguments against *consuetudo*, which is clearly a translation of *sunētheia*. And a passage of Epictetus (*Diss.* 1.27, 15–21) talks of sceptical arguments, by Pyrrhonists and Academics, interchangeably as arguments against the senses and as arguments against *sunētheia*.

It is clearly this usage that is being employed in the present passage of Diogenes. Timon says that he has not gone outside ordinary experience; that is, he has not undermined or contradicted ordinary experience in the way that Pyrrhonists are regularly accused of doing, and are accused of doing at the beginning of the chapter. This is presented as a consequence of the numerous points attributed to the Pyrrhonists in general in the previous sentences. Timon, like other Pyrrhonists, is quite happy to accept that things appear to us in certain ways in certain circumstances (this is precisely what we have seen to be conveyed by the immediately following quotations from Timon); *hence* (*hothen*) he can quite justifiably claim not to have done away with our everyday experience of things—something that, if he had done it, would quite reasonably invite the charge that he had made life itself impossible. As in the other cases, then, we can easily make sense of Timon's words on the assumption that Diogenes knows what he is talking about; and there are no other factors that might cause us to doubt that assumption.[60]

including some preceding the *kai gar*.) In any case, the relevance of Timon's remark, understood as referring to standard linguistic usage, is far from clear if it is a response purely to the previous sentence. Diogenes represents the sceptics as saying, 'When we say that the picture has projections, we are making clear what is apparent; but when we say that it does not have projections, we are no longer speaking of what appears, but of something else.' How is 'Hence Timon in the *Pytho* says that he has not gone outside standard usage' supposed to be a response to this?

[60] Decleva Caizzi (DC 239) objects that, as Antigonus' stories and the Aristocles passage show, Pyrrho did *not* trust sensory experience; hence, if Timon means that he has not gone outside ordinary experience, he must be engaging in self-criticism rather than defending himself

The evidence therefore suggests that in early Pyrrhonism, just as in later Pyrrhonism, acceptance of the appearances was permitted, and used as a basis for choice and action. The description of how things appear was presumably also accepted as a legitimate form of speech. It would not fall under the recommendation in the Aristocles passage, that one should say 'about each single thing that it no more is than is not or both is and is not or neither is nor is not'. As we saw, the assertion that one should not trust one's sensations or opinions cannot sensibly be read as suggesting that one should ignore them altogether in one's everyday behaviour; and the obvious alternative is that it is saying that one should not trust them to reveal how things are in their true natures—as, it might be supposed, people generally do. If so, then the form of words expressing that mistrust should also be read as applying to the natures of things, and not to how they appear—leaving us free to talk about the appearances of things without restriction. Similarly, the 'opinions' from which Timon elsewhere declares Pyrrho to be free (fragments A and B, cf. fragment E) are opinions having to do with the nature of things; specifications of how things appear do not count as opinions any more than they do in Sextus. This interpretation, of course, requires us to explain the relations between how things appear and how they are in their real natures. I shall take up this matter in the next chapter, when I return to the question of the nature and implications of the indeterminacy thesis. For now I shall simply note, first, that it is on the face of it perfectly consistent to hold (*a*) that things are in their natures indeterminate, but (*b*) that they appear to us on given occasions[61] in certain determinate ways, and (*c*) that the ways in which they

---

against an objection—in which case Diogenes has fundamentally misunderstood his point. However, as we have seen, the stories in Antigonus in which Pyrrho has to be rescued by his friends are themselves not to be trusted. And the claim in the Aristocles passage, that we should not trust our sensations, can very well be understood as saying that we should not trust them to reveal the true nature of things (see just below in the main text); it is entirely compatible with this to accept that things *appear* in various ways on various specific occasions, and hence to stay within the bounds of ordinary experience to the extent of allowing it to guide one's action. So if *sunētheia* means 'ordinary experience', it is perfectly possible for Diogenes to be understanding Timon correctly; this does not contradict any credible evidence about either Timon or Pyrrho.

[61] The qualification 'on given occasions' is important. It would be very hard to see why one would be attracted to the thesis that things in their real natures possess no determinate features, if one thought that things *invariably* appeared the same determinate way. Indeed, as we shall see in the next chapter (Sect. 1), it is precisely the fact that things do *not* invariably appear in one particular guise that can most plausibly be thought to motivate the indeterminacy thesis. It is true that Timon's statement 'honey appears sweet' is on the surface a universal claim. But we can easily understand him to mean that this is how honey *usually* appears; in certain circumstances it will appear not-sweet (and after certain chemical changes, it will no longer appear even as honey). As we saw, Sextus uses the same example, with the same apparent universality (*PH* 1.20); yet he also several times draws attention to the fact that honey does *not* appear sweet to people in certain physiological conditions (*PH* 1.101, 211, 213, 2.51, 63), and there is no reason why Timon should not have done the same. See also Aristotle, *Met.* 1009^{b}3–4, 1010^{b}21–3; the example of a generally sweet-tasting thing tasting bitter in certain cases evidently predates Timon.

appear to us on those occasions can and should serve as the basis for our behaviour; and, secondly, that this is the combination of views that, if I am right, best fits the totality of our evidence.

One further issue remains to be discussed in the realm of bases for action. In his initial summary of the views of Pyrrho, which I quoted more extensively in the last chapter, Diogenes says that in Pyrrho's view 'human beings do everything by convention and habit' (*nomōi . . . kai ethei panta tous anthrōpous prattein* (9.61)).[62] However, to repeat, it looks as if Pyrrho's own behaviour was far from conventional or habitual. Supposing we accept the passage of Diogenes as reliable information about Pyrrho,[63] how is the apparent discrepancy to be explained?

A natural explanation would be that when Pyrrho says that 'human beings' do something or other, he does not mean to include himself. It is not necessarily that he considers himself superhuman (even if Timon may sometimes speak as if he is). But his avowed aim, according to one of the stories, was to 'strip off humanity'; so whatever he considers humanity in general to do is not necessarily something that he himself would aspire to do or regard himself as doing. 'Human beings' may shape their behaviour by 'convention and habit'; they probably also take themselves to be doing no such thing, but rather, to be conforming their behaviour to what is *naturally* best.[64] But Pyrrho does not have to follow them in these respects, nor does he have to be read here as saying that he does so; he may very well simply be making a wry comment about how people in general— that is, people other than himself—behave. For his part, he does understand the nature of reality. Hence, according to the Aristocles passage and other evidence, he is without opinions and trouble-free. His freedom from opinions would include freedom from the misguided belief that the way people generally behave has any basis in the nature of things; he sees, instead, that this is based merely on convention and habit—since the nature of things, being indeterminate, could provide no basis for behaviour whatever—and so he sees no particular need to

---

[62] Cf. Suda, s.v. Pyrrho (=DC T1B). Sextus also quotes a line of Timon, 'But these things are judged by mind on the part of humans' (*M* 11.140). As we saw earlier (Ch. 1, Sect. 6), if Sextus' account of the context is to be trusted, 'these things' are the things judged good or bad, and the line follows some comment to the effect that nothing is good or bad by nature. Some scholars (e.g. LS 1I) have altered 'by mind' (*noōi*) to 'by convention' (*nomōi*). If this is correct, the point is very much the same as in the Diogenes passage. But even if not (as I incline to suppose—see Ch. 1 n. 57), the point is not significantly different.

[63] On the doubts that might be cast on Diogenes' reliability in this passage, see again Ch. 1, Sect. 6. However, these doubts had to do mainly with the logic and the precise wording of the various negative claims attributed to Pyrrho ('nothing is either fine or ignoble', etc.), which would seem to leave the present remark unaffected.

[64] The contrast in the Diogenes passage between what is the case in nature or in reality, and how people actually govern their behaviour, suggests that Pyrrho is accusing people of committing some such mistake. Recall that a similar contrast seemed to be implicit in the line of Timon quoted by Sextus (*M* 11.140)—'but these things are judged by mind [or perhaps, "by convention"] on the part of humans'; see Ch. 1, Sect. 6, and above, n. 62.

conform his own behaviour to the same standards. This does not prevent him shaping his behaviour in light of how things appear;[65] for example, he normally spreads honey on his bread because it normally appears sweet (and he, like most other people, generally likes sweet-tasting things). He is not, however, under the illusion that the sweet taste of honey is part of some fixed nature that belongs to it, and he is aware that in certain circumstances it may *not* taste sweet. Nor is it a matter of any great importance to him, in the end, whether it is sweet or not; for again, it is not fixed in the nature of things that tasting sweet things—any more than any other activity—is good.

There is room for some question whether the attitude towards appearances that I have been outlining is to be ascribed to Pyrrho as well as to Timon. In order to leave this question open, I have referred more vaguely in this section to 'early Pyrrhonism'. The texts we have just been looking at never mention Pyrrho by name. Besides, the work *Pytho*, from which the remark about *sunētheia* is taken, was a dialogue between Pyrrho and Timon; Diogenes' report at least makes it sound as if Timon himself is the speaker, and we cannot assume that whatever Timon put into his own mouth, in the role of Pyrrho's possibly inexperienced disciple, was something of which Pyrrho (or even Pyrrho as Timon understood him) would have approved. It is possible, then, that the reliance on appearances is an innovation by Timon himself.[66] However, there is no decisive reason for thinking so unless this reliance is inconsistent with elements of the picture we have assembled of Pyrrho. And this, as we have seen, is not the case; on the contrary, the notion that we can and should rely on appearances seems to be a quite plausible extension of the ideas in the Aristocles passage and elsewhere. The stories depicting Pyrrho as *not* relying on appearances, but relying on his friends to do so, can be rejected as hostile fabrications. And the remainder of the evidence is entirely consistent with a reliance on appearances having been a part of Pyrrho's own outlook as well as Timon's. It may be that Timon is making explicit a point that, in Pyrrho's own account of his ideas, remained implicit; but at any rate, we have no reason to suppose that Timon is substantially modifying or transforming the position adhered to by Pyrrho himself.

[65] This account assumes that conventions themselves are not part of 'the appearances'—that the expression 'the appearances' refers primarily, and perhaps even solely, to sensory appearances. This is quite consistent with the evidence considered just above. But it does mark a contrast with the Pyrrhonism of Sextus, for whom conventions are the source of one of the main species of action-guiding appearances (*PH* 1.23–4); on this, see further below, n. 101.

[66] This is one of two possibilities mentioned by Decleva Caizzi (1984*b*; 93–5) (the other is the one mentioned above in n. 53 and accompanying text). If we take this option, according to Decleva Caizzi, we must see Timon as pressured by his engagement with other philosophers into shifting Pyrrho's original outlook—which did *not* promote a reliance on appearances (see above, nn. 52, 55)—in the direction of later Pyrrhonism. However, if we dismiss the stories suggesting that Pyrrho altogether ignored what his senses told him, we have no reason to posit a major contrast on this point between Pyrrho and Timon.

5. *'The nature of the divine and the good'*

I have presupposed throughout this chapter that Pyrrho's indeterminacy thesis applies to the predicates 'good' and 'bad', and to value predicates in general. Nothing in the Aristocles passage contradicts this supposition; it contains no hint that the indeterminacy thesis is subject to any exceptions having to do with value predicates. Indeed, two of the other texts that were cited in the previous chapter (Section 6) as possible reflections of the indeterminacy thesis seemed especially to emphasize value predicates. The passage from the beginning of Diogenes' life of Pyrrho (9.61) focused specifically on the pairs 'fine'/'ignoble' and 'just'/'unjust' as prime examples of predicates to which Pyrrho's central claims apply; and Sextus at least implies that Timon specifically asserted that nothing was by nature good or bad (*M* 11.140). Besides, we have seen in the present chapter that some of Pyrrho's practical attitudes—in particular, his freedom from passions—are naturally accounted for by supposing that he denies the goodness or badness of anything by nature, just as he denies, quite generally, that there is a determinate nature to things.

However, there is a body of evidence that I have so far left out of the picture, and that seems flatly to contradict this supposition. The philosophical works of Cicero include a number of remarks about Pyrrho; and, in several of these, Pyrrho is portrayed as a particularly severe moralist, holding, along with the unorthodox Stoic Aristo of Chios, that there is nothing of value, positive or negative, except virtue and vice. This clearly implies that there are at any rate two things—virtue and vice themselves—that *are* by nature good and bad respectively. Still more troublesome is a fragment from Timon, quoted by Sextus (*M* 11.20), that speaks explicitly about 'the nature of the divine and the good' (*hē tou theiou te phusis kai t'agathou*), apparently citing this 'nature' as the source of a tranquil life. If the interpretation of Pyrrho's practical attitudes offered in this chapter is to be sustained, I need to show that these texts do not, after all, stand in its way.[67]

---

[67] Another line of Timon, quoted by Athenaeus (337a), might also be thought to pose a problem; it reads 'desire is the very first of all bad things' (*pantōn men prōtista kakōn epithumia estin*). However, this may easily be understood merely as expressing a general opposition to desire. It is perhaps incautious of Timon to speak of desire as a 'bad thing'; but there is no need to read this line as offering a view about the *real nature* of desire, or of anything else. Allowing, then, for a certain looseness of expression, we can accommodate this line without difficulty in the scheme developed so far. The same can be said of the curious anecdote in Diogenes (9.64), according to which Pyrrho was once found talking to himself, and explained that he was 'training to be good' (*meletan chrēstos einai*); again, this is no doubt a careless way of speaking, but need not be seen as a considered philosophical utterance committing Pyrrho to the view that anyone or anything is good *in the real nature of things*. (In any case, even supposing that this story reports a real incident, we need not assume that the words in Diogenes or his source—at this point probably Antigonus (cf. 9.62)—correspond closely to what Pyrrho actually said.)

The fragment of Timon consists of two couplets of elegiac verse. The remark about 'the nature of the divine and the good' occurs in the second couplet. In the first couplet the unidentified speaker announces that he is going to say something, and indicates the status he attributes to what he is going to say. It has always been assumed that the speaker is Pyrrho, and hence that the fragment provides valuable evidence for Pyrrho's views. Both couplets have been understood in at least two ways;[68] and how one understands either one affects the degree of tension between the view here expressed and the views elsewhere attributed to Pyrrho.

The first couplet is impossible to translate as a whole without presupposing crucial interpretive points. I will therefore begin with a version that leaves part of it in the original Greek:

> For I will say, as to me *kataphainetai einai*,
> A word of truth, having a correct standard.[69]

Another, slightly different possibility, is as follows:

> For I will tell an account, as to me *kataphainetai einai*,
> Having a correct standard of truth.[70]

Now Sextus, our sole source for these lines, clearly understands *kataphainetai einai* as meaning 'it appears to be'. He takes Timon to be converting, by means of these words, a statement about the divine and the good that would otherwise be strongly dogmatic into a statement about appearances—just as he himself, in the passage in which the quotation occurs, is proposing to use 'is' in the sense 'appears' when saying, according to a standard scheme of ethical classification, 'some things are good, some are bad, and some are indifferent' (*M* 11.18–20).[71] If this is indeed what Timon intended, then perhaps the conflict with the rest of our evidence about Pyrrho is illusory; and many scholars have read the first couplet in this way. However, we should not assume that Sextus is right about this interpretation of the lines. For *kataphainetai* does not necessarily, or even usually, mean 'appears'; more commonly it means 'plainly is'—just as the corresponding adjective *kataphanēs* means 'manifest' or 'evident'.[72] And in any case, it is clear from

---

[68] I have discussed the fragment, and the numerous scholarly treatments of it, in much more detail in Bett (1994c). The interpretation proposed here corresponds with that argued for in the article; here, however, I confine my discussion of secondary literature to a bare minimum, and omit numerous minor points.

[69] *ē gar egōn ereō, hōs moi kataphainetai einai,*
muthon alētheiēs, orthon echōn kanona.

[70] Reading *alētheiēs* with *kanona* rather than with *muthon*. Elsewhere (Bett 1994c: 317–18) I suggest that both translations are equally possible, and that Timon may very well have intended the ambiguity. [71] See Bett (1997: commentary *ad loc.*)

[72] For evidence, see Bett (1994c: 315–16). Note also that *kataphainetai* is rare after the fourth century BC (and occurs nowhere else in Sextus); it would, therefore, not be surprising for Sextus to misunderstand its use in the current context. On this, see Bett (1994c: 319–20).

the next line that 'appears' is *not* what *kataphainetai* means here. The speaker says that he is going to speak 'having a correct standard', or even perhaps 'having a correct standard of truth'; and this would stand in direct contradiction with the qualification 'as it appears to me to be'. To say that one has a correct standard is to offer a warrant for the *truth* of what one says; to say 'as it appears to me to be', on the other hand, is precisely to give an explicit indication that one is *not* prepared to offer any such warrant. To assert that *P* is to commit oneself to the truth of *P*; to assert that *P*, and to precede this by saying that one has a correct standard in making the assertion, is to strengthen and render overt that commitment. To say that one's forthcoming assertion records how things *appear* to oneself to be is, on the contrary, to *withdraw* from the commitment normally attaching to declarative sentences. It would therefore be self-contradictory to say *both* 'as it appears to me to be' *and* 'having a correct standard'.[73] It follows that *kataphainetai* must be translated in the other fashion mentioned above, by 'plainly is'; the phrase containing this word will therefore become 'as it is evident to me that it is'.[74] In this case, the phrase containing *kataphainetai* and the phrase 'having a correct standard' will reinforce one another; both will emphasize the truth of what is about to be said. And if so, of course, there is no question of taking the first couplet as mitigating the force of whatever is to follow; rather, the entire purpose of the first couplet is to insist that what is to follow really does capture how things actually are.

Now, if this is so, then of course we can expect that the second couplet will issue some declaration that, by Sextus' standards, would be unacceptably dogmatic; it will offer some specification of the real nature of things, which is precisely what Sextus' scepticism is dedicated to avoiding. Indeed, that these lines contain something that at least looked to Sextus like objectionable dogmatism was clear from the outset. For, as we saw, Sextus' purpose in quoting the lines is precisely to show how what *looks* like objectionable dogmatism can be converted, by means of the qualification 'as it appears to me', into something acceptable to the sceptic. However, we cannot assume that what is objectionable to Sextus would also be objectionable to Pyrrho. One of the main points of my argument in the previous chapter was that Pyrrho *was* by

---

[73] It will not do to suggest that the speaker's having a correct standard is itself part of what appears to him to be the case. The speaker says that he will *speak having a correct standard*; the phrase 'as to me *kataphainetai einai*' qualifies 'a word of truth' (or possibly just 'an account'), but it does not qualify 'having a correct standard'—that phrase depends directly on 'I will say'. I here take issue with Long (1978: 85); Burnyeat (1980*b*: 89); and LS ii. 11.

[74] If we translate 'I will say . . . a word of truth, having a correct standard', the phrase 'as it is evident to me that it is' indicates that it is evident to the speaker that the account that is to follow is true; if we translate 'I will tell an account . . . having a correct standard of truth', 'as it is evident to me that it is' indicates that it is evident to the speaker that the things to be reported in the upcoming 'account' really are so (this would be the relatively common 'veridical' use of *einai*).

Sextus' standards dogmatic; for he did offer a specification of the nature of things—namely, the indeterminacy thesis. The question that now needs to be addressed, therefore, is whether the content of the second couplet is inconsistent with the set of ideas we have attributed to Pyrrho; and for the purpose of answering *that* question the attitude and perspective of Sextus are irrelevant.

The second couplet has traditionally been translated along the following lines:

> That the nature of the divine and the good is eternal,
> From which a most even-tempered life for a man is derived.[75]

On this interpretation, the sentiment is clearly incompatible with the view that nothing is by nature of any determinate character, including determinately good or bad. More recently, however, another translation has gained some currency, which, it is claimed, removes or at least greatly reduces the conflict with the other evidence:

> Namely, that the nature of the divine and the good is at any time
> That from which life becomes most equable for a man.[76]

On this reading, the divine and the good are not being hypostasized as eternal entities; rather, 'the nature of the divine and the good' is simply whatever it is that is the source of a tranquil life. Given the rest of what we hear about Pyrrho, it is clear that this would be a certain set of mental attitudes. As we have seen, other verse fragments of Timon tell us that Pyrrho himself achieved his amazing, and even godlike, tranquillity through his lack of passions and his lack of opinions; and the Aristocles passage tells us that the route to tranquillity is acceptance of, and the appropriate attitude towards, the indeterminacy thesis.[77] On this reading, then, the things that are being characterized as divine and good turn out to be human attitudes rather than anything eternal and Platonic.

Does this second reading of the couplet eliminate the contradiction? It

---

[75] *hōs hē tou theiou te phusis kai t'agathou aiei*
   ex hōn isotatos ginetai andri bios,
with a comma placed between the two lines, and existential *esti* understood.

[76] With *aiei* read, as it often may be, as 'at any given time' rather than as 'for ever'; with *esti* again understood, but this time designating identity rather than existence; and with *tauta*, 'those things', also understood, to serve as the antecedent of *ex hōn*, 'from which'. This translation was originally argued for by Burnyeat (1980*b*). Burnyeat's interpretation has also been accepted in full by Long and Sedley (LS 2E); their translation is not identical with Burnyeat's, but the differences are only verbal. Burnyeat is not entirely convincing on the linguistic feasibility of the supplement *tauta*; on this, see Bett (1994*c*: 306–7). However, the existential *esti* supplied in the other translation is also awkward; there will be some linguistic strain however the lines are interpreted. On the point of 'namely' in this translation, and for doubts about it, see Bett (1994*c*: n. 36).

[77] Burnyeat (1980*b*) focuses primarily on emotional indifference as the source of tranquillity, rather than the other points just mentioned. However, this does not affect the force of the criticism about to be introduced.

does not initially appear so. Even though 'the nature of the divine and the good' is no longer being set up as some kind of Platonic entity, it still looks as if a claim is being made that commits the speaker to the view that certain items are *by nature* (divine and) good. The fact that these items are mental attitudes rather than independent and eternal entities does not make this any less troublesome. The other evidence indicates that Pyrrho held that *nothing* is by nature good, and these lines seem to be in conflict with that position;[78] if they imply that there *are* things that are by nature good—and they certainly give every impression of doing so—then they conflict with the view that nothing is by nature good, whether the things in question are mental attitudes or anything else. The only way in which this conflict can be removed is if it can be shown that the phrase 'the nature of the divine and the good' actually commits the speaker to *no* claim to the effect that there are things that are by nature good; but this cannot be done on the basis of anything said so far.

However, there is a further element to this new interpretation of the fragment, which promises to achieve exactly the required result.[79] It is standardly assumed that this fragment gives us Pyrrho's reply, or the beginning of his reply, to the question posed in another fragment of Timon, from the same poem *Images* (*Indalmoi*), that we examined earlier (fragment C); in the latter fragment Pyrrho is asked how he manages to achieve and sustain his amazing and godlike tranquillity. If this is the case, it is argued, the account that Pyrrho is offering in reply is an account about himself; and 'the divine and the good' referred to in the current fragment are the divine and good elements in Pyrrho's own character, the very same qualities referred to as superhuman in the other fragment. Hence the phrase 'the nature of the divine and the good' refers not to the divine and the good in general—let alone the divine and the good *in their real natures*—but simply to certain already identified features of Pyrrho himself. Pyrrho is saying 'those godlike qualities in me that you just asked about—they are the source of my tranquillity (and the same qualities can have the same result for anyone else)'. Though the phrase 'the nature of the divine and the good' sounds suspect at first hearing, it is quite acceptable once one understands the context; the word 'nature' is not being used to refer to anything metaphysical—in fact, it does not really add anything to the terms 'divine' and 'good' themselves.[80]

---

[78] For further discussion of this point, and of Burnyeat's contrary view, see Bett (1994c: n. 25) with accompanying text.

[79] Burnyeat is not entirely consistent in adhering to the line of interpretation I am here introducing; however, it is clearly essential to his case. On this, see further Bett (1994c: n. 12).

[80] This point is not explicitly developed by Burnyeat. But his view requires us to understand 'the nature of the divine and the good' as merely a periphrasis for 'the divine and the good'. Such periphrastic usages of *phusis* are indeed common. On the other hand, it is not clear that, even in such usages, the word *phusis* is entirely innocuous—that is, entirely devoid of implications concerning the nature of things. On this, see Bett (1994c: 311–12).

This completed interpretation certainly does absolve Pyrrho of claiming that anything is divine or good in the real nature of things. However, it does so at the cost of rendering his statement entirely vacuous. Pyrrho's explanation of how he achieves tranquillity cannot be that the godlike qualities *just asked about* (in the other fragment) are what produce tranquillity. For the godlike character asked about in the other fragment *was*, precisely, his tranquillity; the explanation would in effect be 'it is my tranquillity that produces my tranquillity'. If 'the nature of the divine and the good' is really to be the *source* of tranquillity—as it clearly is, on any reading of the fragment—then the phrase 'the nature of the divine and the good' cannot itself refer to Pyrrho's tranquillity, and hence cannot be identified with the godlike character attributed to Pyrrho in the other fragment. But, if this identification collapses, we have no reason to take the phrase as referring to qualities of Pyrrho at all. The text says that the nature of the divine and the good are what produce a tranquil life 'for a man' (*andri*); it appears, that is, to be a quite general statement. We might decide that this impression was misleading if there was good reason in the context to take the immediate topic to be the godlike qualities in Pyrrho himself. But, if the context is indeed given by the other fragment, it supplies no such reason (and no other reasons are readily imaginable); for the link between the two fragments cannot be as just proposed.

It follows that the speaker cannot, after all, be acquitted of saying something that is inconsistent with the early Pyrrhonist outlook (just as much as it is inconsistent with Sextus' own outlook). Whether one translates the second couplet in the traditional manner or according to the recently suggested alternative, we are being told that there are certain entities that are, in their real natures, divine and good; in the former case these entities are eternal and seemingly Platonic in character, in the latter case they are those mental attitudes, whichever exactly they are, that are the source of tranquillity for human beings. Given this result, it is not, for our current purposes, of great importance which of the two readings we adopt. Either way, the original problem remains. The fragment cannot be read in a manner that renders the view its speaker expresses compatible with the view we have elsewhere seen Pyrrho to hold—namely, that nothing is by nature of any particular character, including good and bad.[81] The speaker offers a view according to which there *is* such a thing as 'the nature of the divine and the good'. And, as we saw in examining the first couplet, this view is presented with strong assurances of its truth and correctness—not with cautionary remarks to the effect that what is to be offered is only the way things *appear* to the speaker.

Should we then despair of achieving a consistent picture of Pyrrho's outlook? Certainly not. Though this fragment of Timon has always been

---

[81] For criticism of further attempts to render these views consistent, see Bett (1994c: Sects. IV, V).

taken as a central piece of evidence concerning the ethical or practical attitudes of Pyrrho, there is in fact no reason to connect them with Pyrrho at all. The speaker, as I noted earlier, is not identified within the fragment itself. No one else quotes or mentions this passage of Timon other than Sextus, and Sextus does not say that Pyrrho is the speaker. It is thus perfectly possible that the speaker is someone other than Pyrrho, and that the views this speaker expresses are thoroughly at odds with any views attributed to Pyrrho, either by Timon himself or by anyone else. Now of course, if this is so, it will mean that Sextus is confused about the point and context of the lines. As we saw, he clearly thinks that the lines express a view that belongs in a sceptical style of thinking akin to his own; but, if the speaker is not Pyrrho, but someone who holds, contrary to Pyrrho, that certain things are by nature divine and good, this will not be the case. However, this should come as no great surprise; for we have already seen that Sextus does take the content of the lines to be compatible with scepticism, when in fact it is not. He understands *kataphainetai* to be an example of the sceptics' practice of confining themselves to talk about appearances, whereas in fact the word has precisely the opposite function of reinforcing the truth of the upcoming assertion.[82]

It may be objected that the relation between this fragment and fragment C of Timon, in which Pyrrho is compared with the Sun God and asked for the source of his superhuman tranquillity, guarantees that Pyrrho is indeed the speaker here. But this, too, is entirely questionable. Though, as noted earlier, it is standardly assumed that the present fragment gives Pyrrho's response to the question posed in fragment C, there is no reason why we should accept any such connection. The two fragments came from the same poem *Images* (*Indalmoi*),[83] and Sextus quotes both of them relatively close to one another in his own *Against the Ethicists* (*M* 11.1 and *M* 11.20); that is the extent of the link we can establish between them. There is nothing in the content of the fragment about 'the nature of the divine and the good' that shows that it is the answer to fragment C's question, or an answer to any question. Both fragments speak of tranquillity; but so do a great many other passages from Timon. Both also make some connection between the subjects of tranquillity and divinity; but this connection is common in Greek philosophy as a whole, and does not by any means require us to understand the one fragment as responding to the other.[84]

---

[82] Note that I am not accusing Sextus of failing to realize the *identity* of the speaker—which would be a much grosser error—but rather of misunderstanding the character of the view expressed; more on this in a moment.

[83] At least, if the reading *toisindēmois* (or close variants) in the MSS of Sextus is rightly emended to *tois Indalmois*. For the location of the other fragment, see DL 9.65.

[84] For further discussion of the absence of reasons for connecting the two fragments, including consideration of allegedly relevant lines from the *Odyssey* and from Parmenides, see Bett (1994c: 326–9); the philological issues raised are detailed and technical, and the matter is too tangential to be considered here.

It is therefore entirely open to us to postulate that the speaker in the fragment is not Pyrrho, and that the view expressed therein has nothing to do with any views held by Pyrrho. Since this option is available, we should take it; the alternative, as we have seen, is that there is a glaring contradiction between this fragment and other central evidence concerning Pyrrho. If Pyrrho was not the speaker, we cannot do more than guess at who was. If we assume that Sextus was not simply being careless about the speaker's identity, and that the manuscript to which he had access was not somehow unclear on this point,[85] then presumably—since he takes the fragment as offering support for his own usage—it was someone whom he had reason to believe was an authoritative Pyrrhonist. One possibility is that Timon himself was the speaker, but represented at a stage *prior* to his full initiation into Pyrrho's outlook. Fragment C, also from *Images*, certainly suggests that Timon did portray himself in this poem—as in the dialogue *Pytho*—as a relative novice. He says here that his 'heart longs to hear' how Pyrrho manages to maintain his superhuman tranquillity; someone who is not yet enlightened on this central point can hardly have been deeply initiated into Pyrrho's philosophy.[86] If so, then Sextus would simply need to have misunderstood the *extent* to which Timon has absorbed this philosophy; perhaps Timon has grasped that tranquillity is the goal, but—contrary to what Sextus supposes—still has a lot to learn about the proper way to achieve it.[87] Given Sextus' misunderstanding of the force of the verb *kataphainetai*, such a scenario is not difficult to imagine. It is worth noting that Sextus seems somewhat hesitant about his own interpretation of the lines; he says that the lesson he extracts from the fragment is one that Timon 'seems to indicate' (*eoike dēloun*), which is not his usual manner when discussing the views of others. This may be due to his difficulty with the verb *kataphainetai*, but it could also be connected with some other obscurity about the context of the lines.

All this, however, is bound to remain highly speculative. We know virtually nothing about the character of the poem *Images*; besides the two frag-

---

[85] However, neither possibility can be ruled out. Perhaps Sextus lifted at random a passage that looked as if it suited his purposes, without troubling to check who the speaker was; or perhaps the manuscript was damaged, so that it was unclear who the speaker was. One can imagine all kinds of ways in which it might have escaped Sextus' notice that the speaker actually had no credentials as a spokesman for Pyrrhonism. (Perhaps he did not even have a full text of the *Indalmoi*, but found these lines quoted in isolation, and without indications as to the speaker, by someone else.) However, let us leave these possibilities aside; for, even if he was perfectly aware of the identity of the speaker, it is not hard to see how he could have committed the error I have ascribed to him.

[86] It is, of course, possible that the speaker in fragment C is someone other than Timon. But, if so, the same argument applies to this unknown person; *this* person is devoted to Pyrrho, yet far from fully versed in Pyrrho's outlook—so *this* person could be the speaker of the lines with which we have been occupied.

[87] I develop this possibility in more detail in Bett (1994c: 329–32).

ments already mentioned, almost nothing of the poem survives, and no ancient author gives us any general description of the work. Given this lack of information, a great many other scenarios might be devised, besides the one just sketched, that would cover the data as I have described it. The important point, for our purposes, is this: since we are in no way forced to accept that Pyrrho is the one who speaks about 'the nature of the divine and the good', we need not trouble ourselves with the impossible task of trying to reconcile this fragment with the outlook expounded in the bulk of this chapter and the previous one.

6. Cicero on Pyrrho

The evidence from Cicero poses different problems; but here again, we are not in the end forced to revise the interpretation developed so far. Cicero does ascribe to Pyrrho views about the good that cannot be squared with this interpretation; however, there is good reason to think that Cicero's understanding of Pyrrho's thought is very limited, and that the picture of Pyrrho he presents to us is a distorted one. As noted above, the main point of Cicero's remarks is that Pyrrho, like Aristo of Chios, and sometimes another unorthodox Stoic, Erillus, refuse to admit any distinctions of value among things other than virtue and vice. According to one passage (*Fin.* 3.11–12), Pyrrho held, along with Aristo, that virtue is the sole good; these philosophers thus 'make everything equal' (*omnia exaequant*)—everything, that is, except virtue and vice themselves. Again, Pyrrho and Aristo are said to have held that there was nothing to choose between health and sickness, claiming that the achievement of virtue was the only important thing (*Fin.* 2.43, cf. 4.49, 60); and Pyrrho is said to have been one of the few philosophers to deny that pain was bad—the others being Aristo and Zeno of Citium (*Tusc.* 2.15). For this reason Pyrrho's views, together with Aristo's and Erillus', are said to have been long since neglected, since they do not allow distinctions of a kind that are indispensable, if duty is to be discovered (*Off.* 1.6).[88]

Cicero never mentions Pyrrho without also mentioning Aristo or Erillus or both; and in only two passages does he mark any distinction whatever between Pyrrho and Aristo. First, we are told that, among those who have posited 'living virtuously' (*honeste vivere*) as the highest good, Pyrrho is the most unacceptable because his view leaves nothing worth aiming for besides

---

[88] On the fact that Pyrrho's thought is neglected (though without indications as to the reasons for this), see also *Fin.* 2.35; *Tusc.* 5.85; *De orat.* 3.62; the first two of these texts list Pyrrho with Aristo and Erillus, while the third groups the followers of Pyrrho with the followers of Erillus and various others.

virtue; Aristo, Cicero says, is not much better, but he at least allows as possible motives for the wise man 'whatever enters his mind' or 'whatever occurs to him' (*quodcumque in mentem incideret, quodcumque tamquam occurreret* (*Fin.* 4.43)). Cicero does not elaborate on this account of Aristo[89]—he is not, after all, interested in presenting Aristo in a sympathetic light; but it is clear that he does not regard this distinction between Pyrrho and Aristo as of any great importance, and that, to the extent that the distinction is worth drawing, it centres around a point specific to the philosophy of Aristo rather than to that of Pyrrho. The other passage is the one mentioned near the beginning of this chapter. Aristo is again said to have allowed no distinctions of value among things other than virtue and vice—virtue is the sole good, vice the sole bad, and nothing else counts for anything, positively or negatively—and to have recommended an attitude of indifference (*adiaphoria*) towards these things; Pyrrho, on the other hand, is said to have maintained that the wise man does not even feel these things (*ea ne sentire quidem*), and to have called this attitude *apatheia* (*Acad.* 2.130). As we saw, this comment on Pyrrho probably reflects his reported insensitivity to pain, as well as his extraordinary indifference to events around him; it is in these contexts, and generally in the context of his alleged aspiration to 'strip off humanity', that the term *apatheia* is elsewhere applied to him. There is, then, just one instance in which Cicero shows any sign of knowing about Pyrrho as an individual. Otherwise, he only ever ascribes views to Pyrrho concurrently with Aristo.[90]

The obvious conclusion to draw is that Cicero's knowledge of Pyrrho derives entirely or almost entirely from a source that classifies him alongside Aristo (and probably also Erillus), telling him nothing or almost nothing about how Pyrrho's thought may have differed from that of these others. The likeliest source, as has been noted by commentators,[91] is the *Carneadea divisio*, Carneades' classification of views concerning the good, about which Cicero learned during his youthful studies with the Academics. One passage (*Fin.* 5.16 ff.) is particularly revealing in this context. Cicero tells us that Carneades' classification includes not only all views about the good that have actually been held, but all those that it is possible to hold. Following the

---

[89] For discussion of what Aristo's point may have been, see Ioppolo (1980*b*).

[90] On the other hand, Cicero frequently speaks of Aristo independently of Pyrrho, both on the subjects just mentioned (e.g. *Fin.* 3.50, 4.40, 47, 68–9, 5.73) and on other subjects besides (e.g. *Acad.* 2.123; *Nat d.* 1.37, 3.77). His knowledge of Pyrrho may be limited to what he can gather from a single source with a particular agenda of its own (see below); but the same is clearly not true of his knowledge of Aristo.

[91] See DC 268–71; LS ii. 12. Lévy (1992: 370) suggests that the grouping of Aristo and Erillus with Pyrrho was originally a polemical device of Chrysippus, designed to place these unorthodox Stoics in a bad light, but was later taken over by Carneades for his own purposes. This is an attractive hypothesis. However, since Cicero seems clearly to have derived his picture of Pyrrho from Carneades' taxonomy, we need not concern ourselves with the origins of the tendency to speak in one breath of Aristo and Pyrrho.

Stoics, he speaks of right living as a skill (*ars* (*Fin.* 5.16)), and in particular,
the skill consisting in the virtue of 'practical wisdom' (*prudentia*, which is
Cicero's translation of *phronēsis* (see *Off.* 1.153)).[92] Now, he proposes that,
like any other skill, practical wisdom must have something besides itself to
aim for;[93] and since the purpose of practical wisdom is to enable us to live the
best human life, that which it directs itself towards must be something fundamentally suited to our natures. The three candidates mentioned are pleasure,
freedom from pain, and the 'primary things in accordance with nature' (*prima
secundum naturam* (*Fin.* 5.18)); and the highest good may be defined either
as the *achievement* of these ends, or as the state of *aiming* to achieve them.
There are therefore six actual or possible views about the highest good. Or at
least, these are the views worth discussing. For we are also told that some
views do not fit into this classification, because they do not accept the starting point on which it is based—namely, that discussion of the highest good
must begin from the identification of objects at which we naturally aim;
Pyrrho, Aristo, and Erillus are listed as the main culprits here (*Fin.* 5.23)), for
the familiar reason that they render everything besides virtue itself utterly
indifferent, hence destroying all basis for rational choice.

How, then, does Cicero arrive at the idea that Pyrrho held that virtue was
the sole good, and that everything else (with the exception of vice) was
completely indifferent? Aristo did believe these things; we know this from
sources other than Cicero (DL 7.160; Sextus *M* 11.64–7). And Pyrrho—at any
rate, according to the interpretation I have developed—did believe part of
what Cicero says he believed. He did hold that things are by nature 'indifferent' (*adiaphora*); this is one of the key terms used in the Aristocles passage's
statement of the indeterminacy thesis. And, as we have seen, it looks as if this
thesis was intended to apply just as much to evaluative predicates, such as
'good' and 'bad', as to other kinds of predicates. Hence it is fair to assume
that he would have assented to the view that none of the things other than
virtue or vice is by nature good or bad—or in other words, that all of these
things are, in an ethical sense, indifferent. However, the same evidence
suggests that he would have said exactly the same thing about virtue and vice
themselves; if evaluative predicates were included in the scope of the inde-

[92] On the Stoics' concept of a 'skill relating to life' (*technē peri ton bion*), and the connection
between their notions of skill and of virtue, see Bett (1997: 185–6).

[93] This was denied by the Stoics; according to them practical wisdom is directed simply
towards its own exercise (Cicero, *Fin.* 3.24; cf. Seneca, *Ep.* 85.31–2). This, of course, renders it
problematic how they can at the same time say, as at least some of them did, that the final good
consists in the selection of, or the aiming towards, things in accordance with nature. Carneades'
rejection of the Stoic claim, his inclusion of 'primary things in accordance with nature' among
the things one might aim for, and his distinction between achieving something and the state of
aiming to achieve it (see below), are plainly part of a strategy designed to embarrass the Stoics.
On the details of this debate, see LS i. 406–10; Striker (1991: sect. 3); Lévy (1992: pt. IV, ch.
1).

terminacy thesis, it is very difficult to see how 'virtue is by nature good' and 'vice is by nature bad' could have been singled out as exempt from it. But this important difference between Pyrrho and Aristo might very easily have been glossed over in the context of the *Carneadea divisio*. The *Carneadea divisio* sorts views according to their answers to the question 'What things, *aside from* the "skill relating to life" itself (in which virtue is contained), naturally have value?' Unlike the holders of Carneades' six main actual or possible views, both Pyrrho and Aristo would answer 'nothing'; that is why they are treated together, and why they are excluded from the main classification. The fact that Pyrrho would *also* have denied that virtue is by nature valuable is irrelevant for this purpose; views that answer 'nothing' to the main question—whatever else they may have said besides—are lumped together in the 'reject' category, the category of deluded and uninteresting positions. So, if Cicero's information about Pyrrho is derived almost wholly from his place in the *Carneadea divisio*, it would not be surprising if he assumed that Pyrrho's philosophy was essentially the same as Aristo's, about which he has independent knowledge.[94] And in this way Pyrrho might easily have been saddled with the view that there *is* something by nature good, namely virtue—a view that is deeply at odds with his real position as reconstructed in the light of the other evidence, the evidence whose core and starting point is the Aristocles passage.[95]

7. Comparisons with later Pyrrhonism

Neither Cicero nor Timon's fragment about 'the nature of the divine and the good' should, then, cause us to revise our interpretation of what we can call

---

[94] My wording here assumes that it is Cicero himself who is responsible for the error about Pyrrho, and that the sources from which he learned the *Carneadea divisio* were uninformative about Pyrrho, rather than wrong. It is also quite possible that the near-total conflation of Pyrrho and Aristo took place earlier, and that Cicero is simply perpetuating an error committed by someone else. But it makes no difference, for the present purpose, who is ultimately responsible.

[95] Cicero clearly has no inkling of any evidence, such as the Aristocles passage (and including Aristocles' own hostile commentary), representing Pyrrho as the starting point of what became a sceptical tradition. But this is not in itself surprising, since he also shows no knowledge whatever of his rough contemporary Aenesidemus, the initiator of later Pyrrhonism, and there is no reason to think that anyone else in the first century BC devoted serious attention to understanding or reviving Pyrrho's ideas. Cicero's apparent ignorance of Aenesidemus may itself be seen as surprising, especially if, as Photius appears to show us (*Bibl.* 169b33), Aenesidemus was also originally a member of the Academy; on this latter point see Mansfeld (1995). However, as Mansfeld points out (pp. 245–7), by this time the Academy was in a state of considerable disunity. Cicero's direct exposure to the Academy was strictly temporary and, given his Romanness and his forensic and political ambitions, necessarily of a somewhat dilettante nature; that he may not have been made aware of every strand of this by now fragmented movement is nothing to be wondered at.

Pyrrho's practical philosophy. This therefore concludes my direct examination of Pyrrho's ideas and attitudes. In this chapter and Chapter 1, I have tried to develop an account of those ideas and attitudes that treats the various scraps of evidence at our disposal with appropriate levels of confidence or suspicion, that makes the best possible sense of this evidence, and that hangs together in a plausible and coherent whole. In the following chapters I propose to look further afield, and to consider the relations between Pyrrho's philosophy—supposing it is understood in the way I have proposed—and other philosophies prior to and contemporary with his own, as well as the later Pyrrhonist philosophy that claimed to draw inspiration from him. As noted in the Introduction, this is intended partly to serve as a check on the acceptability of the interpretation of Pyrrho just put forward. The question to be asked is, 'Assuming I am right about the nature of Pyrrho's philosophy, what does this imply about his links with other philosophers?' But if, in attempting to answer that question, it turned out that we could make no good sense of Pyrrho's relations to his predecessors or to later Pyrrhonism, then that would obviously force us to rethink our account of Pyrrho himself.

In preparation for the task just mentioned, I conclude this chapter with a review of the similarities and differences, on the topics that have been our subject in the previous sections, between Pyrrho's outlook—again, assuming that it took the form I have suggested—and that of Sextus' *Outlines of Pyrrhonism*. Evidently there is a certain structural similarity between the two. Both recommend an attitude of *ataraxia*, and both purport to generate this attitude as a result of a certain form of mistrust of the senses, of ordinary opinions, and of philosophers' theories, as guides to the real natures of things. In assessing the extent of the link between Pyrrho and later Pyrrhonism, the *connection* between these two elements is at least as important as the two elements themselves. Other philosophers aim for *ataraxia*, and other philosophers are in various ways mistrustful of standard views of things; but the ambition to generate the former *by means of* the latter seems to be highly distinctive of the Pyrrhonist tradition. We shall say more about this in the final chapter. By the same token, both Pyrrho and Sextus regard other philosophers as being troubled and tormented because of their readiness to engage in theorizing and their rashness in accepting definite conclusions. In addition, both Sextus and Timon (even if Pyrrho himself was not explicit about this) recommend a policy of relying, in one's ordinary behaviour, upon appearances—though, as we shall see, the 'appearances' are not conceived of in exactly the same way in the two periods, either with regard to their possible content or with regard to their status.[96]

These similarities are by no means negligible. But at the same time, of

---

[96] On differences in possible content, see below, n. 101; the other point is discussed at greater length in Chs. 3 and 4.

course, there are numerous differences in the precise nature of the untroubled attitude recommended in each period, and in the precise manner in which it is generated. Several of these differences, as one might expect, are connected with the differences examined in the first chapter; centrally and most notably, Pyrrho accepts the indeterminacy thesis, which to Sextus would have seemed intolerably dogmatic, and this affects a great many aspects of his outlook.

Both Pyrrho and Sextus may be said to have an ethical and a non-ethical component to their *ataraxia*; I begin with the ethical component. Pyrrho's *ataraxia* stems partly from his absence of strong emotional reactions to things; we saw that this was best interpreted as being due to the fact that, in his view, nothing is, in the real nature of things, either good or bad, or in any other way desirable or undesirable—a view that was itself a straightforward consequence of the indeterminacy thesis. *Outlines of Pyrrhonism* proposes a view that is partly reminiscent of this, but only partly. Those who hold the belief that some things are in their real natures good, and that others are in their real natures bad, are tormented, Sextus says, by an obsessive concern for obtaining or keeping the good things, and for warding off or ridding themselves of the bad things; the sceptic, who lacks all such beliefs, is thereby to a large extent trouble-free (*PH* 1.27–30, 3.235–8). The central difference is that *Outlines of Pyrrhonism* does *not* advance the view that *nothing* is really good or bad (which, by its canons, would be just as much a dogmatic belief as the beliefs of the philosophers Sextus is opposing); still less does it advance any general indeterminacy thesis to support that belief. Instead, it *suspends judgement about* the question whether anything is really good or bad.[97] Another difference is that Sextus is very clear that freedom from the belief that things are really good or bad does not suffice to remove *all* disturbance from the sceptic's life. There are still phenomena such as hunger and pain, which afflict us whether or not we are sceptics; the best the sceptic can do here is to attain a state of 'moderate feeling' (*metriopatheia*)—by contrast with the excessive feelings others may be subject to in such circumstances, owing to their belief, over and above the distressing condition itself, that this condition is by nature bad. By contrast, as we saw early in the chapter, some evidence suggests that Pyrrho's *ataraxia* extended even to conditions of physical pain and hardship. No specific justification is offered for this in the surviving records; it seems simply to be one aspect of Pyrrho's general immunity from powerful reactions

---

[97] I have not mentioned *Against the Ethicists* at this point, even though it has much more to say than *PH* about the troubles associated with the dogmatists' 'intense' (*suntonos*) pursuits and avoidances of things, and the sceptics' freedom from such troubles (*M* 11.110–67). This is because, in my view, *Against the Ethicists* represents an earlier, Aenesidemean view distinct from that of *PH*; unlike *PH*, it does advance the view that *nothing* is in reality good or bad (although, in line with *PH*, it does not contain anything like a general indeterminacy thesis). We shall return to this matter in Ch. 4; see also Bett (1997: introduction and commentary). In the latter work I also argue that *PH* contains traces of this earlier Aenesidemean view, inconsistently with the official stance sketched here; but this need not occupy us at present.

to events befalling him, the basis for which appears to be as I have described. But in any case, Sextus goes out of his way to explain that the sceptic's freedom from disturbance is not as all-encompassing as this. This no doubt reflects a long history of debate, including criticism of Pyrrhonist positions, about the extent of the wise person's immunity to trouble; it also seems clearly more plausible than Pyrrho's stance—or at any rate, clearly more attainable for any but the most exceptional of mortals.[98] Yet a further difference is that, closely associated with his general freedom from strong emotional reactions, Pyrrho seems to have maintained a spectacular unconcern for behaving as custom and convention prescribe—whereas for Sextus, as we have already observed a couple of times, laws and customs are one of the main types of factors shaping the sceptic's behaviour. I shall say a little more about this in closing. But first let us address the non-ethical component of Pyrrho's and Sextus' *ataraxia*.

In the case of Pyrrho, as we saw, it was suggested that the very freedom from opinions and from theorizing, whether or not one's opinions or theories had to do with ethical or practical matters, was also a source of *ataraxia*. The explanation for this seemed to be that a dedication to opinions (opinions, that is, about the natures of things) and to theorizing inevitably gave rise to a disturbing instability, and that Pyrrho, who avoided such things, instead enjoyed an exceptionally stable and unruffled state of mind. And this alleged disparity between Pyrrho and the rest was itself readily explicable by means of the indeterminacy thesis; if things really are indeterminate, it is only to be expected that those who seek definite answers to their questions about things in the world around them will fail to find any firm resting point—the only hope for stability is to stay clear of that enterprise altogether.

Outlines of Pyrrhonism contains nothing quite like this—nor could it do so, since it cannot help itself to the indeterminacy thesis. The opening sections of the book do give the impression that it is suspension of judgement in general, not just suspension of judgement about questions of good and bad, that gives rise to *ataraxia* (1.8–10, 26, 29). Unfortunately, though, this is never properly explained; whenever Sextus explicitly discusses why *ataraxia* results from suspension of judgement, the focus is on beliefs, or freedom from beliefs, about good and bad. A couple of reasons are not too hard to reconstruct. But neither of these reasons is closely analogous to anything in the evidence concerning Pyrrho.

First, people's (and especially philosophers') beliefs about ethical matters are often connected with broader beliefs about the nature of the world in which we live. It is therefore possible or even likely that beliefs that are on

---

[98] It is at this point that it becomes particularly attractive to posit an influence on Pyrrho from the Indian thinkers with whom Pyrrho supposedly came into contact during his travels with Alexander; more on this in the next chapter (Sect. 10).

their surface non-ethical will turn out to yield beliefs about what is good and bad, which will give rise to disturbances of the forms already discussed; the only way to be sure of avoiding such disturbances is therefore to steer clear of beliefs (that is, beliefs about the nature of things) altogether. Secondly, Sextus tells us that the sceptic's starting point was the same as that of any dogmatic philosopher. He was troubled precisely by his inability to sort things out; he wanted to discover the truth, and in *that* way to attain *ataraxia*. The story of Apelles the painter (*PH* 1.28–9) is supposed to indicate, by analogy, how the sceptic actually does attain *ataraxia*; he does so, paradoxically, by giving up his original project, which proved to be merely a source of further trouble. But this, clearly, will not work unless it is applied across the board. In order to be released from the trouble associated with the fruitless project of searching for the truth, one must abandon that project altogether; one's disturbance will not disappear unless one ceases quite generally to have a stake in how things really are—not merely on questions having to do with good and bad.

As I said, neither of these lines of thought significantly resembles anything we can attach to Pyrrho—just as Pyrrho's reasoning on this topic does not correspond to anything in Sextus. For both Pyrrho and Sextus, then, the production of *ataraxia* has a non-ethical as well as an ethical component; but the non-ethical components, unlike the ethical ones, have little to do with one another.[99]

Another point of contrast, partly related to the one just discussed, is that Pyrrho seems to have had no great interest in theoretical controversy, or in debates with other philosophers, whereas in *Outlines of Pyrrhonism*[100] Sextus revels in it. But this difference is easily accounted for. Having settled on the indeterminacy thesis, Pyrrho has little need to trouble himself with the views of other philosophers; indeed, he might well think that to involve himself with such views would tend to promote in him the disturbing instability that, as just noted, he takes them to produce in others—so that the less he has to do

---

[99] *Against the Ethicists* (see above, n. 97) contains no hint of a non-ethical component to *ataraxia*; given its subject matter, this is not surprising. It looks, however, as if Aenesidemus did see *ataraxia* as deriving from suspension of judgement in general (in his version of that notion), and not merely from suspension of judgement about good and bad. According to Photius (*Bibl.* 169b26–9), Aenesidemus held that the dogmatist was subjected to 'ceaseless torments', whereas the Pyrrhonist was happy, and that this contrast was due to the fact that the Pyrrhonist, unlike the dogmatist, had come to realize 'that nothing has been firmly grasped by him'. I shall consider this passage in greater detail in the final chapter.

[100] And in most of the rest of his surviving writings. But *Against the Ethicists*, the only one of his books to offer a whole-heartedly Aenesidemean version of Pyrrhonism, is not so clearly in the same camp. Indeed, it has been criticized for *not* engaging in detailed discussion of rival ethical theories—though, if I am right about its Aenesidemean character, the charge can readily be defended against. On this, see Bett (1997: introduction, sect. VI) (and, on the differences between *Against the Ethicists* and the other parts of the same work, *Against the Logicians* and *Against the Physicists*, sect. V).

with them, the better. But Sextus, of course, has settled on no thesis; and for him, on the contrary, it seems as if a constant play of oppositions among impressions and philosophical theories is vital to the maintenance of his *ataraxia*. Scepticism, he says (*PH* 1.8), is a method for producing—literally, an *ability* (*dunamis*) to produce—*ataraxia* by means of such oppositions (between equally balanced alternatives, of course). But this *ataraxia*, it seems, cannot be attained once and for all, because the suspension of judgement from which it follows cannot be attained once and for all; unless one continues to make vivid to oneself the equal force of these various oppositions, one is always in danger of lapsing into a condition of belief. Hence the sceptic's expertise at generating suspension of judgement needs to be exercised repeatedly. Sextus refers to the various sets of Modes as means by which the sceptics generate suspension of judgement *in themselves*—not just in others who are not yet sceptics—and appears to present the Modes as procedures that they habitually employ (*PH* 1.31–4). The juxtaposition of conflicting views advanced by other philosophers seems to be another case of the same type of habitual procedure, having the same effect—at least, if Sextus' evident enthusiasm about this activity is any guide. Maintaining *ataraxia* through suspension of judgement is, then, a life-long project; so the sceptic cannot cease to interest himself in the theories of others, however little he may be tempted to endorse any of them.

Finally, let us return briefly to an issue introduced a few pages back. Pyrrho has no time for convention, and he aspires to 'strip off humanity'. Sextus, on the other hand, takes laws and customs as one of the central means by which a sceptic may guide his life without doctrinal commitments;[101] and sometimes, at least, he presents scepticism as more in tune with ordinary humanity than are other philosophies.[102] Sextus seems eager to blend in with

---

[101] He also thinks of laws and customs as one of the main species of 'appearances' (*PH* 1.23–4). If the policy of regulating one's life by appearances did form part of Pyrrho's outlook as well as Timon's, then in their case laws and customs were presumably not included under the heading of 'appearances'. As Timon put it, 'The appearance is powerful'; but norms and conventions do *not* seem to have had any power at all over Pyrrho, not even the sort of vestigial hold by which one might be prompted (as Sextus apparently was prompted) to act in accordance with them simply as a result of habit or training, and without any commitment to their capturing in some objective sense the *right* way to behave. The only specific example of an 'appearance' given by Timon is the appearance that honey is sweet; we also saw that Timon insisted that he had not deviated from *sunētheia*, where *sunētheia* seemed to mean, at least primarily, 'sensory experience'. This does not prove that 'the appearances', in early Pyrrhonism, included *only* the way things appear to the senses; there is no obvious reason why certain kinds of personal preferences should not have counted as generating 'appearances'—such as 'sweet things appear to me pleasant'—as well. But it is highly unlikely that they included the sort of evaluative appearances, shaped by society's norms, that are important in Sextus.

[102] See e.g. *PH* 2.102, 246, 254, 3.151; *M* 8.158, 9.49. But Sextus is not entirely consistent about this; at *PH* 1.30 ordinary people (*idiōtai*) are said to be afflicted with the same ills as non-sceptical philosophers. For discussion of the sceptic's relation, as Sextus presents it, to the everyday attitudes of ordinary people, see Barnes (1982*a*); Brennan (1994).

the crowd, whereas Pyrrho appears utterly uninterested in doing so. Both are quite intelligible responses to the state at which the two thinkers have arrived (albeit, as we saw, by different routes)—that is, an absence of belief in anything's being by nature good or bad.[103] None the less, it is tempting to try to speculate on *why* Pyrrho and Sextus should have differed in this respect.

There is, of course, the possibility of temperamental differences between the two; however, given our ignorance of both men, we are in no position to say anything genuinely informative about this. But part of the answer may also be that the debunking of convention was far from uncommon in philosophical circles in the fourth and late fifth centuries BC. The Sophists devoted much energy to discussing the distinction between nature (*phusis*) and convention (*nomos*); and some of them, though not all, adopted as a consequence views according to which conventional modes of behaviour are to be rejected, and some form of behaviour 'according to nature' is to be adopted instead.[104] And in Pyrrho's own day and shortly before, the Cynics very visibly put into practice a view of this kind; for them the life according to nature was the ideal, and this entailed paying no attention either to conventional proprieties or to conventional conceptions of what kinds of things (wealth, social position, and the like) were worth having. So the philosophical climate of Pyrrho's time (but surely not of Sextus' time—despite our uncertainty over exactly when and where he lived)[105] was one in which a disregard of convention, or a refusal to see it as authoritative over one's behaviour, was a live and vocally expressed option; Pyrrho's own attitude towards convention, though perhaps eccentric by later standards, does not seem especially odd when seen in that context. The further exploration of that philosophical climate, and of possible influences upon Pyrrho's thinking, is the subject of the next chapter.

---

[103] On this, see further above, n. 101.
[104] On the variety of views taken by the Sophists in this area, see Bett (1989*b*: sect. V).
[105] On this, see House (1980).

3

Looking Backwards

Pyrrho's philosophical affiliations and antecedents are far from clear. And a bewildering variety of claims has been made on the topic, in both ancient and modern times. In the ancient period these frequently take the form of locating Pyrrho in a certain 'succession' of philosophers—that is, a chronological sequence of philosophers, each member of which is alleged to have been the teacher of the next member. As was noted at the outset, such 'succession' stories deserve to be treated with a large measure of suspicion.[1] However, in so far as they reflect views as to the like-mindedness of Pyrrho and other philosophers before and after him, they may deserve consideration. More clearly worthy of serious attention are the verdicts on other philosophers offered by Timon in his poem *Silloi*, 'Lampoons'. Most of the surviving fragments of this poem consist of thumbnail sketches of other philosophers. Most of these sketches, in turn, are largely or wholly hostile to the philosophers in question. But, though Timon never expresses unreserved admiration for any philosopher other than Pyrrho himself, he does offer qualified praise of several of Pyrrho's predecessors. These fragments will need to be looked at carefully; for it is plausible to read him as suggesting that each of these people anticipated Pyrrho's outlook in some significant respect.

Modern scholars, by contrast, typically offer such claims explicitly, and as part and parcel of an interpretation of Pyrrho's philosophy; the best way to understand Pyrrho, it is suggested, is to see him as responding to philosopher *X*, or as engaged in a project comparable to that of philosopher *Y*. Since we know little about which other philosophers Pyrrho was actually acquainted with or impressed by, these connections, though subject to the constraints of chronological possibility, are again generally based on the scholar's perception of common ground between Pyrrho and the other philosopher in question. There is nothing inherently wrong with this. However, there is always a danger, in this kind of account, that one's perception of common ground may be too hasty and superficial, and may itself shape one's interpretation of Pyrrho to an unwarranted extent, distracting one's attention from, or distorting one's reading of, the finer details of the evidence relating to Pyrrho

[1] See Introduction, n. 2.

himself.[2] I have tried to avoid this trap by developing an interpretation of Pyrrho's philosophy derived, as far as possible, from *nothing but* the evidence relating to Pyrrho himself. The aim in the present chapter will be to use this already developed interpretation as a starting point in seeking to understand how Pyrrho's philosophy connects with the philosophies of those around him and preceding him. This enterprise might, of course, prove impossible to carry out in the form just suggested; the attempt might instead force us to revise our opinions about Pyrrho's philosophy itself. Clearly the plausibility of our account of Pyrrho's philosophy, and of our account of the relations between that philosophy and earlier or contemporaneous philosophies, are not entirely separate issues. However, for the most part I shall proceed as if our account of Pyrrho's philosophy has been settled by the argument of the previous chapters, and try to see what this philosophy has to do with the ideas of a number of other thinkers. This approach will, I believe, prove to be justified by the extent of the connections that we are able to draw in this area; Pyrrho's philosophy, understood as I have proposed, will turn out to be by no means extraordinary for its time and place.

Some people think that it is pointless, or worse, to try to detect the *influences* on a certain philosopher in the absence of detailed knowledge of who that philosopher read or met[3]—knowledge of a sort that, again, is very scanty in Pyrrho's case. I disagree. It seems to me that, if the similarities in thought between two philosophers are sufficiently distinctive, and if we know enough to be able to say at least that the later philosopher *could have* been familiar with the work of the earlier philosopher (and assuming, too, that we know which is which), then it is not unreasonable to conclude that the earlier philosopher influenced the later one. In what follows, I shall be casting doubt on a number of such claims of influence—claims that have received a large measure of acceptance in the literature on Pyrrho; but I shall also try to show that there are others that can be respectably argued for, and that, if accepted, make a difference to our picture of the development of Pyrrhonism. However, even if the question 'What were the major influences on Pyrrho's philosophy?' were a misguided one, it would still be worth asking how much he shares with his contemporaries and predecessors. For we do not have a comprehensive picture of Pyrrho (nor, therefore, of the Pyrrhonian tradition as a whole) without some sense of the context in which his philosophy arose, and of the uniqueness of his contribution.

---

[2] Numerous cases of this phenomenon are discussed and criticized in Bett (1994*a*).

[3] See e.g. Barnes (1982*b*: p. xvi), where this enterprise is described as 'either merely impertinent or grossly speculative'.

1. The indeterminacy thesis: its nature and motivations

We have seen that the difficulty or impossibility of acquiring *knowledge* does not seem to have been a central concern for Pyrrho—as the history of what later came to be called scepticism might have led us to expect. His mistrust of sensations and opinions as guides to the true nature of things derives, if I am right, from a metaphysical thesis—the indeterminacy thesis—and not, or at least not directly, from epistemological worries. We might expect, then, that those earlier philosophers who did, in one way or another, express worries about our prospects for achieving knowledge would not be of any great significance as forerunners of Pyrrho (even though it is these who have usually been singled out as 'precursors' to the Greek sceptical tradition).[4] More important, one might think, would be whoever may have maintained something resembling the indeterminacy thesis. Yet, as we shall see, two of the earlier thinkers about whom Timon expresses his kindest verdicts are Xenophanes and Democritus—precisely the two early figures most commonly cited by modern interpreters as prone to doubts about the possibility of knowledge. The issue, then, is complicated. The best place to begin is perhaps to ask, in a more detailed manner than we have so far done, why Pyrrho might have been attracted to the indeterminacy thesis, and what the thesis commits him to. This will put us in a better position to discern who are the other philosophers with whom he has the most common ground, with respect to his central claims. And this, in turn, will make it easier for us to assess the many other hints, in the ancient evidence, concerning associations between Pyrrho and other philosophers, as well as claims concerning such associations in modern scholarship.

What, then, were Pyrrho's grounds for maintaining the indeterminacy thesis? As we saw, the Aristocles passage is silent on this, and none of the other reports on Pyrrho discusses the question either. This does not mean that Pyrrho had no such grounds; the Aristocles passage is avowedly only a brief summary of the central points in Pyrrho's philosophy, and there is no other summary that comes close even to that level of detail. But it does mean that the question must take a somewhat abstract form: why might someone, and particularly someone in Pyrrho's time and place, have been attracted to the indeterminacy thesis?

The answer, I suggest, is that the thesis must somehow or other have had its basis in the variable and often conflicting ways in which things strike us—the differing impressions of the same objects experienced by different people,

---

[4] On this, see again Introduction, n. 10 and accompanying text. In addition to the scholars cited there, this tendency is also very noticeable in di Marco (1989). This is not, however, surprising, since di Marco seems uncritically to assume that Pyrrho's position is that of a sceptic practising later Pyrrhonist-style suspension of judgement.

or by the same people at different times, owing to changes in the objects themselves, to differences or changes in the circumstances or perspectives of the viewers, and to a variety of other causes. I shall use the term 'variability' to refer generically to this cluster of phenomena.[5] Now, there are a number of reasons why it is plausible that the indeterminacy thesis derived in some way from considerations concerning variability. First, purely in the abstract, it is hard to imagine that such considerations did not play *some* role in motivating the thesis. Pyrrho holds that things are 'indifferent and unstable and indeterminate'; an obvious starting point for such a view would seem to be the observation that things do not present themselves to us in fixed and stable ways. Secondly, it is clear that numerous other philosophers prior to Pyrrho had used similar observations to support novel and even radical metaphysical views; Heraclitus, Protagoras, and Plato had all done so, and so perhaps had Democritus. We need not go into detail at this stage; all of these figures will be considered later for their possible links with Pyrrho. For now, it is sufficient to note that the idea that variability creates difficulties for any straightforward, common-sense view of the world was certainly rife in the fifth and fourth centuries BC; if Pyrrho based his indeterminacy thesis on the variability with which things strike us, he would thus be in good company. Thirdly, if this was the basis for his thesis, that would also put him into closer proximity with the later Pyrrhonists. Both Aenesidemus and Sextus clearly attach a great deal of importance to the implications of conflicts in our impressions of things. There is very little in the surviving evidence on Pyrrho indicating explicitly that he accorded these conflicts a similar degree of importance. In Chapter 1 we did discuss a claim of Aenesidemus, reported in Diogenes Laertius (9.106), that seemed to point in this direction—namely, that Pyrrho 'determines nothing dogmatically because of contradiction'; but we also saw that either Aenesidemus' claim or Diogenes' report of it may well be to some degree a distortion. However, if considerations having to do with a 'contradiction' in our impressions of things did indeed motivate the indeterminacy thesis, this would mark an important point of contact between the earlier and the later periods of Pyrrhonism—despite the fact that the indeterminacy thesis itself was not countenanced in the later period. (Again, we shall take up this matter in greater detail later on—in this case, in Chapter 4.) Fourthly, if this was the motivation, that would fit neatly with Pyrrho's reported use of phrases

---

[5] This obviously skates over a great many subtleties—subtleties that have received extensive discussion in the literature on several other Greek philosophers, most especially Plato. In the present context, however, it would be pointless to adopt anything other than a very broad-brushed approach. The aim is to reconstruct the sort of reasoning that may have led Pyrrho to his indeterminacy thesis; in the absence of any direct evidence on this subject, the reconstruction is bound to remain at a highly general level, and the finer details of (and the differences among) the numerous species of what I am calling 'variability' can hardly be expected to help us. I say a little more about different forms of variability in Sect. 3 and Appendix B.

of the form 'no more F than not-F'. In the Aristocles passage, he is supposed to have recommended such phrases as an appropriate form of speech for one who accepts the indeterminacy thesis; this recommendation would be very natural if the indeterminacy thesis itself was a response to the fact that things very often strike us as F in one situation and as not-F in another.[6]

None of these considerations, of course, amounts to anything more than circumstantial evidence. However, it is readily intelligible, historically and philosophically, that the indeterminacy thesis should have been argued for by appeal to the variability with which things strike us; and it is quite unclear what *other* kind of justification Pyrrho might have offered for this thesis.[7] We have no way of telling whether any particular *type* of variability—changeability in the intrinsic features of things, for example—impressed Pyrrho more forcefully than other types;[8] but that variability of some kinds or other was the motivating force behind the indeterminacy thesis seems, at the very least, an attractive hypothesis.

But, if this is correct, how, more precisely, did the argument work? Here matters get more complicated, as well as more speculative. In *Outlines of Pyrrhonism*, variability is a route to suspension of judgement about how things really are; things strike us in a multitude of conflicting ways, we are unable to settle upon any one of these ways, rather than the others, as being the true reflection of the natures of these things, and so we are forced to suspend judgement about this question. But for Pyrrho—or so I have argued—the end point is not *suspension* of judgement about the nature of things, but the *judgement that* things are in their nature indeterminate. For Pyrrho, therefore, it could not be our inability to determine the accuracy or inaccuracy of the conflicting ways in which things strike us that was the intended moral of variability; that would yield not a judgement, but a withdrawal from judgement.[9] Rather, in order to yield the indeterminacy thesis,

---

[6] On the accusation of circularity that this may invoke, see below, n. 10.

[7] Of those interpreters who accept that Pyrrho maintained some form of indeterminacy thesis, few have attempted to identify the grounds he may have had for maintaining it (as opposed to identifying the other philosophers to whom he may have been responding, either positively or negatively, by means of it). But those who have tackled the question of its grounds seem uniformly to appeal to some type of considerations concerning variability. The most explicit example I have found is LS ii. 6 (though the reconstruction here is framed in terms of a conflict among competing *theories* of the nature of things, rather than among impressions of things generally); another example is Ferrari (1981: 364–5).

[8] We shall see later (Sect. 3) that this question may be of some interest in connection with the possible parallel between Pyrrho's reasoning and certain arguments in Plato.

[9] This is the main difficulty with LS's reconstruction of Pyrrho's reasoning (see n. 7 above), which proceeds by way of the notion that there is *no reason to prefer* any one of the conflicting theories about the world over the others. As so reconstructed, the reasoning is invalid—but unnecessarily so. We do not need to attribute to Pyrrho any dubious slide from epistemological to metaphysical considerations, since we have no need to assume that his thinking must have started out on an epistemological plane.

the reasoning would somehow have to run along the following lines: things present themselves to us in various and conflicting ways; so there is no single, fixed way things are; so reality is indeterminate.

Suppose that a certain rock looks brown at one time of day, but that at other times of day, when the light is of a different quality, it looks other than brown—orange, for example, or grey. Pyrrho's inference from this state of affairs could not be that we cannot tell whether the rock is really brown or other than brown—that it might be either, but that we are not in a position to say. On the contrary, he would have to infer that we *are* able to say something about the colour of the rock, and that is that, in its true nature, the rock cannot be *either* brown *or* other than brown. And the reason would presumably be that, since it presents itself in some circumstances as brown and in others circumstances as other than brown, neither predicate can be descriptive of its true nature.

Now, one might conclude in this case that the rock is in its true nature uncoloured; other philosophers have reached analogous conclusions in similar conditions. But Pyrrho's way of thinking would have to be different from this as well. For this would not get us any closer to the indeterminacy thesis— at least, if that thesis is as broad in scope as the Aristocles passage makes it sound. On this view it would still be the case that the rock *has* a determinate nature, though a determinate nature in which colours play no part. Pyrrho's thought, rather, would have to be that the rock is not in its true nature either brown or other than brown, but that nor is it, in its true nature, *neither* brown *nor* other than brown. Rather, as regards the presence or absence of brown-ness or other colours, the rock is in its true nature purely indeterminate; the predicates 'brown' and 'other than brown' *neither apply to it nor fail to apply to it*. And, if this way of thinking was applied to all the potentially conflicting pairs of predicates that might be applied to the rock, or to any other rock, or to any other object whatever, we would arrive at the conclusion that reality quite generally is indeterminate. And this, in turn, would yield all the consequences of the indeterminacy thesis that we saw related in the Aristocles passage. Our sensations and opinions are neither true nor false, in that they neither capture this indeterminate reality, nor represent it as the simple *negation* of how it really is; we should not trust them as revelatory of the true nature of things, since that is not what they are; and we should say of any given thing (again, as regards its true nature, should the question arise) that it 'no more is than is not or both is and is not or neither is nor is not' any particular way—which amounts, precisely, to the claim that no particular predicate either applies or fails to apply to the thing.[10]

---

[10] It might be objected that I am here attributing to Pyrrho a circular form of reasoning: the claim that no predicate applies or fails to apply to anything is presented as a consequence of the indeterminacy thesis, and the indeterminacy thesis is presented as a consequence of the idea that

We have, then, a rough sketch of how the indeterminacy thesis could be motivated by means of considerations concerning variability. It is clear that the use to which variability is put must be substantially different from its use in *Outlines of Pyrrhonism*, in order for the indeterminacy thesis, rather than suspension of judgement about the nature of things, to be the result. For both Pyrrho and Sextus, there is a sense in which no member of some set of conflicting appearances can be judged more veridical than any other member; but the *way* in which this is so must differ importantly in the two cases. But now, why might someone be tempted by Pyrrho's approach (if this was indeed his approach) rather than Sextus'? The inference that things are, in their real natures, *none* of the variable ways they strike us as being—and not the negations of those ways, either—looks at first sight like a far less attractive move, in the face of variability, than the decision not to commit oneself at all as to the real natures of things. But perhaps the inference would seem more attractive if one held some additional view about what it is for an object to be *by nature* a certain way. Obviously it would be absurd to try to reconstruct Pyrrho's reasoning in this area down to the last detail. We can, however, suggest one general idea that, together with a simple supplementary assumption, would make the route from variability to the indeterminacy thesis seem plausible and even compelling.

The general idea is this: in order for an object to be a certain way *by nature*, it must be that way *invariably* or *without qualification*. Hence something that is *F* only *in some circumstances* (but not-*F* in other circumstances), or *F* only *in certain respects* (but not-*F* in certain other respects), is thereby *not* by nature *F*. The thing might admit of these merely qualified predications through undergoing internal change, through standing in opposite relations to certain other objects (for example, *A* might be heavy compared with *B* but light compared with *C*), or in other ways; but, in any case, a predicate that

---

no predicate either applies or fails to apply to anything (itself presented as a consequence of variability on a global scale). But there is no difficulty here. The indeterminacy thesis is not a *consequence* of the idea that no predicate either applies or fails to apply to anything; rather, as hinted in the main text, it *is* that very idea, stated in a somewhat more compendious form. And the 'no more' locution is not a plain inference from the indeterminacy thesis, but is Pyrrho's account of *what we should say*, given the indeterminacy thesis. The reasoning is therefore as follows: (1) things strike us in variable and conflicting ways; so (2) any predicate that we might be inclined to apply to something in fact neither applies to it nor fails to apply to it—in other words, reality is indeterminate; so (3) we should speak in a way that reflects this indeterminacy, neither applying nor refusing to apply any particular predicate to any particular thing. Hence the closeness of step (3) to step (2) is a virtue, not a vice; just as we would hope, the recommended mode of speech is true to the thinking that, according to Pyrrho, makes it advisable. (Hence, too, it was not misguided of me to cite the 'no more' locution as one reason for thinking that considerations concerning variability were at the root of the indeterminacy thesis—see above, n. 6 and accompanying text. A mode of speech that is supposed to be desirable in the light of a certain thesis might well be expected to echo to some degree the considerations that motivated that thesis; and this is no exception.)

belongs to an object in some merely qualified fashion is not, according to this view, any part of the object's true nature. The object's true nature, then, will comprise only those features that belong to it *un*qualifiedly—that is, constantly or intrinsically or both, independently of any particular circumstances, or any particular relations with other things, in which it may stand. This idea may seem to us peculiar and unintuitive. However, as may already be apparent, and as we shall be seeing in more detail later, similar ideas are not uncommon in Greek philosophy; that someone in Pyrrho's time and place might have adhered to it is not an outlandish supposition.

Suppose, then, that Pyrrho accepts some version of this condition[11]— which I shall refer to for convenience as the invariability condition—on a feature's being part of an object's true nature. Then, clearly, he will take the variability of some feature of an object as *excluding* that feature from any catalogue of features comprising the object's true nature. *A*'s heaviness compared with *B*, or the rock's brownness at certain times of day, is therefore not a feature belonging to the real nature of *A*, or of the rock; for it applies only in *some* relations or in *some* circumstances, not without qualification. So *A* is not *by nature* either heavy or light; the rock is not *by nature* either brown or other than brown. Nor, indeed, can *A* be said to be by nature *both* heavy *and* light, or by nature *neither* heavy *nor* light (or the rock by nature both brown and other than brown, or by nature neither of the two); for *those* composite features plainly do not belong to the objects in any invariable or unqualified way either—if, indeed, they belong to them in any way at all. Thus a focus on the phenomenon of variability, coupled with an acceptance of the invariability condition, will indeed encourage Pyrrho to regard things as purely indeterminate, as far as their natures are concerned, with respect to those features of the things that he perceives as variable. And if he thinks that variability operates quite unrestrictedly—that is, if he cannot find *any* feature that belongs to things entirely unqualifiedly—then the natural consequence will be a quite general indeterminacy thesis such as the Aristocles passage appears to report. If *none* of the perceived features of things is other than variable, in the sense discussed, then, as far as one can tell, there are simply no features—or at any rate, no determinate features—that are in a position to qualify as constituting anything's true nature. But, if this is the conclusion to which one is driven, then the answer one will give to the question 'What is

---

[11] Again, I deliberately present the condition with some looseness, offering alternative formulations and alternative examples throughout; see above, n. 5, on variability. What precisely the invariability condition amounts to depends on what types of variability Pyrrho had in mind as favouring the indeterminacy thesis; and this, as I said, we are in no position to settle. But in whatever respects he took things to be variable—and it could of course be a conjunction of many different respects—the argument for the indeterminacy thesis will go through if he assumes, as a condition for some property's belonging to a thing *by nature*, that the property's attachment to the thing be *in those respects* invariable or unqualified.

the nature of things?' will have to be 'things are indeterminate'; as far as the nature of things is concerned, that is all that there is left to say.[12] So, if Pyrrho was impressed by the phenomenon of variability, then this would very easily motivate the indeterminacy thesis when conjoined with the invariability condition; wherever there are variabilities, the indeterminacy thesis will apply, and if variability is thought of as ubiquitous, the indeterminacy thesis will be unlimited in scope.

The supplementary assumption needed for this line of thought to be complete is simply that the temporary and contingent character of an object, as it stands in certain specific circumstances, or in certain specific relations with other objects, is not, at least in general, itself a matter of obscurity. Thus *A*'s heaviness compared with *B* and its lightness compared with *C*, or the rock's brownness at certain times of day and lack of brownness at other times of day, are matters of plain experience; we do not need to worry, at *this* level, about whether we are being deceived. This is not necessarily to rule out the possibility of rare cases of optical illusion or the like; but we are at any rate not subject to pervasive or systematic illusion in our everyday encounters with things. Now this is, of course, quite compatible with our sensations and opinions being neither true nor false, as the Aristocles passage tells us, and with our needing to mistrust them—if those remarks are understood in the manner suggested in the last chapter. That is, we should not take our sensations and opinions to capture the real nature of things; at that level the only possible thing to say is that things are indeterminate, and hence the determinate content of our sensations and opinions in specific cases is neither true to things in their real natures, nor false to them.[13] But the character of an object in its specific circumstances, or its specific relations with other objects, in any given case, is a very different matter from this. Given the invariability condition, features that belong to an object in a merely qualified way are no part of the object's true nature (if it has any true nature at all); they are *just* temporary and contingent features, which puts them in another category altogether.

---

[12] Is the statement 'things are indifferent and unstable and indeterminate' to be understood as itself a *description* of the nature of things? Or is it, rather, a way of denying that *there is any* genuine nature to things? If we stick with the idea that, in order for a certain feature to belong to a thing by nature, it must belong to the thing unqualifiedly, we will incline to the second option. There may be no determinate features that belong to things unqualifiedly; but, equally, it is difficult to see *in*determinacy as a feature that belongs to things unqualifiedly. So it seems better to understand 'things are indeterminate' as amounting simply to the claim that there are *no* features belonging to things unqualifiedly—that is, as denying that things have any true nature, in the sense explained. However, the line between these two readings is a fine one, and the point is of no great importance; either way, the statement is a metaphysical thesis specifying what is the case, as far as the natures of things are concerned.

[13] To recall: in order to be false, our sensations and opinions would have to represent things as having features that were the *negations* of their actual features—which would require things to be determinate in their real natures, just as they would have to be in order for our sensations and opinions to be true.

Nevertheless, for this reasoning to issue in the indeterminacy thesis, it does need to be assumed that our grasp of these temporary and contingent features, as they confront us in our ordinary experience, is itself unproblematic. Otherwise, there would be room for the speculation that some feature that *seemed to us* merely temporary and contingent might *in fact* belong to an object invariably and unqualifiedly, and so be part of that object's true nature. The phenomenon of variability, plus the invariability condition, does yield the indeterminacy thesis; but the argument would of course collapse if the phenomenon of variability itself was put into question. Pyrrho may mistrust the senses in one way; but he cannot subject ordinary experience to any truly hyperbolic doubt without cutting off the route to his conclusion. However, in not entertaining hyperbolic doubts, he would hardly be doing anything very adventurous or surprising.

Again, much of the last few pages has been highly speculative. But, as I noted earlier, the hypothesis that Pyrrho's indeterminacy thesis was motivated—somehow or other—by way of considerations concerning variability seems to have much to recommend it. And the remaining ideas that I have tentatively attributed to him are merely an attempt to find the shortest and most plausible route between the two. It is, of course, possible that Pyrrho was just confused, or that his reasoning was more circuitous or more objectionable than I have suggested. But, if a way of understanding him is available that does not convict him of confusion or philosophical incompetence, but takes us some way towards making sense of his position, then the principle of charity should dictate that we at least try this out. And, if we do so, I shall argue, Pyrrho's links with both his predecessors and his successors appear in a new and intriguing light.

Before we get to Pyrrho's predecessors, there is one more thread to be picked up. We saw in the previous chapter that early Pyrrhonism, at least in the person of Timon, seemed to include the idea that we can and should rely on appearances. Now, if Pyrrho did adhere to the conception that I have just outlined, this policy would seem to make very good sense. If one assumes that ordinary experience is not systematically deceptive about what I called the 'temporary and contingent' features of things—as opposed to their real natures—it is clear that one will see no difficulty in using the various ways in which things appear in ordinary experience as a perfectly adequate basis for decision-making. If, for example, honey (normally) appears sweet, that gives us very good reason (normally) to spread it on our bread. Since in certain circumstances honey will present itself as not-sweet, we cannot claim that it is sweet in its true nature; but, if it tastes sweet today, and on most other days, then the fact that it is not *in its true nature* sweet is no obstacle to our regularly eating it. There is no need to worry that we might be *deceived* about the sweetness that it displays most of the time; and, as far as our everyday reactions to honey are concerned, the sweetness that it displays most of the time is all that matters. It is only when one is discussing the real nature of things that the fact that honey does not present itself as sweet invariably or without qualification becomes an important issue. And the indeterminate nature of things, and the consequent need to rely on 'appearances', would be a problem only if one thought that a well-lived human life needed to be anchored in the nature of things. But that is precisely the illusion from which Pyrrho, as reported in the Aristocles passage, frees us. Once one grasps the indeterminacy thesis, and what follows from it, one sees that the nature of things neither can nor needs to furnish one with any prescriptions for one's behaviour; one is, so to speak, on one's own in the world. But this realization, for reasons considered in the previous chapter, is liberating rather than disturbing; and once this has been understood, the appearances of things are quite enough to go on.

My reconstruction in this section thus offers us a possible way of filling out and justifying the picture suggested by the evidence on the subject of appearances—which, as we saw, was rather exiguous. It is not quite clear whether we should say that the term 'the appearances', according to this picture, is simply a *name* for those variable characteristics that objects exhibit, temporarily or qualifiedly, in ordinary experience—or whether, on the other hand, we should say that objects *appear* to exhibit these variable characteristics, but that, in addition, it is unproblematic (except perhaps in a few special cases) to infer that they *do* exhibit these characteristics (again, temporarily or qualifiedly, not as part of their real natures). Either way, the policy of relying on appearances in one's everyday behaviour, which the evidence seemed to suggest, turns out to fit neatly into the early Pyrrhonist philosophy. Finally, if there is any merit to my reconstruction of Pyrrho's reasoning in support of the indeterminacy thesis, then that tends to favour the hypothesis that the attitude towards appearances recorded in the evidence considered in the last chapter belonged not only to Timon—which is all that the evidence itself allowed us to conclude—but also to Pyrrho himself.

This conception of the appearances of things is not the same as the one we are familiar with from *Outlines of Pyrrhonism*. There is certainly room for dispute about precisely how Sextus conceives of appearances.[14] In particular, it is unclear in his case, too, to what extent one is allowed, when one restricts one's speech to the realm of appearances, to talk about *objects* in the world, or to what extent, on the other hand, one is compelled to limit oneself to talking about one's own subjective *impressions*. But it is at least clear that the distinction between the appearances and the underlying nature of a thing displayed in the opening chapters of book I of *Outlines of Pyrrhonism* is not couched in terms of any distinction between temporary and qualified features

---

[14] On this vexed topic, see most recently Brennan (1994); also Frede (1979); Burnyeat (1980a); Barnes (1982a).

and invariable or unqualified features.[15] Moreover, it is clear that Sextus does not allow us to make any inferences *from* the appearances *to* the nature of things. Pyrrho, according to my reconstruction, is considerably less cautious; from the variable appearances, he infers that reality is indeterminate. But then, given that he does hold the indeterminacy thesis, some such audacious move was perhaps only to be expected. We shall come back to this contrast, and other similar ones, in this chapter and the next. Let us now turn directly to the question of Pyrrho's predecessors.

2. *Pyrrho and Aristotle's opponents in* Metaphysics *IV*

If I am right that variability is the starting point of the indeterminacy thesis, and that the route to the indeterminacy thesis, and the nature of the thesis itself, was along somewhat the lines suggested, the next question to ask is what other philosophies of the same or the immediately preceding period the resulting outlook most resembles. And the best place to begin that enquiry is to ask who else besides Pyrrho maintained or discussed some form of indeterminacy thesis, and why they did so.

Two texts immediately strike one as being especially likely to be relevant in this connection: Aristotle's discussion in *Metaphysics* IV.4 ff. of those who claim to deny, or who in his view are committed to denying, the Law of Non-Contradiction, and Plato's treatment in the *Theaetetus* (181a–183b) of what may be called a 'thesis of total instability'. Aristotle specifically points out that one consequence of rejecting the Law of Non-Contradiction would be that everything is indeterminate (*aoriston* (1007^{b}27)).[16] And Socrates' criticism of the thesis of total instability is that it makes it impossible to assert of anything that it is any particular way; in fact, language in general becomes impossible, except perhaps for a peculiar form of words, *oud'houtōs* (183^{b}4,

---

[15] Sextus' summary of the Ten Modes does sometimes seem to employ a distinction of this kind. But this is clearly inconsistent with his usual procedure—and represents, as I shall argue, an isolated survival of an earlier conception distinct from Sextus' usual one; see Ch. 4, Sect. 3.

[16] Cf. 1009^{a}4–5, 'preventing us from determining [*horisai*] anything in our thought'; and 1008^{a}34, where Aristotle details the kind of language (an impossible kind, in his view) that the denier of the Law is bound to use—because, if he did not use such language, 'already something would be definite' (*ēdē an ti eiē hōrismenon*). The Aristocles passage does not use *horizō* or cognates to express Pyrrho's indeterminacy thesis. But we did observe that Timon explains the term *ou mallon* as conveying the notion of 'determining nothing [*to mēden horizein*] and withholding assent' (DL 9.76)—where this, in turn, is best understood not in later Pyrrhonist terms, but as an expression of the indeterminacy thesis of the Aristocles passage (see Ch. 1, Sect. 3). In any case, Aristotle's point is that, if one denies the Law, things will cease to have definite predicates attaching to them; and this clearly bears at least a family resemblance to Pyrrho's indeterminacy thesis and its purported consequences.

translated 'not at all thus' in the Burnyeat/Levett translation),[17] that is apparently designed precisely to signal that there is no definite way things are. In addition, it is clear that variability, of one kind or another, is at the root of both positions. Aristotle explains that the fact of conflicting opinions and conflicting appearances of things, together with a misinterpretation of the significance of these conflicts, is what has led some people to deny the Law of Non-Contradiction (1009^a9-12, $22-6$, 1009^b2-11). And the *Theaetetus'* thesis of total instability is precisely the view that everything is constantly changing in every respect.

Both Plato and Aristotle, then, considered some variety of indeterminacy thesis important enough to pay some attention to. Both, of course, have their own philosophical motivations for discussing these theses; Plato sees the thesis of total instability as the logical end point of Protagoreanism, and his own *reductio* of the thesis as a means for the latter's final dismissal, while Aristotle is in the business of establishing the Law of Non-Contradiction as the most indubitable principle of all, and clarifying exactly what forms of justification it does and does not admit of (and does and does not need). None the less, it is clear that both Plato and Aristotle regard the theses they are criticizing as having been upheld by historically live opponents, and not just as theoretical possibilities to mull over for their own purposes. This is already enough to suggest that Pyrrho's indeterminacy thesis need not have appeared wildly eccentric in his own time and place; views recognizably akin to his had evidently been aired by certain of his predecessors. But can we pin down the antecedents of his indeterminacy thesis any more precisely than this?

The idea that the views of Pyrrho reported in the Aristocles passage are especially closely related to views criticized by Aristotle in *Metaphysics* IV has been accepted by a number of scholars. If one is impressed by the similarity between the two, one might be tempted to suppose that Pyrrho is among those to whom Aristotle is responding. But it is usually assumed— almost certainly correctly—that this is chronologically impossible;[18] according to Diogenes Laertius (9.61), Pyrrho developed his philosophy after, and as a result of, his trip to India with Alexander,[19] from which he presumably would not have returned until after the composition of *Metaphysics* IV. (And it might be added that, even if, contrary to Diogenes' report, Pyrrho had developed his distinctive outlook before joining Alexander's expedition, he would probably have been too young and insignificant a figure to have attracted Aristotle's attention.) Several scholars have proposed, instead, that it is Pyrrho who is responding to Aristotle. One version of this hypothesis

---

[17] Burnyeat (1990: 313).

[18] Not, however, by DeLacy (1958) who suggests (p. 64 n. 1) that Pyrrho may have influenced Aristotle's use of the term *ou mallon* in *Metaphysics* IV.

[19] We shall return to the possible Indian connection in Sect. 10 of this chapter.

has it that Pyrrho actually studied with Aristotle for a year or two (between 334 and 332, prior to his departure with Alexander).[20] According to another version, Pyrrho knew Aristotle's writings without knowing Aristotle; he became acquainted with them either through his contact with Aristotle's nephew and student Callisthenes while on Alexander's expedition,[21] or by searching them out in Athens after his return.[22] In any case, the suggestion is that Pyrrho developed his philosophy in self-conscious opposition to Aristotle—that he accepted the challenge of espousing and embodying an attitude claimed in *Metaphysics* IV to be both theoretically and practically untenable.[23] Another explanation offered for the correspondences detected between the two sets of ideas is that Aristotle is responding to predecessors of Pyrrho who substantially anticipated his ideas, and who perhaps influenced him; specifically, the Megarians, one of whom may have been a teacher of Pyrrho, have been proposed as the unnamed targets of Aristotle's polemic.[24] One may of course adopt both these explanations in conjunction; Pyrrho's desire to respond to Aristotle's arguments naturally makes good sense if the original targets of those arguments were people whose views he shared, and from whom he may have learned those views. In fact, it would be difficult to see why Pyrrho would have set himself in opposition to Aristotle's ideas *unless* he had seen at least some significant kinship between his own ideas and those of Aristotle's opponents.

This proposed assimilation between Pyrrho and Aristotle's opponents is, however, more than a little problematic. First, the identification of the Megarians as Aristotle's opponents is tenuous at best. Indeed, it is very unclear whom Aristotle is primarily attacking; at a few points he names people whom he takes to be victims of erroneous reasoning, but most of the time his opponents remain anonymous—and they seem to have left no other traces. Still, this is not the central issue (and for this reason I discuss it separately, in Appendix A); for, even if we cannot say who Aristotle's main opponents were, it would still be worth knowing that *someone* anticipated Pyrrho's

---

[20] This is tentatively proposed by Conche (1994: 31, 69).

[21] See Plutarch, *Alexander* 52, for Callisthenes' presence on the expedition.

[22] The first hypothesis is also suggested by Conche (1994: 69–70); both hypotheses are suggested by Reale (1981: 316).

[23] This is also accepted by Decleva Caizzi (DC 152–5); this does not, however, advance any particular theory of how Pyrrho came to know Aristotle's work. See also Decleva Caizzi (1984*a*), which speaks of the anti-Aristotelianism of Pyrrho. The suggestion is also mentioned by Long (1981: n. 31); but Long does not commit himself on this issue, saying that, despite the 'almost identical language' used by Aristotle and by Pyrrho (as reported in the Aristocles passage), 'the two descriptions may well be independent of each other'. Cf. LS ii. 6, which again speaks of the 'striking similarity' between the two texts, while offering no specific explanation.

[24] By Reale (1981: 305, 312–15), and by Berti (1981). The view that Aristotle's opponents were the Megarians was originally proposed (independently of any possible connections with Pyrrho) by Maier (1900: ii, pt. 2, 6 ff.), and is viewed sympathetically by Ross (1924: i. 268).

ideas in important respects. The central difficulty is simply that the view attacked in *Metaphysics* IV is not, in fact, particularly close to that of Pyrrho. It is true that in some passages Aristotle seems to be attacking ideas that sound like later Pyrrhonism; in particular, he sometimes criticizes his opponents' unending demand for justification.[25] But that point is not relevant here. As we have seen, the ideas of Pyrrho and the ideas of later Pyrrhonists diverge considerably in a number of places, and this is an example. The unending demand for justification may be characteristic of the later Pyrrhonists; the Five Modes of Agrippa seem especially to embody this type of attitude. But none of the evidence relating to Pyrrho suggests that he would press people relentlessly to justify their claims; on the contrary, he seems to have had very little interest in challenging people about their claims at all. Rather, he seems simply to have assumed, from an early stage in his own argumentation, that they were misguided, and to have ignored them after that. However, it is the denial of the Law of Non-Contradiction itself that has especially been thought to represent an important point of contact with Pyrrho; and this requires more detailed attention.

Here too, though, there is an immediate difficulty. We have seen that, according to the Aristocles passage, our sensations and opinions are neither true nor false. But it is very hard to see how someone who held that sensations and opinions are neither true nor false could *also* hold that things may possess both members of a pair of contradictory properties—that a human being both is and is not pale, or is and is not a trireme (the examples are Aristotle's). If the latter statements are accepted, the following 'sensations and opinions' must all be acknowledged to be *true*, not neither true nor false: (1) the person is pale, (2) the person is not pale, (3) the person is a trireme, and (4) the person is not a trireme. Aristotle himself, in fact, takes the denial of the Law of Non-Contradiction to be equivalent to the view, discussed in chapters 5 and 6 of *Metaphysics* IV, that all opinions and appearances are true. If everything is both *F* and not-*F*, he argues, then any two conflicting opinions and appearances will both be true ($1009^{a}12$–15); similarly, if all opinions and appearances are true, then any opinion *A*, to the effect that some other opinion *B* is mistaken, will be true, so that it will be true that opinion *B* is false—yet opinion *B* will also be true, so that the subject of opinion *B* will both be and not be whatever opinion *B* says that it is ($1009^{a}7$–12). This argument has the further corollary that, if all opinions and appearances are true, all of them are also *both* true *and* false. But this is all quite distinct from saying that they are *neither* true *nor* false, as Pyrrho is supposed to have said.[26]

---

[25] He also puts in their mouths observations that sound reminiscent of the Ten Modes; see $1009^{b}1$ ff., $1010^{b}1$ ff., $1011^{a}3$ ff., with Long (1981). As we shall see, however (below, n. 28), this similarity with later Pyrrhonism is only superficial.

[26] It might be replied that the claim that sensations and opinions are neither true nor false is *equivalent* to the claim that they are both true and false. But this equivalence works only if the principle of bivalence is accepted. As we saw, however, Pyrrho's claim is a consequence of the

Again, according to the Aristocles passage, the inference Pyrrho drew from the claim that our sensations and opinions are neither true nor false is that we should not trust them. But the problem with the deniers of the Law of Non-Contradiction seems to be precisely the opposite; they end up accepting that the same thing may possess contradictory properties because they are *too* trusting of the opposing impressions that often occur concerning the same thing (1009^a22–6, 1009^b1 ff.). Aristotle maintains that the denial of the Law of Non-Contradiction is equivalent to the position of Protagoras, that things are however they appear to any perceiver (1009^a6 ff.);[27] but the problem with Protagoras' view seems to be that there is *no* reason to mistrust *any* opinions, not that they should all be mistrusted. One of the persisting problems in the first part of Plato's *Theaetetus*, where Protagoras' position is under discussion, is to see how this position can make room for the notion of experts, whose views about some subject are more deserving of trust than those of most people (161d–e, 166d–167d, 169d–170b, 172a–b, 177c–179b); if Protagoras is correct, it seems as if everyone is right about everything, and there is no reason for people to mistrust their own, or anyone else's, opinions. Aristotle has the *Theaetetus* in mind in this chapter (see 1010^b11–14); and he argues in response that *not* all appearances are true, but that some should be accepted and some (such as those of the sick, or the sleeping) should not (1010^b3–9)[28]—and also that no one is, in practice, as universally trusting of appearances as his opponents purport to be (1010^b9–11). In any case, his

indeterminacy thesis, and attributes to sensations and opinions an indeterminate status that is, precisely, neither truth nor falsehood. To attribute *this* status to them is not at all the same as saying that they have *both* of the two regularly opposed truth-values. Though, as we noted earlier, Aristotle does say that the denial of the Law of Non-Contradiction has the consequence that things are indeterminate, there is no sign that he here envisages the possibility of claims lacking either of the two standard truth-values. (In fact, in ch. 7 he argues that his opponent at this point is committed to the consequence that 'a person will neither tell the truth nor not tell the truth' (1012^a6–7). He assumes that 'not tell the truth' is equivalent to 'speak falsely', and he assumes the consequence itself to be a *reductio*, not needing further discussion; this would be plainly question-begging against a view like Pyrrho's.) Rather, Aristotle thinks that things will, on his opponents' view, be indeterminate in the sense that statements about them will fail to have just *one* truth-value out of the standard two.

[27] This, at any rate, is how Aristotle understands Protagoras' position. See Burnyeat (1976: esp. 46–7); Fine (1994: esp. 218–19 and n. 65). Burnyeat thinks that Aristotle's interpretation of Protagoras (and that of everyone else subsequently) differs from Plato's, and that Plato's is the correct one; Fine thinks that Plato's is the same as Aristotle's, but suspends judgement on the question of correctness.

[28] This is one of the passages reminiscent of material from the later Pyrrhonists' Ten Modes (see above, n. 25). It should now be clear that, though many of the examples are the same, and though both the Pyrrhonists and Aristotle's opponents hold that neither one of two contradictory impressions should be preferred to the other, there is an important difference between the two outlooks. For the later Pyrrhonists, neither one should be preferred to the other because both are equally *likely* to be correct, but at most one *can* be correct (for the later Pyrrhonists are not at all inclined to deny the Law of Non-Contradiction). For Aristotle's opponents, on the other hand, neither one should be preferred to the other because both *actually are* correct.

target is not Pyrrho's blanket mistrust of sensations and opinions, but, on the contrary, an indiscriminate *acceptance* of opinions and appearances.

It will be objected that, according to my own reconstruction of the reasoning that led Pyrrho to his indeterminacy thesis, there is another level at which Pyrrho is far less mistrustful of appearances. I suggested in the previous section that, in order to generate the indeterminacy thesis from the phenomenon of variability, Pyrrho must assume that our everyday experience of things is not systematically misleading, at least as concerns the characteristics exhibited by things temporarily and qualifiedly. But, it may be said, how is this different from saying that at a certain level—even if not at the level of the real nature of things—the appearances are true? And, if so, what is to prevent some forerunner of Pyrrho from being among Aristotle's opponents—even if it is not the Aristocles passage itself that reveals this?

But to this question at least two replies are available. First, the Law of Non-Contradiction, as Aristotle states it, is that 'It is impossible for the same attribute both to belong and not to belong to the same thing *at the same time and in the same respect*' (1005^b19–20). My reconstruction of Pyrrho's reasoning in no way required him to violate *this* principle. On the contrary, if the phenomenon of variability did lead Pyrrho to the indeterminacy thesis in something like the way I suggested, then this would require him to be particularly sensitive to the fact that the variable characteristics of things belong to them *only in certain respects but not in others*; for it is precisely this fact that leads him, according to my reconstruction, to disqualify these characteristics from being part of the *natures* of the things. So even if I do attribute to him, at a certain level, an acceptance of the appearances of things,[29] this is in a way that plainly does not lead to the principal fault of which Aristotle is accusing his opponents. Secondly, and perhaps more importantly, it is in any case clear that Aristotle has no inkling of a view that distinguishes between *levels* at which appearances may be accepted or mistrusted. His opponents in this passage are accused of holding, or attempting to hold, a certain view about reality—the Law of Non-Contradiction that they violate is, after all, the most basic principle in the science of 'being *qua* being'—and of arriving at this view by means of a simplistic inference from appearance to reality. The distinction my reconstruction attributed to Pyrrho, between the true nature of a thing and its temporary and contingent characteristics, and the resulting need for one's attitude towards the appearances to vary depending on which of these domains one is considering, are quite remote from anything Aristotle has in mind in discussing the violators of the Law of Non-Contradiction. One

---

[29] In addition, it is not clear (and I touched on this in the previous section) that Pyrrho needs to accept the view that *all* appearances are true; it may well be sufficient for him to accept the common-sense attitude that ordinary experience is not *systematically* misleading—even if it may be so in certain special cases.

could take issue with my reconstruction for various reasons; but at least it does not cause Pyrrho to fall afoul of the arguments of *Metaphysics* IV.

So far, then, it seems difficult to accept the hypothesis that Aristotle is attacking a position that was a forerunner of Pyrrho's. Whether one focuses on the Aristocles passage itself, as has generally been done in this context, or on the ideas I introduced more speculatively in the last section, Pyrrho's outlook seems significantly at odds with the views discussed by Aristotle. However, the defenders of that hypothesis have pointed to one passage in *Metaphysics* IV that, it has been alleged, employs 'almost identical language' to Pyrrho, as reported by Aristocles.[30] This parallel needs to be examined before the matter can be properly decided. Here is what Aristotle says about his unnamed opponent: 'He says neither "thus" nor "not thus", but "both thus and not thus"; and again he denies both of these, saying "neither thus nor not thus"; for otherwise there would already be something definite' ($1008^{a}31$–4). And here is the relevant portion of what Aristocles presents as Timon's summary of Pyrrho's position: 'One should be without opinions . . . saying about each single thing that it no more is than is not or both is and is not or neither is nor is not' (XIV.18.3). There is certainly some verbal similarity between the two passages. But whether the ideas being summarized are closely related is another question.

Aristotle's opponent is taken to be asserting that some object both is and is not of a certain character, and also that it neither is nor is not of that character. But, as we saw in Chapter 1, Pyrrho's prescription concerning what we should say 'about each single thing' cannot coherently be read as containing the recommendation that we *assert* that each thing 'both is and is not' and that it 'neither is nor is not'.[31] For that, again, would violate the conclusion that our sensations and opinions are neither true nor false; the first assertion would follow from our sensations and opinions being true, and the second from their being false, but both would be inconsistent with their being *neither* true *nor* false. Rather, to recall, the way to read Pyrrho's rule about what we should say so that it fits coherently into the logic of the whole passage is as follows: we should say of each thing that it no more (1) is than (2) is not or (3) both is and is not or (4) neither is nor is not, where each of these four alternatives is

---

[30] The phrase is from Long (1981: 92); the parallelism is also insisted upon by LS ii. 6; Reale (1981: 318–21); DC 230; Conche (1994: 80–1).

[31] Aristocles, in his criticism of Pyrrho, does at one point suggest that he might 'say that the same thing both is and is not' (XIV.18.9). But this is clearly one of a series of unwelcome possibilities Aristocles is presenting to Pyrrho in a polemical construction of his own—a construction obviously derived from arguments in *Metaphysics* IV itself. It does not show that Pyrrho actually did say this, or that Aristocles thought that he did. As a Peripatetic, Aristocles naturally uses Aristotelian argument whenever he thinks it will be effective. At this point he is trying to prove, in the spirit of *Metaphysics* IV, that Pyrrho's position cannot be intelligibly stated; he offers Pyrrho a number of apparent refuges from this conclusion, and it is unsurprising that the view that is the main subject in *Metaphysics* IV would be one of these.

'no more' true than any of the others; and, further, the only way in which it could be the case that each of the four is 'no more' true than any of the others is if none of them is either true or false—with the result that no determinate features are attributed to the object at all. So the assertions Aristotle attributes to his opponent are assertions that Pyrrho cannot consistently have made, and that there is no reason to believe he did make.

None the less, it may be felt that the linguistic similarity is so strong that something must have been overlooked in the preceding argument. But how strong, in fact, is the linguistic similarity? Aristotle's opponent says 'thus and not thus' and also 'neither thus nor not thus'; and Pyrrho's statement about what we should say contains the words 'both is and is not' and also 'neither is nor is not'. But Pyrrho first tells us to say that each thing 'no more is than is not', whereas Aristotle's opponent is never presented as saying 'thus no more than not thus'. Aristotle does claim that his opponent 'says neither "thus" nor "not thus" '. But this does not constitute an additional component, possibly parallel with Pyrrho's 'no more is than is not', that the opponent says; on the contrary, it clearly specifies what he does *not* say. Aristotle's point is that, whereas normal sane people will state either that something *is* a certain way, or that it is not that way, his opponent *rejects* these ordinary utterances in favour of saying that the thing *both* is *and* is not that way. So Pyrrho's statement contains two components verbally resembling claims attributed by Aristotle to his opponent; but it contains a further component—arguably the most important, since it contains the crucial phrase 'no more'—for which there is no equivalent in the passage of Aristotle.

Moreover, one of the two claims Aristotle does put in his opponent's mouth is arguably not something that he takes his opponent actually to have said, but rather something that he, Aristotle, thinks his opponent is *committed* to saying. Earlier in the same chapter, Aristotle himself argues that someone who is prepared to say '*A* is both a human being and not a human being' must also accept the statement '*A* is neither a human being nor not a human being' (1008^a2–7). So, when Aristotle's opponent says 'thus and not thus', and then 'denies both of these, saying "neither thus nor not thus" ' (1008^a32–3), it is entirely possible that Aristotle is referring not to his opponent's expressed position, but to his own argument shortly before. Throughout the chapter, the main doctrine under scrutiny is that something can be both F and not-F; the addition 'neither F nor not-F' is plausibly understood, then, as an embarrassing consequence that Aristotle seeks to foist on his opponent, not as a further element in the opponent's own understanding of the view. But, if so, the parallel with Pyrrho becomes even more slender. The only remaining point of contact is that Pyrrho uses the words 'both is and is not', and Aristotle's opponent the words 'thus and not thus'. But since, as we have seen, Pyrrho cannot mean to *assert* that each thing 'both is and is not'—as Aristotle's opponent clearly does—this verbal similarity by itself becomes insignificant; it does not indicate any philosophical common ground. Hence, whoever are the people whom Aristotle is attacking, there is no serious basis for the belief that they were associates of Pyrrho, or that they and Pyrrho were of like mind.[32]

As was noted earlier, Aristotle does accuse his opponent of failing or refusing to say anything determinate. But it should be clear by now that this does not show that the view in question is identical with Pyrrho's view. Aristotle's opponent 'determines nothing' in the sense that he both asserts and denies the same predicates of the same subjects, and hence, as Aristotle argues, fails to say anything definite at all. Pyrrho's indeterminacy thesis is different, and in a way more radical; it neither asserts nor denies any predicates of any subjects.[33] It is also true, as we saw in Chapter 2, that Pyrrho's view is attacked on the grounds that it cannot be embodied in action; and Aristotle attacks his opponent in very similar terms. But this too shows nothing about the identity of the two views; a wide variety of philosophical positions might be thought to invite the criticism that action consistent with them is impossible. Lucretius argues against someone 'who thinks that nothing is known' (*nil sciri . . . putat* (4.469)), by saying that he would be unable to avoid precipices if he really lived what he claimed to accept (4.507–510); Plutarch reports the Epicurean Colotes as asking an Academic sceptic,[34] who claims to suspend judgement about everything, why he does not walk towards the wall rather than the door when he wants to leave the house (*Adv. Col.* 1122e), and as objecting against the Megarian Stilpo, who denies the possibility of predicating one thing of another, that 'life is destroyed' if his philosophy is accepted (1119c). The resemblance between Pyrrho's indeterminacy thesis and the position attacked by Aristotle is not non-existent; but it is too broad to be historically significant—except, as I said earlier, to suggest that positions of this general type were not unpopular in this phase of Greek philosophy. There is no good reason for thinking that Pyrrho is responding to Aristotle, or that he learned from the specific thinkers, whoever they were, whom Aristotle is opposing.

[32] One might abandon the idea that Aristotle's opponents were associates or kindred spirits of Pyrrho, but still claim that Pyrrho is, so to speak, accepting Aristotle's challenge, framing a position claimed by Aristotle to be impossible. In this case, it might be said, it is irrelevant whether or not 'neither thus nor not thus' is a polemical addition by Aristotle himself. However, as hinted earlier, this would make no sense at all unless the position being attacked was one that Pyrrho might have *thought* was akin to his own. And, to repeat, there is no reason why he would have thought so, since he does not and should not assert that the same thing 'both is and is not'.

[33] Cf. above, n. 26, on the difference between these two. The closest parallel to Pyrrho's thesis in *Metaphysics* IV is the reference to Cratylus, who 'thought that one should say nothing but just moved his finger' (1010[a]12–13). But this reference is merely incidental; Aristotle's main opponents certainly do think that it possible to say things—even contradictory things. We shall return to Cratylus in a moment.

[34] Almost certainly Arcesilaus; see LS i. 455–7, ii. 444.

3. Pyrrho and Plato

If Aristotle's discussion of the Law of Non-Contradiction proves to be unil-luminating on the question of Pyrrho's antecedents, what of the other text mentioned earlier? As we said, the 'thesis of total instability' in the *Theaetetus* is that everything is constantly changing in every respect; and Socrates criticizes it by arguing that it renders language impossible. The thesis is ascribed to some unidentified followers of Heraclitus. One thinks immediately of Cratylus, whom Aristotle presents as refusing to say anything, on the grounds that the extreme changeableness of things makes it impossi-ble to attribute any definite qualities to anything (*Met.* 1010^{a}7–15);[35] but there were no doubt other Heracliteans whose names are now lost to us. The thesis also appears to be presented as what Protagoras, with his 'man the measure' doctrine, is ultimately committed to.[36]

Nothing in our treatment of Pyrrho so far has suggested that he thought that everything was constantly *changing*. Variability may, as I argued, be at the root of the indeterminacy thesis; but there are other forms of variability besides changeability, and there is no obvious way of telling whether any particular form of variability loomed especially large in Pyrrho's thinking. Despite this apparent difference, however, Socrates' various assertions about what the extreme Heracliteans can consistently say seem to line up rather closely with Pyrrho's assertions as reported in the Aristocles passage. It is noteworthy, first, that the same term 'no more' is used here as in the Aristocles passage (*oute/oude/ouden mallon* (182e3, 4, 10)). But more important than the mere use of the term—which, as we saw in Chapter 1, can admit of numerous further implications, some of them incompatible with Pyrrho's position—is the precise character of the view employing this language. According to Socrates, the extreme Heraclitean thesis entails that nothing is any particular way any more than the opposite; this consequence is developed to the point where what we would previously have called seeing is 'no more' seeing than not-seeing, or than any other form of sense perception—and the same applies to knowledge, the main subject of the dialogue (182e).

Now, Socrates clearly does not mean to accuse the extreme Heracliteans of violating the Law of Non-Contradiction; although 'no more *P* than not-*P*' can

---

[35] See also *Met.* 987^{a}32–4, and Plato, *Cratylus* 439d–440e.

[36] This is not entirely uncontroversial, but seems to me to be clearly implied by the text. The connection between Protagoras and a Heraclitean view of reality has been drawn much earlier, when the 'man the measure' doctrine is introduced (152a–e); see also 160d–e, where the two positions are said to 'come together to the same point' (*eis t'auton sumpeptōken*). And as soon as the 'thesis of total instability' has been dismissed, the 'man the measure' doctrine is dismissed on the same grounds (183b–c). See also Day (1997). However, nothing in the current argument turns on this issue.

in some contexts be taken to imply 'both *P* and not-*P*', this is not the intention here. Socrates does say that it follows from their position that, for any question, the answer 'it is thus' and the answer 'it is not thus' are 'equally correct' (*homoiōs orthē* (183a5–6)). But to say that both answers are *equally* correct is not necessarily to say that both are correct. Rather, it is to say that both are correct to the same degree—a degree that has to be specified by means of other considerations; and it is clear from other considerations in *this* passage that the correctness of the statements 'it is thus' and 'it is not thus' will never be other than seriously defective. The constant change to which everything is subjected means, first, that 'is' is a less suitable term than 'becomes' (183a6–7), and, secondly and more crucially, that even to use the terms 'thus' (whatever specific feature that stands for on any given occasion) and 'not thus' is to attribute a fixity to things beyond what is warranted by the phenomena (183a9–b3). No pair of statements 'it is thus' and 'it is not thus' can, therefore, be said to be jointly true. Yet neither can they be said to be jointly *false*—if that is taken, as it normally would be taken, to imply that their negations are true; for that will be simply *equivalent* to saying that they are both true. The two statements—that is, *any* given pair of contradictory statements—will thus be incorrect for the reasons given, but in a sense that does *not* imply that their negations are correct; and this is precisely the point of the one form of words Socrates tentatively permits the Heracliteans to use. They may, if they wish, say ' "not at all thus", *spoken indefinitely*' (*oud'houtōs . . . apeiron legomenon* (183^{b}4–5)); that is, they may deny that something is some particular way, but *without* this carrying the implication that there is some *other*, contrary but still definite, way the thing is. The effect, then, is to refuse to attribute any definite features to anything, and to consign all definite claims about things to an ambivalent status that is neither truth nor falsehood. In other words, the effect is precisely the same as that of the form of words Pyrrho recommends that we use—namely, that each thing 'no more is than is not or both is and is not or neither is nor is not'.

In the *Theaetetus*, this consequence is presented as a *reductio* of the thesis of total instability. But it is not a *reductio* that would have impressed Pyrrho. Pyrrho is happy to insist that, at least as regards the nature of things, nothing definite can be said; indeed, the expression he recommends that we use to signal the utter indefiniteness of things might well be seen as an improvement on the obscure form of words 'not at all thus'. In order for his position to be sustainable, there has to be some other way of using language that does *not* purport to describe the real nature of things—a point not envisaged in Socrates' criticism. But, as we have seen, there is every reason to suppose that early Pyrrhonism found a way to accommodate this; it allows us to describe the *appearances* of things without restriction[37]—or, rather, with the sole

---

[37] This presumably entails that, at least at the level of appearances, there is not *constant* change in *every* respect; but this is not difficult to grant. In fact, one of the problems for the

restriction that one not confuse the application of language to appearances with its application to the real natures of things.

The consequences of the extreme Heraclitean thesis discussed in the *Theaetetus* seem, then, to have much more in common with Pyrrho's indeterminacy thesis than does the position of Aristotle's opponents in *Metaphysics* IV. Pyrrho's indeterminacy thesis may not have been inspired by the notion that everything is constantly *changing*. But, if there is a difference here, it is not, in the end, a very important one. The structure of Pyrrho's reasoning would be the same whether it was, specifically, constant change that impressed him (as it impressed the extreme Heracliteans), or some other type or types of variability. In either case, he infers that things are in their true nature indeterminate, and hence that statements of the form 'it is thus' and 'it is not thus' are 'equally correct'—but in the special sense that each of them is neither true nor false. And it is in the details of this exploration of the logic of indeterminacy (as one might call it), and of the linguistic constraints imposed by indeterminacy, that the striking parallel between Pyrrho and the *Theaetetus* passage lies.[38]

This does not, of course, prove that Pyrrho actually knew the *Theaetetus*, or any other works of Plato; I have simply suggested that Pyrrho's thought ran along lines very similar to those of Socrates' criticism of the thesis of total instability, while drawing from this train of thought a radically different moral. However, it is at least tempting to speculate at this point that Pyrrho may actually have been inspired by Plato. And this speculation becomes all the more attractive if one looks beyond the *Theaetetus*. It has often been thought that the discussion of the thesis of total instability in that dialogue has something to do with Plato's own conception of sensible things, as proposed

extreme Heraclitean view would seem to be precisely that, though things do indeed appear to undergo many kinds of change, this change does not appear to be anything like as breakneck or all-pervasive as the Heracliteans claim. As noted above, however, there is no reason to think that Pyrrho was in this respect in the Heracliteans' camp. He does say that things are in their nature 'unstable' (*astathmēta*). But 'unstable' need not be simply equivalent to 'changeable'—it might refer more generally to what I am calling the phenomenon of variability; and, in any case, to say that things are changeable is not to say that they are changing in every respect at every instant.

[38] Hippolytus (*Haer.* 1.23.2) and Philoponus (*In Ar. Cat. prooem.* 2, 7 ff.) associate Pyrrho with the Heraclitean view that reality is in flux. Both texts are historically confused; Hippolytus makes Pyrrho an Academic, and Philoponus makes Heraclitus a *student* of Pyrrho (*contra* Decleva Caizzi (DC 123, 281), who seems to understand *mathētēs* as 'teacher')—and also attributes to Heraclitus the extreme view elsewhere associated with Cratylus but *not* Heraclitus that it is not possible to step into the same river even once. Still, if my argument has been sound, this association between Pyrrho and Heraclitean views is not entirely fanciful. Pyrrho seems to have adopted a view of things as subject to extreme variability, and he may have been inspired in this in part by Plato's treatment of the Heracliteans in the *Theaetetus*—even though we need not suppose that he himself construed this variability as, specifically, susceptibility to change. (It is notable that Philoponus refers immediately afterwards to Plato's refutation of these ideas (*In Ar. Cat. prooem.* 2, 20 ff.). Decleva Caizzi (DC 281) asserts that he is thinking of the *Theaetetus*, and this may very well be correct.)

in other dialogues.[39] But leaving aside that issue for the moment, it is in any case surely correct to say that a number of other dialogues suggest a conception of sensibles as suffering from a certain kind of indeterminacy; and here too, it turns out, there is a considerable degree of overlap with Pyrrho's indeterminacy thesis.

The term 'no more' occurs elsewhere besides the *Theaetetus*, as part of a characterization of sensible things firmly endorsed by Socrates. The most conspicuous example is perhaps the end of *Republic* book V.[40] Here sensible things are said to be 'no more' beautiful than ugly, large than small, light than heavy, and so on (479a–b), because, for any such pair of opposite predicates, there are circumstances in which each of the two applies.[41] As in the *Theaetetus*, this does not mean that such things may be said to be *both* beautiful *and* ugly.[42] Rather, it is taken to show that sensible things cannot be said really to *be* either beautiful or ugly, large or small, light or heavy, and so on. Socrates asks whether any of these things '*is*, any more than it *is not*, that which one says it is' (479b9–10); and the answer, according to his interlocutor Glaucon, is in the negative. Instead, they are said to 'be double' or 'be ambiguous' (*epamphoterizein* (479c3)),[43] which is explained by saying that 'none of them can be fixedly [*pagiōs*] conceived as either being or not being or both or neither' (479c4–5). The parallel with Pyrrho's recommended four-part way of speaking in the Aristocles passage could hardly be closer. As we saw, the only possible outcome if, as that passage tells us, none of the four locutions 'is', 'is not', 'both is and is not', and 'neither is nor is not' is any more correct than any other, is that none of them is *either* true *or* false; and Plato here takes us to a precisely analogous result. In glossing the conclusion

---

[39] Some have thought that Plato is here obliquely demonstrating that, given the radical degree of instability in the sensible world, it is necessary to postulate some other, stable entities—namely, the Forms—in order for anything to make sense. See Cornford (1935); Cherniss (1936, 1957). Others have thought that Plato is here criticizing his own earlier conception of the sensible world, showing that it cannot be subject to the degree of instability he had previously supposed; see Owen (1953), endorsed by White (1976: 188 n.19).

[40] Another notable case is *Hippias Major* 289c—assuming that this is by Plato. On the question of authenticity see Woodruff (1982).

[41] There has been considerable dispute about whether the 'things' to which Socrates is referring are particular sensible *objects* (such as Helen, or a certain redwood tree) or sensible *properties* (such as the property of being brightly coloured, or 200 feet tall). For opposing views on this subject, with references to earlier literature, see Annas (1981: ch. 8, esp. 204); Fine (1990: esp. 91). For my purposes it is not necessary to resolve this question; the structural similarity that I hope to exhibit between Plato's reasoning and Pyrrho's will be just as close either way.

[42] 478d5–6 does speak of the need to find something that 'as it were both is and is not'. But the 'as it were' (*hoion*) makes clear that this is an inaccurate way of speaking; this is cleared up in the characterization just below (478e1–3)—'that which participates in both being and not being, and would not correctly be called either one purely [*eilikrines*]'.

[43] We shall see later that Timon several times uses epithets containing the elements *amphi-* or *amphotero-* to describe philosophers of whom he (at least partially) approves; the verbal similarity is, I think, no accident.

that none of the items under discussion 'is, any more than it is not' some particular way with the suggestion that these items are 'ambiguous', he indicates that none of them can straightforwardly *be* either one particular way (say, beautiful) to the exclusion of its opposite (ugly), or vice versa. But, to return again to the discussion in Chapter 1, this by itself would leave open the possibility that an object might be *both* beautiful *and* ugly, or *neither* beautiful *nor* ugly. By adding that 'none of them can be fixedly conceived as either being or not being *or both or neither*', Plato rules out these possibilities as well, and takes us to a deeper level of indeterminacy—Pyrrho's level—at which, at least as concerns its true being, the predicates 'beautiful' and 'ugly' can neither be asserted nor denied of an object, either separately or together.

One might object that the word 'fixedly' suggests that there is some *other*, less stringent sense in which one *can* say that such things 'are' or 'are not' a certain way. But this is not the route taken by Plato. Socrates immediately responds to Glaucon's statement by saying that sensible things are *between* being and not being (479c7); so, if we are to be precise, we should not say that they are either. Indeed, the implication of the whole passage is that only 'fixed' or 'pure' being is strictly speaking to count as being; hence only the Forms qualify as truly *being* a certain way, because, unlike the sensible things just discussed, Forms by definition are whatever they are *without qualification*. And here again, if my earlier reconstruction was on the right lines, we have a point of contact with Pyrrho. I suggested that Pyrrho's adoption of the indeterminacy thesis is best understood as a response to the phenomenon of variability; and, further, that the easiest way of explaining how it might have seemed to him a cogent response is to suppose that he too takes the view that, in order for something to be *by nature* a certain definite way, it must present itself that way invariably or without qualification. The difference, of course, is that Pyrrho does not think anything actually meets this standard. But with the proviso, again, that the specific *types* of variability (and invariability or unqualifiedness) with which the two authors are dealing may not be identical,[44] the standard itself seems to be essentially the same in Pyrrho and in Plato.

Instead of having Socrates and Glaucon say that sensible things may (even on some single occasion) *be* beautiful, large, light, or whatever, Plato is careful to have them use the word 'appear'. 'Of the many beautiful things', Socrates imagines himself asking his opponent, 'is there any that will not also appear ugly?', and so on; and Glaucon agrees that they are bound to 'appear' both ways (479a6–b2). The point of 'appear', in this passage of the *Republic*, is not to express doubt or caution about whether, in a specific case where one of a pair of opposite predicates (say, 'beautiful') would normally be applied, it is really *that* member of the pair that is appropriate rather than the other

---

[44] I say a little more about Plato's stance on this matter in Appendix B.

member (say, 'ugly'). Socrates is not denying that on particular occasions, or in particular respects, one may quite confidently and accurately apply the labels 'beautiful', 'large', 'light', or their opposites to things; the notion that these 'appearances' may be (in that sense)[45] *deceptive* would be simply irrelevant to his thinking at this point. The point, rather, is that, when one does so, one is not referring to how the things in question *really are*. Precisely because *each* of the labels 'beautiful' and 'ugly', 'large' and 'small', and so on is (in certain circumstances or in certain respects) appropriate to the same sensible things, one cannot truly say that they *are* either one of these opposite ways. Because of the variability of sensible things—because of their merely qualified or temporary possession of certain predicates—one can speak of these predicates only as 'appearing' to belong to these things. But to talk of their 'appearing' to belong to the things is not a way of avoiding any definite claims; rather, it is a way of making clear that one is not speaking of the *true being* of the things in question, but *only* of their temporary and contingent character on specific occasions or in specific respects.

Now here we have yet another area of overlap between Plato and the ideas I have attributed to Pyrrho. We saw that the fragments of Timon included some talk of the appearances of things, and I suggested that this could be connected with the central claims of the Aristocles passage as follows: though the true nature of things may be indeterminate, it is still quite legitimate to accept at face value the variable ways in which things strike us—to accept them not as reflecting the true natures of the things (their variability itself rules that out), but as exhibiting, quite simply, the characteristics of the things on one occasion or another, or in one respect or another. To make clear that no claim is being made as to the nature of things, we are to speak of things 'appearing' in these various ways; as in *Republic* V, 'appears' signals not a withdrawal from definite commitment, but a definite claim of a certain specific type—namely, one having to do with things' characteristics *in particular circumstances or respects*—as opposed to a claim of another type—namely, one having to do with the true nature of the things in question.

Again, there are obvious differences. First, to repeat, Plato also has the Forms, which do meet his standards for true being; indeed, he thinks it is vitally important that we have access to these Forms, if we are to achieve any kind of genuine understanding. Pyrrho, by contrast, regards the search for Forms, or any other determinate true natures in things, as a wild-goose chase (in fact, he thinks that when, and only when, one realizes this will one be able to achieve *ataraxia*); and either he, or Timon in a sympathetic extension of his ideas, declares attention to the appearances to be quite sufficient for practical purposes. Secondly, Plato never suggests that the kind of variability that

---

[45] This is not to deny that Plato (like Pyrrho) *would* see them as deceptive in so far as they masquerade as capturing the true being of the items so described.

applies to predicates such as 'beautiful', 'large,' or 'heavy' applies to all predicates whatever. Later in the *Republic*, in fact, he makes quite clear that there
are many predicates about which there is no 'ambiguity', and for which ordinary sensory experience gives us all the understanding we need; the question
whether or not something is a finger, for example, admits of a straightforward, unambiguous answer (*Rep.* 523c–d). It is only certain classes of predicates that apply 'ambiguously' to sensible things, and that therefore require
recourse to purely intelligible Forms in order for us to have a proper understanding of them. Precisely *which* classes is a question of some difficulty for
interpreters of Plato. But it is at any rate clear that Plato is not inclined to
anything like as sweeping a conception of the variability of things as the
Aristocles passage suggests that we should ascribe to Pyrrho. None the less,
if one starts with the metaphysics of the *Republic*, and subtracts the Forms,
then what one is left with is a way of thinking bearing a strong structural similarity to Pyrrho's conception of what things are like and of how one should
describe them.

There are reasons for supposing, then, that for a key portion of his philosophy Pyrrho is indebted, directly or indirectly, to Plato. Perhaps he was
acquainted with Plato's dialogues, or perhaps he came to know about the
ideas discussed in those dialogues through other sources. At any rate, if my
interpretation of the Aristocles passage is accepted, the connection between
Pyrrho's ideas and certain ideas in Plato looks too close, and too distinctive,
to be accidental;[46] and the hypothesis (which is not in itself a daring one) that
Pyrrho knew about Plato's ideas would seem to be the easiest way to explain
this. Now, I have suggested a connection between Pyrrho and the view of the

---

[46] Some of the parallels to which I have drawn attention admittedly depend on my reconstruction of the ideas *behind* the indeterminacy thesis, rather than on the Aristocles passage
itself. But the central points, with respect to both the texts of Plato on which I have focused,
have to do with parallels between those texts and ideas directly present in the Aristocles passage.
Obviously, the further parallels between ideas in Plato and ideas in my reconstruction add
weight to my conclusion only to the extent that this reconstruction is itself judged plausible.
However, these parallels actually offer some help in that direction as well; that is, they suggest
that the reconstruction—which was based in large part on considerations of theoretical simplicity—is also unobjectionable from a historical point of view. This is not circular reasoning, but
is an attempt to fill a gap in our knowledge in a way that connects as well as possible with the
evidence we do have. To return to a point from the Introduction, much of my interpretation of
Pyrrho and Pyrrhonism should be seen as an exercise in reflective equilibrium. Given the state
of the evidence, there are many issues that we cannot hope to settle with the force of demon-
stration; the question, rather, is what picture of Pyrrho, his antecedents, and his legacy fits
together, all things considered, in the best way. My reconstruction in Sect. 1 of this chapter
should be seen in this light. It is speculative, but it accounts economically for the indeterminacy
thesis, and it fits nicely with the Platonic parallel *both* in that it thereby acquires some historical credibility, *and* in that it helps to flesh out a picture of Pyrrho's relation to Plato that already
looks attractive—all of which recommends it as the best way to fill this particular gap in the
evidence. (We shall see in the next chapter that something similar is true with respect to the
parallel with Aenesidemus.)

sensible world discussed in *Republic* V (and amplified in later books, as well as in related dialogues, notably the *Phaedo* and *Symposium*), and also a connection between Pyrrho and the thesis of total instability criticized in the *Theaetetus*. But are these two pieces of the Platonic corpus themselves connected? It is not strictly necessary that we answer this question. Since Pyrrho's debt to Plato, assuming that there is one, is clearly in any case selective, it would be perfectly possible for him to be indebted to two aspects of Plato's writings whether or not they are connected, and whether or not he took them to be connected. On the other hand, it is the very *same* area of Pyrrho's philosophy—the indeterminacy thesis and its immediate ramifications—that, as I have argued, it is plausible to see as indebted, and in closely related ways, to these two parts of Plato's work; and, if that is correct, it suggests that Pyrrho, at least, *did* consider them to be themselves closely related to one another. Of course, that does not mean that they are in fact connected in Plato's own thinking. But it would clearly be better for Pyrrho's philosophical reputation if his indebtedness to Plato—assuming that I am right that there is indebtedness—did not involve a misunderstanding.

The question is a disputed one, and the matter is too complicated, and too tangential, to be handled in the main body of the text; I discuss it briefly in Appendix B. My conclusion is that a decent case can be made for saying that the *Theaetetus* passage and the ideas about sensible things considered in *Republic* V and elsewhere are indeed connected in Plato's thought; the *Theaetetus* passage may plausibly be understood as partly an exercise in self-criticism. If this is right, then Pyrrho's apparent indebtedness, in the same context, to the ideas in both the *Theaetetus* passage and the end of *Republic* V need not be simply fortuitous, and need not betoken any gross misunderstanding of Plato, on his or anyone else's part. However, to repeat, it is not really important that we settle this question. The important point for our purposes is not the internal connection, or lack of it, between different parts of Plato's writings, but the connection between Plato and Pyrrho, which may be summed up as follows. Pyrrho accepts an extreme view of the indeterminacy of things, as far as their true natures are concerned; and it is plausible to see this view as deriving from an emphasis on the phenomenon of variability. To what extent this variability consisted, for Pyrrho, in changeability is not clear, though there is no reason why it should not have been one important component. If we ask what earlier ideas may have inspired him, one probable answer seems to be a cluster of ideas about sensible things, revealed especially in these two passages of Plato but also in others—ideas that Plato himself gives the impression of accepting, in some version, but of rejecting as incoherent if developed too far in certain directions. Pyrrho, by contrast, sees no danger in an extreme version of these ideas. But then, despite the parallels I have been emphasizing, it is surely in any case obvious that the philosophical temperaments of the two were extremely different.

If Pyrrho has an important forerunner in Plato, one might expect Timon's verdict on Plato in the *Silloi* to be at least in part a positive one. What we find is in fact more negative than positive, but not to such a degree as to put in doubt the conclusions just argued for. Plato is referred to directly in three fragments, of which two are clearly critical; and in a fourth we are told by our source, Sextus (*M* 7.10), that Timon is criticizing Plato for misrepresenting Socrates. Several of these fragments, and two others that do not specifically mention Plato, also make puns with his name, using forms or cognates of the verb *plattō*, 'fabricate', the adjective *platus*, 'broad', and perhaps (if this is the correct text) *platistakos*, the name of a fish.[47] However, of the three fragments that specifically mention Plato, one (30) expresses clear admiration for Plato's style; another (19) talks of Plato's 'fabricated wonders' (*peplasmena thaumata*), which, though accusing him of manufacturing fictions, also acknowledges that these fictions have a certain appeal; and even a third (54), which accuses him of plagiarizing the *Timaeus*, begins 'You too, Plato'—which can be (even if it does not have to be) read as expressing surprise that someone of Plato's calibre would resort to such measures (compare Julius Caesar's 'Et tu, Brute?').[48] The tenor of Timon's remarks about Plato is, then, at least consistent with the suggestion that Pyrrho adopted one element of Plato's metaphysical scheme. As we said, Pyrrho would clearly have had nothing to do with Platonic Forms—or with the physical theorizing of the *Timaeus*; these would indeed qualify, from his point of view, as 'fabricated wonders', and would make quite understandable Timon's scorn and sarcasm. But this in no way excludes the possibility that Pyrrho might have been indebted to Plato in certain other respects.[49]

4. *Pyrrho and the Eleatics*

Another set of philosophers on whom Timon bestows some favourable verdicts is the Eleatics. This fits nicely with the picture I have just been developing,

---

[47] See frs. 19, 20, 30, 34, 54, 62 in di Marco (1989). (For the remainder of this chapter I shall refer to the fragments of the *Silloi* by the numbers in di Marco's edition.)

[48] For further development of these points, see the commentary of di Marco (1989) on these fragments, also his introduction, p. 37.

[49] Now that we have introduced Timon's *Silloi* into the story, it might be wondered whether he has anything to say about a Heraclitean position such as that criticized in the *Theaetetus* passage. The answer is that there is nothing in the surviving fragments that bears upon this issue. Heraclitus is referred to in just one fragment of the *Silloi* (fr. 43 di Marco), which makes fun of his characteristic style and attitude; he is described as a 'screamer' (*kokkustēs*), a 'reviler of the mob' (*ochloloidoros*), and as 'enigmatic' (*ainiktēs*). But this is clearly unhelpful for our purposes; and there are no fragments referring to Cratylus or any other extremist Heracliteans.

since the Eleatics' view of sensibles is clearly an ancestor of Plato's.[50] Timon describes Parmenides as 'high-minded' (*megalophrōn*) and 'not full of opinions' (*ou poludoxon*), and says that he 'elevated our thought-processes from the deception of appearance'.[51] That a follower of Pyrrho would approve of Parmenides' rejection of opinion is understandable; but the reference to appearance is more subtle. What Parmenides does, by removing the operations of the intellect from the domain of appearances, is to prevent us from taking the appearances as a guide to the true nature of things. This is how appearances 'deceive'; if one is not careful, one is liable to assume that things are, in their true natures,[52] as they appear to be—a notion accepted neither by Parmenides nor, as we have frequently observed, by Pyrrho.

This does not mean that we should not in *any* circumstances be guided by appearances. We have seen that early Pyrrhonism included a willingness to rely on appearances in the ordinary course of life; and the attention given to the Way of Opinion in Parmenides' poem has often been taken to suggest that he also thought some kind of acceptance of the appearances, short of taking them as revealing true reality, was inevitable. But such an agreement on the way in which, and the extent to which, appearances are deceptive does not, of course, imply that the views of Pyrrho and Parmenides about the true nature of things also overlapped. An Eleatic conception of reality would have been just as profoundly opposed to Pyrrho's own conception as Platonic Forms. What Timon is doing, then, is singling out Parmenides for praise on certain

---

[50] The connection between Parmenides and Plato, on the issues with which we have been concerned, is even closer than usually thought, according to the recent argument of Curd (1998). According to Curd, Parmenides was not a numerical monist, but what she calls a 'predicational monist'; that is, he thinks that the real nature of a thing must consist of just one predicate, a predicate that belongs to the thing unqualifiedly. Parmenides' real entities thus become very like Platonic Forms—a connection that is explored in the final section of the book (ch. VI, sect. 2, entitled 'The Last Presocratic: Plato and the Legacy of Parmenides'). If so, of course, they also become much closer to what, according to my reconstruction in Sect. 1, Pyrrho thinks determinate real natures *would* have to be like, if there were any. However, I will not pursue these intriguing possibilities any further, since it is doubtful that this is the understanding of Parmenides that was current in the time of Pyrrho and Timon—see below.

[51] Fr. 44 di Marco. I accept Long and Sedley's emendation *ek* in the second line for the MSS *epi* (LS 3H; see also Long (1978: n. 31)). Di Marco's attempt to salvage *epi* is tortuous and unconvincing; the most serious problem is that he is forced to read *nōseis*, 'thought-processes', as referring not to the operations of the intellect, but to ordinary opinions influenced by the senses. It is true that in other authors, such as Homer, *noein* and cognates need not be restricted to intellectual activity independent of the senses. But in Parmenides' own writing, to which Timon is obviously paying attention at this point, the distinction between *nous* and the senses is fundamental.

[52] On the importance in Parmenides of the concept of the *nature* of a thing, see Curd (1998: esp. ch. 1, sect. 2); again (cf. above, n. 50), if Curd is right, Parmenides is assimilated to Pyrrho (and Plato) even more closely than one might have suspected. But, if not, the contrast in Parmenides between what truly is, and what we are usually inclined to think, still clearly bears more than a passing resemblance to Pyrrho's contrast between the true nature of things and the deliverances of opinion.

important counts; we need not take him to be suggesting that Parmenides' views corresponded with Pyrrho's in every respect.[53]

Similarly, Melissus is praised for being 'above many illusions [*phantasmōn*] and yielding to few' (fr. 45 di Marco). This is not unqualified praise, since it does entail that Melissus went wrong in certain respects. But again, among the many 'illusions' resisted by Melissus will surely have been those stemming from a thoughtless trust in appearances as revealing ultimate reality—something that a long fragment of Melissus warns us against doing.[54] And Zeno is praised in the same fragment for being 'double-tongued' (*amphoteroglōssos*). Not all of the numerous ancient authors who cite this term seem to have realized that it was a term of praise.[55] However, this is clear from the use of the phrases 'great strength' (*mega sthenos*) and 'no weakling' (*ouk alapadnon*)—phrases applied by Homer to heroes[56]—in connection with Zeno in the same context; literally, the passage reads 'the non-weak great strength of double-tongued Zeno', so that the quality of being 'double-tongued' is an inextricable aspect of the heroic character that is being attributed to him.

The point of calling Zeno 'double-tongued' is clearly that many of his paradoxes argued for two opposing conclusions—that things are both finite and infinite in number, for example, or both infinitely large and infinitely small. The reason why Timon would see this as a good point is also not hard to understand; it discourages a view of things—or at least, of the ordinary things perceived by the senses—as fixed and determinate in nature. This is not to suggest that Pyrrho or Timon would have endorsed a view of the nature of things according to which they actually do possess both members of some pair of contradictory features; as we saw in Section 2, there is no reason to suppose that Pyrrho was interested in denying the Law of Non-Contradiction. But neither, of course, was this Zeno's own purpose in propounding the paradoxes. Several views about this question are possible, but the view by which Timon is likely to have been influenced is the one that appears most prominently at the opening of Plato's *Parmenides*.[57] According to this account, the

---

[53] On Timon's use of Parmenidean language in his description of Pyrrho himself, see Ch. 2 n. 41.

[54] DK 30B8. The parallel is noted by LS ii. 16, and Long (1978: n. 32).

[55] See the lengthy list in di Marco (1989: *ad loc.*). In particular, Elias, *In Ar. Cat.* 109, 6 ff. says that the term refers to the fact that Zeno said one thing and thought another—presumably a feature Elias would both himself regard as undesirable and assume that Timon would regard as undesirable. Proclus seems to have a clearer understanding of the fragment; he sees that the lines express admiration of Zeno, and at least does not regard the epithet 'double-tongued' as detracting from this (*In Pl. Parm.* 632, 13 ff.; 684, 26 f.). Di Marco himself seems to have a less than complete grasp of the significance of the term; he claims that it reflects an ambivalence about Zeno on Timon's part (1989: 213, cf. 35).

[56] For the Homeric parallels, see again di Marco (1989: *ad loc.*).

[57] For another view of this (and discussion of further views), see Curd (1998: ch. IV, sect.

purpose of the paradoxes was to support the Eleatic view of reality as unchanging and numerically one; the paradoxes are prefaced by a conditional—the paradoxical conclusions hold 'if there are many things'—and the 'double-tongued' conclusions are meant to demonstrate the falsehood of this antecedent. Again, Timon was no devotee of Eleatic monism[58]—quite the opposite, as we shall see in the next section. But an obvious corollary of the monistic conclusion is that the ordinary world around us, which appears to consist of a plurality of things in motion, resists any coherent account being given of it; and such immunity to any coherent account is precisely the effect of Pyrrho's indeterminacy thesis as well. As with the other Eleatics, Timon's sketch emphasizes the points of sympathy, as he sees them, between Zeno and Pyrrho's outlook. They may be opposed to one another on crucial issues; but just as importantly—or so Timon seems, not unreasonably, to have viewed the matter—they share a suspicion of the way things appear, and a disdain for most theoretical opinions other than their own, as based on fundamental misunderstandings.

5. Pyrrho and Xenophanes

I have been developing an account of Pyrrho as heir to a conception of the world around us that is to be found in Plato and, more distantly, in the Eleatics; to put it very crudely indeed, Pyrrho's indeterminacy thesis is, as it were, Plato without the Forms. But now, having begun to examine Timon's thumbnail sketches of other philosophers, we may seem to be faced with an obstacle. Several fragments from the *Silloi* appear to offer qualified praise of philosophers who are now commonly regarded as noteworthy in large part because of their sceptical epistemologies; and this may seem to run counter to the picture I have just laid out—as well as, more generally, to my account of the Aristocles passage, and indeed of Pyrrho's whole philosophy, as contrasting with later Pyrrhonism in its emphasis on metaphysical concerns rather than epistemological ones. The matter therefore needs further consideration.

The most obvious case of this kind is Xenophanes, who occupied a central role in the *Silloi*. Sextus says (*PH* 1.224) that Timon dedicated the work to Xenophanes. More specific information is offered by Diogenes Laertius

4). It should also be noted that Curd interprets both Zeno and Melissus as differing on some important points with Parmenides. Again, since Timon would probably not have agreed, we need not pursue this matter.

[58] Here I mean, of course, Eleatic monism as described in the *Parmenides*, and as traditionally understood—though presumably, in fact, Timon would not have accepted that anything met Parmenides' standards for true being *however* those standards are understood.

(9.111), who says that the work consisted of three books; the first book was a monologue by Timon himself, and in the second and third he represented himself as questioning and receiving answers from Xenophanes about a number of philosophers. Clearly Xenophanes was portrayed as a figure of special authority. Part of the reason for this was no doubt that Xenophanes was also the author of satirical verses with philosophical content. Later sources even give *Silloi* as the title of a poem by Xenophanes—a title shared by no one else besides Timon; however, it is difficult to tell whether this was a title assigned to the poem by Xenophanes himself (or by someone else prior to Timon's own day), or whether the title was later applied to Xenophanes' poem on the basis of the association with Timon.[59] But, in any case, Xenophanes could plausibly be seen as the originator of the genre in which Timon was writing. This would surely not have been enough, though, for Timon to have given him such an important role if his philosophy had seemed to Timon to be entirely at odds with Pyrrho's; there must have been some perception of philosophical kinship as well. And this is borne out by one of the two surviving fragments of the *Silloi* dealing with Xenophanes (quoted by Sextus, *PH* 1.224, fr. 60 di Marco), where he is described as *hupatuphos*, 'partly free from *tuphos*'; *tuphos*, a term widely used in Cynic diatribe, and applied by Timon to Zeno of Citium (DL 7.15, fr. 38 di Marco), can mean 'conceit', 'vanity', or 'humbug'.[60] The only one who is fully 'free from *tuphos*' is Pyrrho;[61] to call someone 'partly free from *tuphos*' is, then, already high praise from Timon, compared with his verdicts on most other philosophers. But what, more precisely, is the basis for this partly favourable judgement?

The answer that has usually been given is that Xenophanes is the earliest philosopher whom it is reasonable to see as anticipating the sceptical outlook. In a well-known fragment (DK 21B34), quoted by Sextus in his discussion of the criterion of truth (*M* 7.49), Xenophanes appears to deny the possibility of knowledge, and to hold, instead, that all we can have is belief (*dokos*). Another fragment suggests worries about the relativity of sense perception: 'If god had not created yellow honey, [people] would say that figs were far sweeter' (DK 21B38). On the basis of these remarks, Xenophanes has often been interpreted as the first proponent of some form of philosophical scepticism; and this, it has been alleged, is why Timon finds his philosophy somewhat, even if not wholly, congenial.[62]

---

[59] For views on this question, with reference to further treatments, see Long (1978: esp. 77), and di Marco (1989: 17 ff.).

[60] See LSJ, and, on the use of the term by Cynics and others, Decleva Caizzi (1980), also Long (1978: 74–5).

[61] DC T58 (=LS 2B, fr. 9 di Marco), l. 1; this fragment was translated and discussed in the previous chapter (see Sects. 2 and 3, where it was referred to as fragment A).

[62] For this view, see e.g. Long (1978: 77–78); di Marco (1989: 38); and implicitly Barnes (1982*b*: 137–8).

But there are at least three problems with this view. Let us suppose, to begin with, that Xenophanes' position does indeed deserve the label 'scepticism'. If so, it was a scepticism that consisted in *denying* the possibility of knowledge in some domain. This, of course, is the type of position that nowadays tends to be called scepticism. But it is not what the later Pyrrhonists, at any rate, would have recognized as scepticism. For Sextus, scepticism consists in suspension of judgement (on any subject, including the question whether knowledge is possible) brought about by the assembling of equally convincing opposed arguments or impressions on the subject in question; and his very first point in *Outlines of Pyrrhonism* (1.1–3) is that scepticism is to be *distinguished* from two other positions, one of which is the view that knowledge is impossible. When he quotes the famous fragment, Sextus does not claim Xenophanes as a fellow-sceptic.[63] Rather, he cites it as evidence that Xenophanes denied that there is any criterion of truth—which is not Sextus' own position on the matter; on this question, as on any other, Sextus himself suspends judgement. And elsewhere he explicitly denies that Xenophanes is a sceptic (*PH* 1.223–5). So, even if, contrary to my interpretation, Pyrrho and Timon did adhere to a sceptical outlook of the same general type as Sextus, it does not look as if they would have had any good reason to think of Xenophanes' sceptical fragments as expressing ideas akin to their own.[64]

One might reply that Pyrrho and Timon would no doubt not have been so sophisticated, or so alert to the risk of self-refutation, as Sextus. Sextus may

---

[63] As suggested by Barnes (1982*b*: 138), and Annas and Barnes (1994: 59 n. 247). Sextus does quote the same fragment two more times in the same work. At *M* 7.110 he mentions that others have interpreted the fragment as expressing a less pessimistic view (in fact, a view similar to the one I propose in the next paragraph in the main text); but clearly this is not relevant to the question of his own understanding of Xenophanes. And at *M* 8.326 he quotes it in support of his own argument for the conclusion that proof is something 'non-evident'—a conclusion that plays a role in his subsequent argument to the effect that there is no such thing as proof. But this argument, as he makes clear at the end of the book (*M* 8.476–7), is itself not one that he personally endorses; it is brought in to provide a counterbalance to the Dogmatists' arguments in favour of the existence of proof, the intended result being, as always, suspension of judgement.

[64] Diogenes Laertius (9.72) does mention the opinion that Xenophanes was a sceptic as one that had been held (on the basis of the same well-known fragment, part of which he quotes) by 'some people' (*enioi* (9.71)). But we do not need to assume that these 'some people' were themselves sceptics. The passage on the alleged forerunners of scepticism begins *tautēs de tēs haireseōs enioi phasin Homēron katarxai* (9.71), which is far more naturally translated 'Some people [i.e. unidentified people] say that Homer began this school', with *tautēs tēs haireseōs* the object of *katarxai*, than 'Some [members] of this school [i.e. the sceptical school] say that Homer began [it]'. Galen *In Hipp. de off. med. comm.* (18b.658K) does claim that the Pyrrhonists traced back their school *eis palaiotatous andras*. But it is not clear who these Pyrrhonists are; Sextus, in his discussion at the end of *PH* 1 of the various philosophies that had been thought similar to Pyrrhonism, is extremely resistant to doing what Galen describes (unless Pyrrho and Timon themselves qualify, from Galen's point of view, as *palaiotatoi*.) In any case, neither Diogenes nor Galen provides any support for the notion that *Timon* thought of Xenophanes as a sceptic.

refuse to assert that knowledge is impossible, but Pyrrho and Timon could very well have been willing to do so; indeed, to return to the beginning of the first chapter, this *was* in effect what they did according to the epistemological reading of the Aristocles passage. If so, it would not be at all surprising for them to have associated themselves with Xenophanes' denial of the possibility of knowledge. But now, the second difficulty is that it is actually by no means clear that Xenophanes' 'scepticism' goes deep enough to motivate such an association. The famous fragment does indeed deny that knowledge is possible. But the knowledge that is beyond our reach is explicitly said to be 'about the gods and what I say about all things'—that is, about the gods and about cosmology (the two main subjects of his own theoretical enquiries);[65] this leaves it quite open that knowledge about, say, everyday mundane matters might be perfectly attainable. Besides, there is no indication that Xenophanes thought that belief as such was suspect; he might, for example, have held that some beliefs, while admittedly falling short of knowledge, are none the less better justified than others. In fact, another fragment, which appears to sum up some set of conclusions, reads 'Let these things be believed [*dedoxastho*] as like the truth' (DK 21B35); this appears precisely to assume that it is quite acceptable to adopt beliefs, despite the fact that they fall short of knowledge, provided one recognizes their limited status.[66] This would hardly have been acceptable to the Pyrrho who, according to numerous testimonia, held that opinions (*doxai*) were to be mistrusted and avoided.

But it is the third difficulty that is perhaps the most significant. This is that the specific point for which Timon expresses his highly qualified approval of Xenophanes has nothing to do with his position on knowledge. Apparently Xenophanes is commendable, in Timon's eyes, and deserving of the label 'partly free from *tuphos*', in so far as he was a 'mocker of Homeric deception'; but he is also said to have 'fashioned a god apart from humanity, equal on all sides, unblemished, more thoughtful than thought'.[67] This latter point is evidently cause for criticism. For in the other fragment on Xenophanes, quoted by Sextus immediately before (*PH* 1.224, fr. 59 di Marco), Xenophanes is portrayed as the speaker, and as engaging in self-criticism on the grounds that he believed that the whole of reality formed a single, uniform nature. Timon thus interprets Xenophanes as a radical monist and

---

[65] On the term 'all things' as referring specifically to scientific or cosmological matters, see Lesher (1992: 167–8). (This appears to represent a change of view from Lesher 1978.) More generally, see Lesher's entire discussion of this fragment (1992: 156–69); also Barnes (1982*b*: 139–40), who cites close parallels from the Hippocratic treatise *On Ancient Medicine* in support of a similar reading of Xenophanes' sceptical-sounding fragments.

[66] See Lesher (1992: 170–6).

[67] The final line of the fragment is incomplete; metrical considerations show that something must have been lost either before or after the word 'unblemished' (*askēthē*). For the various supplements that have been proposed, see di Marco (1989: 96). None of these, however, adds importantly to the sense, and I have not included any of them in my translation.

proto-Eleatic,[68] and this must be on the basis of his positive theological remarks, some of which do have an Eleatic ring; this god is said to be motionless, and to do everything 'as a whole' (DK 21B26, 21B24). Xenophanes, on this view, identifies his one unchanging god with the whole of reality—an interpretation for which there is no clear support in the surviving fragments, though it was a common interpretation from Aristotle onwards,[69] and is shared by Sextus in his comments on the fragments he has quoted (*PH* 1.225). Xenophanes is only partly free from *tuphos*, then, because he has an objectionable positive view about the divine reality; so it must be solely the other point—namely, his criticism of Homer—that in Timon's eyes merits partial admiration. But now, the juxtaposition of these two points in the fragment suggests what is in any case likely enough—that the specific 'deceptions' in Homer that Xenophanes is being praised for denouncing also have to do with the gods. One of the things for which Xenophanes was best known was his criticism of the traditional view of the gods as anthropomorphic and morally imperfect (DK 21B11–16). And one of the numerous fragments of Xenophanes on this topic (DK 21B11) attacks Homer and Hesiod by name for portraying the gods themselves as engaging in deception (*apateuein*), alongside various other typically human faults.[70] It is at least quite possible that Timon's coinage *Homērapatēs*, which I have translated 'of Homeric deception', was inspired by this very passage of Xenophanes. In any case, given that it is because of his criticism of Homer that Timon expresses approval of Xenophanes, there is no reason to think that this approval has anything at all to do with a view about knowledge, sceptical or otherwise.

The other fragment, where Xenophanes criticizes himself for having held a monistic position, also shows him expressing regret at failing to be *amphoterobleptos*—that is, for failing to 'look both ways'. Again, as in the case of Zeno, a word containing the element *amphotero-*, 'both' or 'double', is used to signal a quality deemed desirable by Timon. Now this term, too, has been read as indicating that Timon favours a sceptical outlook resembling that of later Pyrrhonism[71] (though in this case, of course, Xenophanes is not being praised for anticipating this outlook—quite the reverse); the desirable activity of 'looking both ways' is interpreted as the activity of assembling or

[68] Again I assume a traditional interpretation of the Eleatic position, because this is clearly what Timon is assuming; cf. above, nn. 50, 57, 58.

[69] Aristotle subscribes to it somewhat hesitantly at *Met.* 986^{b}10–27; the pseudo-Aristotelian *On Melissus, Xenophanes and Gorgias* adopts it wholesale. For Xenophanes as the starting point of the Eleatic school, see also Cicero, *Acad.* 2.129.

[70] Another fragment (B12) is said by Sextus, our source, to be talking about Homer and Hesiod (*M* 1.289), though they are not actually named in the lines he quotes.

[71] By Long (1978: 78) and di Marco (1989: 247). These are among the *same* authors who think that Timon approves of Xenophanes because of his sceptical tendencies, as revealed especially in the fragment on the impossibility of knowledge; there is at least a potential inconsistency in their also claiming that Timon has Xenophanes criticize himself for *not* being sceptical.

concentrating on opposing arguments, in the manner of Sextus, with a view to inducing suspension of judgement. But there is no need to read the term 'looking both ways' in this fashion. It is precisely because of his monism that Xenophanes accuses himself of not 'looking both ways'. This *might* be on the grounds that he failed to consider the arguments tending to undermine monism, as well as those tending to support it—in other words, that he failed to take into account equally powerful opposing arguments. But it might just as well be simply on the grounds that he viewed reality as single, uniform, and unchanging, rather than attending to the two-sidedness of everything. According to the indeterminacy thesis that I have argued that Pyrrho held, things have no stable and definite natures; and I have suggested that he held this view on the basis of the fact that things strike us in multiple and conflicting ways. In a certain sense, monism is the polar opposite of the indeterminacy thesis; is it not merely the case that *each* of the many things in the universe has a single definite nature—the universe as a *whole* is single, and *this* unitary item has a fixed and definite nature. 'Looking both ways', in the sense of attending to the variegated character in which things present themselves to us, would be precisely the first step needed to drive someone out of the demented thesis (as Timon would see it) of monism, and towards the indeterminacy thesis.

In the same passage Xenophanes is pictured as regretting the fact that he was devoid 'of all *skeptosunē*'; the text here is corrupt, but *skeptosunē* is clearly something he wishes he had attained.[72] Does *skeptosunē* here mean 'scepticism', as that term was understood by the later Pyrrhonists? It is probable that Sextus thought so. For he introduces Timon's lines on Xenophanes in support of his claim that someone who is dogmatic on just one point qualifies as a dogmatist and not as a sceptic (*PH* 1.223). The fragments show Xenophanes subscribing to monism, and this one point is sufficient to disqualify him from scepticism; this is what Sextus interprets Timon to be saying. Presumably, then, Sextus took *skeptosunē* to mean 'scepticism'.[73] However, we do not have to follow him. *Skeptikos*, 'enquirer', is a label for the later Pyrrhonists; the first person clearly to use the term in this way is Philo of Alexandria, several centuries after Timon.[74] There is no reason to suppose that in Timon's day 'scepticism' was already a technical term, designating the specific type of 'enquiry' engaged in by Pyrrhonists.[75] *Skeptosunē* here can very well mean simply 'careful consideration'; Xenophanes failed to

[72] The manuscripts read *apenthēristos hapasēs skeptosunēs*. Bergk's emendation *amenthēristos* has been, as far as I know, universally accepted, yielding the sense 'heedless of all *skeptosunē*'.

[73] He is followed in this by Bury, his translator in the Loeb series.

[74] *Congr.* 52; *Fug.* 209; *QG* 3.33; and for discussion see Tarrant (1985: 23–6). As Tarrant emphasizes, Philo elsewhere uses *skeptikos* in its original broad sense, without meaning to identify a specific group of philosophers.

[75] As supposed by Mansfeld (1987: 295). For the contrary view, see di Marco (1989: 248); also Spinelli (2000).

'look both ways', and so ended up with the ill-considered hypothesis of monism. In summary, there is nothing in the fragments of Timon relating to Xenophanes suggesting that his attitudes towards him, positive or negative, have anything to do with Xenophanes' epistemological ideas, sceptical or not.

6. *Pyrrho and Protagoras*

Another thinker who is singled out by Timon on account of his view about the gods is Protagoras. Protagoras was well known for the agnostic statement about the existence and the nature of the gods with which he opened his book *On the Gods*;[76] and, in contrast to most other ancient commentators, Timon singles out Protagoras for praise on this count (quoted in Sextus, *M* 9.57, fr. 5 di Marco). Protagoras is called 'not unclear of voice nor without vision or versatility', and is cited as having written 'that he did not know and could not observe what any of the gods are like and whether there are any,[77] keeping all guard on his reasonableness'[78]—even in the face of book-burnings and pros-ecutions. Here, then, unlike in Xenophanes' case, the point is in some sense epistemological; and, not surprisingly, this is sometimes interpreted as mark-ing Timon's approval of a sceptical or suspensive attitude similar to what we find in Sextus.[79] This interpretation is at least not subject to one of the objec-tions raised just now in the case of Xenophanes. Protagoras does not say that *it cannot be known* whether there are gods or what they are like—which by later Pyrrhonist standards would be negative dogmatism, not scepticism; he

---

[76] The statement is quoted in its fullest form in DL 9.51, and partially in (among others) Sextus, *M* 9.56 and Eusebius, *Praep. evang.* XIV.3.7. It is referred to as early as Plato (*Tht.* 162d6–e2), and continues to be referred to for many centuries; see e.g. Cicero, *Nat. d.* 1.2, 63, 117; Philostratus, *Vit. soph.* 1.10, 2. It has sometimes been wondered how a book about the gods could *begin* with such a forthright statement of agnosticism. The most likely answer would seem to be that the book went on to deal with such questions as the origins, and the socially benefi-cial functions, of religious belief—topics that we know to have interested other Sophists. On this see Guthrie (1971: 234–5); Kerferd (1981: 167–9).

[77] With most editors, I follow Bekker's conjecture *ei tines* for the MSS *hoi tines*, 'whoever they are'. The latter would be somewhat remote from any of the quoted versions of Protagoras' sentence, and would also add little to 'what any of the gods are like', whereas 'whether there are any' conforms to at least one possible interpretation of Protagoras' *hōs eisin outh' hōs ouk eisin*. On the question whether Protagoras did in fact mean here to deny knowledge of the *exis-tence* of the gods (as has usually been assumed in both ancient and modern times), see Kerferd (1981: 165–7). Kerferd oddly refers to the fragment of Timon as a 'hostile parody' (p. 167).

[78] 'Reasonableness' is a translation of *epieikeia*. This word is regularly used in ethical contexts, and may there be translated by 'fairness', 'equity', 'decency', and related terms. But the related adjective *epieikēs* is also used of statements or arguments, and there it means 'reasonable' or 'plausible' (e.g. Thuc. 3.9; Pl. *Tim.* 67d2; *Apol.* 34d2); this seems the most likely connotation of the noun in the present context.

[79] So di Marco (1989: 36), and implicitly Long (1978: 78–9).

merely says that *he* does not know this. Nevertheless, we should not assume that this fragment, either, supports an understanding of early Pyrrhonism as advocating a general suspension of judgement, or as dominated by epistemological concerns.

First, it may be that the important point for Timon is not so much Protagoras' agnostic attitude *per se* as his freedom from the constraints of ordinary opinion. Ordinary opinions about the gods were shaped by the 'Homeric deception' that he elsewhere praises Xenophanes for mocking; in declaring that he does not know about the gods, Protagoras is expressing his mistrust of these opinions. A mistrust of opinions—which must surely include, even if it is not restricted to, everyday non-philosophical opinions[80]—is just what the Aristocles passage recommends; so whatever Timon might think of other things that Protagoras said, or even of agnosticism itself, he would have good reason for approving of Protagoras on this score. Secondly, we have no definite evidence concerning the early Pyrrhonists' own theological attitudes;[81] and it is not impossible that, on this specific subject, Pyrrho and Timon were themselves undecided. Pyrrho asserted that things are in their nature indeterminate. But, while we have seen that the scope of the 'things' to which the indeterminacy thesis is intended to apply is clearly very broad, it is not obvious that the thesis admits of no exceptions whatever. Whether it was thought to apply to the gods, in particular, might depend on the extent to which the gods were conceived of as part of nature (*phusis*); and this is an issue on which Greek philosophers differ considerably. On many conceptions the divine is in some sense embodied in the world with which we are familiar, but on many others (such as, for example, Xenophanes') God is detached from the rest of nature, and not subject to its laws or constraints— even if exerting important influences on it. So it might well have seemed to Pyrrho and Timon an open question whether, in declaring that the nature of things is indeterminate, they had captured the whole truth about the gods; the 'things' that comprise the ordinary world around us might be indeterminate in their nature, but a God or gods might none the less exist in some other realm. Hence, on the particular issue of the existence and nature of the gods, an agnostic attitude might well seem the most sensible—especially since, if the

---

[80] On this, see again Ch. 1, Sect. 2. I argue there that 'opinion', in the usage of early Pyrrhonism, is best understood as encompassing both everyday opinions and the opinions of cosmologists. Most of the cosmologies prior to Protagoras include opinions about the divine; these too, then, will be among the opinions Protagoras can be credited with mistrusting.

[81] Some scholars have ascribed positive theological views to Pyrrho on the basis of the fragment about the 'nature of the divine and the good' (LS 2E; DC T62). See esp. Reale (1981: 309 ff., 324–5). However, as I argued in the previous chapter, there is no good reason to take this fragment as summarizing the views of Pyrrho, and strong reasons not to do so. On the other hand, Conche (1994: chs. X.1, XIII) argues, largely on the basis of the Aristocles passage, that there is no room for any positive conception of the divine in Pyrrho's philosophy, and supposes that he was in a certain sense an atheist. But this is too hasty, for reasons that I explain below.

nature of 'things' is indeterminate, the prospects for inferring anything at all about the gods (including whether there are any) on the basis of our interactions with these 'things' would be dim indeed. And if so, of course, Timon would naturally see an ally (and a rare one) in Protagoras. I do not propose this as anything more than a possibility. My point is simply that there are other ways of reading this fragment, the context of which is unknown to us, than as implying approval of the kind of global epistemological caution characteristic of later Pyrrhonism.

There is no reason to suppose that Timon's approval of Protagoras extended beyond his remark about the gods. In another fragment (quoted in DL 9.52, fr. 47 di Marco) Protagoras is described as 'skilled in contentiousness' (*erizemenai eu eidōs*); as we saw in Chapter 2, Timon considers one of the most striking and praiseworthy traits of Pyrrho, and also of his pupil Philo, to be precisely their avoidance of verbal 'contests' of the sort that the Sophists were renowned for.[82] And, even in the fragment concerning his view of the gods, Protagoras is referred to as a 'sophist'. In the *Silloi* the term is not limited to the group of thinkers we now refer to as the Sophists, but appears to cover any kind of purveyor of theoretical ideas; however, it is clearly a term of abuse, as is apparent from what, according to Diogenes Laertius (9.112), was the very first line of the poem: 'Tell me now, all you busybody sophists.'[83] As we noted earlier, Protagoras' 'man the measure' doctrine would have had no attractions for Pyrrho and Timon, since, however precisely it is interpreted,[84] it has the consequence that all our sensations are purely and simply *correct*. Things are however they appear to any given perceiver, and that is all there is to be said; whatever exactly the 'are' amounts to here, there is clearly no room for a level at which the truth of appearances can be doubted or denied. Mistrust of our sensations and opinions, such as Pyrrho is reported as advocating in the Aristocles passage, thus takes us in precisely the opposite direction from that of Protagoras.[85] In short, Timon's

---

[82] Timon's judgement of other Sophists, to the extent that it is discernible from the surviving fragments, seems similarly negative. Prodicus is described (Athenaeus 406e, fr. 18 di Marco) as a 'money-grabbing discourser on Hours' (*labarguros hōrologētēs* (*Hours* was the title of one of Prodicus' books)); and Antisthenes, whom some classify with the Sophists, is dismissed with the label 'all-spawning chatterbox' (*pantophuē phledona* (quoted in DL 6.18)). Whatever the Sophists' influence on the later development of Pyrrhonism—and that there is some such influence has recently been argued by Striker (1996: esp. 18–21)—Timon evidently does not see them as kindred spirits.

[83] LS's translation (3A), which I cannot improve on. Another pejorative use of 'sophist' occurred in a fragment of Timon discussed in Ch. 2, Sects 2 and 3 (it was listed there as fragment B).

[84] For differing views on this, see again the works cited above, n. 27; also Fine (1996).

[85] This is true despite the fact that both Pyrrho's indeterminacy thesis and Protagoras' 'man the measure' doctrine seem to be responses to the kinds of phenomena I have grouped under the label 'variability'; such phenomena can and did inspire many different and incompatible responses, and this is just one example. There is also no inconsistency in saying *both* that Pyrrho

favourable attitude towards Protagoras seems to be strictly limited; and the precise significance of the one favourable point he does make about him is not obvious. Again, we have found no good reason to revise our understanding of early Pyrrhonism.

7. *Pyrrho and Democritus*

The sources also indicate a connection between Pyrrho and the atomists; and this too may be thought to reopen the question as to whether Pyrrho's thinking ran fundamentally along epistemological lines or metaphysical ones—and hence, too, as to how far it resembled the sort of scepticism familiar from *Outlines of Pyrrhonism*. In this case we are not solely dependent on the partially favourable verdicts to be inferred from Timon's caricatures; the evidence referring to Pyrrho himself connects him with a variety of figures in the atomist tradition. Several authors report 'successions' of philosophers stretching from Leucippus and Democritus back through the Eleatics to Xenophanes, and forward, through numerous little-known members of the atomist tradition, to Pyrrho; one of these also continues the succession past Pyrrho to Nausiphanes and then Epicurus.[86] Pyrrho's connection with Nausiphanes, and Nausiphanes' with Epicurus, seem to be well attested in other sources.[87] However, the successions prior to Pyrrho are much more

and Timon would have seen little to admire in Protagoras' thought, *and* that the criticism of the extreme Heraclitean thesis in *Theaetetus* 181–3, a thesis apparently represented by Plato as the logical end point of Protagoras' 'man the measure' doctrine, *can* plausibly be seen as anticipating Pyrrho's indeterminacy thesis (see above, Sect. 3). First, it was in Socrates' polemical exploration of the *consequences* of the Heraclitean thesis, much more than in the thesis itself as originally presented, that the striking connections with the indeterminacy thesis seemed to be found. And, secondly, neither Protagoras nor Pyrrho needs to have gone along with Plato's suggestion that the 'man the measure' doctrine commits one to the extreme Heraclitean position. Decleva Caizzi (DC 280) is right to say that Plato takes Protagoras in a direction that prepares the way for Pyrrho's philosophy; but this does not impose on Pyrrho or Timon any obligation to endorse Protagoras' views.

[86] Clement, *Strom.* 1.14.64, 2–4; Eusebius, *Praep. evang.* XIV.17.10; [Galen], *Hist. phil.,* ch. 3, p. 601 Diels (=DC T25A–C); Nausiphanes and Epicurus are included in the first of these. A garbled version of part of the atomist succession also occurs in the Suda under 'Pyrrho' (see DC T1B with commentary).

[87] DL 9.64, 69; Sextus, *M* 1.1–3; Eusebius, *Praep. evang.* XIV.20.14. Some of these texts are uncertain about whether Epicurus studied with Nausiphanes; but this appears to be related to an apocryphal story started by Epicurus himself, according to which he was self-taught, on which see Blank (1998: 77–8). On Nausiphanes, see also Seneca, *Ep.* 88.43, where Nausiphanes is said to have held that *ex his quae videntur nihil magis esse quam non esse*; though this no doubt admits of various interpretations, it is at least tempting (despite the fact that Nausiphanes is supposed to have said that one should follow Pyrrho's disposition, rather than his doctrine (see Ch. 2 n. 31)) to connect it with Pyrrho's use of *ou mallon*, as reported in the Aristocles passage and elsewhere.

dubious; aside from the suspiciously neat connections between Xenophanes and the Eleatics, and between the Eleatics and the atomists, there seem to be too many members of the atomist tradition in these lists to occupy the relatively short period between Democritus and Pyrrho.[88] None the less, there are further reasons for connecting Pyrrho with two members of this tradition— Democritus himself and Anaxarchus. Pyrrho is reported by his associate Philo (DL 9.67) to have 'mentioned Democritus most often';[89] Timon also refers to Democritus as *periphrona*, 'very thoughtful' (DL 9.40, fr. 46 di Marco). As for Anaxarchus, we noted at the very start that several sources mention Pyrrho's association with him, and travel with him on Alexander's expedition to India.[90] Given the differences in the issues involved, it is best to discuss these two separately; we shall begin with Democritus.

What, then, is the basis for Pyrrho's and Timon's apparent admiration for Democritus? The answer is plainly not that they were attracted to a view of reality as consisting of atoms and void;[91] as we saw in Chapter 2, Timon emphasizes Pyrrho's disdain for all kinds of detailed physical theorizing, and the atomic theory would undoubtedly be an example. A far more attractive answer is that their admiration for Democritus has something to do with his epistemology—either his view that properties such as colours and tastes, in contrast to atoms and void, exist only *nomōi*, 'by convention',[92] or the sceptical-sounding

---

[88] On this point, see von Fritz (1963: 93–5); Giannantoni (1981); DC 181.

[89] Cf. Aristocles (in Eusebius, *Praep. evang.* XIV.18.27), who states that Pyrrho learned from Anaxarchus, and then that he later encountered Democritus' books; also Numenius in Eusebius, *Praep. evang.* XIV.6.4.

[90] A claim by Eusebius (*Praep. evang.* XIV.19.9), that the atomist Metrodorus of Chios gave Pyrrho 'bad beginnings' (*kakas aphormas*) with his insistence on the impossibility of knowledge, may be discounted. There is no reason to read this as anything other than Eusebius' own speculation; he claims that Metrodorus exerted an influence on Pyrrho, but this may very well be based purely on his own perception of a similarity between the two philosophies.

[91] According to Decleva Caizzi (1984*a*), Pyrrho's admiration for Democritus *was* based on the latter's atomism, but interpreted in a particular way. I discuss this suggestion in Appendix C.

[92] Sextus, *M* 7.135 (=DK 68B9); DL 9.72 (=DK 68B117); Galen, *Med. emp.* 15.7–8 (=DK 68B125), *De el. ex Hipp.* I.417K. The purpose of the term *nomōi*, 'by convention', has not generally received sufficient scrutiny. The point cannot be that it is a matter of convention whether, for example, a thing looks brown to us; that would be absurd. What is 'conventional' on Democritus' view is, rather, the linguistic practice of saying that a certain rock *is brown*, or that honey *is sweet*; strictly speaking this is incorrect—since in reality rock and honey are just atoms and void, without any colours or tastes intrinsic to them—but the usage is convenient and entrenched. For this interpretation, see Furley (1993). Makin (1993) has a very different interpretation; using the example of a green olive, he suggests that the point is that, 'given the way most perceivers are constituted, the common human agreement about this olive is that it is green' (p. 72). But *nomos* does not mean simply 'agreement'. A *nomos*, rather, is a practice laid down by some form of *evaluative prescription*—a prescription issued by some specific individual, by society collectively, or occasionally by nature itself. A *nomos* tells us *what to do*; the term can properly apply to linguistic norms, but it could not apply to the spontaneous shared deliverances of most people's senses. On this see Kerferd (1981: ch. 10, esp. p. 112).

There is also room for dispute about precisely *which* are the properties that are regarded by

remarks about the possibility of knowledge that appear to be a development from that view (DK 68B6–10, 68B117, 68B125), or both.[93] But here again we have to be very careful. First, any appeal that his remark about colours and tastes might have had for Pyrrho and Timon must have been strictly limited. For this remark also appears to be connected with a theory of the physiology of sense perception in terms of the atomic make-up of the things, and the interaction between the things' atoms and the atoms of which we ourselves are composed.[94] Though this seems to have included some recognition of conflicts among different people's sense perceptions, it also seems to have included an attempt to account for these conflicts in atomic terms[95]—a procedure for which the early Pyrrhonists, on any reasonable interpretation of their views, would have felt no affinity at all. Suppose, then, that we focus solely on the sceptical, rather than the constructive, tendencies in Democritus' thinking; is this where the links with early Pyrrhonism are to be sought?

As in the case of Xenophanes, there is room for some doubt as to whether

Democritus as belonging to things only 'by convention'. Democritus has frequently been assumed to anticipate the early modern distinction between primary and secondary qualities; but the matter is more complicated than this, and here Makin's discussion (ch. 3, sect. 3) is very helpful.

[93] Both aspects are cited by von Fritz (1963: 93–5), and by Dal Pra (1989: 47–51) (though Dal Pra does also go on to emphasize the connection between Democritus' and Pyrrho's ethical outlooks, on which more below); the first alone is cited by Long (1978: 78–9).

[94] Most of our evidence for Democritus' treatment of this topic comes from Theophrastus' lengthy summary and critique of Democritus' account of sense perception and its objects in *De sensibus* 49–58, 61–82; see also Sextus, *M* 7.136 (=DK 68B9).

[95] Certain passages in Theophrastus' account seem clearly to indicate that Democritus did offer the beginnings of an atomic explanation of differences in sense impressions of the same objects on the part of different people; see especially *De sensibus* 64, 67, 69–70—and cf. *De causis plantarum* 6.2.1–3, which discusses Democritus' account of flavours. The nature of the explanation, though, is difficult to reconstruct. In both books Theophrastus objects that Democritus (*a*) assigns various sensory qualities to particular atomic shapes—sweet taste is caused by round atoms that are not too small, bitter taste is caused by small, smooth, round atoms with hooks on them (*De sensibus* 65–6), and so on—and yet also (*b*) insists that the same object may give rise to opposite sensory experiences in different people (or in members of different species), depending on the atomic composition of the perceivers. On the face of it, this does appear inconsistent, or at the very least seriously incomplete (for the accusation of inconsistency, see esp. *De sensibus* 69, for the accusation of incompleteness see esp. *De causis plantarum* 6.2.1–3, 6.7.2). The matter is discussed by Furley (1993: 79–80). In Furley's view, Democritus never claims that the very same *atomic shapes* may give rise to different sensory experiences—only that the same *objects* may do so; and he suggests that this was accounted for by the presence of *multiple* atomic shapes in each 'perceptible compound', the differing dispos-itions of the perceivers causing them to be receptive to different shapes within this multiplicity. But the passage he quotes in support of this, from *De sensibus* 67, seems to me to suggest the opposite; 'Whatever [shape] there is most of in it, that has most strength with regard to sensation and power [i.e. power to cause sensations]' is surely incompatible with the idea that *different* shapes in the object are determinative of the quality of different people's sensations of the object. Whatever may be the truth on this issue, however, it is clear that Democritus would have needed to take his account much further than, as far as we can tell from Theophrastus, he did.

Democritus' 'scepticism' extends as far as has often been alleged;[96] and this might lead one to question whether Pyrrho and Timon would have approved of *any* part of his epistemology. One fragment tells us that reason can provide us with a form of knowledge superior to that provided by the senses, and can take over when the resources of the senses run out.[97] And a famous fragment represents the senses addressing the mind: 'Poor mind! Do you take your confirmation from us and then throw us down? The throwing down is a fall for *you*' (DK 68B125). This is often read as a despairing comment about the self-refuting character of a theory, like atomism itself, that starts from sensory evidence but has the consequence that the senses falsify the nature of things. But it may just as well be read as a warning that such damaging self-refutation had *better not* be allowed to happen—a warning that Democritus, with his explanation *in atomic terms* of how it is that the senses present things to us in the ways they do, could easily have thought that his own theory had adequately heeded.[98] However, one may reply that not all the sceptical-sounding fragments can so easily be explained away[99]—and that in any case, whatever Democritus' own intentions, his pupil Metrodorus of Chios, whose main claim to fame seems to have been precisely that he insisted in the strongest possible terms on the impossibility of knowledge,[100] would surely have encouraged a reading of Democritus' epistemology that emphasized its sceptical tendencies.

[96] This is a very complicated matter, and I cannot hope to do it justice in the present context. One possibility is that Democritus' epistemology is internally inconsistent (as alleged by Sextus, our source for many of the important fragments—*M* 7.135 ff.). This is the view of Barnes (1982*b*: 559–64), who puts greater stress on the sceptical aspect, and also appears to be conceded by Kirk, *et al.* (1983: 409–13), and by McKirahan (1994: 333–7), both of whom give at least as much weight to the optimistic as to the sceptical side. Readings of Democritus' epistemology as consistently non-sceptical include Salem (1996: ch. III), and Farrar (1988: 197–215).

I leave aside the fact that, if Democritus was a sceptic, his scepticism was of a kind that consisted in *denying* the possibility of knowledge, rather than in suspending judgement. Though this may differentiate him from the later Pyrrhonists, it does not follow, as we saw in Sect. 5, that the same can be said of the early Pyrrhonists.

[97] Sextus *M* 7.139 (=DK 68B11). The text at the end of the fragment is usually taken to be corrupt—though see Sedley (1992: 41–2); but the general sense is not in doubt. The claim that it is *reason* that is the superior form of knowledge is not present in the fragment itself, but is an editorial comment by Sextus; however, it is difficult to see what else Democritus could have in mind.

[98] Jacques Brunschwig has suggested that there is a contradiction between the dependence of the mind on the senses in this fragment, and the claim in DK 68B11 that the superior form of knowledge is 'separated' (*apokekrimenē*) from the senses; see Brunschwig (1984: 122–3). But 'separated from' need not mean 'operating without reference to the evidence provided by'. It could just as well mean 'distinct in character from, and operating by methods not available to'—which would be quite compatible with a need to build on, and to remain consistent with, sensory evidence.

[99] The most difficult is perhaps 'in reality we know nothing about anything, but belief in every case is a changing of shape' (Sextus, *M* 7.137 (=DK 68B7)).

[100] See Cicero, *Acad.* 2.73; Sextus, *M* 7.88; Eusebius, *Praep. evang.* XIV.19.9.

On the other hand (and here again we return to a point from the discussion of Xenophanes), there is no explicit indication that the reason for Pyrrho's and Timon's admiration for Democritus had anything to do with his epistemology, sceptical or otherwise; Diogenes does not tell us which aspects of Democritus' many-sided philosophy Pyrrho 'mentioned most', and the one fragment of Timon relating to Democritus does not specify why he is deserving of praise. However, this is not quite the end of the story. One phrase in these two lines of Timon calls for special attention: Timon calls Democritus *amphinoon leschēna*, 'two-minded discusser'. Since this comes immediately after the description *periphrona poimena muthōn*, 'very thoughtful shepherd of discourses', it seems likely that this, too, should be understood as a positive appellation. Besides, we have already seen two cases in the *Silloi* where thought or speech that tends in some way in two opposite directions is regarded as desirable.[101] What, then, might there be about Democritus' thought that might merit the label 'two-minded', and that would be regarded favourably by Pyrrho or Timon? At least two possible answers spring to mind, both from Democritus' epistemology.

First, Democritus is reported to have used the term *ou mallon*, 'no more', in various contexts. One of these has to do with the truth-value of our sense perceptions; the contrary impressions of people in different physiological conditions are said to be 'no more' true than each other (Aristotle, *Met.* 1009^{b}10–11; Theophrastus, *De sensibus* 69; Sextus, *PH* 1.213)—and this could certainly be considered a 'two-minded' way of speaking. Sextus tells us that, in saying this, Democritus meant that *neither* of these contrary impressions is true; given that neither of them actually exhibits the atoms and void of which, on Democritus' view, reality truly consists, this seems plausible enough.[102] This usage of *ou mallon* is, of course, different from Sextus' own,

---

[101] Di Marco (1989: 36), sees this phrase as critical (see above, n. 55, on his interpretation of *amphoteroglōssos* as applied to Zeno), and 'shepherd of discourses' in the previous line as ironic. However, he omits to mention the word *periphrona*, 'very thoughtful', in the same phrase, which is surely complimentary (and also omits it in his translation of the fragment). *Pace* di Marco, *leschēn* needed not be understood in the negative sense 'chatterer'. The word appears nowhere else, and is probably Timon's own coinage. But *leschē*, from which it is derived, can be used either negatively ('chatter', 'gossip'), or neutrally in the sense 'discussion' or 'conversation'; see LSJ.

[102] Aristotle says that Democritus inferred from this point 'either that nothing is true, or at least that it [the truth] is unclear to us' (*Met.* 1009^{b}11–12); presumably this means that nothing *shown to us by the senses* is true, or that, for all that the senses show us, it is unclear what is true—which would be consistent with Sextus' report. Cf. Salem (1996: 162). Makin (1993: 65–6) reads 'it is unclear to us' as meaning that it is unclear *which* of these competing perceptions is correct. But Democritus need not mean to suggest that either one of these perceptions may be correct; the point may just as well be that the truth is unclear given that *both* perceptions (and indeed the senses quite generally) *fail* to show us the truth, at least directly. Makin seems to be drawing support from the sentence containing the 'no more' statement; the text reads 'Which of these [competing perceptions] is true or false, then, is unclear; for these are no more true than those, but equally so'. But Democritus' inference may be understood to be drawn from

as he does not hesitate to point out; but, if we were on the right track in Chapter 1, it is a good deal closer to the usage of Pyrrho. For Pyrrho, as we saw, *ou mallon* has its natural sense of 'to no greater extent', and the form of words using *ou mallon* in the Aristocles passage is designed precisely as a way of expressing the failure of sensations and opinions to be true, given the indeterminacy thesis.

It may be said that the correspondence is not exact; for Pyrrho, according to the Aristocles passage, held that sensations and opinions are not false either, whereas Democritus will have held that sensory impressions do falsify the true nature of things. But this contrast is not as clear-cut as one might expect—which leads us to the second possible way in which Democritus might approvingly be described as 'two-minded'. Though sensory impressions, in his view, may not be true—in the sense that they do not directly reveal to us the atoms and void of which things are composed—it is plausible, as noted a few paragraphs back, that he thought of them as at least a necessary *guide* in our search for the truth, a guide whose credentials had better not be called too radically into question.[103] In what appears to be an expression of this point, Democritus is said by Aristotle to have thought that 'the truth lies in the appearance' (*Gen. et corr.* 315^{b}9–10; cf. *De an.* 404^{a}27–9),[104] and by Sextus to have approved of Anaxagoras' saying

the second half of this sentence alone—the 'no more' statement itself—rather than from the sentence as a whole. And the 'no more' statement itself cannot be read as having to do with 'our inability to adjudicate between conflicting perceptions', as Makin suggests; whatever may be the case in the Pyrrhonist tradition, the words 'but equally so' (*all'homoiōs*) in this passage guarantee that this is a *definite verdict* to the effect that the truth-value of these competing perceptions is the same. The first half of the sentence, 'which of these is true or false, then, is unclear', is in any case hard to explain in the context. The point of the whole passage is that (on a view to which Aristotle is opposed) the perceptions of the majority are not more correct than those of the minority, nor those of the healthy or sane more correct than those of the sick or insane, but they are all on a par—in fact, that they are *all true* (so that Democritus' claim that *nothing* is true is actually a parenthetical aside (cf. n. 104 below)). The best sense I can make of 'which of these is true or false, then, is unclear' in this context is as a warning against taking for granted the usual view that the perceptions of the majority, the healthy, and the sane are true and those of the others false. But, regardless of how it is to be interpreted, we do not have to take *this* claim to be connected with the report about Democritus' inference.

103 DK 68B11 (Sextus, *M* 7.139) seems to speak of the need for reason to take over when the senses *can do no more*; this implies that the senses do take us at least some of the way towards the truth, and that they need to be supplemented rather than simply replaced by reason. The senses are also referred to here as a 'bastard' (*skotiē*) form of knowledge, as opposed to the 'legitimate' (*gnēsiē*) form, reason. But a bastard form of knowledge is still a form of *knowledge* (*gnōmē*). And a bastard does have *one* parent of the favoured lineage, even though the other parent is of different and usually humbler origins; if we take this metaphor seriously, it suggests that the senses are in part to be trusted and in part to be mistrusted—or (recalling Timon's description of Democritus' words) that they are two-sided. The implications of the term 'bastard' are especially emphasized by Salem (1996: 152–4).

104 Aristotle elsewhere even attributes to Democritus, among others, the view that 'what appears to the senses is of necessity true' (*Met.* 1009^{b}13–15). Aristotle is here reporting in rather

'appearances are a sight of the non-evident' (*M* 7.140).[105] So it is certainly within reason to suggest that Democritus accords to sensations an ambiguous status.[106] They are in a sense neither wholly accurate nor wholly inaccurate; we should not trust them as reflecting the nature of things in any direct way, but we should be prepared to use them as a basis for more complicated *inferences* concerning the nature of things. And Pyrrho and Timon could easily have regarded *this* 'two-minded' attitude as a sign of superior insight.

Again, of course, it has to be stressed that much else that, in Democritus' thinking, was *connected* with this attitude would have been rejected by them immediately. However, some aspects of Democritus' epistemology may after all have something to do with Pyrrho's and Timon's approval of him. It does not matter for this purpose (and it obviously cannot be settled in the current context) whether or not the ideas about Democritus' epistemology that I have been discussing are correct. What is important is just that they constitute *one* possible way of understanding his epistemology, and that parts of this epistemology, so understood, could reasonably have seemed appealing to Pyrrho and Timon. But now—to return to the question raised at the opening of this section—none of this forms any support for the view that Pyrrho's philosophy was centred especially on epistemological problems, or that it was essentially the same as later Pyrrhonism. On the contrary, the above speculations (for that is all that they are) fit squarely within the rather different interpretation of Pyrrho offered in the previous chapters; the possible affinities I have pointed to have to do with the immediate consequences of the indeterminacy

broad strokes a number of positions that in his view are liable to similar pitfalls (and note that just a few lines earlier he attributed to Democritus the view that *nothing* is true—see n. 102). Whatever the other thinkers, named and unnamed, may have said, this cannot be literally correct for Democritus; 'true' in his case must mean 'capable of leading us to the truth' (or perhaps 'based in reality', as opposed to fictional, as suggested by McKirahan (1994: 336)).

[105] It has been suggested by Gisela Striker that the report on Democritus in which this occurs should properly refer to Epicurus and *not* to Democritus. See Striker (1974); the relevant passage is at pp. 28–9 in the English version. Sextus is reproducing a report from a certain Diotimus, and Striker proposes that the views summarized were in fact held by Epicurus, and ascribed by Diotimus to Democritus because Epicurus was held to have followed Democritus. It is certainly true that the views in question do line up neatly with those Epicurus is known from other sources to have held—and also that the report contains much terminology that would be anachronistic if applied to Democritus. But even if some set of doctrines might be ascribed to one philosopher purely on the basis of their having been held by another philosopher who was thought to be somehow connected with the first, such a transference would be very surprising in the case of the approval of a specific statement made by some third person; I find it hard to believe that any doxographer would write 'as Anaxagoras says, and Democritus praises him for this', if it was actually Epicurus and *not* Democritus who had praised the statement in question.

[106] Decleva Caizzi (1984*a*: 152 (18–19 in the Italian version)), also understands *amphinoon* as 'ambiguous'. However, in her view the ambiguity in question is the susceptibility of Democritus' philosophy to conflicting interpretations, that of the early Pyrrhonists themselves and that of the Peripatetics or Epicureans. But in this case it is hard to see why Timon would regard 'ambiguousness' as a *positive* characteristic, as he seems to do.

thesis, as reported in the Aristocles passage. It has been clear from the start that some of these consequences are epistemological in character; so there would be nothing surprising if, at this particular point, Pyrrho's ideas turned out to have something in common with ideas from Democritus' epistemology. That the indeterminacy thesis is none the less at the centre of Pyrrho's thinking would not thereby be put into question in any way. If it could be shown that Pyrrho approved of other aspects of Democritus' epistemology from the ones I have suggested, then we might need to change our minds. But, with the minuscule amount of evidence on this issue that is at our disposal, it is hard to see how that could be done.

Now, we have still not achieved a satisfactory picture of Pyrrho's relation to Democritus. A qualified approval of a few aspects of Democritus' epistemological outlook hardly seems sufficient to explain why Timon would call Democritus 'very thoughtful', or why Pyrrho would have 'mentioned Democritus most often'. To find a better explanation, it may help to attend to the context in which the latter report occurs. Diogenes has just been reporting various anecdotes that illustrate Pyrrho's indifference to convention and to hardship. He then tells us (9.67), as we saw in Chapter 2, that Philo said that Pyrrho referred most to Democritus and to Homer—particularly to those passages of Homer that talk of human foolishness and the frailty and instability of human life. Democritus is mentioned, then, in the course of an account of Pyrrho's attitudes to life; so we might expect that it would be Democritus' attitudes to life for which Pyrrho particularly admired him. And, in fact, Democritus' ethical thinking seems to contain plenty with which Pyrrho could have found himself at home.

Democritus' ideal of *euthumia* or *euestō*—'good spirit' or 'well-being'— is closely related to the *ataraxia* recommended and aimed for by Pyrrho. One text even says that Democritus called it *ataraxia*, in addition to *euthumia*, *euestō*, *harmonia* ('harmony'), *summetria* ('symmetry'), and *eudaimonia* ('happiness') (Stobaeus 2.52, 15–19);[107] Cicero also says that he called it *athambia*, 'imperturbability' (*Fin.* 5.87). As this cluster of terms, and the brief descriptions of this ideal in Cicero (*Fin.* 5.23, 87) and Diogenes Laertius (9.45) make clear, Democritus' goal was an untroubled, stable life, as far as possible immune from large reversals of fortune and large swings of mood. The ethical fragments ascribed to Democritus of course support this; in particular, two lengthy fragments in Stobaeus (5.907,17–908,3 (=DK 68B3),[108] 3.176,9–177,12 (=DK 68B191)) expound upon the character of *euthumia*. In addition, there is a sizeable number of fragments pointing at

---

[107] It has usually been thought that this is from a passage taken by Stobaeus from Arius Didymus. For effective arguments against this, see Görannson (1995: ch. 11). Still, whoever Stobaeus' source may be, he does claim to be basing his information on Democritus' own writings, and there is no reason not to believe him.

[108] Part of this is also preserved in Plutarch, *De tranq. an.* 465c.

cases of human folly. Unfortunately, there are serious questions about the authenticity of at least a substantial proportion of the ethical fragments ascribed to Democritus (or in many cases to 'Democrates').[109] But, even if we take the most sceptical possible view of these fragments, there is enough evidence from elsewhere to show that Democritus espoused an ethical ideal whose similarity with Pyrrho's *ataraxia* is plain to see. Aside from the evidence already mentioned, it is noteworthy that among the titles of ethical works in the list reproduced (from Thrasyllus) by Diogenes Laertius (9.46) are *On the Disposition of the Wise Man, On Good Spirit,* and *Well-Being* (though he says that the last one 'is not found');[110] presumably these would have contained material particularly congenial to Pyrrho. Of course, not everything in Democritus' ethics would have appealed to him;[111] the fragments on political topics, for example—if they are genuine—would surely not have struck a chord. But in a central respect Democritus' ethics would have seemed to him to be on the right lines; moreover, there is no one else, prior to Pyrrho and his contemporaries, of whom it is clear that the same can be said. Here, then, is a fuller and more adequate explanation for why Pyrrho would have felt a particular affinity for Democritus; though we may well suspect that Democritus' epistemology is not irrelevant, it looks as if his ethical outlook is much more significant.

8. *Pyrrho, Anaxarchus, and the Cynics*

Ethical outlooks also seem to constitute a clear area of agreement, if again only partial agreement, between Pyrrho and Anaxarchus, with whom he travelled on Alexander's expedition. It is true that Timon's verdict, in his single fragment on Anaxarchus (Plut., *Virt. mor.* 446b–c, fr. 58 di Marco), is decidedly mixed. He is called 'daring and tenacious' (*tharsaleon kai emmenes*) and is said to have 'doglike [or "Cynic"] strength' (*kuneon menos*); but the fragment

---

[109] For a brief overview of this issue, see Farrar (1988: 193–5).

[110] Diogenes appends to his list of titles the comment 'Of the others which some attribute to him, some are compiled from his own works, while others are by common consent not his' (9.49). Evidently questions of authenticity had already arisen with respect to Democritus' writings.

[111] The idiosyncratic interpretation of Decleva Caizzi (1984*a*) (see Appendix C to this chapter) is based in part on her dissatisfaction with other possible points of contact between Pyrrho and Democritus; among other things, she insists (though without really arguing) that there are major differences in their ethical outlooks. But the ethical parallel need not be exact; there merely has to be an important area of agreement, and this seems to be the case here. It may be added that, given the clear division of topics implied in the titles of Democritus' books (DL 9.46–9), there need not be anything surprising in a compartmentalized approval by the early Pyrrhonists of certain portions of Democritus' thinking, to the exclusion of others.

goes on to say that 'though wise, so they said, he was unhappy' (*ra kai eidōs, hōs phasan, athlios eske*) because he was 'pleasure-struck' (*hēdonoplēx*). As Timon's scathing lines on the Cyrenaic Aristippus (DL 2.66, fr. 27 di Marco), and on Epicurus (Athenaeus 279f, fr. 7 di Marco), make clear, he has no sympathy for the dedicated pursuit of pleasure[112]—as one would in any case expect, given the antipathy to strong desires of any kind that we noted in Chapter 2. But still, whatever the nature and extent of Anaxarchus' addiction to pleasure, we are also told by Diogenes Laertius that 'he was called Mr Happiness (*Eudaimonikos*) because of the freedom from emotion and contentedness of his life' (9.60).[113] As we have seen, *apatheia*, 'freedom from emotion', is a term used numerous times in connection with Pyrrho; and, though the term may have different connotations in the context of different philosophies (think of *apatheia* in the Stoic context, for example), the combination of *apatheia* and *eukolia*, 'contentedness', does seem to suggest an attitude closely related to that which we have seen ascribed to Pyrrho.

Besides this, little is to be gathered about Anaxarchus' philosophy. Most of the surviving evidence about him consists of anecdotes concerning his conversations with Alexander; we are also told of his defiance while being pounded to death at the orders of the tyrant Nicocreon, as punishment for a joke at his expense in Alexander's presence (DL 9.58–9; cf. Cicero, *Nat. d.* 3.82). As in the case of Pyrrho, it would be unwise to be too confident of the detailed and literal truth of these stories.[114] The only obvious point they allow us to be sure of is that Anaxarchus spent a good deal of time in the company

---

[112] It may seem ironic that Epicurus is lambasted in this fashion, since Epicurus also espoused an ideal of *ataraxia*, and may even have been influenced in this by Pyrrho himself (via Nausiphanes). However, Timon is only an early example of the widespread ancient tendency to depict Epicurus as a hedonist in the vulgar sense. And it must be admitted that Epicurus sometimes seems to invite such erroneous or one-sided interpretations. Timon criticizes Epicurus for 'gratifying his stomach'; Epicurus is quoted as saying 'The beginning and root of all good are the pleasure of the stomach' (Athenaeus 546f).

There are no other references in Timon to Aristippus or any other Cyrenaic. In particular, there is no mention of the Cyrenaics' pessimistic epistemology, which has sometimes been thought relevant to the early history of Pyrrhonism (see e.g. Görler 1994: 749–50). But, if Pyrrho's outlook was, as I have argued, not primarily oriented towards epistemological questions, this is just what we would expect; see also DC 194–6.

[113] The title *Eudaimonikos* is also recorded in other sources (Athenaeus 548b; Aelian, *Var. hist.* 9.37), but without the explanation; [Galen], *Hist. phil.*, ch. 4, p. 602 Diels, even claims that *Eudaimonikē* was the name of a school stemming from Anaxarchus. See also Plutarch, *Alex. fort. virt.* 331e, where according to the MSS Anaxarchus is called *harmonikon*, 'Mr Harmony'; Menagius suggested altering this to *eudaimonikon*, and this may be correct, but the point is not greatly different either way.

[114] They may none the less tell us a good deal about the image, or perhaps the contrasting images, that came to be attached to Anaxarchus in later antiquity; and this may in turn allow us to speculate on the character of the man himself. An engaging account of this subject is given in Brunschwig (1993). However, little or nothing in the way of philosophical contacts between Anaxarchus and Pyrrho can be gleaned from this material.

of kings; and this itself, according to Diogenes Laertius, was what encouraged Pyrrho to take the opposite path, towards a life of reclusiveness and obscurity. Pyrrho withdrew from human society, and even largely from his own household, because he had 'heard an Indian reproach Anaxarchus, saying that he could not teach anyone else to be good while himself playing the attendant at royal courts' (9.63).[115] Although Anaxarchus is connected with the atomists in the sources—besides the 'successions' cited earlier, Diogenes (9.58) says that he studied with Diogenes of Smyrna (who studied with Metrodorus), and Cicero (*Nat. d.* 3.82) calls him a 'Democritean'—there is in fact no reason to believe that he personally subscribed to the atomic theory,[116] or indeed to a systematic philosophy of any kind.[117]

There is just one further scrap of evidence with a possible bearing on Pyrrho's affiliations with Anaxarchus. We are told by Sextus that Anaxarchus, along with the Cynic Monimus, 'likened existing things to stage-painting and took them to be similar to the things which strike us while asleep or insane' (*M* 7.88). The temptation to assimilate this to the sceptical arguments in Descartes's *First Meditation*, exploiting the possibility (among others) that one might now be dreaming, is almost irresistible; at the same time, one is tempted to see it as a further development, yet more extreme than Metrodorus', of the tendency towards a scepticism about the senses in Democritus.[118] Nevertheless, these temptations *should*, I think, be resisted. The report does not say that Anaxarchus likened *our experience* of the world to viewing a fictional world, dreaming, or being insane; instead, the comparison is between *existing things* (*ta onta*) and stage-sets, the content of our dreams and the content of an insane person's delusions. What we have here, at least on the face of it, is a deflationary comment about the ontological status of the world around us, not a despairing remark about our inability to penetrate behind the veil of a possibly delusive experience; reality itself, it is suggested, is much less solid than we usually take it to be. If one wants a

[115] If our sources are to be believed, however, Pyrrho himself must have acted in somewhat the same way in his younger days. According to Sextus, *M* 1.281–2, he wrote a poem for Alexander and was rewarded with 'thousands of gold pieces' (cf. Plutarch, *Alex. fort. virt.* 331e; also above, Introduction, n. 4). This perhaps supports Diogenes' contention that Pyrrho arrived at his philosophy after and as a result of the Indian expedition (9.61).

[116] Only one anecdote seems to show any connection with atomism at all. Anaxarchus is supposed to have told Alexander of the atomists' view that there are multiple worlds, prompting the lament from Alexander that he had not yet conquered even one (Plutarch, *Tranq. an.* 466d; Valerius Maximus 8.14—both texts appear as DK 72A11). But, even here, it is not clear that Anaxarchus is putting forward the multiplicity of worlds as his own view, rather than simply reporting it as a view held by Democritus and others.

[117] In this sense the comment of Plutarch (*Alexander* 52,4), that Anaxarchus pursued a 'private road' (*idian tina hodon*) in philosophy, may have some justification.

[118] For this type of interpretation, see e.g. von Fritz (1963: 94); Hankinson (1995: 54–5); and the fascinating unpublished paper by Myles Burnyeat, 'All the World's a Stage Painting: Scenery, Optics and Greek Epistemology'.

modern comparison, it can better be found in such remarks as 'All the world's a stage' and 'Life is but a dream'. Whatever may be the origins of these remarks, they are routinely understood nowadays to be emphasizing the fleeting, insubstantial, and senseless character of everything; the point here is not that there is or may be some *other*, more genuine reality *behind* the stage-set or dream, but simply that the ordinary reality with which we are familiar is not as real as it may once have seemed. If something like this was the point of Anaxarchus' similes, the anticipation of Pyrrho's philosophy is obvious; Anaxarchus is telling us something about how things are—and something with which Pyrrho would very naturally have been in sympathy—not something about our being cut off from knowledge of things.[119] There is, of course, room for some doubt about whether Anaxarchus meant this as a serious metaphysical claim, or more loosely as a comment to the effect that nothing is worth caring about; comments such as 'All the world's a stage' or 'Life is but a dream' are not usually understood as contributions to metaphysics, but rather as expressions of a disengaged attitude to life, and Anaxarchus' remark may be another example of the same thing. But either way—and perhaps Anaxarchus did not clearly distinguish between the two—it looks as if Pyrrho did indeed learn a good deal, at least in terms of general orientation, from his teacher and travelling companion. If the remark is a piece of metaphysics, it clearly has more than a little in common with Pyrrho's indeterminacy thesis;[120] but if it has a looser ethical significance, there is an equally clear connection with the attitudes we saw ascribed to Pyrrho in the texts examined in Chapter 2.

As I said, Sextus also ascribes the stage-set, dream, and insanity similes to the Cynic Monimus. This too makes much better sense if the remark is understood as a comment about the vanity of things or of human life than if it is thought of as a kind of epistemological scepticism. There is no other indication that the Cynics had any interest whatever in epistemology; on the other hand, as we observed earlier, remarks about *tuphos*, 'vanity', were commonplace in Cynic diatribe. Indeed, Monimus himself is elsewhere recorded by

[119] It is no objection to this interpretation that, according to Sextus (*M* 7.87), Anaxarchus' statement was widely understood as amounting to the abolition of any criterion of truth—even if we accept, as Sextus carefully refrains from doing, that this widespread understanding was correct. For, as we saw in Chapter 1, claims about the nature of things can have epistemological consequences. Pyrrho's indeterminacy thesis does have the consequence that knowledge, at least most normal kinds, is impossible; similarly, if it were true that reality is fleeting, insubstantial, and senseless, then any prospects for reliably distinguishing what is true from what is false might well be diminished or eliminated.

[120] Supposing that this is so, however, there is no indication that Anaxarchus' 'happiness' was *derived from* the attitude reflected in his similes—as Pyrrho's *ataraxia* is derived from his withdrawal of trust in sensations and opinions, which in turn is derived from the indeterminacy thesis. It is in this respect that Pyrrho is most distinctive and most original; we shall be returning to this point in the next chapter (Sect. 4).

Sextus (*M* 8.5) as universalizing this Cynic attitude, saying that 'all is vanity' (*tuphon einai ta panta*);[121] this would in fact be equivalent to the stage-set and other similes, on the reading just proposed. Sextus' information also suggests a link between the Cynics and Anaxarchus,[122] a link apparently confirmed by Timon's reference to Anaxarchus' 'Cynic strength' (*kuneon menos*). As we saw, the tone of this reference seems to be one of approval, which in turn suggests the possibility of a link between the Cynics and early Pyrrhonism. Such a link has, in fact, been thoroughly investigated by others, and so little needs to be said here;[123] we may simply note a few of the salient points.

First, the Cynic Onesicritus also joined Alexander's expedition, and wrote an account of it. Like Pyrrho, he even visited some 'naked wise men' in India; his report of this incident is summarized in Strabo's *Geography* (15.1.63–5).[124] We can reasonably assume that Pyrrho and Onesicritus were at least acquainted. Secondly, as noted at the end of Chapter 2, Pyrrho and the Cynics seem to share a disregard of conventional mores, and of conventional conceptions of what things in life are worth striving for; in addition, both Pyrrho and the Cynics seem to have espoused, and to some degree achieved, an exceptional toughness or indifference in the face of life's hardships. Some of this, of course, can be seen as an aspect of the legacy bequeathed to later philosophy by Socrates; but whatever Pyrrho's knowledge of or attitude towards Socrates,[125] the Cynics constituted a clear and present model for this side of his own outlook. Thirdly, the Cynics repudiated theoretical enquiry, to the extent that Diogenes Laertius reports it as a point of contention whether Cynicism should be considered a 'philosophy' at all, rather than just a way of life (6.103). Pyrrho's disavowal of philosophical theorizing does not go quite as far as this; the Aristocles passage, at least, shows that he did have a certain set of theoretical ideas, coherently connected and precisely articulated, on the basis of which his attitudes to life were developed. However, as we have also seen, these attitudes included a contempt for and withdrawal from almost everything that passed for theoretical enquiry among more conventional thinkers; to this extent he would

[121] This statement is also attributed to Monimus in a fragment of Menander recorded in Diogenes' brief life of Monimus (6.82–3); this fact, coupled with the fact that Diogenes names him as a pupil of Diogenes the Cynic, seems to place him as a rough contemporary of Pyrrho.

[122] On this connection, see Ioppolo (1980*a*).

[123] See Long (1978); Brancacci (1981).

[124] There is also a reference to Onesicritus' meeting with Indian philosophers in Plutarch, *Alexander* 65 (which states that he was a Cynic). In addition, Onesicritus' account of the expedition is referred to in Arrian's *Anabasis* (e.g. 6.2.3).

[125] Timon's words on Socrates (DL 2.19, fr. 25 di Marco) are ambiguous in tone; for discussion see Long (1988: 150–2); di Marco (1989: 36–8, 165–71); Ioppolo (1995: 110–11). But at any rate there is no mention here of the particular side of Socrates emphasized especially by the Cynics.

again have found the Cynics' attitude agreeable. Finally, we noted earlier that Timon, like the Cynics, is keen to criticize the *tuphos*, 'vanity', of other philosophers, and also praises Pyrrho for being free from *tuphos*; and it has been plausibly argued that Timon's writing owes a far more extensive debt to Cynic postures and even Cynic writings, especially the satirical poems of the Cynic Crates.[126] It is highly probable, then, that the Cynics served as an encouragement to certain of the attitudes characteristic of early Pyrrhonism.

9. Pyrrho and the Megarians

We may conclude this survey with a look at two other groups, each of whom has been alleged to have exerted an important influence on Pyrrho's ideas, in both the theoretical and the practical arenas. These are the Megarians, among whom one of Pyrrho's teachers may have been numbered, and the 'naked wise men' whom Pyrrho is supposed to have met in India. In both cases the evidence is scanty and confusing. And in both cases this evidence has been handled, I think, in a somewhat over-enthusiastic fashion.

The initial impetus for seeing Pyrrho as having been influenced by the Megarians comes from the report in Diogenes Laertius (9.61) that Pyrrho studied with (if the manuscripts are to be accepted) 'Bryson son of Stilpo'. One of the best-known Megarian thinkers was called Stilpo, and there is also evidence connecting a certain Bryson with the Megarians. The Suda under 'Pyrrho' again names Bryson as the teacher of Pyrrho, and says that he studied with the Megarian Clinomachus; the same work under 'Socrates' lists him as a pupil of Socrates and co-founder, with the Megarian Euclides, of 'eristic dialectic', which Clinomachus is said to have further developed—but then adds that some people say Bryson studied not with Socrates but with Euclides (and again names him as the teacher of Pyrrho).[127] Now, as we noted at the beginning of the Introduction, there is considerable difficulty in supposing that Pyrrho studied with a *son* of Stilpo, since Pyrrho and Stilpo appear to

---

[126] On this see Long (1978).

[127] The first entry appears as DC T1B. Part of the second appears as DC T2; a fuller reproduction occurs in Döring (1972: text 34). The discrepancies between the two texts are evidently serious, and have led some to suspect that the entire connection of Bryson with the Megarians is a fabrication designed to show Pyrrho as connected with Socrates; see e.g. LS ii. 1–2, Döring (1972: 157–64), and Giannantoni (1981: 29). In addition, it is not at all clear whether Bryson is one person or more than one; on this, see also Giannantoni (1990: iv, Note 10). The waters are muddied still further by another entry in the Suda, under Theodorus (DC T36), in which Theodorus is said to have had both *Bryson* and *Pyrrho* for teachers. In the main text I ignore these (admittedly real) problems; for, even if they can somehow be solved, there is, I claim, absolutely no reason for thinking that Pyrrho would have felt any affinity for any *philosophical* ideas ascribed in our sources to anyone named Bryson.

have been rough contemporaries.[128] It has been suggested that the text should be emended to 'Bryson *or* Stilpo'; but the notion that Stilpo himself could have taught Pyrrho is still unlikely—elsewhere Diogenes tells us, with greater chronological plausibility, that *Timon* associated with him for a time (9.109). However, let us leave aside the problems besetting Diogenes' mention of 'Bryson son of Stilpo'; what is there in what we know of Megarian thought to justify the idea of a Megarian influence on Pyrrho?

The answer would appear to be 'very little'. The Megarians are best known for formulating a variety of logical and linguistic puzzles, and for subjecting their listeners to dazzling and/or mind-numbing dialectic. Our sources associate all of the well-known Megarians with one or both of these kinds of activity—Euclides, Euboulides, Stilpo, Clinomachus, Diodorus Cronus, and others besides.[129] Stilpo, for example, seems to have been quite generally opposed to predication, holding that the only term correctly to be applied to a thing is its name.[130] And the Megarians are supposed collectively to have claimed that things whose definitions are different are themselves different— so that Socrates the pale and Socrates the musical are two different entities.[131] As for Bryson, the only ideas ever ascribed to a person bearing that name are that obscenity is impossible (because the allegedly obscene language signifies the same thing as its non-obscene counterpart (Aristotle, *Rhet.* 1405^{b}6–11)) and that it is possible to square the circle (Aristotle, *An. post.* 75^{b}37–76^{a}1, *Soph. el.* 171^{b}16–22, 172^{a}2–7).[132] But all of this is exceedingly remote from the kinds of interests and concerns that we have seen to be characteristic of Pyrrho and Timon. Once he has arrived at his own theoretical position, Pyrrho, as portrayed by Timon and others, is happy to regard from afar the contentious theoretical debates (*erides*) of other philosophers; and these same debates are the object of scorn and derision from Timon himself. One would naturally assume that the Megarians, who look as if they relished abstruse dialectical activity more than most, would for the early Pyrrhonists be objects of particular contempt. And this assumption seems to be confirmed by a fragment of Timon referring in thoroughly dismissive terms to Euclides and the

---

[128] For the evidence on Stilpo's dates, see Muller (1988: 56–61).

[129] See the texts, with commentary, collected in Döring (1972); also the French translation of these texts, with commentary, in Muller (1985). In listing these names, I have assumed the traditional, broad conception of the extent of the Megarian school (assumed by Döring and defended by Muller). Sedley (1977) argues that, properly understood, the Megarians include only Euclides, a certain Ichthyas, and Stilpo, together with their immediate followers (that is, pupils who did not themselves initiate new lines of thought). It does not matter for my purposes whether or not this is correct; either way, the Megarians were best known for logic-chopping.

[130] See DL 2.119; Plutarch, *Adv. Col.* 1120a–b; and for discussion Denyer (1991: 33–7).

[131] This thesis is further discussed in Appendix A, in connection with the question whether the Megarians are Aristotle's unnamed opponents in *Metaphysics* IV.

[132] A number of the Aristotelian commentators expand upon both these points; see Döring (1972: texts 208A–210C).

Megarians (DL 2.107, fr. 28 di Marco): 'But I do not care about[133] these chat-terboxes, nor anyone else[134]—not about Phaedo, whoever he was, nor about the contentious [*eridanteō*] Euclides, who instilled in the Megarians a fanat-ical love of wrangling [*erismou*].' So, whatever Pyrrho or Timon may have learned from Stilpo or any other Megarian, it can hardly have had anything to do with what was generally regarded as their main concern.[135]

We are also told that Euclides held that 'The good is one, though called by many names—sometimes practical wisdom, sometimes god, and at other times mind, etc. But the things opposed to the good he abolished, saying that they do not exist' (DL 2.106, cf. 7.161). It has been claimed that there is an echo of this in the fragment of Timon concerning 'the nature of the divine and the good',[136] which we examined at some length in the previous chapter. But even if one rejects the conclusion I urged—that this fragment cannot be taken to be summarizing the ideas of Pyrrho at all—there is simply no clear connec-tion between this doctrine and what is said in Timon's fragment about the good. According to one possible translation of the latter, we are told that 'the nature of the divine and the good is eternal', and that it is the source of a tran-quil life; according to another translation, we are told that the nature of the divine and the good is whatever it is that is the source of a tranquil life, with no reference to eternity. But neither of these claims implies, is implied by, or is in any other obvious way related to, the claim that the good is one (though called by many names), or the claim that the opposite of the good does not exist.[137]

---

[133] Both LS and the Loeb translation of DL translate *ou moi . . . melei* as 'I do not care *for*' (my emphasis). This would suit the context nicely; however, 'care for' means something rather different from 'care about', and I am not convinced that *melei* can mean the former as well as the latter.

[134] i.e., as Diogenes informs us, any other member of a 'Socratic' school.

[135] Long (1978: 72) suggests a connection between Megarian logico-linguistic positions (especially Stilpo's rejection of predication), and a remark about time attributed to Timon by Sextus (*M* 10.197, *M* 6.66); LS ii. 17 suggests that Timon may be influenced here by Diodorus Cronus' theory of partless magnitudes (*amerē*). But neither of these suggestions is compelling, since the remark attributed to Timon is not a substantive claim of any kind, Megarian or other-wise; rather, it is a simple tautology. Timon says that no process divisible into temporal parts (such as coming-into-being, perishing, and the like) can take place in a partless period of time; who could possibly disagree? We may very well ask what may have been the *point* of this remark (Sextus offers no clue here); for some speculations on this, see Decleva Caizzi (1984*b*: 101–5). Any attempt to detect *influences* on Timon in this case is, however, liable to be fruit-less.

[136] See Reale (1981: 311).

[137] Of course the Eleatics, at least as standardly interpreted, would have seen oneness and eter-nity as related predicates. But, since neither Euclides nor 'Pyrrho' mentions oneness and eter-nity *both together* in connection with the good—Euclides stresses the oneness of the good, 'Pyrrho' (on one possible translation) its eternity—there is no reason for assuming that either one of them is thinking about the good along Eleatic lines. The Megarians have often been asso-ciated with the Eleatics, and particularly on the basis of this testimony on Euclides; however, as

So is there nothing that might justify our seeing a connection between Pyrrho and the Megarians? A passage of Seneca appears to associate Stilpo with (though it does not specifically list him among) 'those to whom the highest good seemed to be a soul free from suffering [*impatiens*]' (*Ep.* 9.1). *Impatiens* is surely a rendering into Latin of the Greek *apathēs*; the people Seneca refers to thus have *apatheia* as an ideal, as did Pyrrho. Plutarch, too, claims that Stilpo was renowned for his 'mildness and moderation of feeling' (*praotētos kai metriopatheias (Adv. Col.* 1119c)); these terms, though not identical in meaning with *apatheia*, come to be used in descriptions of the goal of life promoted in later Pyrrhonism, a goal that is plainly a close relative of Pyrrho's own. Finally, Alexander of Aphrodisias (*De anima* 2.150,34–5) attributes to the Megarians in general an ideal of *aochlēsia*, 'freedom from disturbance'.[138] All this suggests that there would have been a good deal of common ground between Pyrrho and Stilpo (and perhaps other Megarians) on the question what was most worth seeking in life. However, as we have seen, there are other possible antecedents for Pyrrho's position on this question; if there was any influence here, it need not have been of any great importance.

With this possible exception, then, the connection between Pyrrho and the Megarians seems to be a red herring. While we need not doubt that Pyrrho and Timon knew some Megarians, their philosophy does not show any significant Megarian influence. And this, in addition to the evident confusion in the sources claiming a student–teacher relationship between Pyrrho and Megarians, leads one to suspect that this story was simply concocted by later writers who liked to fit as many philosophers as possible into lines of 'succession', without troubling themselves over historical accuracy. A similar but more blatant case of this phenomenon is the report of Strabo (9.1.8), that Pyrrho belonged to an 'Elean' school started by Phaedo of Elis.[139] Historical and philosophical grounds for this are, as far as we can tell, non-existent; and recall that Phaedo is also singled out in the same fragment of Timon in which the Megarians are criticized for their pointless 'wrangling'. The report is surely inspired by the common birthplace of Pyrrho and Phaedo, and has the

a number of recent studies have shown, such a connection, though vouched for by Aristocles (*Praep. evang.* XIV.17.1) and Cicero (*Acad.* 2.129), is in fact very dubious. See Moraux (1984: 198–201); Muller (1988: 71–5); Giannantoni (1990: iv, Notes 4, 5, 9); the last of these contains an extensive review of modern scholarship on the subject. Note, finally, that this alleged connection between the Eleatics and the Megarians has to do with their supposed common adoption of some form of monism. It has nothing to do with the points on which I earlier suggested common ground between the Eleatics and Pyrrho (see Sect. 4); nor do those latter points seem to be echoed in the slightest in any of the ideas attributed to the Megarians.

[138] This text appears as fr. 196 in Döring (1972). As Döring points out, however (p. 154), its reliability is questionable, given the views ascribed, in the passage of which it forms a part, to other thinkers about whom we are better informed.

[139] The Suda, under 'Socrates' (DC T4), includes the same piece of information.

felicitous effect (as does the Megarian connection) of linking Pyrrho by philo-sophical 'succession' to Socrates; but, in the absence of any corroborating detail, either historical or philosophical—such as one has with, for example, the connection between Pyrrho and Anaxarchus—it is valueless.

10. Pyrrho and the Indians

What, then, of Pyrrho and the 'naked wise men'—the unnamed Indian thinkers he is said to have met on his travels with Alexander? There is no obvious difficulty in accepting the historicity of the reported encounter. Though Diogenes Laertius is the only one who actually says that Pyrrho met these Indian thinkers, we do, as already noted, have other evidence corrobor-ating the fact that Pyrrho did go on Alexander's expedition, and we have evidence of another philosopher, the Cynic Onesicritus, meeting and talking with 'naked wise men' on the same expedition. So, on this point, at least, there seems to be no good reason to suspect Diogenes' source. The more diffi-cult question is what, if anything, Pyrrho may have learned from this encounter; is it also true, as Diogenes goes on to say, that Pyrrho developed his distinctive philosophy as a *result* of talking with the Indian thinkers? It is not uncommon for students, on encountering Pyrrhonian scepticism for the first time, to notice a resemblance between it and certain attitudes generally associated with Eastern thought. In particular, both are thought to share a certain detachment from the sensible or material world, and a special tran-quillity, or inner peace, that stems from this detachment. At this level of generality, such attitudes may be said to belong equally to Pyrrho and to the later Pyrrhonists; hence the Eastern parallel tends equally to receive mention whichever period of Pyrrhonism one is discussing. And at this level of gener-ality, again, the resemblance is hard to deny. Suggestive as this is, however—especially when combined with the report that Pyrrho actually met some Indian thinkers—it is also uncomfortably vague; one would like to see more specific similarities before postulating an influence on Pyrrho (let alone on Pyrrhonism more generally) from the East.

In Pyrrho's case, though, we can perhaps do a little better than this. We saw in the previous chapter that Pyrrho was supposed to have shown an extraor-dinary insensitivity to physical pain—unlike the later Pyrrhonists, who admit-ted that the sceptic was just as liable to suffering on this score as the non-sceptic. Another aspect of the image of the Indian wise man popular in the West is that he can walk on hot coals without batting an eyelid, survive on three beans a day, and generally ignore bodily demands. Though this picture can easily descend to caricature, it is not *merely* a Western invention; and it is notable that this type of behaviour is a salient feature of the ascetically inclined 'naked wise men' whom the Cynic Onesicritus reports having met (Strabo 15.1.63–5). They stand, sit or lie naked on the ground, which is so hot that no one else can even walk on it easily (15.1.63); and Calanus, one of those who actually spoke to Onesicritus, says that if they think that they are ill, they commit suicide by building a pyre, lighting it, and sitting on it motionless (15.1.65)—an action that Calanus himself is subsequently reported as carrying out in Alexander's presence (15.1.68).[140] Here, then, is a striking and distinctive element in the image of Pyrrho transmitted in our sources, and an element for which it is highly tempting to postulate an Eastern influence.[141] On a somewhat different note, the idea is widespread in Buddhist and other Indian thought that the world of ordinary experience is insubstantial or impermanent; and this idea seems to be connected with—indeed, a cause of—the detachment and inner peace that, according to these traditions, is characteristic of the higher stage of enlightenment.[142] It is natural to speculate that the way in which, in Pyrrho's thought, the view that things are in their nature indeterminate results in a withdrawal of trust in sensations and opinions, which in turn results in *ataraxia*, may have been at least partially inspired by this; as we have mentioned before, this particular route to a trouble-free existence sets Pyrrho conspicuously apart from the main current of Greek philosophy. In broad terms, then, the notion that Pyrrho's attitudes and outlook were shaped to some degree by his encounter with Indian thinkers has something to recommend it, and has been widely accepted by scholars writing on Pyrrho.[143]

But others have proposed a much more definite and detailed connection

---

[140] The historicity of this meeting—or, at least, of Onesicritus' report of it—has been questioned; some have thought that he is simply putting Cynic doctrine into the mouths of these Indians. The matter has been thoroughly discussed by Stoneman (1994, 1995). Despite difficulties having to do with the details of Indian philosophical doctrine, and with matters of literary genre, Stoneman inclines to regard the report as containing genuine information about the 'naked wise men'. See also the following note.

[141] This is, of course, not unrelated to the Cynics' own toughness or indifference, and we have already mentioned that Pyrrho also exhibited an attitude comparable to this (Sect. 8). However, our sources suggest that Pyrrho on occasion went beyond mere toughness, not seeming even to *notice* physical pain (see esp. DL 9.67); and this is where the Indian parallel immediately springs to mind. The Cynics prided themselves on satisfying their bodily needs with maximum simplicity, and developed exercises to *train* themselves in the endurance of pain (e.g. DL 6.23); but neither is quite the same as Pyrrho's reported *obliviousness* to burns or incisions.

[142] I admit that in making this claim I relied, in the first instance, on the woefully inadequate and cartoon-like image of Indian thought that I have picked up by osmosis (and heard expressed by my students). The following are among the works I have consulted to check that this image has some basis in historical fact: Murti (1955); Smart (1967a, b); Organ (1975).

[143] See e.g. Conche (1994: 36–8) and, more tentatively, LS i. 17; a broader survey of scholarly opinion appears in DC 136–43. For a cautionary note, however, see Hadot (1995: 152–4, 419), who observes that the number of possible attitudes to life is not unlimited—so that apparent similarities need not always indicate influences—and that, even if certain attitudes of the 'naked wise men' did strike a chord with Pyrrho, Anaxarchus, or Onesicritus, this may simply have had the effect of reinforcing attitudes to which they themselves were already inclined, owing to legacies internal to the Greek tradition.

between Pyrrho and Indian thought. In Buddhist and other ancient Indian writings one frequently encounters a set of questions, or alternatives, posed in the form of a 'quadrilemma'; schematically, the questions are in the form '*P*? Or not *P*? Or both *P* and not *P*? Or neither *P* nor not *P*?' Two uses of this 'quadrilemmatic' procedure, both probably predating Pyrrho, are adduced as likely influences.[144] First, the Buddha[145] is said to have refused any definite answer to any of a set of 'quadrilemmatic' questions. Secondly, one of the Buddhist scriptures, the *Brahma-Gala Sutta* from the *Digha Nikaya* (*Long Dialogues*), mentions four sets of 'recluses and Brahmans who wriggle like eels; and when a question is put to them on this or that they resort to equivocation, to eel-wriggling'.[146] These 'eel-wrigglers' are clearly sceptics of a kind,[147] whose 'equivocation' or verbal legerdemain is again a way of refusing to answer certain questions; and those in the last of the four groups, identified by scholars with the school of the sceptical thinker Sanjaya, a rough contemporary of the Buddha,[148] apply their 'eel-wriggling' to every member

---

[144] See Flintoff (1980); also Frenkian (1957, 1958 (both of these being condensed versions of a book-length Romanian study of Greek scepticism and Indian Philosophy)); Jayatilleke (1963: 129–30); Piantelli (1978: esp. 148–50). The Indian quadrilemma is also mentioned in connection with Pyrrho by Patrick (1929: 61). Frenkian (1957) cites several other examples of quadrilemmatic reasoning besides the ones mentioned below; but these are all from innovative writers of the early centuries of the Christian era (Nagarjuna, Gaudapada, and Vasubandhu, on whom see Murti (1955)). Frenkian refers to these later writers as part of his thoroughly unconvincing attempt to show that *later* Pyrrhonism was also directly influenced by Indian thought— in addition to the supposed indirect influence via Pyrrho—as a result of visitors from India to Greece and Rome.

In addition to the quadrilemma, both Flintoff and Piantelli adduce a number of parallels of a more general character, having to do with attitude and practical orientation, between Pyrrho and Indian thought. These partly overlap with, and seem to be generally complementary to, the observations of the previous paragraph—though they are clearly based, in both cases, on a much more extensive reading of the ancient Indian texts. As such, I have no quarrel with them in principle; but see again the cautions of Hadot (see above, n. 143).

[145] Gautama, the Buddha or Enlightened One, seems to have lived in the sixth and early fifth centuries BC. The oldest Buddhist scriptures date only from the first century BC; but it is generally accepted that they reflect an oral tradition going back to the Buddha himself.

[146] *Brahma-Gala Sutta,* sect. 23, p. 37 in Rhys Davids (1899). Flintoff (1980: 101–3) also refers to discussions of sceptical positions by the Jain writer Silanka, but these are much less relevant; Silanka wrote in the ninth century (see Jayatilleke 1963: 113), and seems, as Flintoff admits, to have distorted the positions in question by forcing them into characteristically Jain categories. According to Jayatilleke (p. 121), Silanka does mention a kind of quadrilemma, but it is not the same as the one we have referred to so far; instead of 'neither *P* nor not-*P*' it has '*P* is inexpressible'—a difference later glossed over by Jayatilleke himself (pp. 139–40). So, if we are interested in possible influences on Pyrrho, it is the much earlier Buddhist texts which are of primary importance. (Flintoff is also confusing in speaking of 'Jainist Scepticism' and 'Buddhist Scepticism'; it is in fact the *representations* of sceptical positions in Jain and Buddhist texts that is at issue.)

[147] On the term, and its association with sceptical ways of thinking, see Jayatilleke (1963: 121–2).

[148] See Piantelli (1978: 149) and Flintoff (1980: 102–3), both citing Barua (1921), a work to which I have not had access; Jayatilleke (1963: 130–1).

of several quadrilemmas of questions. Now these procedures, it has been argued, are extremely similar to Pyrrho's preferred mode of speech, according to the Aristocles passage, in which the four alternatives 'It is', 'It is not', 'It both is and is not' and 'It neither is nor is not', are all on a par, and none of them endorsed; in fact, it is *too* similar for coincidence—Pyrrho must have picked up this very specific form of language from Buddhists or 'eel-wrigglers' during his Eastern travels. The attractiveness of this hypothesis, of course, depends in part on the idea that the quadrilemma is 'a mode of thinking hitherto without precedent in Greek philosophical or indeed any other thinking';[149] but as we saw, this is not quite true. Plato uses a quadrilemmatic form of speech—in a context bearing other significant similarities to the position described in the Aristocles passage (*Rep.* 479c). However, it must be conceded that this is not typical of Plato or any other Greek philosopher before Pyrrho—whereas quadrilemmas appear to be common in Buddhist and other Indian texts.[150] Still, the view that Pyrrho learned of the quadrilemma in India and incorporated it into his own thinking is plausible only if the *ways* in which the quadrilemma is used in Indian thought are noticeably similar to its occurrence in the Aristocles passage.

Here, it seems to me, the matter is not as clear-cut as has been claimed by the proponents of this view. I shall begin with the Buddhists. The quadrilemmas, as expounded in Buddhist contexts, occur as part of a series of questions known as the *avyakrta*—'inexpressible', 'undetermined', or 'unanswered' questions.[151] Not every text that discusses these questions includes the complete set; but the complete set consists of fourteen such questions, composed of three quadrilemmas and one dilemma.[152] The four topics dealt with in these questions are (1) whether the world is eternal, (2) whether the world is (spatially) finite, (3) whether the *Tathagata* (perfect being, person

---

[149] Flintoff (1980: 92).

[150] See Murti (1955: 36). For Buddhist examples, see Sutta 63 and Sutta 72 of the *Majjhima-Nikaya*, in Warren (1896: 117–28); *Potthapada Sutta*, in Rhys Davids (1899: 244–64, esp. 254); *Pasadika Suttanta*, in Rhys Davids and Rhys Davids (1921: 111–31, esp. 127–30); *Milinda Panha* (*The Questions of King Milinda*) IV, 2, 4–5, in Rhys Davids (1890: 204–6).

[151] Murti (1955: 36), translates 'inexpressible'; Organ (1975: 181) translates 'undetermined' or 'unelucidated'. Jayatilleke (1963: 470–1) criticizes Murti and translates 'unexplained' or 'unanswered'.

[152] Sutta 63 of the *Majjhima-Nikaya* (see above, n. 150) contains ten, with just one quadrilemma; the *Potthapada Sutta* contains the same ten; the *Milinda Panha* contains twelve, with two quadrilemmas; and the *Pasadika Suttanta* contains a quadrilemma on topic 3 (see below), but then mentions four further quadrilemmas that appear to be minor variations on (and combinations of) topics 1 and 3. It looks as if there is considerably less uniformity in the presentation of these questions than is suggested by Flintoff (1980: 93), or Murti (1955: 38), from whom Flintoff is quoting at this point. Here too, Jayatilleke (1963) criticizes Murti (see the previous note). However, his claim (p. 471) that 'only ten questions are mentioned in the Pali Canon, and it is in the Buddhist Sanskrit literature that the list is extended to fourteen' also appears not to be quite accurate, if the translators of these texts are to be trusted; all of the texts just mentioned are in Pali.

who has penetrated to the truth) survives death, and (4) whether the soul and the body are identical. With respect to the last topic, the questions are just 'Are the soul and the body identical?' and 'Are the soul and the body non-identical?'; with respect to the other three (in complete versions), there are four questions, in the quadrilemmatic form mentioned above—for example, 'Is the world eternal?', 'Is the world non-eternal?', 'Is the world both eternal and non-eternal?', and 'Is the world neither eternal nor non-eternal?'. And the questions are called 'inexpressible', 'undetermined', or 'unanswered' because the proper response to them is no response at all. The reason, to put it roughly, is that answering any of them is useless for the development of true wisdom, and even a hindrance to it; according to one version, a positive answer to any of these questions 'is a jungle, a wilderness, a puppet-show, a writhing and a fetter, and is coupled with misery, ruin, despair and agony, and does not tend to aversion, absence of passion, cessation, quiescence, knowledge, supreme wisdom and Nirvana'.[153]

Clearly there are some similarities with Pyrrho's recommended form of speech. The Buddha gives no definite answers to these questions; and Pyrrho's recommended form of speech is a way of expressing the indefiniteness of things. In addition, refusing to answer the questions is the only way to achieve 'absence of passion' and 'quiescence'; and for Pyrrho the result of adopting the attitude expressed by the recommended form of speech is *ataraxia* or *apatheia*. But there are also some notable differences. First, the Buddha's questions apply only to four specific metaphysical topics.[154] Pyrrho's recommended form of speech, on the other hand, applies to 'each single thing'—that is, to everything in the ordinary world presented to us in our 'sensations and opinions'. A second and perhaps more important difference is that for the Buddha the rejection of these questions opens up the path to enlightenment and Nirvana, which is to occur at an altogether different level; true wisdom and true reality are to be found by renouncing what passes for such among those who misguidedly seek to answer these questions. For Pyrrho, on the other hand, there is no question of finding the truth at a different level. If my interpretation of the Aristocles passage has been correct, the recommended form of speech is, precisely, *about* the real nature of things; it does not release us to seek the truth somewhere else, but is itself a statement of the truth.[155] Relatedly, we are not presented here with a set of four ques-

[153] *Majjhima-Nikaya*, Sutta 72, in Warren (1896: 124–5). For an interpretation, and a review of other possible interpretations, of *why* the questions are left unanswered, see Jayatilleke (1963: 471–6). For our purposes, however, the broad-brush explanation just given is adequate.
[154] According to Jayatilleke (1963: 344–7), there are other uses of quadrilemmatic reasoning in the Pali scriptures. However, these do not involve *refusing* to answer a set of questions, but *assenting* to one of the four alternatives and denying the others, or (rarely) denying all four; clearly these are not relevant to the connection with Pyrrho.
[155] Suppose, on the other hand, that I have been wrong throughout, and that some form of

tions that Pyrrho *refuses* to answer—which is the whole point of the Buddha's questions. Rather, we are presented with a report of what, in Pyrrho's view, we *should say*; our speech (when dealing with the nature of things) should be of the form '*X* no more is *F* than is not *F* or both *F* and not *F* or neither *F* nor not *F*'.[156] The Buddha is refusing to be embroiled in metaphysical questions at all, whereas Pyrrho *has* a metaphysical view, of which the four-part form of speech is one expression. A consequence of all these differences is that for the Buddha the realization that these questions are not to be answered is an important stage in one's progress, but a stage that it is also important to move *beyond* as soon as possible. For Pyrrho, on the other hand, the adoption of the four-part form of speech is not a temporary expedient, but an important part of one's terminal stage of understanding. It leads to *ataraxia*, but it is not *replaced* by *ataraxia*; on the contrary, *ataraxia* is achieved, precisely, by making it part of one's permanent view of things.

The case of the 'eel-wrigglers' is slightly different; there are also differences between the fourth group of 'eel-wrigglers', the school of Sanjaya, and the others. The members of this fourth group also refuse, by means of 'equivocation', to answer any of several quadrilemmas of questions;[157] but in their case there is no indication that this refusal is a preliminary stage towards a higher wisdom, so that one of the disanalogies with Pyrrho that I just noted for the Buddha would not apply to them. However, one of the important analogies does not seem to apply, either; for there is also no indication, in their case, that this verbal slipperiness is any kind of route towards tranquillity. And the other two disanalogies do seem to apply to them just as much as

epistemological interpretation of Pyrrho's thinking is correct. Then the recommended form of speech is a way of renouncing the search for the truth altogether—not displacing it to some other higher level; there is still an obvious contrast with the Buddha's procedure.

[156] Both Frenkian (1957: 124) and Flintoff (1980: 92) mistranslate this part of the Aristocles passage, in such a way as to obscure this difference. Flintoff's version is 'We must not say about any one thing (1) that it is or (2) that it is not', etc.; Frenkian's is identical except that (for no apparent reason) he has 'must not incline to say' instead of 'must not say'. As was emphasized in Chapter 1, Pyrrho maintains that our condition must be one of '*saying* about *each* single thing that it no more is than is not', etc.

[157] Piantelli (1978: 149–50) denies that this constitutes a parallel with Pyrrho (in contrast to the Buddhist parallel, by which he is impressed); but his focus seems to be in the wrong place. The text contains a list of four quadrilemmas, and this set of 'eel-wrigglers' is said to 'equivocate' about *each member* of each quadrilemma (*Brahma-Gāla Sutta* sect. 27, in Rhys Davids (1899: 39)); but, in addition to this, the *form* of the 'equivocations' that they are said to employ in each of these cases is highly structured, and is spelled out with an example (p. 39). (The other sets of 'eel-wrigglers' also 'equivocate' according to the same structure; more on this in a moment.) It too involves a complicated sequence of affirmations and negations, but not one that takes a precisely quadrilemmatic shape. Piantelli's verdict in this case appears to result from his focusing on the form of the 'equivocations' and not on the quadrilemmas of propositions that are said to be subjected to these 'equivocations'. His observations, however, would have been very much to the point if applied to the attempt to assimilate Pyrrho to the other three sets of 'eel-wrigglers'; see below.

to the Buddha. The fourth group of 'eel-wrigglers' refuses to say anything, whereas Pyrrho's four-part form of speech is, if I have been right, a statement of the truth; and the subjects on which they refuse to answer questions seem to be a relatively limited cluster of metaphysical-cum-moral questions,[158] whereas Pyrrho is telling us to use the four-part form of speech 'about each single thing'. Finally, a point raised in the previous section, in connection with the Megarians, seems to be pertinent here as well. All the evidence suggests that Pyrrho was quite uninterested in, and even suspicious of, verbal pyrotechnics such as these Indian thinkers are reported to have employed; it is easy enough to think of Greek philosophers for whom the title 'eel-wriggler' would be appropriate, but Pyrrho is certainly not one of them.

The other three sets of 'eel-wrigglers' are people who refuse to answer questions on the grounds that (1) they might be wrong, that (2) they might become involved in the world, and that (3) they might be unable to respond to captious critics; in all three cases, the feared result is a kind of psychological trauma referred to as 'remorse' and 'hindrance'. It is not too great a leap, then, to assume that they set a high value on some kind of mental stability or tranquillity. In addition, it is arguable that the subject matter on which they are prepared to resort to this 'equivocation' is unrestricted. The one example given, in all three cases, is the question what the good and the evil really are. However, all of them are said to engage in their 'eel-wriggling' when questioned 'on this or that'; and there is no indication in their cases, as there is in the case of the school of Sanjaya, that 'this or that' actually covers a strictly defined set of topics.[159] One may feel, then, that the first three sets of 'eel-wrigglers' are rather closer to Pyrrho's outlook than the fourth set.[160]

---

[158] All four sets of 'eel-wrigglers' are said to resort to their tricks 'when a question is put to them on this or that' (sects. 23, 24, 27, in Rhys Davids (1899: 37–9)). Jayatilleke (1963) translates these words both by 'when questioned on this or that matter' (p. 124) and 'when questioned on each and every matter' (p. 129). (In both cases the original, *tattha tattha panham puttho*, is quoted.) But, although, in either translation, these words may suggest a certain generality, the text (Rhys Davids 1899: 39–40) gives a specific list of topics on which the fourth set of 'eel-wrigglers' adopt their procedure: whether there is another world, whether there are Chance Beings (that is, spontaneously generated beings), whether good and bad actions have consequences, and whether the *Tathagata* survives after death. (According to the Rhys Davids translation, their 'equivocations' are about '*such propositions as* the following' (p. 39, my emphasis); this may suggest that they were not confined to these very four sets of questions, but it does not suggest a significantly broader subject matter.)

[159] See again n. 158.

[160] This is the view of Jayatilleke (1963: 129–30, cf. 124, 133–4), for the two reasons just given. He also claims (p. 130) that both Pyrrho and the 'eel-wrigglers' 'hold that there were no beliefs or opinions which were true or false'; but this is itself false of the 'eel-wrigglers', on his own account. They, like all the other Indian thinkers we have discussed, *refuse* to make any claims as to the truth-value of some set of statements. Pyrrho, on the other hand, is indeed prepared to 'hold' a certain view about the truth-value of opinions; that was precisely the point of the crucial phrase in the Aristocles passage, 'neither our sensations nor our opinions tell the truth or lie'—see above Ch. 1, Sect. 2 and Appendix.

However, this feeling should evaporate when it is pointed out that no quadrilemmas are ascribed to these 'eel-wrigglers' at all. Instead, each group is ascribed *five* forms of words, the interpretation and translation of which appear to be very difficult; a version that is avowedly trying to be as literal as possible is the following: '(1) I do not say so. (2) I do not say thus. (3) I do not say otherwise. (4) I do not say no. (5) I do not say no, no.'[161] The fit with Pyrrho's fourfold form of speech in the Aristocles passage is very far from exact. It seems fair to say that equivalents of Pyrrho's 'is' and 'is not' occur here (1 and 4, or perhaps 1 and 2—if 'so' and 'thus' represent alternatives), and also perhaps 'neither is nor is not' (5), though this is far less obvious. But there is nothing corresponding to 'both is and is not'; and this leaves (at least) two components, whichever exactly they are and whatever exactly they mean, that have *no* equivalent in Pyrrho's form of speech.[162]

It is not clear, then, that any of these parallels is so precise as to compel the conclusion that Pyrrho adopted the quadrilemma from the 'naked wise men' he met in India. To this one might answer, however, that we should not expect the parallel to be precise;[163] Pyrrho might easily have adapted the quadrilemma for his own use, and in any case, the translation from whatever Indian language the 'naked wise men' spoke into Greek would not necessarily be without flaws. But now we come to the most serious problem with the hypothesis of a detailed Indian influence. To say that the translation would not be flawless is in fact a major understatement. It is extremely difficult to believe that anything as abstruse as a quadrilemma could possibly have been communicated in any remotely intact form from the Indian 'naked wise men' to Pyrrho. The ancient Greeks are notorious for their dismissiveness of all

---

[161] Jayatilleke (1963: 135). Rhys Davids (1899: 38) translates 'I don't take it thus. I don't take it the other way. But I advance no different opinion. And I don't deny your position. And I don't say it is neither one, nor the other.' Piantelli's Italian translation (Piantelli 1978: 149) seems to be logically equivalent to Jayatilleke's, except in the fifth component, which he renders by 'Per me non è che non sia non così'. It should be noted again (see n. 157) that this five-part 'equivocation' is also mentioned in connection with the school of Sanjaya; the difference is that in their case the statements to which their 'equivocation' was *applied* are specified as a list of quadrilemmas.

[162] Jayatilleke's attempt to assimilate the five-part 'equivocation' to the standard quadrilemma (Jayatilleke 1963: 135–8) is at least as hard to accept as the two suggestions of an ancient commentator that he rightly criticizes. He takes 5 as 'a denial of the rejection of all the possible logical alternatives' (p. 137)—that is, as a denial that 1–4 themselves constitute denials—and takes 1–4 as amounting to the standard quadrilemma in the standard order. The first and second elements, as we saw, might be equivalent to 'is' and 'is not'. But the idea that 'otherwise' is equivalent to 'both is and is not', or that 'no' is equivalent to 'neither is nor is not', seems to have no justification whatever.

[163] One might also object that I did not let obvious differences between Pyrrho and Plato prevent me from postulating an influence. But the connection in that case, though applying in an admittedly limited area of each man's philosophy, had to do with some precise verbal and philosophical parallels; and that, it seems to me, is what has not clearly been shown in the Indian case.

languages other than Greek; and Indian languages, in particular, would certainly not be among those with which, prior to Alexander's expedition, they would have come into regular contact. Later, in the Eastern territories conquered by Alexander, there appears to have been some cross-fertilization of cultures between the Greeks who settled there and the native peoples, which would presumably require some degree of bilingualism.[164] But it is inconceivable that an educated Greek in Pyrrho's day would have known Sanskrit, Pali (the language of the Buddhist scriptures), or any spoken Indian dialect. It is equally inconceivable, given the previous lack of contact between the two peoples, that the Indian thinkers knew Greek. Whatever conversation Pyrrho had with the Indians, then, must have taken place by means of a translation from an Indian language to Greek by some additional party or parties. Now, the people who served as translators on Alexander's expedition will presumably have been people from borderline linguistic territories, people who needed, for trading or other practical reasons, to deal with speakers of more than one language; and they will almost certainly have had no previous acquaintance with any philosophical tradition, Indian or Greek. Moreover, since there is no borderline territory linking Greece and India, any conversation between the Indian 'naked wise men' and Pyrrho must have required at least *two* of these philosophically unsophisticated translators—Greek to Persian, and Persian to whatever Indian language the 'naked wise men' may have spoken. Onesicritus states that he actually required *three* such translators—all people 'of no greater understanding than the masses' (*mēden sunientōn pleon ē hoi polloi*)—in his meeting with 'naked wise men'; not surprisingly the result was, as he says, as clear as mud (Strabo 15.1.64).

But Pyrrho's situation would have been even worse than this. Onesicritus' discussion, as he reports it, has to do with the way of life of the 'naked wise men', and with a few rather general ethical matters. There is no abstract argument, and nothing else that would require great intellectual subtlety to comprehend, at least in its general outline. No doubt a great deal in the way of nuance would have been lost; but it is imaginable that at least *something* could have been transmitted from the Indians to Onesicritus even in the circumstances of a cumbersome three-way translation by non-philosophers. But the way of thinking and speaking that Pyrrho supposedly picked up in India is in an altogether different category. Philosophers tend to forget (or wilfully deny) how wildly unnatural and extraordinary much of their activity is in the eyes of most outsiders. Quadrilemmas are not part of any non-philosopher's everyday speech; and, as anyone knows who has ever taught an

---

[164] See Tarn (1985: esp. ch. IX). The *Milinda Panha*, to which reference was made above (Rhys Davids 1890), may be a case in point. It has been argued that this shows traces of Greek influence—and also that it exerted influence on some Greek writings. See the Excursus in Tarn (1985: 414 ff.), and Stoneman (1995: 111). In any case, 'King Milinda' in this Buddhist text is the Bactrian Greek king Menander (155–130 BC).

introductory philosophy course, it is when philosophers start using bizarre, complicated, and non-standard forms of language that people are most apt to find them unintelligible (and so, not surprisingly, uninteresting). There is no reason to think that matters were any different in the ancient world; indeed, given how much more restricted education of any kind was in this period, the perceived remoteness of technical philosophizing would if anything have been even greater than it is today. So, let us suppose that the unidentified 'naked wise men' with whom Pyrrho spoke actually were devotees of the quadrilemma. In fact we have no idea who they were; but it makes no difference one way or the other. For the notion that the two or more translators who would have had to be employed by Pyrrho and the Indians would have been capable of communicating even a garbled account of the nature and purpose of the quadrilemma—or willing to struggle for any length of time at the task—is simply too fantastic to entertain.[165]

This in no way excludes the possibility of a more general influence of the kind discussed earlier—an influence at the level of lifestyle and broad philosophical attitude. This might in part be achieved without any linguistic communication at all; in any case, it would not require translators possessed of logical refinement or bilingual philosophical experience. However, the case for an influence at a detailed doctrinal level is shaky. The parallels of language and doctrine do not seem to be as exact as has been alleged— though, as an outsider to the field of Indian philosophy, that is clearly not a point on which I can rest with any great assurance. But the fundamental problem is a very simple one: there is no plausible medium by which this alleged influence, having to do with a technical form of language to be used for a precise philosophical purpose, could have been exerted.

11. Summary and conclusion

We have seen by now that the practical attitudes characteristic of early Pyrrhonism are, if anything, overdetermined by the other philosophies with which Pyrrho had some acquaintance; it would really not be out of the ordinary for someone in Pyrrho's time and place to have leaned towards an ideal of life of the same general kind as his *ataraxia* or *apatheia*. For the indeterminacy thesis, and its accompanying mistrust of sensation, precedents in Greek philosophy are not so plentiful; but, here again, they are by no means non-existent. The view encompassed in Anaxarchus' stage-set simile may have served, broadly speaking, as an inspiration here; Aristotle's discussion

---

[165] Decleva Caizzi (DC 139–40) also notes the difficulty of translation, but does not, I think, state it as forcefully as it deserves.

of the Law of Non-Contradiction also shows that some variety of indeterminacy thesis was proposed in the immediately preceding period. But I have argued that the clearest antecedent, if one looks in greater detail, is to be seen in the attitude towards sensible things exhibited in some dialogues of Plato and, more remotely, in the Eleatics. At any rate, the presence of these parallels makes clear that the interpretation of Pyrrho's central ideas offered in Chapter 1 is not historically implausible; it is certainly no more difficult, in terms of the historical context, to picture him as the exponent of the indeterminacy thesis than as promoting some form of suspension of judgement.[166]

What is most distinctive about Pyrrho, however, is the way in which the indeterminacy thesis and *ataraxia* are *combined*; neither Plato and the Eleatics nor Anaxarchus furnish a parallel here,[167] and nor, with the possible exception of the Indian sages, does anyone else. As Sextus points out centuries later (*PH* 1.12, 26), the usual orientation of Greek philosophy is to try to achieve a desirable attitude to life by means of successful theoretical enquiry, in which one comes to understand certain of the ways in which things present themselves to us as true to their real natures, and certain others as false; by renouncing any such attempt to discriminate among the appearances as indicators of the real natures of things, and by claiming to achieve *ataraxia by way of* this very renunciation, Pyrrho is charting what is, within Greek philosophy, a very unusual course, a course that was later to be followed by Aenesidemus and Sextus. This is true even though this renunciation is itself derived, in Pyrrho's case, from a thesis about the real nature of things—namely, that it is indeterminate. We have already frequently remarked that the later Pyrrhonists did not allow themselves even this much—indeed, that they would have regarded Pyrrho's indeterminacy thesis as a species of objectionable dogmatism. I have hinted at how they could nevertheless have regarded Pyrrho as their forerunner, and reasonably so. A more detailed account of the nature of the inspiration the later Pyrrhonists saw in Pyrrho—in other words, of why they called themselves 'Pyrrhonists' in the first place—will be elaborated in the final chapter.

---

[166] Slightly later, Arcesilaus is supposed to have appealed to Plato as an inspiration for his own sceptical practice (Cicero, *Acad.* 1.44–6). Presumably Pyrrho could have made a similar appeal, if suspension of judgement had been at the centre of his philosophy. It should, however, be noted that the extent to which Plato's dialogues—even just the aporetic ones—exhibit anything like a sceptical suspension of judgement is limited at best, and that there is an air of special pleading about Arcesilaus' claim; as head of the Academy, he *had to* place himself in the Platonic tradition—as Pyrrho did not. Still, since Arcesilaus *did* practise suspension of judgement only a generation or so after Pyrrho, it would be hard to maintain that Pyrrho could not have done so, with or without historical precedents. What I have argued is more cautious: first (in Chs. 1 and 2), that the evidence suggests that this was not in fact his approach, and, secondly (in this chapter), that the approach that the evidence suggests he did take is by no means unexpected in historical terms.

[167] On the difference between Pyrrho and Anaxarchus in this respect, see above, n. 120.

APPENDIX A.

Can we identify Aristotle's opponents in *Metaphysics* IV?

As was mentioned in Chapter 3, Section 2, some have thought that the people primarily under attack in Aristotle's discussion of the Law of Non-Contradiction are the Megarians; and, since it has also been thought that there is some connection between the Megarians and Pyrrho, this has been taken to favour the view that Pyrrho's indeterminacy thesis is a response to Aristotle. The identification was based[168] on a passage of Simplicius (*In Phys.* 120.12–17). The Megarians are said to hold 'that those things are different of which the definitions are different, and that things that are different are separated from one another'; on this basis they are said to have argued that 'each thing is separated from itself. For since the definition of Socrates the musical is different from the definition of Socrates the pale, Socrates would be separated from himself.' Now, the view attributed to the Megarians in this passage was thought to be highly reminiscent of a view criticized by Aristotle in the following two passages of *Metaphysics* IV: (1) 'It is not possible, then, that "being a human being" should signify what "not being a human being" signifies, if "human being" signifies not only *in respect of* one thing but also one thing (for we do not consider signifying *in respect of* one thing as signifying one thing, since in that case "musical" and "pale" and "human being" would signify one thing)' ($1006^{b}13$–17), and (2) 'But if, when one asks the question simply, he [i.e. Aristotle's imagined opponent] adds the denials also, he is not answering what was asked. For nothing prevents the same thing being a human being and pale and indefinitely many other things; but still, when one is asked whether it is true to say that this thing is a human being or not, one's answer should signify one thing—one should not add that it is also pale and large' ($1007^{a}8$–14).

However, apart from the use of the examples of 'musical' and 'pale' in passage 1, and 'pale' alone in passage 2, there is nothing at all to connect these passages to the Megarian view reported by Simplicius. The first passage points out that, if the term 'human being' has a single meaning, it cannot mean the same as its opposite, and also (as a point of clarification) that meaning the same should not be identified with being applicable to the same object. The second passage points out that an unambiguous question should receive an unambiguous answer—and that this is not altered by the fact that many different predicates may apply to the same object. Neither of these points has anything to do with the view that things whose definitions are different are themselves different.[169] To this one may add that nothing in any text relating to the Megarians suggests that any of them ever attempted to do what Aristotle is funda-

---

[168] By Maier (1900: ii, pt. 2, 6 ff.). As noted above, n. 24, Maier himself does not attempt to build a connection with Pyrrho on this identification; it is others who have taken that further step.

[169] The Megarians would of course deny that the same thing can be 'a human being and pale and indefinitely many other things'. But Aristotle's point is that, despite the obvious *truth* of this claim, it does not have the consequence his opponent needs. The implication, then, is that the opponent also accepts it as obviously true.

mentally claiming in this text to be impossible—that is, to deny the Law of Non-Contradiction. In fact the Simplicius passage suggests quite the opposite. On the view reported there, the same thing cannot even have a *plurality* of (non-synonymous) predicates, let alone contradictory predicates; if Socrates the musical is not even the same entity as Socrates the pale, it can hardly be supposed that Socrates the musical would be the same entity as Socrates the non-musical.

There is, then, no reason to think that the Megarians are the unnamed targets of Aristotle's polemic.[170] Indeed, it is very hard to know who they are. At the beginning of *Metaphysics* IV.4, Aristotle tells us that some people 'both themselves say that it is possible for the same thing to be and not to be, and say that it is possible to suppose so' (1005^{b}35–1006^{a}2). He then adds that 'many even of the physicists use this language' (1006^{a}2–3); and in the subsequent discussion, particularly in the later chapters of the book, a number of physical thinkers are indeed referred to (in addition to Protagoras).[171] But these thinkers seem to be mentioned primarily as examples of people whose views *commit* them to the denial of the Law of Non-Contradiction, or who may incidentally have denied it, not as people who explicitly made a virtue of denying it. The unusual phrase 'use this language' (*chrōntai . . . tōi logōi toutōi*), in the sentence just quoted, seems to fit with this attitude; to *use* a certain form of words is by no means necessarily the same as putting forward the ideas contained in those words as a considered doctrine. Besides, the phrase 'many *even* of the physicists' (*polloi kai tōn peri phuseōs*) indicates that Aristotle's main target is some other group of people who are not physicists. And, in keeping with this, the vast majority of the discussion is directed against unnamed opponents. We may be able to say a good deal about the nature of the view or views being criticized; but, since none of our sources names any set of philosophers who 'both themselves say that it is possible for the same thing to be and not to be, and say that it is possible to suppose so', we are in no position to identify the authors of this view.

Only one of the Aristotelian commentators offers any clue as to their identity. Asclepius (*In Met.* 222, 11–13) says that one of the goals of *Metaphysics* IV is to attack 'those called "suspensive" [*ephektikous*]' on the subject of 'inapprehensibility' (*akatalēpsias*), and to show 'that there is no inapprehensibility, but things are apprehensible [*katalēpta*]'. But this tells us little or nothing. 'Suspensive' was one of the

---

[170] The identification of the Megarians as Aristotle's opponents is also criticized by Stopper (1983: 267). On the question whether there are other reasons for connecting Pyrrho with the Megarians, see Ch. 3. Sect. 9.

[171] Among these is Heraclitus (1012a24–5, 34–5). However, despite Heraclitus' widely reported penchant for statements attributing opposite properties to the same thing, Aristotle seems hesitant about whether to include him among the offenders. In introducing the subject at the end of *Metaphysics* IV.3, Aristotle says that '*some think* that Heraclitus said' that the same thing can both be and not be a certain way (1005^{b}25). And, in referring later to the extreme view of the Heraclitean Cratylus, to the effect that everything is constantly changing in every respect, he is careful to avoid any implication that Heraclitus himself accepted this view. The view is said to be that of 'those who declare themselves to be Heraclitizing' (*tōn phaskontōn Hērakleitizein* (1010^{a}11)); and Cratylus is recorded as criticizing Heraclitus for not holding a sufficiently radical doctrine of flux (1010^{a}13–15). These reservations on Aristotle's part are probably justified; there is in fact no good reason to believe that Heraclitus intended to attribute contradictory properties to the same things in the same respects. See Kahn (1979: 192, 267 ff.); Graham (1997: esp. sect. I).

terms used in self-description by the later Pyrrhonists (see Sextus, *PH* 1.7), but in Aristotle's day the term had not been invented;[172] nor was the term 'apprehensible' or its opposite standard philosophical vocabulary until the Hellenistic era. Aristotle does several times complain that certain people continue their demands for justification beyond the point where they are legitimate (so as to demand a justification even of the Law of Non-Contradiction); and this may perhaps put us in mind of a sceptic of the later Pyrrhonist mold.[173] But Asclepius' anachronistic terminology and his general vagueness strongly suggests that he was simply guessing at the identity of Aristotle's opponents, based on his knowledge of the range of positions that had been adopted at some point in the history of philosophy. In any case, his comment takes us no closer to identifying them ourselves.

[172] On this, see Ch. 1 n. 75.

[173] In addition, some passages attribute to the opponents considerations reminiscent of those employed in the Ten Modes of later Pyrrhonism; see 1009^{b}1 ff., 1010^{b}1 ff., 1011^{a}3 ff., and for discussion Long (1981). However, this similarity proves to be a rather limited one; the outlook sketched there is in fact considerably different from later Pyrrhonism (see above, n. 28). Modern commentators have also sometimes referred to Aristotle's opponents as sceptics. See Annas and Barnes (1985: 11–12); Irwin (1988: ch. 9). But in this case no historical claim is being made about their identity; the term 'sceptic' is employed simply as a convenient label for the position being attacked.

APPENDIX B.

Is *Theaetetus* 181a–183b connected with *Republic* V, etc.?

As was pointed out in Chapter 3, Section 3, it has often been thought that Socrates' criticism of the extreme Heraclitean thesis in the *Theaetetus* is related to the conception of sensible things discussed in the *Republic* and certain other dialogues generally thought to belong to the same period of Plato's life—a conception that Plato himself appears to find compelling. For the reasons mentioned in the main text, it is not essential for my argument that we settle whether or not there is a connection between these two parts of Plato's *œuvre*; but the question is not irrelevant to our assessment of Pyrrho, and is also of some intrinsic interest. The answer to the question turns on whether there is ever any sign that Plato himself accepts, or is committed to, a view of sensible things as radically subject to change, in something like the manner described in the *Theaetetus* passage.

The passage from *Republic* V on which we have focused certainly does not need to be interpreted as entailing such a view. For the variability to which, according to that passage, sensible things are subject need not take the specific form of changeability. When Socrates says that the same things will sometimes appear beautiful and sometimes appear ugly, this need not mean that the things will undergo some *internal alteration* such that one epithet will cease to be applicable and the other will become applicable; it may mean, for example, that the same thing may be beautiful in one setting, ugly in another—depending, for example, on the lighting conditions, on the other things with which it is juxtaposed, and so on. Again, the same thing may simultaneously warrant the epithets 'large' and 'small', depending on the other things with which it is being compared. Opposite epithets may, then, be applicable to the thing without its undergoing any intrinsic change. What I have been including under the general heading of 'variability' is by no means confined to change; there are numerous types of variability that do not include change, but instead consist purely in what has been called 'compresence of opposites'.[174] Thus it is possible to read the entire passage at the end of *Republic* V as claiming that sensible things have a lower status than Forms because, unlike Forms, they admit the compresence of opposites—and not as claiming that sensible things are changing, constantly or otherwise. And, if one reads it in this way, one will not be inclined to see any connection between the view of sensible things in the *Republic* and the thesis of total instability in the *Theaetetus*.

---

[174] See Irwin (1977); Fine (1993: ch. 4, esp. pp. 54–7). Fine says that Plato counts compresence as a kind of change; Irwin defines a form of change, 'a-change', which is either equivalent to or includes the compresence of opposites. I would prefer to say that what Plato means by *kinēsis*, *metabolē*, etc., if he is indeed prepared to use these terms to characterize the compresence of opposites, is not quite the same as what we mean by 'change'; to call the compresence of opposites a species of change seems to strain the meaning of the English word. (This is why I have instead chosen 'variability'—a word not in ordinary use at all—as the general term.)

On the other hand, it is clearly true that sensible things are at least *subject* to change; and clearly *one* possible way in which sensible things can come to have opposite epithets applicable to them is by changing. We may accept that the *Republic* passage in no way implies the presence of *constant* change among sensible things; but it is far less obvious that the changeability of sensible things is not in his mind in this passage at all—even if this is not actually required for the argument at this point. For one thing, Plato in this passage appears to draw conspicuously on Parmenidean reasoning;[175] and Parmenides certainly does consider various species of change—'coming into being and perishing . . . changing place and altering bright colour' (DK 28B8, ll. 40–1)—as among the reasons why sensible things are to be disqualified from the status of *to eon*, 'that which is'. But, if changeability is naturally understood as at least one component of the variability Plato emphasizes about sensibles, we may also wonder whether he may not at times have been attracted to a more extreme thesis concerning their changeability. At least two passages from other dialogues have been thought to suggest that he was.

At *Phaedo* 78e, speaking of 'the many beautiful things, such as human beings or horses or clothes or any other such things'—that is, beautiful sensible particulars, as opposed to the Form of Beauty (or sensible equals, as opposed to Form of Equality, and so on)—Socrates asks whether they 'are never, so to speak, in any way in the same state in relation to themselves or to each other', and receives the answer that this is correct; they are never in the same state.[176] Once agreed upon, this point is then exploited in an argument for the soul's immortality, based on the similarity between souls and Forms, on the one hand, and bodies and sensible things, on the other. Is this an endorsement of some kind of extreme changeability in the sensible world? It certainly looks like it. It has been suggested that here too, as in the *Republic* passage, Plato means us to understand only a reference to the comprecence of opposites;[177] sensible things are 'never in the same state' in that opposite predications are always (in some respects or other) true of them. But this seems not to take into account the context of the argument. Socrates' point is that souls are to bodies as Forms are to sensibles. The body is conspicuously subject to change—specifically and worryingly, to decay and dissolution; the question is whether the soul can be shown to be exempt from this fate. It is argued that the soul is exempt, because, out of the two types of entities, Forms and sensibles, souls, being invisible, are more like Forms, and Forms are not subject to dissolution or decay. It is only the body that is like—indeed, is an instance of—the class of sensibles; so, while the body may be liable to dissolution, the soul need not be. The feature of sensibles that is relevant to the argument, then, is

---

[175] For some verbal parallels with Parmenides, and their significance, see Crystal (1996).

[176] The words 'so to speak' (*hōs epos eipein*) may appear to weaken or qualify the claim (cf. above, n. 42). But there is no indication anywhere else that this is the intention; cf. 79a9–10, 80b4–5, where the visible realm is said without qualification to be 'never in the same state'.

[177] By Irwin (1977) and Fine (1993: 54–7). Both also claim that, by 'the many beautifuls, such as human beings or horses or clothes, etc.', Socrates is referring to *classes* of human beings, horses, clothes, etc.—for example, the class of dark-complexioned men—and not to individuals. But without some clear indication to the contrary—of which there is none—'human beings or horses or clothes' is naturally taken to refer to individual human beings, horses, and items of clothing. (In the *Republic* passage, by contrast, there is some possible textual warrant for taking 'the many beautiful things' to refer to properties rather than to individuals (see above, n. 41)).

precisely their susceptibility to a certain kind of change. So, when the speakers talk of sensibles in general as being 'never in the same state', and aligning them for this reason with the body rather than with the soul, it is difficult to read them as referring to compresence of opposites *rather than* to change; for that would make the reference to sensibles useless for the purpose for which it is introduced. The fact that sensibles undergo change has an obvious connection with the body's mortality; the fact that, for example, a baseball is heavier than a tennis ball but lighter than a bowling ball has, on the face of it, no connection with the issue of mortality whatsoever.

Again, at *Symposium* 207d–208b Diotima talks of the processes of decay and renewal constantly undergone by all living beings—in multiple respects, both physical and psychological. Now, it is true that the changes in question are ordered[178]— they explain how a living being can at least seem to be the same individual (208a6–7) over time—whereas the constant and all-consuming change believed in by the extreme Heracliteans in the *Theaetetus* seems to preclude any kind of orderly processes, and any reference to any individuals whatsoever. However, the *Symposium* passage, along with the passage from the *Phaedo*, does suggest that Plato was at times tempted by views to the effect that sensible things are in some sense radically changeable or unstable. And this also fits with what Aristotle has to say on the subject. In *Metaphysics* I Aristotle says that Plato in his youth became 'familiar with Cratylus and the Heraclitean doctrines, that all sensible things are always in flux and that there is no knowledge about them', and that 'later, too, he held these views' (987ᵃ32–ᵇ1). Now, as we have seen, both Plato and Aristotle elsewhere make clear that the view of Cratylus is that things are constantly undergoing change. It is therefore not open to us to interpret 'are always in flux' as referring merely to the compresence of opposites;[179] 'in flux' (*reontōn*) must mean 'undergoing change', and Aristotle is telling us that, both in his youth and in his maturity—though not necessarily for the whole of either period—Plato accepted the view that sensible things are constantly undergoing change. It may well be that he did not need to hold this view, in order for his central contrasts between sensible things and Forms to be made out; but the evidence appears to suggest that he did hold it. For him, it seems, change and the compresence of opposites are both defects suffered by sensible things, and they are both defects for the same reason; in both cases, predicates fail to belong to sensibles unqualifiedly. And, if this is correct, it is not unreasonable to suppose that the passage in the *Theaetetus*, in which an extreme Heraclitean view is shown to be incoherent, does have some connection with the conception of sensible things revealed in the *Republic* and elsewhere.

We need not suppose that Plato ever subscribed to the idea that sensibles are constantly changing in *every respect*; none of the passages we have looked at goes as far as that. But the passages from the *Phaedo* and *Symposium* might easily be seen as

---

[178] As is pointed out by Irwin (1977: 6).

[179] As do Irwin (1977) and Fine (1993: 54–7), who maintain both that Plato does not hold that sensibles are constantly changing and that Aristotle does not misinterpret him. They cannot have it both ways. Aristotle associates Plato with Cratylus, and Cratylus did hold that sensibles are constantly changing (or, in Irwin's terminology, are constantly undergoing s-change); either Aristotle is wrong, or change does have a role in Plato's thinking about sensibles and their relations to Forms.

at least pushing him in that direction;[180] and, if so, it could well have seemed to him important to make clear—as he had failed to do so far—that there are limits to how far one's view as to the changeability of sensibles can coherently go. The *Theaetetus* passage has its function within the structure of the dialogue, and the precise determination of that function is a complex and controversial matter. But the echoes that so many have detected between this passage and others, in which Plato is apparently offering for serious consideration a certain conception of sensibles, need not after all be accidental. It makes sense (I do not claim anything stronger) to see this passage as, among other things, self-criticism or at least self-clarification.[181]

[180] By contrast, he need not have felt any pressure to generalize his picture of the 'compresence of opposites'. For, as noted in Ch. 3, Sect. 3, he makes plain that a wide range of questions, such as whether or not a certain object is a finger, do not admit any of the 'ambiguity' by which he is troubled in the case of predicates such as beautiful, large, or heavy. There are no such obvious limits to Pyrrho's conception of the variability of things—which is why the parallel with the *Theaetetus* passage seemed plausible in the first place. But, in Plato's case, it was *only* his ideas about change that might have threatened to get out of control; his ideas about other forms of variability seem to be far more clearly restricted, stopping well short of any danger of a breakdown in coherence.

[181] Arguably, this development is taken further in the *Timaeus*, where it is claimed that sensible things do have a certain minimal level of stability that makes reference to them, and hence coherent thought about them, possible. See Gill (1987).

APPENDIX C.

On the interpretation of atomism as a 'myth'

As noted in Chapter 3, Section 7, on any literal interpretation of atomism, Pyrrho would have wanted nothing to do with it. However, Fernanda Decleva Caizzi (1984*a*) has argued that, according to a certain *non*-literal interpretation, he could have found atomism much more appealing—and that this could have been the primary basis for his attested admiration for Democritus. Pyrrho, it is suggested, viewed the atomic theory as an expression of the fundamental disorder and purposelessness of the world. The world does not tend in any direction, according to atomism, but is simply a collection of atoms, thrown together by chance; and we humans are the same way. Democritus' atomism was read by Pyrrho, then, as a 'myth' or metaphor for the vanity of human life.

But against this ingenious suggestion various objections can be made. First, for him to have understood atomism *merely* as mythical or metaphorical would be a misreading so gross as to be incredible; the surviving words of Democritus—even though few of them are on the subject of atomism—make it clear that it was intended as a theory of the nature of reality, and the recorded titles of his physical works, as well as the accounts of the theory in Aristotle, Theophrastus, and others, make it clear that this theory was expounded in considerable detail. Decleva Caizzi at one point speaks of Pyrrho's interpretation and the cosmological interpretation as *alternative* readings of Democritus' atomic theory.[182] However, the two are really not on a par; the one is an account of the specifics of the theory, while the other is no more than a lesson that might possibly be derived from it.

But neither would it have made sense for Pyrrho to have extracted a mythical message from Democritus' atomism and discarded the physics. As a way of explaining or promoting his own ideas, a reference to atomism would be thoroughly perverse, since his audience would surely have understood atomism as a cosmology; as far as we can tell, this is how everyone else in the ancient world understood it. And in any case, as was observed in the main text, Pyrrho could not have been merely indifferent to atomism, understood as a theory of the true nature of things; he must have been opposed to it, since it conflicts with his own indeterminacy thesis. In fact, while he held that things were 'indifferent and unstable and indeterminate', atoms are paradigmatically the opposite; every atom has a fixed and precise character, and retains that character throughout time. No matter how much he might have stressed his own idiosyncratic metaphorical understanding of atomism, it seems highly unlikely that Pyrrho would have been attracted to atomism in the first place, given that, understood literally, it ought to have been anathema to someone with the views that he held.

Finally, the word *muthōn*, in Timon's description of Democritus as *periphrona*

---

[182] Decleva Caizi (1984*a*: 150 in the French version, 16–17 in the Italian version).

poimena muthōn, can very well be understood in the sense 'words' or 'discourses' rather than in the sense 'myths'. This would not be a weakened sense of the term, as alleged by Decleva Caizzi;[183] it is standard in Homer, and Timon's *Silloi* are full of Homeric and mock-Homeric language.

[183] Decleva Caizzi (1984*a*: 151–2 in the French version, 18 in the Italian version).

4

Looking Forwards

If Pyrrho's outlook was as different from that of Sextus as I have suggested, why did Sextus call himself a Pyrrhonist? That, in brief, is the remaining question that I need to address. Even in the course of underlining the differences, I have also drawn attention to some similarities between the two outlooks. But these similarities, it may well be felt, are by no means sufficient to explain why the obscure[1] figure of Pyrrho should have been seized upon by the later Pyrrhonists as an inspiration or founding father. Sextus insists that, as far as the real nature of things is concerned, the sceptic suspends judgement. Yet, if I argued correctly in Chapter 1, this is precisely what Pyrrho does *not* do. By propounding a metaphysical thesis, he disqualifies himself from the title 'sceptic', as understood by Sextus; and this, one might think, would be enough to ensure that he would not be a thinker with whom Sextus would want to associate himself. It is true, as we also saw in Chapter 1, Section 7, that Sextus only once attempts to *explain* the point of the term 'Pyrrhonist', and that his comment in this one passage is surprisingly cautious and vague; the sceptical movement is called Pyrrhonism, he tells us, 'from the fact that Pyrrho appears to us to have approached scepticism in a more bodily fashion and more manifestly than those who preceded him' (*PH* 1.7). But elsewhere he is happy to count himself among the Pyrrhonians (*Purrōneioi*), as if this needed no defence (*PH* 1.11, 13, 217); and even the passage just quoted, for all its caution, indicates clearly that Pyrrho was the figure from the past with whom Sextus' tradition felt itself to have the greatest philosophical kinship. Why should this be?

A satisfying answer to this question, I shall suggest, requires that we distinguish two phases within the later Pyrrhonist tradition: a terminal phase, represented by most of the writings of Sextus himself, and an initial phase, represented by the founder of the tradition, Aenesidemus. Aenesidemus' variety of Pyrrhonism seems to have used slogans similar to those used by Sextus; the Pyrrhonist is said to be without dogma, and to 'determine nothing', and

---

[1] As we have seen, Cicero several times remarks on the fact that Pyrrho is a little-known figure; see Ch. 2 n. 88 and accompanying text. Apparently the later Pyrrhonist movement itself did not significantly change this state of affairs; Seneca, too, refers to Pyrrho as a neglected thinker without a following (*Nat. Q.* 7.32.2).

this posture may easily be assumed to be identical with the suspension of judgement adopted by Sextus. But a closer inspection reveals that freedom from dogma amounts, in Aenesidemus' eyes, to something considerably different from what it amounts to in Sextus' *Outlines of Pyrrhonism*—and something considerably closer to the position held by Pyrrho. The problem of why the later Pyrrhonists chose to give themselves that title is a good deal easier to solve, then, if we recognize that later Pyrrhonism itself, in its initial phase, was by no means identical with what is presented to us—most of the time, at any rate—in the pages of Sextus. Of course, this presents us with the further problem of explaining the transition between the initial and terminal phases of later Pyrrhonism; but this problem can also be solved, I shall argue, in a comparatively straightforward way.

This chapter will begin, then, with an interpretation of the philosophy of Aenesidemus, and of the ways in which it differs from that of the later phase known to us primarily through Sextus. This will include some discussion of the extent to which Aenesidemus' version of Pyrrhonism is discernible even in some parts of Sextus' own writings, despite its incompatibility with the Pyrrhonism to which Sextus himself mostly claims allegiance. The task will then be to explain the connection between the ideas of Pyrrho and of Aenesidemus, and the connection between the initial and terminal phases of later Pyrrhonism. In the course of this discussion, we shall also need to tackle one other thorny issue—namely, a connection between Aenesidemus and Heraclitus that is apparently alluded to in a number of places by Sextus. As we saw in Chapter 3, a Heraclitean view attacked by Plato seemed to be of some importance in the discussion of Pyrrho's antecedents; so it is natural to wonder whether the alleged 'Heracliteanism' of Aenesidemus may also have some bearing on the question why he regarded himself as following in Pyrrho's footsteps.

1. Aenesidemus: relativities and the invariability condition

As was noted in the Introduction, Pyrrho's direct personal influence seems to have been short-lived; he had a number of disciples, but there is no indication that any of these went on to found a Pyrrhonist school. It is possible that his younger contemporary Arcesilaus, who was the first to take the Academy in a sceptical direction, was in some way indebted to his ideas or his example; satirical verses by two other contemporaries, Timon and the Stoic Aristo, point to Pyrrho as one of the figures on whom Arcesilaus relied in assembling his philosophy.[2] But, whatever the nature and extent of this influence, it was

---

[2] The verses are quoted in several places; see DL 4.33; Sextus, *PH* 1.234; Numenius in Eusebius, *Praep. evang.* XIV.5.13 (and cf. XIV.6.4–6, which alleges an association between

never acknowledged, as far as we can tell, within the Academy. So Pyrrho quickly passed into obscurity, where he was to remain for some two centuries. It was not until Aenesidemus that there came to be anything we could call a Pyrrhonian tradition.

Aenesidemus may be dated with fair security to the first century BC. The passage that is our single most important source of evidence for Aenesidemus' views—a chapter from the *Bibliotheca*, or *Library*, of Photius, the ninth-century Patriarch of Constantinople (169b18–171a4)—tells us that his book *Pyrrhonist Discourses* (*Purrōnioi Logoi*) was dedicated to a certain Lucius Tubero (169b32–5), who is plausibly identified with a known acquaintance of Cicero.[3] The passage does not actually say that Aenesidemus was the *first* to use the term 'Pyrrhonist'. But there is no earlier evidence of this practice;[4] and Aristocles says that it was Aenesidemus who revived the Pyrrhonian way of thinking after it had lain dormant for a considerable length of time (Eusebius, *Praep. evang.* XIV.18.29). Aenesidemus' use of the term 'Pyrrhonist' is clearly not casual. In addition to the title of what must have been a central work of his, Photius frequently has Aenesidemus refer to himself and his associates (whoever they may have been) as 'Pyrrhonists' (169b21, 36–7, 170a11, 40, 170b2) or as 'followers of Pyrrho' (*hoi apo Purrōnos* (169b40, 170a22–3)); he also characterizes himself as 'philosophizing in the manner of Pyrrho' (*kata Purrōna philosophōn* (169b26–7)). One can hardly doubt that these expressions were liberally scattered through Aenesidemus' own writing. Again, as in Sextus' case, they do not show that Aenesidemus took himself to be reproducing Pyrrho's philosophy in every detail. But they do show that he took Pyrrho to have anticipated his own ideas in crucial respects. And, unlike Sextus, he is not being fed this notion by way of an already existing tradition; on the contrary, since he is the *initiator* of the later Pyrrhonist tradition, it must be his own deliberate policy to appropriate the name of Pyrrho in this way. In order to understand why this policy might have made good sense, we need to examine his own distinctive variety of Pyrrhonism.

Photius writes two or three pages summarizing Aenesidemus' *Pyrrhonist*

Arcesilaus and Pyrrho, probably on the basis of nothing more than the verses themselves). For contrasting views on the extent to which the ideas or example of Pyrrho actually were a factor in the development of Arcesilaus' sceptical posture, see Sedley (1983*a*); Decleva Caizzi (1986); LS i. 445–6; Görler (1994: 812–15).

[3] The most detailed recent examination of the evidence is Decleva Caizzi (1992*a*). Some of the details of Decleva Caizzi's account are, however, plausibly challenged by Lévy (1997: 115–17). In particular, Lévy argues for a date of composition for Aenesidemus' *Purrōnioi Logoi* of around 80 BC, rather than the 50s BC, as suggested by Decleva Caizzi; this would place it considerably closer to the period in which Philo and Antiochus were active, and hence would make better sense of Aenesidemus' special antipathy to the Academics of his own day (see below).

[4] On the list of 'Pyrrhonists' at DL 9.115–16, see again Introduction, n. 6.

Discourses—a work also referred to by Sextus (*M* 8.215) and Diogenes (9.106)—followed by some very brief and largely dismissive criticism. As just suggested, this is by far the most extensive surviving passage devoted directly to the description of Aenesidemus' views. It might well be wondered whether a late, hostile, and non-philosophical source such as this should be taken seriously. However, comparisons between the language of the Photius passage and language employed in numerous briefer allusions to Aenesidemus in Sextus and in Diogenes Laertius, as well as comparisons between this passage of Photius and his summaries of some other books, suggest that Photius is taking good care to keep his summary objective, and that frequently, at least, he is employing Aenesidemus' actual words.[5] Besides, the view Photius ascribes to Aenesidemus is internally coherent, philosophically interesting, and clearly comparable to ideas that appear periodically in Sextus and in Diogenes—not always, admittedly, under the name of Aenesidemus, but often as characteristic of Pyrrhonism more generally. The view that emerges, however, is noticeably distinct from that of the official programme promoted by Sextus' *Outlines of Pyrrhonism*.

As already noted, Aenesidemus maintains, according to Photius, that the Pyrrhonist 'determines nothing' (not even that nothing is determined (170a11–12)) and is 'free from all dogma' (169b41). This stance is contrasted with that of the Academics, and especially those of his own day, who are accused of being 'dogmatic' (169b39), and of accepting so much Stoic doctrine that they seem like 'Stoics fighting with Stoics' (170a14–17). It is not clear whether this refers to the ongoing dispute between the Stoa and the sceptical Academy, or to a dispute internal to the Academy (*both* of the parties to which seemed to Aenesidemus not significantly different from Stoics). The latter interpretation seems thoroughly appropriate to the dispute between Philo of Larissa and Antiochus of Ascalon in the early first century BC, the period of the Academy's demise as a formal institution—and also the period that we have already seen, on other grounds, to be probably Aenesidemus' own. But that would make the remark apply *exclusively*, and not just 'especially' (*malista*), to the contemporary situation. The other interpretation perhaps fits better with the whole history of the sceptical Academy; for dialectical purposes the Academics had always allowed their debates with the Stoics to be framed by the terms of Stoic doctrine, but in different ways Philo and Antiochus had effected a degree of *rapprochement* with Stoicism far beyond anything countenanced by Arcesilaus or Carneades.[6] In any case, Aenesidemus is proclaiming his own new Pyrrhonist movement as a

---

[5] On this see Janáček (1976).

[6] The story of the Academy under Philo and Antiochus (or Academies, since Antiochus founded a breakaway school) is complex and disputed; but the points just alluded to are not controversial. See Glucker (1978); Sedley (1981); Tarrant (1985); Barnes (1989); Striker (1997); Hankinson (1997: sects. II–IV, IX–XI).

genuinely sceptical outlook, and contrasting it unfavourably with the Academy, which, he suggests, was never properly sceptical, but which certainly could not be considered sceptical in his own time. The passage appears to imply that Aenesidemus was himself once a member of the Academy;[7] if so, his adoption of the label Pyrrhonism is his way of marking a decisive break with his own former allegiances.

Aenesidemus draws another contrast between his own movement and not only the Academics, but dogmatic philosophers in general. Dogmatists are said to 'wear themselves out to no purpose' (*heautous matēn katatribein*) and to be exercised by 'ceaseless torments' (*sunechesin aniais*), while the Pyrrhonist is said to be happy, and his policy of determining nothing is clearly what is supposed to be responsible for this (169b22–9). The Pyrrhonist's happiness is not specifically described as *ataraxia*; but the nature of the contrast with the dogmatists' situation at least suggests that this is how Aenesidemus conceives of the Pyrrhonist's more desirable state. So far, then, there is nothing to which the Sextus of *Outlines of Pyrrhonism* could object; his own depiction both of the Academy (*PH* 1.3, 220–35) and of Pyrrhonism itself seems quite compatible with Aenesidemus' pronouncements. However, on further inspection of the Photius passage, it turns out that Aenesidemus' form of 'freedom of dogma' permits him to hold views, and to make assertions, that *Outlines of Pyrrhonism* could not possibly allow.

First, the Pyrrhonist is said to assert that things are 'no more of this kind than that, or sometimes of this kind and sometimes not, or for one person of this kind, for another not of this kind, and for someone else not even existent at all' (170a1–3).[8] Now, as in the case of Pyrrho and the Aristocles passage,

---

[7] Lucius Tubero, the man to whom *Pyrrhonist Discourses* was dedicated, is referred to as one of Aenesidemus' *sunairesiōtai* in the Academy (169b33). *Sunairesiōtēs* was always assumed to mean 'fellow-member' or 'colleague'. Decleva Caizzi, however, has argued (1992a) that *sunairesiōtēs* can mean simply 'member', rather than 'fellow-member'—in which case the sole evidence for Aenesidemus' having ever belonged to the Academy disappears. But Jaap Mansfeld has replied with a counter-argument that seems to establish that, here at least, *sunairesiōtēs* must mean 'fellow-member'; see Mansfeld (1995). It may seem to have been a benefit of Decleva Caizzi's position that it accounted for the fact that Cicero, himself a student of the Academy, never once refers to Aenesidemus. But Cicero was not a professional philosopher, and his direct engagement with the Academy was sporadic; it is entirely possible that Aenesidemus made his decisive move at a time when Cicero was occupied with Roman politics rather than the Academy's politics. On this see also Brochard (1923: 245), and above, Ch. 2, n. 95.

[8] The preceding line reads 'Absolutely none of them [i.e. Pyrrhonists, as opposed to Academics] has said that all things are inapprehensible, nor that they are apprehensible'; the passage then continues 'but no more of this kind than that', etc. I am assuming that a comma belongs before 'but no more of this kind than that', and hence that what follows 'but' summarizes what the Pyrrhonist *does* say ('but no more of this kind than that' being read as 'but [the Pyrrhonist says that they are] no more of this kind than that'), by *contrast* with his refusal to say that 'all things are inapprehensible' or 'all things are apprehensible'. If one omits this comma, then 'but that they are no more of this kind than that', etc. becomes a further component of what

there is a question as to how 'no more' (*ouden mallon*) is to be interpreted. Does 'no more of this kind than that'—or, in contemporary philosophical parlance, 'no more F than not-F', where F stands for any arbitrary predicate[9]—express suspension of judgement as between the alternatives F and not-F? As we saw, that is how Sextus explains the term 'no more' in *Outlines of Pyrrhonism*. Or should 'no more' be taken in its natural sense of 'to no greater extent than'? The other phrases—sometimes F, sometimes not-F, and F for one person, not-F for another, and non-existent for a third—make clear that the latter is the correct reading.[10] For these other phrases express not

the Pyrrhonist does *not* say (but the Academic does say); the Pyrrhonist refuses to say that things are 'apprehensible-but-no-more-of-this-kind-than-that', etc. However, this cannot be the right way to read the text. Aside from the difficulty of understanding what it would mean for 'but no more of this kind than that', etc. to be a *qualification* on 'apprehensible', the next sentence reads 'nor [has any of the Pyrrhonists said] that all things . . . are accessible [*ephikta*] nor that they are not accessible, but [they say that they are] no more accessible than not accessible, or sometimes', etc. (170a3–5). Here it is undeniable that there is a comma before 'but', and that the words after 'but' give what the Pyrrhonist *does* say ('not-accessible-but-no-more-accessible-than-not-accessible' would obviously be nonsense); and the strict parallelism of the passage makes clear that the same must be true of the previous sentence. See also Hankinson (1995: 336–7 n. 19).

9 It might be objected that, since the previous clauses have been about inapprehensibility or apprehensibility (see the previous note), 'of this kind than that' (*toiade ē toiade*) should be read as meaning specifically 'inapprehensible than apprehensible', and not as substituting for any arbitrary predicates F and not-F. However (as Hankinson 1995: 337 n. 20 points out), the words 'not even existent at all' have nothing to do with apprehensibility or its opposite, which suggests that the immediately preceding words are also of more general application. Besides, as we shall see in the next section, Aenesidemus is very emphatic that *none* of us have *katalēpsis*, 'apprehension', of *anything*; in view of this, it is very hard to see how he could be willing to assert that things are 'sometimes apprehensible, sometimes inapprehensible' or 'apprehensible for one person, inapprehensible for another' (I leave aside the 'no more' clause for the moment, since we have not yet sorted out its function). On why he none the less refuses to assert that 'all things are inapprehensible', see the next section.

If I am right in reading *toiade* as standing for any arbitrary predicate, a further question arises as to the point of the contrast; why would Aenesidemus say that the Pyrrhonist refuses to assert that things are inapprehensible or that they are apprehensible, *but* is willing to assert that they are no more F than not-F, etc.? Again, this question will be taken up in the next section.

10 James Allen has suggested to me that the 'sometimes' and 'for this person' phrases might be understood as falling within the scope of the 'no more'; that is, the Pyrrhonist might be saying that things are no more (1) of this kind than (2) of that kind or (3) sometimes of this kind, sometimes of that kind, or (4) of this kind for one person, of that kind for another, and not even existent for a third. The effect of this would be that the 'sometimes' and 'for this person' phrases would no longer represent direct assertions of the Pyrrhonist, as I am assuming that they are. This would of course be a very cumbersome form of words (much more so than the analogous four-part 'no more' statement that is to be found, according to my interpretation, in the Aristocles passage). But the decisive consideration against this reading comes, again, from a parallel formulation just below. At the end of this catalogue of what the Pyrrhonist will and will not say, we are told that the Pyrrhonist will say that 'the same thing . . . is no more true than false, or [no more] persuasive than unpersuasive, or [no more] existent than non-existent, or sometimes of this kind, sometimes of that kind, or for one person of this kind, for another person of that kind' (170a8–11). Here 'of this kind' and 'of that kind' (*toion, toiondi*) clearly stand for

suspension of judgement, but certain types of relativity. Things are not *invariably F*, the point seems to be, but *F* in certain circumstances and not in others; this is not suspension of judgement as to whether or not things are *F*, but the confident *assertion* that things are *F* only in a relative or qualified sense. The 'no more' locution is evidently supposed to be interchangeable with these others, and it would *not* be interchangeable with them if it was intended to convey suspension of judgement. Hence it should be read in its natural sense 'to no greater extent than', which can be readily understood, like the 'sometimes' and 'for this person' restrictions, as qualifying the claim that things are *F*; things may be in a certain sense *F*, but to no greater extent than they are not-*F*—for each alternative, there are circumstances in which that alternative obtains, and circumstances in which it does not.[11] Aenesidemus twice accuses the Academics of making assertions 'unambiguously' (*anamphibolōs* (169b40, 170a29)); it is by relativizing or qualifying his assertions with the phrase 'no more', or with 'sometimes' or 'for this person', that he and the Pyrrhonists avoid this trap.[12]

any one of the pairs 'true/false', 'persuasive/unpersuasive', and 'existent/non-existent'; by this point Photius is compressing his account, and for the sake of brevity applies the 'sometimes' and 'for this person' phrases to all three pairs simultaneously. But in this case 'sometimes of this kind, sometimes of that kind' and 'for one person of this kind, for another person of that kind' must represent detachable assertions, *not* within the scope of any 'no more' statement. To read them in the way Allen suggests would require them to go with '[no more] existent than non-existent' alone; but the structure of the whole sentence shows that that is not the intention. But if the 'sometimes' and 'for this person' phrases represent detachable assertions in this case, then the parallelism of this entire portion of the passage indicates that the same must be true throughout.

[11] Another possibility is that the point is this: things are 'no more' *F* than not-*F* in that they are not, *in their real natures*, either (the least bit) *F* or (the least bit) not-*F*. As we shall see shortly, this point is entirely complementary to the reading given in the main text; indeed, the two readings are really just opposite sides of the same coin. It is worth noting that Diogenes Laertius mentions that 'no more' may be used either positively or negatively—'*A* no more than *B*' is true if *A* and *B* either both obtain or both fail to obtain—and says that the sceptics use it negatively; here, as elsewhere (see Sect. 3), it looks as if Diogenes has preserved an element of Aenesidemus' Pyrrhonism rather than the later variety represented in most of Sextus' writings. See also Ch. 1 nn. 34, 36.

[12] After a long sequence of such relativized or qualified assertions (170a1–11), Photius cites Aenesidemus as apologizing for his form of speech (170a12–14). This apology might be taken to apply to an intervening statement (170a11–12) to the effect that the Pyrrhonist determines nothing, not even that nothing is determined (Long and Sedley seem to assume as much in their translation (LS 71C8)). But that statement is itself an explanatory comment on the sequence of relativized assertions that has just preceded; and it is at least as natural to read the accompanying apology, too, as applying to this previous sequence of assertions. Aenesidemus is reported as saying 'But we speak in this way, not having any means with which to blurt out [*eklalēsōmen*] the thought'. *Eklalein* does not mean simply 'express' (as regularly assumed in translations of this passage); *eklalein* is to say bluntly and publicly things that would be better left *unsaid*—for reasons of decency, secrecy, religious prohibition, and so on. The word occurs in the Hippocratic Oath; see also Demosthenes 1.26 and, for indications that the word kept this sense long after the classical period was over, Libanius 18.213 and Aeneas of Gaza, *Ep.* 7. Aenesidemus is thus

Yet the Photius passage also represents Aenesidemus himself as making a number of negative assertions that would seem to be thoroughly 'unambiguous'. Aenesidemus is said to argue that signs—that is, observable phenomena affording reliable inferences to the unobservable features of things—'do not exist at all' (170b12–14); he is described as 'refusing to concede that anything is the cause of anything' (170b18–19); and he is said to have argued that there is simply no such thing as the *telos*, the ethical end (170b30–5). How is this consistent with his ban on assertions made 'unambiguously'? And how is either this or the relative or qualified assertions that we have seen he does admit consistent with the claim with which we began—namely, that the Pyrrhonist 'determines nothing' and is 'free from all dogma'?

The answer, I believe, has to do with a certain conception of what it is for something to be *by nature*, or *in reality*, a certain way[13]—a conception already touched on, in fact, in the previous chapter (Sections 1 and 3). To recall, according to this conception, an object is by nature *F* only if it is *F* *invariably* or *without qualification*.[14] Thus an object which is *F* only sometimes, or for some people, is *thereby not* by nature *F*. This does not mean that one cannot refer to it as *F* on those specific occasions; it means that, when one does so, one is not ascribing to it any features that belong to its nature. We referred to this in Chapter 3 as the 'invariability condition'.[15] Now, the invari-

apologizing for the impossibility of stating the ideas under consideration in a forthright, no-nonsense manner—as his readers might have hoped—and for the need to resort, instead, to these prolix and circumspect locutions, which are the very opposite of 'blurting out' one's thought.

[13] This idea is not original with me; similar interpretations are pursued in Woodruff (1988) and in Hankinson (1995: ch. 7).

[14] As we noted earlier (Ch. 3 n. 11), what exactly 'invariably' and 'without qualification' amount to may vary depending on what types of variability are cited as evidence *against* certain features' belonging to objects by nature. The forms of variability mentioned in the Photius passage are relativity to times and to persons; and the same two are drawn attention to in the Aenesidemus-influenced portion of Sextus' *Against the Ethicists* (M 11.69–78, 114, 118), on which see below, Sect. 3; see also Bett (1997: pp. xiv–xv, 138–9). In order to be *by nature* a certain way, then, a thing must (at least) be that way *always* and *for all persons*. This leaves it open that other forms of variability may *not* disqualify the thing from being by nature that way; but the evidence is too scanty for us to be sure. There is also some ambiguity in 'for all persons'; is this to be opposed to 'differing from person to person depending on their physiological and psychological states', or '... depending on their circumstances', or '... depending on their beliefs and background assumptions', or something else again, or some combination of the above? Though we are clearly better off here than we were in the case of Pyrrho—for in his case we had no indication at all as to the types of variability by which he may have been impressed—we are not in a position to resolve these finer details, and I shall again gloss over them. More important than the precise species of variability and invariability with which Aenesidemus is concerned is the general structure of his reasoning; and here, unlike in the case of Pyrrho, we are not purely dependent on speculative reconstruction.

[15] In Bett (1997), speaking of this condition in connection with Aenesidemus' view and the Aenesidemus-like view expressed by Sextus in *Against the Ethicists*, I referred to it as the Universality Requirement. This label now seems to me less helpful than the proposed replacement.

ability condition certainly has precedents in Greek philosophy. As we saw, Plato appears to have Socrates subscribe to it in the *Republic* and elsewhere. The Stoics also subscribe to a version of it, at least for the concepts of good and bad; the reason why virtue and vice are the only things, according to them, that are genuinely good and bad respectively—whereas everything else is indifferent—is that virtue is the only thing that is good, and vice the only thing that is bad, *in all circumstances and without qualification* (see e.g. DL 7.103). Again, the Epicurean Polystratus, of the third century BC, takes it for granted as a quite general condition on 'those things being said in accordance with a thing's own nature' (*tois kata tēn idian phusin legomenois* (*De contemptu* 25,19–20)).[16] And later, too, Galen takes for granted that natural things are 'common to all' (*koina pantōn* (*PHP* 9.1.11))—that whatever is *by nature* true (of human beings, in the case discussed) must be true in all instances. Finally, according to my reconstruction of the reasoning behind the indeterminacy thesis, Pyrrho assumed some version of the invariability condition as well. But we can leave this last parallel aside until later. Quite apart from the possibility of a precedent within the Pyrrhonist tradition, it would not be at all surprising, historically speaking, if Aenesidemus adopted this way of thinking—peculiar as it may seem to us.

There is no certain evidence that Aenesidemus did accept the invariability condition. However, there is a passage of Sextus, reporting Aenesidemus' ideas, which at least seems to come close to doing so (*M* 8.8). According to Sextus, Aenesidemus said that 'those things which appear to all in common are true, whereas those that are not such are false'; again, in order for something genuinely to count as part of reality, it must manifest itself in a way that is 'common to all'.[17] In any case, if we assume that Aenesidemus did

---

[16] Polystratus would, however, emphatically reject the equation of 'by nature' and 'in reality'; his whole point in this section of *De contemptu* (23,26–26,23 (=LS 7D)) is that predicates that apply to a thing only relatively speaking none the less apply to it just as genuinely and truly (in those cases, that is, where they do apply) as predicates that apply 'by nature'—that is, invariably or without qualification. I use 'by nature' and 'in reality' interchangeably in this chapter because Sextus uses them interchangeably in a central argument of *Against the Ethicists* (*M* 11.68–78), an argument relying quite explicitly on the invariability condition; on this argument, see further below, Sect. 3; also Bett (1997: commentary *ad loc*). On the contrast between Sextus and Polystratus in this respect, see Bett (1994*b*: sect. III). My attribution of the invariability condition to Pyrrho, if accepted, may seem to speak in favour of identifying the early Pyrrhonists as Polystratus' opponents in this passage. However, other implied features of these opponents' position are difficult to square with this identification; on this see Sedley (1983*b* (a review of Indelli 1978)).

[17] I hesitate to place much weight on this passage as evidence for Aenesidemus' acceptance of the invariability condition (the best evidence, I think, is simply the way in which this explains what otherwise seems thoroughly obscure and inconsistent in Aenesidemus' view), for the passage is problematic in at least two ways. First, it is implied in the quoted passage, and stated just before this, that Aenesidemus claimed that some things actually do meet the requirement in question; if so, it would seem to follow, contrary to the Photius passage, that he did permit some 'unambiguous' assertions. (The inclusion of Aenesidemus' ideas in a list of *dogmatists'* views

accept the invariability condition, this immediately makes sense of the points that seemed so intractable a moment ago. Given the invariability condition, the practice of restricting oneself to relative or qualified assertions is, precisely, a way of *refraining* from all claims to the effect that things are *by nature* any particular way; it is only when one starts speaking 'unambiguously', as the Academics allegedly do, that one's words have the force of attributing features to things by nature. Nor are the claims that there are no such things as signs, causes, or the ethical end claims to the effect that anything is of any particular character *by nature*. Aenesidemus is prepared to deny that anything is by nature a sign, a cause, or an end; or at least, his conclusions about signs, causes, and ends may very easily be read this way. But this is not to assert that anything is *by nature* a non-sign, non-cause, or non-end; for, in order for those assertions to be true, by the invariability condition, things would have *invariably* to be *not* signs, *not* causes, or *not* ends—which Aenesidemus may again very easily deny. The denials that anything is a sign, a cause, or an end, then, are not, after all, examples of 'unambiguous' assertions. Finally, to 'determine nothing' is to refrain from positing that any particular feature holds of any particular thing by nature;[18]

---

about truth (*M* 8.3) is consistent with this.) However, this could well be the result of a misunderstanding on the part of Sextus or his source. Aenesidemus might have been explicating *what it would be* for a certain set of appearances to be true (i.e. true of the real natures of the things in question)—or, in other words, stating something very like the invariability condition itself—without meaning to suggest that any of them actually meet this standard; it would not be hard for someone to twist this into the account given in Sextus. The Photius passage (170a6–7) has Aenesidemus refusing to say that anything is true (or false), and this fits far better with the rest of the evidence. Compare *M* 10.38–9, where a classification of various types of motion is attributed to Aenesidemus (again contrary to Photius (170b9–12)). Again, Sextus makes it sound as if Aenesidemus holds a dogmatic theory about what types of motion really exist; but the report can easily be understood to derive from an analysis of the *concept* of motion, and of various related concepts—an analysis that could have been used for anti-dogmatic purposes as much as for dogmatic ones.

Secondly, the quoted passage is introduced, according to the manuscripts, by a reference to 'Aenesidemus and Heraclitus' (*hoi de peri ton Ainēsidēmon kai Hērakleiton*)—though the specific view described is then attributed to Aenesidemus alone. Bekker, followed by Mutschmann, altered *kai* to *kath'*, by analogy with the puzzling expression *Ainēsidēmos kata Hērakleiton* that appears elsewhere in Sextus. On this issue, see below, n. 68; on the expression *Ainēsidēmos kata Hērakleiton* in general, and the question of the relations between Aenesidemus and Heraclitus, see below, Sect. 5.

[18] As noted earlier, Aenesidemus makes the claim self-applicable; the Pyrrhonist 'determines nothing, not even this very thing, that nothing is determined' (170a11–12). This will then turn out to mean the following: the Pyrrhonist issues no specification of the nature of anything, not even specifications to the effect that it is part of the *nature* of things not to have their nature specified. The force of this is thus similar to what, as we shall see in the next section, Aenesidemus means by denying that things are inapprehensible. This is of course rather different from Sextus' explanation of 'I determine nothing', including its self-applicability (*PH* 1.197). But this need not be a surprise; we have already seen a significant difference in their usages of another stock Pyrrhonist expression, 'no more'. Besides, the self-applicability is

both Aenesidemus' denials and his relativized assertions are consistent with this.[19]

There is, then, a form of suspension of judgement—or, as the Photius passage has it, freedom from dogma—in the position attributed to Aenesidemus. It is a suspension of judgement that consists in refusing to offer any specifications of how things are by nature. But, because of Aenesidemus' acceptance of the invariability condition as a test for something's being a certain way by nature, the forms of speech he permits himself are substantially broader than those permitted under the regime of *Outlines of Pyrrhonism*. Assertions that are relativized to time or person do not violate suspension of judgement, as so understood; and nor do certain assertions, having to do with the nature of things, that *Outlines of Pyrrhonism* would stigmatize as 'negatively dogmatic'—for from 'nothing is by nature F', or 'X is not by nature F', no statement of the form 'X is by nature G' (not even 'X is by nature not-F') follows. As we shall see, Sextus sometimes appears confused about how to classify Aenesidemus, despite their membership in a common tradition. If I am right that the central notion of suspension of judgement underwent this significant change within the Pyrrhonist tradition, such confusion is not surprising.

stated differently in the two cases. Sextus says that the Pyrrhonist determines nothing, 'not even "I determine nothing" itself' (*oude auto to ouden horizō*)—which he explains by saying that the Pyrrhonist's statement 'I determine nothing' is not itself any kind of dogmatic assertion, but is simply an expression of his current state of mind. Aenesidemus, on the other hand—if Photius is summarizing him accurately—says that he determines nothing, 'not even this very thing, *that nothing is determined*', (*oude auto touto, hoti ouden diorizetai*), which is *not* naturally understood as placing the focus on the speaker's state of mind. (DL 9.74, 104 are ambiguous as between the two versions; both say 'not even this very thing', without saying what exactly 'this very thing' is.)

[19] What of the invariability condition itself? Does this not constitute a specification of the nature of things? One might say that an assertion about *what it is* for something to be F by nature is not itself an assertion to the effect that anything in particular is F by nature. But the invariability condition does allow us to attribute the following second-order feature to everything indiscriminately: being such that whatever features belong to them by nature belong to them invariably. Aenesidemus may have regarded this as unproblematic; a very general constraint such as this, he might say, leaves it an entirely open question what features *in particular* belong to the nature of each individual entity. (In the same way, in accepting the Law of Non-Contradiction, one attributes to all things the feature 'being such that contradictory features cannot belong to them at the same time and in the same respect'; again, this takes us nowhere towards specifying the nature of any one thing as against any other.) However, Aenesidemus seems not to have inspired lasting agreement on this point; for the invariability condition is dispensed with in the terminal phase of later Pyrrhonism. In fact, I shall suggest below (Sect. 6) that it is a discomfort with this very condition, on the part of some Pyrrhonists after Aenesidemus, that by itself suffices to explain the shift from the initial phase of later Pyrrhonism to the terminal phase.

2. *Aenesidemus on appearances and on knowledge*

The evidence on Aenesidemus presents some other puzzling features that need scrutiny. First, we saw in earlier chapters that, according to Diogenes Laertius (9.106), Aenesidemus attributed to Pyrrho (rightly, if we can infer backwards from Timon's pronouncements on the subject) the practice of following appearances; Diogenes goes on to say that Aenesidemus himself designated 'the appearance' (*to phainomenon*) as the sceptic's criterion. Presumably this means the same as what Sextus means when he says that *to phainomenon* is the sceptic's criterion (*PH* 1.22)—namely, that the sceptic relies on appearances in deciding what to do in any given circumstances. That the initial phase of later Pyrrhonism made widespread use of the notion of appearance is suggested, again, by a passage (also referred to in Chapters 1 and 2) of the Anonymous Commentary on the *Theaetetus* (60.48–61.46 (=LS 71D)), in which Pyrrhonism is said to eschew dogmatism, and to restrict us, instead, to stating how things appear to us.²⁰ In addition, Sextus' brief account of Aenesidemus' Eight Modes against causal explanation (*PH* 1.180–5) several times draws attention to the same contrast.²¹ But now, how is this consistent with the Photius passage, which allows the Pyrrhonist to employ relativized or qualified assertions?

---

²⁰ The Anonymous Commentary is plausibly dated to the late first century BC—in other words, to a time relatively soon after Aenesidemus' revival of Pyrrhonism; see Ch. 1 n. 83. It may seem to be a problem for my interpretation of Aenesidemus that the Commentator refers to the Pyrrhonists as thinking that opposing arguments are 'equally strong' (*isokrateis* (61.26)), and as 'putting appearances on a par' (*exomalizein tas phantasias* (61.28–30)). Does this not clearly anticipate Sextus' concept of *isostheneia*; and does that not suggest that Aenesidemus' position is not significantly different from that of *PH*? But to say that opposing arguments and appearances are on a par is perfectly consistent with the position that emerges from the Photius passage. It is quite true, according to this position—though for different reasons from those offered in *PH*—that no one member of a pair of opposing arguments or appearances has any greater claim than any other member to representing the way things are by nature. Besides, a few columns later (63.1–40, on which more in the next section) the author attributes to the Pyrrhonists an interest in relativities, and a willingness to advance relativized assertions, that is plainly much more in line with the Photius passage than with *PH*. Finally, even if the earlier passage was inconsistent with the view apparent in the Photius passage, this might very well have been due to the Commentator's own misunderstandings or wilful distortions. (On his highly idiosyncratic and agenda-driven reading of Plato, see Sedley 1997.) The sceptical Academy of Arcesilaus and Carneades seems clearly to have employed something close to Sextus' procedure of *isostheneia*, even if not the term itself (see e.g. DL 4.28; Cicero, *Acad.* 1.45); and the Commentator was certainly aware of a sceptical phase in the history of the Academy (even though he greatly downplays its importance (54.38–55.13)). So it would not have been at all surprising if his acquaintance with Academic styles of scepticism had affected his reading of Aenesidemus.

²¹ See also the occurrence of the term *phainomena* in *M* 8.8, the passage in which, as I suggested earlier, Sextus attributes to Aenesidemus something resembling the invariability condition.

The most economical answer—indeed, the obvious one, if it can be worked out—is that the distinction between relativized assertions and assertions purporting to specify the nature of things, and the distinction between assertions having to do with appearances and assertions committing one to a picture of how things really are, are in fact one and the same distinction. This may seem counter-intuitive—to relativize and to confine oneself to appearance-statements may look like very different tactics; yet we saw something similar to this Chapter 3, in connection with Plato and also, according to my reconstruction of his reasoning, in connection with Pyrrho himself. The idea is that the relativized statements employed by Aenesidemus, precisely because they make no claim to be specifications of the natures of things, qualify as appearance-statements. Given the invariability condition, they do not purport to capture how things really are; what they do, rather, is record the characteristics manifested by things in specific circumstances or on specific occasions. In view of this condition, 'Tylenol is good for people with headaches' says nothing at all about the underlying nature of Tylenol; the qualification 'for people with headaches' guarantees that the statement is not attributing *goodness* to Tylenol as a feature of its real nature, and no other feature of Tylenol is mentioned. But if the statement 'Tylenol is good for people with headaches' is not about how Tylenol is in its real nature, then it is not unreasonable to speak of it as having to do with Tylenol's 'appearance'; it has to do, that is, with how Tylenol strikes us as a matter of ordinary experience. It is not a statement purely about our *subjective impressions*; 'Tylenol is good for people with headaches' tells us something about Tylenol, and not merely about impressions of ours that have Tylenol as part of their content.[22] But what this statement tells us about Tylenol is a characteristic, or an effect, that it displays in certain specific circumstances, as opposed to some feature of its true nature or underlying structure.

So, when we are told that Aenesidemus followed appearances, this need not be taken as conflicting with Photius' claim that he restricted himself to assertions qualified by relativities; on the contrary, it can be understood as a shorthand version of that claim. If this is correct, what does the work of restricting a certain statement to the domain of 'appearances'—that is, the domain of plain experience, as opposed to the obscure domain of underlying natures—is not so much the word 'appears' itself; the crucial element, rather, is a relativizing phrase such as 'for people with headaches'. One might want to use the word 'appears' in such contexts in any case, just to emphasize one's 'freedom from dogma'—that is, one's lack of commitment to any statements

---

[22] This way of proceeding of course assumes that our impressions of things are not systematically misleading as regards the features manifested by things on specific occasions or in specific respects. Again, a similar point was raised in Chapter 3 in connection with both Plato and Pyrrho. We shall return to this issue in Sect. 6, in considering the transition to the terminal phase of later Pyrrhonism.

purporting to specify the natures of things—just as Plato at the end of
Republic V uses 'appears' in his sample statements concerning sensible
things, to emphasize the gulf between these statements and those capturing reality (see Chapter 3, Section 3). We cannot be certain whether
Aenesidemus made a similar move,[23] for the passage of Photius that might
have settled the question in fact contains no verbs at all. Though I have been
assuming that Aenesidemus was prepared to make assertions of the form '*X*
is no more *F* than not-*F*', etc., the text does not specify this; what Photius
says is simply that he *declared things* 'no more *F* than not-*F*', etc., without
saying whether he used 'is'/'are' or 'appear(s)' to do so. Still, I suspect that
Aenesidemus was not squeamish about using 'is' or 'are' in such contexts.[24]
To say that someone declared (*eirēken* (169b42–170a1)) something *F*
would standardly be taken to mean that he or she *said that it is F*; if
Aenesidemus had strictly confined himself to the word 'appear(s)', one
would expect Photius to have taken account of this fact in his summary. But
the point is of no great importance; if I am right that Aenesidemus was
prepared to use 'is' in the contexts we are discussing, he would still be
restricting himself, in a quite comprehensible sense, to the domain of
'appearances'. This use of the notion of appearances is not, of course, the
same as the one assumed in *Outlines of Pyrrhonism*, which—officially at
least—has nothing to do with relativities.[25] However, as I suggested, it is
not without precedent in Greek philosophy. Furthermore, we saw in the
previous chapter that there is some reason to think that a similar conception

---

[23] The use of the term *phainomena* in Sextus *M* 8.8 (see above, n. 21) possibly suggests that
he did; however, we have seen that this text is difficult to assess (n. 17), so it should not be relied
on too heavily. It is worth noting that Sextus in *Against the Ethicists*, which offers a version of
Pyrrhonism essentially the same as that of Aenesidemus (see the following section), does *not*
seem to adopt any comparable move. He says that 'is' (*esti*) can be used to mean either 'actually is' (*huparchei*) or 'appears' (*M* 11.18); but he is quite happy to use 'is' in the sense 'actually is' in statements such as 'it is day'. 'Is' needs to be used in the sense 'appears' only when
there is some danger that a set of words used by the sceptic might be taken as a pronouncement
on the nature of things—as is not the case with 'it is day', with its implied relativization to the
present time. On this, see further Bett (1997: commentary on sects. 18–20). However, if there is
a difference here between Aenesidemus and the Sextus of *Against the Ethicists*, it is a minor
one, concerning matters of terminology rather than of substance.

[24] Note also that there could still be some purpose to a distinction between 'Tylenol is good
for people with headaches' and 'Tylenol seems good for people with headaches'. If the domain
of 'appearances' is the domain of ordinary experience, then statements in this domain may be
issued with widely differing levels of confidence. For example, one's observation of the beneficial effects of Tylenol on people with headaches might so far be very limited or hasty; until one
has looked at these effects more extensively, one might prefer to use 'seems' rather than 'is',
and, once one has looked at them extensively, one might prefer 'is' over 'seems'. But this does
not in any way detract from the idea that nothing at all is being said, in either statement, about
the real nature of Tylenol (or of people with headaches); in that sense, both are arrived at by
'following appearances' and nothing more.

[25] I say 'officially' because, as we shall see in the next section, there are occasional relics of
the Aenesidemean view to be found even in *Outlines of Pyrrhonism*.

of the 'appearances' occurred, in particular, in the philosophy of Pyrrho. I shall come back to this point later.

One more set of issues needs to be added to complete this survey of Aenesidemus' outlook. The Photius passage frequently reports that, according to Aenesidemus, certain things are beyond our grasp, beyond our knowledge, or beyond our apprehension (170b7–8, 11–12, 16–17, 25–6). This too seems to be different from the position of *Outlines of Pyrrhonism*, which specifically *distinguishes* Pyrrhonism from the assertion that things cannot be known (an assertion associated by Sextus, rightly or wrongly, with the Academics), holding that this is as much a violation of sceptical principles as the assertion that things *can* be known (*PH* 1.1–3). But the Photius passage is very insistent on this matter. Near the outset, it also says that the whole point of the book is 'to confirm that there is no firm means to apprehension' (*bebaiōsai hoti ouden bebaion eis katalēpsin* (169b19–20)); that, according to Aenesidemus, neither the Pyrrhonist nor anyone else 'knows the truth in the things that are' (*eidenai tēn en tois ousin alētheian* (169b22)); and that the Pyrrhonist, unlike other thinkers, is in the happy position of 'knowing [*eidenai*] that nothing has been firmly apprehended [*kateilēptai*] by him' (169b28–9). Clearly Aenesidemus had a considerable interest in describing (in unpromising terms) our cognitive situation; and this may seem surprising, given the approach we have so far seen him adopt, with its forthright assertions having to do with relativities and the non-existence of various items. However, Aenesidemus' strong denial that we have apprehension (*katalēpsis*) of anything, or that we know the way things are in reality, is in fact readily understandable in light of the preceding points. First, if it is only 'unambiguous' specifications of the features of things that are of the right type to be specifications of the *natures* of those things, and if, as Aenesidemus clearly thinks, we are in no position to issue any such 'unambiguous' specifications (but are confined instead to relative or qualified specifications), then it is quite correct to say that we are cut off from knowledge or apprehension—that is, knowledge or apprehension of the nature of things. Secondly, it is quite correct to say, concerning the items said by Aenesidemus not to exist, that they too are not to be apprehended or known; a thing that does not even exist certainly cannot be known about.[26] In general, since accounts of the nature of things are precisely what Aenesidemus refuses to allow, then if apprehension or knowledge is taken in a strong sense, as applying solely to a grasp of how things are by nature, then 'apprehension' or 'knowledge' is bound to be disallowed at the same time. And, finally, these various *assertions* to the effect that

---

[26] Note that the negative epistemological claims in the Photius passage are all of the form 'X cannot be known', or 'X is closed off from our apprehension'—and not of the form 'It cannot be known whether or not X exists', (or '. . . whether or not X is F', or '. . . whether or not X is a Y'). The latter kinds of claims *would* clearly be inconsistent with 'There is no such thing as X'; but 'there is no such thing as X' and 'X cannot be known' are quite compatible.

knowledge of the nature of things is not to be had are not themselves problematic for Aenesidemus (as they are for Sextus); for to assert that a certain item is beyond our apprehension is not *eo ipso* to offer any specification of the item's nature. I shall return to this point in a moment.

This does not, of course, rule out the possibility of some form of knowledge applying to topics *other* than the real nature of things; and the Photius passage suggests that Aenesidemus was prepared to allow some such notion. It is never suggested that 'apprehension' (*katalēpsis*) of any kind is possible—that term seems to be rigorously reserved for a grasp of the nature of things; but Photius does represent Aenesidemus as using *eidenai*, a much older, non-technical Greek word for 'know', of the Pyrrhonist. The passage has Aenesidemus saying that 'even the things he [i.e. the Pyrrhonist] knows [*eideiē*], he is well-bred enough to assent no more to their affirmation than to their denial' (169b29–30). I take it that this refers to the Pyrrhonist's 'no more *F* than not-*F*' locution, which Photius is going to introduce a little further on; if so, the suggestion here is that the kinds of relativized assertions for which the 'no more *F* than not-*F*' locution is a shorthand may, for the Pyrrhonist, be objects of a certain kind of knowledge. That is, one can *know* that *X* is *F* in circumstances *C*—though, as a good Pyrrhonist, one will be careful to make clear that one is not claiming that *X* is *F* *irrespective* of circumstances. As I mentioned above, Photius also has Aenesidemus saying that the Pyrrhonist *knows* (*eidenai*) that he does not have 'apprehension'. Even this is consistent with the position as described so far; for the *assertion that* one does not have 'apprehension' (that is, a grasp of the nature of things) is a meta-level assertion not itself having the nature of things as its subject matter, and hence is not ruled out as a possible object of knowledge (*eidenai*). What one *cannot* know (*eidenai*), as we saw, is simply 'the truth in the things that are'; but here it is the subject matter itself—namely, the real nature of things—that creates the obstacle, not any general problem having to do with knowledge (*eidenai*). Now, it is possible that the use of *eidenai* in these contexts is Photius', not Aenesidemus'; his clearly ironic language in this part of the passage (note especially the word 'well-bred' (*gennaios*) and the wordplay of 'confirm [*bebaiōsai*] that there is no firm [*bebaion*] means') might well suggest that he is foisting knowledge claims on Aenesidemus without warrant, in order to make him look silly.[27] On the other hand, there is no inconsistency in the view just outlined; and, as we have seen, Aenesidemus seems quite willing to issue confident assertions of several types. It would not be especially surprising, then, if he were to claim *knowledge*, in a generous and non-technical use of the word, in these areas.

'Apprehension', or knowledge of the nature of things, is not available;

---

[27] Cf. e.g. Lucretius 4.469–77, which relies on the idea that someone who claims that nothing can be known must also presume to *know* the content of that very claim.

knowledge of a more mundane form—or so the Photius passage suggests—is possible. All this seems tidy enough, and easy enough to incorporate into the rest of the ideas attributed to Aenesidemus. But there is yet a further twist to the remarks having to do with apprehension or knowledge. In the course of explaining the Pyrrhonist's use of the qualifications 'no more', 'sometimes', and 'for this person', Aenesidemus is also reported as saying that the Pyrrhonist, unlike the Academic, claims *neither* that everything is inapprehensible *nor* that everything is apprehensible (169b42–170a1); and the first part of this looks in flat contradiction with the denial of apprehension that we have seen to be a prominent feature of the passage.

Here again, though, the appearance of contradiction can be removed without any great strain. The best way to read the text just cited is as yet another point about the nature of things—we are not in a position to assert that things are *of such a nature* as to be either inapprehensible or apprehensible; this is quite compatible with our in fact being cut off from apprehension of things, and with our being in a position to say so.[28] In favour of this reading is a puzzling statement of Aenesidemus' probable contemporary Philo of Larissa, reported by Sextus (*PH* 1.235). Philo is said to hold that, as far as the nature of things themselves is concerned, things are apprehensible—whereas, as far as the Stoic criterion (that is, the *phantasia kataleptike*, 'apprehensive impression') is concerned, they are inapprehensible. What exactly Philo meant by this, and why he said it, is a much disputed matter.[29] But it at least looks as if

---

[28] Note that Sextus (*PH* 1.215) distinguishes the Pyrrhonists from the Cyrenaics on the basis that the Cyrenaics *assert* that things have an *inapprehensible nature* (*phusin . . . akatalepton*). Aenesidemus would no doubt also distinguish himself from the Cyrenaics in this respect—even though he, unlike Sextus, does seem prepared to deny that apprehension is possible. For the reason *why* apprehension of things is not possible need not be any intrinsic feature of the things themselves; indeed, it would be self-refuting to say that some intrinsic feature of things *was* responsible—for then one would need to have achieved apprehension of that very feature. The reason why apprehension is impossible might simply be the inadequacy of our faculties, rather than anything about the natures of the things themselves; and this is what Photius suggests that Aenesidemus thought, when he says that the point of the book is 'to confirm that there is no firm means to apprehension, *neither through sensation nor even through the intellect*' (169b19–21). Cf. above, Ch. 1 n. 14 and accompanying text on Pyrrho. If the epistemological interpretation of the Aristocles passage (which I rejected) had been correct, Pyrrho *would* have been liable to the same charge as Sextus levels at the Cyrenaics; for he would have been stating, in answer to the question 'What is the *nature* of things?' that things are 'undifferentiable, unmeasurable and indeterminable'. One might object, along the lines of an objection considered in that earlier discussion, that Aenesidemus too—if he really does hold that apprehension is *impossible*—is committed at least to things' having, as part of their *nature*, the feature of 'inapprehensibility to humans'. However, given his view of the status of relativities, and his acceptance of some version of the invariability condition, it is doubtful whether he would have considered 'inapprehensibility *to humans*' as even a candidate for belonging to anything's *nature*.

[29] One possibility is that, by contrasting things apprehended in their own nature with things apprehended by the empiricist Stoic criterion, Philo is reintroducing into the Academy something like Platonic Forms; for this reading see Sharples (1996: 28–9), drawing upon Tarrant

part of what he is saying is that it belongs to things, in their *natures*, to be apprehensible.[30] And, if so, it makes good sense to see Aenesidemus as responding to Philo. That he has Philo's claim in mind is already suggested by the fact that at one point he attributes a number of dogmatic assertions to the Academics, but then says that 'it is only about the apprehensive impression that they say that they are in dispute' (170a21–2). But the claim on which we are currently focusing would constitute a direct response to Philo, on the reading that I have suggested; Aenesidemus would be refusing to attribute either apprehensibility or inapprehensibility to *things in their own nature* (while implying that the Academics thought otherwise).[31]

This reading also makes good sense of the fact that these words are followed by the ones with which we began: 'but that they are no more of this kind than that, or sometimes of this kind and sometimes not, or for one person of this kind, for another not of this kind, and for someone else not even existent at all' (170a1–3). The Pyrrhonist (unlike the Academic) does not say that

---

(1985: 53–62). If this is correct, and if my interpretation of Pyrrho as 'Plato without the Forms' has been on the right lines, then there is a special appropriateness in Aenesidemus' taking Pyrrho as his inspiration as he reacts against Philo's position. However, this matter is too complicated for me to hope to settle here. For some other recent interpretations of Philo's statement, see Hankinson (1995: 116–20); Glidden (1996); Striker (1997) .

[30] I agree with Striker (1997: n. 2) that the first part of Philo's statement does not need to be understood as the strong and general claim that the nature of things is apprehensible. But he does seem to be asserting that the characteristic of apprehensibility itself is part of the natures of things. Striker also argues that Philo is pressing for a less stringent conception of what 'apprehensibility' involves than is assumed in discussions of the Stoic apprehensive impression. But that does not affect my present point; what Aenesidemus is objecting to here, if I am right, is not any particular view of what apprehensibility consists in, but the attribution of the feature 'apprehensibility' (whatever precisely that may amount to) to things as part of their real natures.

[31] This is stated explicitly in another place in the Photius passage—if the text is correct; the Academics are accused of 'stating in general terms that there exist apprehensible things' (*phanai koinōs huparchein katalēpta* (170a29–30)). Most people have assumed, on the other hand, that the text must be faulty. The immediate context reads 'proposing and denying a thing unambiguously, and at the same time stating in general terms that there exist apprehensible things, introduces an undeniable conflict'; and it has generally been assumed that the 'conflict' in question must be *between* the two immediately preceding points, which makes no sense as the text stands. The proposed solutions all involve somehow altering the second point in such a way that it includes, or consists of, the claim that things are *in*apprehensible (the simplest version being the addition of a negation); see the apparatus criticus to LS 71C (vol. 2), also Hankinson (1995: 335 n. 7). However, if we take the 'conflict' to be not between these two points themselves, but between *both* of them taken together and *other*, more sceptical-sounding pronouncements of the Academics mentioned just below (170a32–3), then the text needs no alteration; in that case one would expect the two points to be complementary, as indeed they are. It is true that the words 'at the same time' (*hama . . . hama . . .*) incline one to think that the conflict is between *these* two simultaneous utterances. But there are other reasons why one might draw attention to the fact that two utterances are made 'at the same time', besides their being in conflict; the point might be to emphasize the multifaceted nature of the Academics' anti-sceptical position, and their effrontery in promoting it (despite also professing the sceptical attitudes referred to just below).

things are, in their real natures, inapprehensible or that they are apprehensible; *but* the Pyrrhonist does say that things are no more *F* than not-*F*, etc.[32] Now, why should stating that things are no more *F* than not-*F*—where *F* is any arbitrary predicate—be placed in *contrast* with the refusal to state that they are either inapprehensible or apprehensible? The answer is that it is precisely *because* relativized assertions are the *only* type of positive assertions the Pyrrhonist permits himself that he cannot be accused of making any blanket assertion—that is, any assertion that might be suspected of applying to the *natures* of the things in question—concerning inapprehensibility or apprehensibility. The Pyrrhonist makes assertions of the form '*X* is no more *F* than not-*F*', and that is all. By contrast, he does *not* make unguarded assertions of the form '*X* is *F*' or '*X* is not-*F*'; and this applies in the particular case where *F* stands for 'apprehensible'. (It would also apply, of course, for any other value of F; but that is not to the point here.)[33]

3. *Traces of Aenesidemus in Sextus and Diogenes Laertius*

The position attributed to Aenesidemus can also be detected—or, at least, aspects of it can be detected—in a number of places in Sextus and in Diogenes. Both authors preserve versions of a set of Ten Modes, or standardized forms of sceptical argumentation, that are attributed to Aenesidemus (*PH* 1.35–163; DL 9.79–88).[34] Now, Sextus' official presentation of the workings

---

[32] On this, see above, n. 9; 'no more of this kind than that' cannot easily be understood to mean 'no more apprehensible than inapprehensible'—a generalized 'no more *F* than not-*F*' is much more plausible.

[33] As we saw (see above, n. 8), the passage continues by saying that the Pyrrhonist will not assert that things are accessible (*ephikta*) or that they are inaccessible, but will assert that they are *no more accessible than inaccessible*. Why is Aenesidemus willing to claim that things are no more accessible than inaccessible, but not (if I am right) that they are no more apprehensible than inapprehensible? The reason, I suggest, is that, again, the concept of apprehension is distinctive in applying specifically to the act of grasping the nature of things. Apprehension, so understood, is what he repeatedly denies that we *ever* have; so it would make no sense for him to claim that things are 'no more apprehensible than inapprehensible' or 'sometimes apprehensible and sometimes inapprehensible'. But the notion of being 'accessible' (*ephikton*) is arguably a looser and less technical one—like the notion of 'knowing' (*eidenai*) employed elsewhere in the passage—which covers more than just the case of something's nature being grasped. (It may, however, *include* this case, so that if the proposition in question does have to do with the natures of things, *that* proposition will *not* be 'accessible' (170b11)—just as it will not be a candidate for *eidenai* (169b22)). If so, it would be quite possible for Aenesidemus to assert that things are in some circumstances 'accessible' and in other circumstances not (where a thing's being 'accessible' does not require a grasp of its real nature), while also refusing to assert categorically (that is, in virtue of the *natures* of the things in question) that they are either accessible or inaccessible.

[34] The attribution to Aenesidemus occurs at Sextus, *M* 7.345.

of these Modes, in book I of *Outlines of Pyrrhonism*, conforms to the pattern one would expect from that book; the Modes assemble sets of opposing appearances that, according to Sextus, strike one as having 'equal strength', and so one is forced to suspend judgement as to the real nature of the objects of which these are the appearances. However, as commentators have noticed,[35] we not infrequently find, even in the Ten Modes as presented by Sextus himself, an emphasis on relativity, and on the contrast between how things are relatively speaking and how they are by nature—the latter state being deemed inaccessible to us because our awareness is restricted to instances of the former. The most obvious case is the Mode from Relativity itself (which appears eighth in Sextus' account), the outcome of which is that 'we will not be able to say what each of the underlying things is like in its own nature and purely [*eilikrinōs*], but how it appears in relative terms' (*PH* 1.140).[36] But the same kind of remark occurs at the end of Sextus' tenth Mode, the one having to do with laws and customs: 'we will not be in a position to say what the underlying thing is like in its nature, but how it appears in relation to this way of life or in relation to this law or in relation to this custom and all the rest' (*PH* 1.163). And similar points are made in other places (*PH* 1.132, 134, 144). All this seems at odds with appeals to the unresolvability of the conflict among appearances; but it seems thoroughly compatible with the kind of approach that we have seen from the Photius passage to be characteristic of Aenesidemus. The point is not that attempts to *decide among* these conflicting appearances all fail—as if one of them might after all be the correct one, and the problem is to decide *which* it is. Rather, the point is that the very fact that these 'appearances' obtain in some specific and limited set of circumstances, and that the character of the 'appearances' varies with the circumstances, itself guarantees that *none* of them captures the object in its true nature; an object that presents itself in a certain way only in a specific set of circumstances is *thereby not* by nature that way. Sextus' periodic inclusion of this point creates problems for the consistency of his version of the Ten Modes. However, it also supports the idea that the variety of Pyrrhonism officially promoted by *Outlines of Pyrrhonism* itself is not the only variety that existed. If Aenesidemus' thinking was indeed along the rather different lines suggested in the previous sections, then Sextus is here preserving relics of that distinct earlier view—relics of the Ten Modes as they originally looked when Aenesidemus compiled them.[37]

---

[35] See Striker (1983); Annas and Barnes (1985).

[36] The Mode from Relativity is puzzling for a number of reasons, the most significant of which are that (*a*) while listing it as *one* of the Ten Modes, Sextus also claims that relativity is the general form common to *all* the Ten Modes (*PH* 1.39), and (*b*) the versions of the Relativity Mode in Sextus, in Diogenes, and in Philo of Alexandria are extremely diverse, probably more so than in any other case. For discussion of these and other difficulties, see Annas and Barnes (1985: ch. 11).

[37] I say 'compiled' rather than 'created' or 'thought up' because, as is well known, the Ten

Moreover, even when Sextus does introduce the notion of unresolvability in the Ten Modes, it is often, or even usually, in connection with considerations derived from another set of Five Modes, attributed to a certain Agrippa and belonging to a later phase of the Pyrrhonist tradition (*PH* 1.60–1, 88–90, 114–17, 121–3).[38] The notion of unresolvable conflict, that is, tends to be associated with material that cannot originally have belonged to Aenesidemus' Ten Modes; this adds weight to the supposition that, as Aenesidemus himself presented them, they expressed a different outlook, one akin to that which occurs in the Photius passage.

Finally, the Ten Modes as presented by Diogenes—who seems clearly to be drawing for his account of Pyrrhonism on sources other than Sextus[39]—nowhere mention the notions of 'equal strength' or unresolvability. Instead, they seem to be wholly interpretable along the lines of the Photius passage. Diogenes throughout emphasizes the relativity of phenomena, or their variability with circumstances; and he consistently makes a direct inference from observations concerning this relativity or variability to a pessimistic conclusion about our access to the nature of things.[40] What is an occasional anomaly in Sextus is standard practice in Diogenes. Moreover, the conclusions to the Modes in Diogenes as often take the form of an assertion that the nature of things, in the area in question, is not or cannot be known (9.85, 86, 88),[41]

Modes draw on material that is to be found in much earlier phases of Greek philosophy; see Ch. 3 nn. 25, 28. Clearly, what Aenesidemus did was not so much to *invent* a set of arguments as to collect, systematize, and reformulate them for a specific purpose.

[38] The Five Modes are attributed to Agrippa by Diogenes Laertius (9.88); Sextus (*PH* 1.164) says that they come from 'the later sceptics', by contrast with 'the older sceptics' (*PH* 1.36) who are responsible for the Ten Modes.

[39] On this point, see Barnes (1992: esp. 4250–6, 4268–70).

[40] Such direct inferences occur in Modes 1, 2, 3, 5, 6, 7, and 10 (in Diogenes' order, which is not the same as Sextus'); the others simply lay out some examples of relativity or variability, and leave the conclusion implicit. It might, of course, be maintained that Diogenes' presentation of the Modes is merely more compressed than that of Sextus—that the notion of unresolvability is not mentioned in Diogenes' telegraphic treatment, but that it is none the less operating behind the scenes. But if unresolvability was important to the workings of the Modes in Diogenes, it would be very surprising that it should receive *no mention at all*. If we assume, on the other hand, that a different variety of Pyrrhonism is being presented here, the variety apparent in the Photius passage, then everything is in order; on that view, the omnipresence of relativity does by itself prevent us from grasping the nature of things. Besides, as we shall see in a moment, the terms in which Diogenes states the results of the Modes are often clearly inconsistent with the outlook of *Outlines of Pyrrhonism*, but quite consistent with the view sketched in the Photius passage.

[41] In the last of these cases the manuscripts vary as between *agnōsta oun ta pros ti hōs kath'heauta* and *agnōsta oun ta pros ti kath'heauta*. Both the OCT and the Loeb editions of Diogenes bracket *hōs*. But, if it is retained, yet another point from the Photius passage is recalled. The sense will then be 'relatives are unknown *as* things in themselves'. And this seems to leave room, as the Photius passage seemed to leave room, for another, weaker sense in which knowledge of relatives *is* possible; though no amount of accuracy about relativities can yield knowledge of the nature of things, *that* an object is *F* in circumstances *C*, and not-*F* in some other set of circumstances, may itself be something known, in a less demanding usage of 'know'.

as that suspension of judgement is necessary (9.79, 81, 84); indeed, no clear distinction seems to be drawn between these two types of assertions—they appear to be interchangeable.[42] Once more, this is disastrously confused by the standards of *Outlines of Pyrrhonism*, but perfectly sensible by the standards of the Photius passage. In that passage, as we saw, Aenesidemus is represented as holding that apprehension, or knowledge of the nature of things, was beyond our reach; and this conclusion[43] was quite compatible with (and indeed, closely connected with) the refusal to 'make determinations', in Aenesidemus' specific understanding of that notion.[44]

It is not only in his summary of the Ten Modes that Diogenes attributes to the Pyrrhonists the claim that things are unknown or unknowable (*agnōsta*). Elsewhere in his account of Pyrrhonism he says the same thing about the criterion, and about truth itself (9.95), and also about that which is by nature good (9.101). But in the part of his account following the Modes, where he summarizes the Pyrrhonists' treatment of the various topics that have been the subject of dogmatic philosophers' theories, another term is also common. We are several times told that the Pyrrhonists 'did away with' (*anēiroun*) a certain

---

[42] The one other example of a concluding statement in Diogenes' Ten Modes is 'Therefore it follows that what appears is "no more" of this kind than of another kind' (*akolouthei oun mē mallon einai toion to phainomenon ē alloion* (9.81)). How one understands this depends on whether *ou mallon* is understood in the manner of the Photius passage or in the manner of *Outlines of Pyrrhonism*. Naturally, in view of the many other indications that Diogenes' version of the Ten Modes is different from that of *Outlines of Pyrrhonism*, but in line with the Aenesidemus of the Photius passage, I am inclined to read *ou mallon* in its natural sense of 'no more'; in this case, as in the Photius passage, the statement becomes a generalized assertion of the relativity of things. But I admit that the sentence by itself does not force this interpretation.

[43] It is often observed, concerning the Ten Modes in Sextus, that their aim is to generate not a certain *conclusion*, but a certain *effect* on the reader. They do not offer premises that are supposed to *entail* that *judgement must be suspended*; rather, they offer considerations to which suspension of judgement is supposed to be the inevitable *psychological reaction*. Aenesidemus' variety of Pyrrhonism, however, does license certain kinds of conclusions, including the conclusion that such-and-such cannot be known; and the various statements of the form 'such-and-such cannot be known', in the Ten Modes as presented by Diogenes, can also fairly be labelled conclusions.

[44] Many of the same points might be made about the Ten Modes as they appear in Philo's *On Drunkenness* 169–205. There is a heavy emphasis on relativities, and no explicit mention of 'equal strength' or the unresolvability of conflicts among appearances; in addition, at one point it is asserted that a set of such conflicting appearances are 'clear confirmations of inapprehensibility' (*pisteis enargeis akatalēpsias* (175))—even though elsewhere (192, 205) it is the necessity for suspension of judgement that is insisted upon. However, since Philo does not purport to be describing the Pyrrhonist outlook, but has appropriated the Ten Modes for his own purposes, it is hazardous to use this text as detailed evidence for the Pyrrhonists' own practice. This is a pity, since Philo is by far the earliest extended witness to this material. (Aristocles is quite possibly earlier than Philo—see Ch. 1 n. 1—but his mention of Aenesidemus' Modes (in Eusebius, *Praep. evang.* XIV.18.11–12) is very brief, and unhelpful for our purposes. It does include the notion that 'everything is confused and spoken of relatively' (*panta . . . einai sugkechumena kai pros ti legomena*). But this tells us nothing we did not already know; as we saw, even Sextus includes a mode having to do with relativity.)

item (9.90, 94, 97, 100). Presumably this means that they argued for its non-existence; in several other places conclusions of the form 'there is no such thing as *X*' or '*X* does not exist' are specifically attributed to them (9.96, 98, 99, 100, 101), and 'they did away with *X*' seems to be simply an alternative to this.[45] On Diogenes' account, then, the Pyrrhonists alternate between the claim that things cannot be known and the claim that things do not exist; in fact, in one place the very same items (things by nature good or bad) are said *both* not to exist *and* to be unknowable (9.101). Yet again, Diogenes appears to be talking nonsense if one approaches him through the lens of *Outlines of Pyrrhonism*; that text, in addition to treating these types of claims as quite distinct, bans the Pyrrhonist from uttering either one. But, according to the Photius passage, as we saw in Section 2, Aenesidemus seems to regard both of these types of assertions as important parts of the Pyrrhonist's repertoire— and also as intimately connected with one another. So it looks as if, in these respects as well, Diogenes is preserving the initial phase of Pyrrhonism as propounded by Aenesidemus, rather than the terminal phase represented by most of Sextus.[46]

But the strongest evidence of a version of Pyrrhonism distinct from that of *Outlines of Pyrrhonism* occurs in Sextus' own *Against the Ethicists*, a book from one of his other two surviving works.[47] Sextus does not tell us in *Against the Ethicists* that he is reproducing the views of Aenesidemus; he expresses

---

[45] In one case, an argument is introduced 'They do away with cause as follows'; then, after a brief argument, the conclusion given is 'so there is no such thing as cause' (9.97–8).

[46] It has been observed that Sextus' *M* 7–11 often give the initial impression that the sceptic, rather than suspending judgement about the reality of the items under consideration, is arguing for their unreality. Among other things, the word *anairein*, 'do away with', is often used in these books (as it is used by Diogenes) to refer to the sceptic's activity; by contrast, *Outlines of Pyrrhonism* never uses the word in this type of context. See Janáček (1972: 54–60, 132). However, except in the case of *Against the Ethicists* (*M* 11, on which see the next paragraph in the main text), this is *only* an initial impression. As Sextus frequently makes clear, the policy of *M* 7–10, like that of *Outlines of Pyrrhonism*, is after all to suspend judgement about the reality of the objects under discussion. Since this is so, for Sextus to speak of the sceptic 'doing away with' these objects is odd and misleading. But the oddity may easily be explained by the supposition that this term, in this usage, is an isolated element surviving from an earlier and different form of Pyrrhonism—the form represented by the Photius passage and by some aspects of Diogenes' summary—in which 'doing away with' the items posited by the dogmatists was precisely the Pyrrhonist's aim. (Sextus' use of *anairein* would in this case be similar to his use of *ou mallon*; in order to fit this established piece of Pyrrhonist vocabulary into the terminal phase of Pyrrhonism, he has to use it in a strained and unnatural fashion.) On the consequences of this for one's views about the order of composition of Sextus' works, and about the relations between *M* 7–10 and *M* 11, see Bett (1997: introduction, sects. IV and V).

[47] The claims advanced in this paragraph are argued for in much more detail in Bett (1997). I also argue there that the Aenesidemean character of *Against the Ethicists* is one reason for thinking that it, and the composite work to which it belongs, is earlier than *Outlines of Pyrrhonism*. This runs counter to the standard view about the order of composition of Sextus' works; but the standard view is highly questionable for other reasons besides the one just mentioned.

agreement with Aenesidemus on one specific point (*M* 11.42), but that is the only mention Aenesidemus receives. However, the view expressed in *Against the Ethicists*—or, at least, in the first of its two major parts[48]—is in all essentials the same as the one Photius attributes to Aenesidemus. Again, the term 'equal strength' (*isostheneia*) nowhere appears in *Against the Ethicists*.[49] Sextus argues not that we should suspend judgement about what, if anything, is really good or bad, but that *nothing is* really, or by nature, good or bad (*M* 11.68–95); and this definite negative conclusion is one to which he is committed in his own person, since he presents its acceptance as crucial to the attainment of the sceptic's own goal of *ataraxia* (*M* 11.118, 130, 140). He also presents the sceptic as referring to things as good or bad in the same relative or qualified manner that we have discussed, while simultaneously denying that anything is good or bad *by nature*; the view that he recommends adopting is that, 'in relation to this person this thing is to be chosen or to be avoided, but in relation to the nature of things it is neither to be chosen nor to be avoided' (*M* 11.114). This view is rephrased a little later, and here there is a use of the 'no more' (*ou mallon*) locution; the sceptic's view, the one that leads to tranquillity, is the view that 'a certain thing is no more by nature to be chosen than to be avoided, nor more to be avoided than to be chosen, every event being in a certain state in relation to something and, in accordance with differing states of affairs and circumstances, turning out as at one time to be chosen and at another time to be avoided' (*M* 11.118). Since the second passage is deliberately recalling the first one, 'no more by nature to be chosen than to be avoided' must be intended as equivalent to 'by nature neither to be chosen nor to be avoided'. Hence 'no more' has to be understood—as in the Photius passage, but *not* as Sextus himself explains the term in *Outlines of Pyrrhonism*—in its natural usage, as meaning 'to no greater extent than'; things are (by nature) 'no more' to be chosen than to be avoided in that they are not (by nature) either (the least bit) to be chosen or (the least bit) to be avoided.[50] Furthermore, Sextus' arguments for the conclusion that nothing is by nature good or bad include an explicit mention of what I have called the

---

[48] The final portion of the book (*M* 11.168–257) is almost entirely distinct in subject matter from the portion that precedes it. It is probable that these two main portions derive from different sources, and it is possible that they derive from different phases in the history of Pyrrhonism; on this, see Bett (1997).

[49] The term 'unresolvable disagreement' (*anepikritos diaphōnia*) does appear (*M* 11.229, 230), but only in the second major part; see the previous note.

[50] We saw earlier (see n. 11) that this was one possible construal of the *ou mallon* locutions in the Photius passage; the other possibility was that they were equivalent to an assertion of the relativity of things. Sextus' inclusion of 'by nature' *within* his 'no more' locutions shows that he must have the first reading in mind. But since, as I noted earlier, the points being made on each of the two readings are closely connected with one another, this makes no serious difference. The crucial point is that 'no more' really does mean 'no more'; and this, as we have seen several times in this chapter, is characteristic of the initial phase of later Pyrrhonism, by contrast with the terminal phase.

invariability condition (*M* 11.69–71); he is very clear that, in order for something to be *by nature* a certain way (in this case, by nature good or bad), it must be that way invariably.[51] Finally, as in the Photius passage, all this is assumed to be consistent with the refusal to 'make determinations' (or, as Sextus also puts it, with the suspending of judgement—e.g. *M* 11.111); again, the refusal to 'make determinations' must here mean, and can unproblematically be taken as meaning, the refusal to issue any specifications of the way things are by nature—a refusal with which, given the invariability condition, the denial that anything is by nature good or bad and the accompanying assertion of relativities are quite consistent.

We have evidence, then, from a variety of sources—from Photius, from Diogenes Laertius, and from Sextus himself—suggesting that the outlook of Aenesidemus, and of the initial phase of later Pyrrhonism, was significantly different from that represented most of the time by Sextus. It is perhaps true that none of these sources, considered by itself, would be especially trustworthy; but the cumulative force of all three of them—since they are all clearly independent of one another—is considerable. Aulus Gellius (11.5.7) says that the Pyrrhonists 'say that absolutely everything which affects people's senses is relative'. Here Gellius uses the Greek term *pros ti*, and adds in explanation: 'This term signifies that there is nothing whatever that exists in itself or has its own force and nature, but everything is referred to something else.' Similarly, the Anonymous Commentator on the *Theaetetus* claims (63.2–6) that 'the Pyrrhonists say that everything is relative, in as much as nothing exists in itself, but everything is considered in relation to other things', and goes on to elaborate this position with reference to numerous examples reminiscent of Aenesidemus' Ten Modes. Again, either of these texts taken by itself might be dismissed as being due to a simple misunderstanding. Aulus Gellius dubiously attributes the view in question to the Academics as well as the Pyrrhonists; and the Anonymous Commentator is not an author on whom one is in general happy to have to rely.[52] However, both authors attribute to the Pyrrhonists a view that seems to correspond easily enough with the position we have observed in Photius, Diogenes, and Sextus; so it seems preferable to see their remarks, too, as genuine reflections of the state of affairs on which I have been insisting throughout this chapter— that later Pyrrhonism at its inception, in the hands of Aenesidemus, was by no means the same as (and, indeed, was in important ways incompatible with) the Pyrrhonism portrayed by Sextus in *Outlines of Pyrrhonism* and elsewhere.

[51] Specifically, for all persons as opposed to only some; cf. above, n. 14. The presence of what I call the invariability condition in this passage is also drawn attention to by Decleva Caizzi (1995). Despite the title, this article has very little to do with Pyrrho; what is of interest for my purposes, however, is that Decleva Caizzi convincingly connects the style of reasoning in this passage of *Against the Ethicists* to Aenesidemus.

[52] On the Anonymous Commentator's less than complete reliability, see above, n. 20.

4. *Aenesidemus' relations with Pyrrho*

Now that we have looked at the initial phase of later Pyrrhonism, represented especially by Aenesidemus, and the ways in which it differs from the much more familiar terminal phase, it is time to return to the central question of this chapter. Why did the later Pyrrhonists adopt *Pyrrho* as their figurehead? As I suggested earlier, it was presumably Aenesidemus, the initiator of the revived Pyrrhonist movement, who was above all responsible for this choice. Now, part of the explanation is no doubt that Aenesidemus wanted someone clearly distinct from the entire Academic tradition; as we have seen, he presents the new Pyrrhonism as standing in opposition to the Academy in particular, and his choice of forerunners would be expected to reflect this. However, this is plainly not an adequate explanation by itself. For, first, the Pyrrhonists were not obligated to choose anyone at all in the role of forerunner or figurehead. And, secondly, given that they did choose someone, the mere need to avoid anyone with Academic connections would not have dictated the choice of Pyrrho in particular. A satisfactory explanation of Aenesidemus' choice of Pyrrho must, then, make clear the nature of the philosophical common ground between the two, in such a way that it becomes understandable why Aenesidemus should have thought of Pyrrho as a model to whom it was worth drawing special attention. As I suggested at the beginning of the chapter, this is much easier to achieve if one recognizes the significant differences between the initial phase of later Pyrrhonism and its terminal phase; Aenesidemus is in several respects closer to Pyrrho than is the Sextus of *Outlines of Pyrrhonism*. But the story that needs to be told at this point is none the less not without complications.

As I have interpreted them, the views of Pyrrho and Aenesidemus differ in at least one important way. Pyrrho advances the metaphysical thesis that reality is indeterminate, whereas Aenesidemus refuses any attempt to specify the nature of reality. Accompanying this difference is a second one, having to do with their employment of sentences containing the term 'no more'. Both are prepared to assert, apparently for a very wide range of predicates,[53] that things are 'no more' *F* than not-*F*. But in Pyrrho's case the use of assertions of this form is best understood as a way of stating the inherent indeterminacy of things; to say that each thing 'no more is than is not or both is and is not or neither is nor is not' is to say that, for the predicates under consideration, those predicates neither apply nor fail to apply to the things in question—in other words, that the things are purely indeterminate with respect to their

---

[53] Precisely *how* widely the 'no more' locutions are supposed to apply is never made clear in either case. But there is no indication, in either case, of any strict limitations on their applicability.

possession or non-possession of those predicates (see Chapter 1, Section 3, and Chapter 3, Section 1). In Aenesidemus' case, on the other hand, such assertions are best understood as conveying two complementary points: first, that, as a matter of ordinary experience, the things in question are in some circumstances *F*, in other circumstances not-*F*, and, secondly, that they are not, in their *real nature*, either *F* or not-*F*. The 'no more' locution is thus used by Pyrrho as a way of speaking about the real nature of things, but by Aenesidemus as a way of avoiding any claims purporting to specify their real nature (see above, Section 1).[54] Despite this difference, though, there are also a number of notable similarities between the outlooks of the two men—similarities that collectively make it easy enough to see how Pyrrho might have seemed to Aenesidemus a uniquely appropriate figure to point to as a forerunner. Moreover, when one takes into account the rather different philosophical climates of the periods in which they each lived, the difference to which I have just drawn attention proves to be unsurprising.

First of all, the views of both are driven to a large extent, if my reading of them has been correct, by a preoccupation with what I have called variability, or what one of the ancient sources called 'contradiction' (*antilogian* (DL 9.106)). Both are impressed, that is, by the fact that different and incompatible predicates may apply to the same object in different situations, in different respects, or in relation to different people. In Aenesidemus' case this is obvious from the evidence I have reviewed in the last few sections—most notably the Ten Modes and the Photius passage. In Pyrrho's case it cannot be read quite so straightforwardly from the available evidence. However, I argued in the Chapter 3, Section 1, that by far the best way to make sense of Pyrrho's central philosophical attitudes, as revealed especially by the Aristocles passage, is to see them as stemming from reflection on some form or forms of variability; the indeterminacy thesis, in particular, is most naturally understood as deriving from the idea that there is simply no fixed and stable way in which things present themselves to us—an idea that Pyrrho was certainly not the first in Greek philosophy to find compelling.

Secondly, both Pyrrho and Aenesidemus react to variability, or to certain species of variability, by refusing to trust our ordinary experience of things as revelatory of how those things are in their real natures. So far, of course, the same could be said of the terminal phase of Pyrrhonism represented by most of the writings of Sextus. However, as we have seen, the specific *way* in which Pyrrho's and Aenesidemus' reasoning works in this case is importantly different from what one finds in most of Sextus. For both Pyrrho and Aenesidemus, the point is *not* that, since a thing strikes us in two or more

---

[54] A related difference, of course, is that Aenesidemus uses only the form of words 'no more *F* than not-*F*', and not the extended form of words 'no more *F* than not-*F or both or neither*' employed by Pyrrho; again see the sections of earlier chapters cited in the main text.

different and incompatible ways, either one (or any one) of these ways in which it strikes us may be the way it really is (but there is no non-question-begging method for determining which this is). That is the kind of account characteristic of Sextus, an account centred around the concept of *isostheneia*, 'equal strength'. Rather, for Pyrrho and Aenesidemus—again, if my reconstructions of their thinking have been on the right lines—the very *existence* of multiple ways in which the thing presents itself guarantees that *none* of these ways is the way the thing is in its true nature. This is because of their common acceptance of what I called the invariability condition: nothing can be *really*, or *by nature*, a certain way unless it is that way in all circumstances without exception.[55] Except in *Against the Ethicists*, the book that espouses an essentially Aenesidemean outlook, Sextus shows no sign of accepting the invariability condition; nor would one expect him to accept it—it would surely look to him like a dogmatic philosophical view.[56] But both Pyrrho and Aenesidemus do seem to accept it; or, at any rate, the assumption that they accept it makes readily intelligible what would otherwise be thoroughly obscure in their reasoning. And again, if they do accept it, they are certainly not alone among Greek philosophers.

Thirdly, as a way of expressing their mistrust of our everyday impressions of things as guides to the true natures of those things, both adopt forms of words including phrases of the type 'no more *F* than not-*F*'. Despite the difference in their usage of these phrases referred to above, Pyrrho and Aenesidemus have far more in common with each other in this respect, too, than they have with Sextus (again with the exception of *Against the Ethicists*). For both of them, as we have seen, 'no more' has to be understood in its natural sense of 'to no greater extent than', rather than in the more convoluted fashion described in *Outlines of Pyrrhonism*; and, for both of them, statements of the form '*X* is no more *F* than not-*F*' are to be understood as straightforward assertions. *X*'s being *F* or not-*F*, that is, is not thereby being proposed as a topic on which judgement is to be suspended (as it is according to the explanation of the term 'no more' in *Outlines of Pyrrhonism*); to say '*X* is no more *F* than not-*F*' is simply to assert that *X* has the one property to no greater extent than it has the other. For Pyrrho, this is an assertion of the indeterminacy of the thing, as far as its real nature is concerned, whereas for Aenesidemus it is either an assertion concerning how things present themselves in varying circumstances, or an assertion to the effect that the thing does not, in its real nature, have either property; but it is in both cases a response to the phenomenon of variability, and a response that is

---

55 Again, the slide between 'presents itself' and 'is' depends on the assumption that the characteristics of things *in specific circumstances*—as opposed to their real natures—are not themselves (except perhaps in certain special cases) a matter for doubt; cf. above, n. 22, and see further Sect. 6.

56 More on this, too, in Sect. 6 (and cf. above, n. 19).

shaped, if I am right, by acceptance of the invariability condition. Given this condition, a thing cannot be determinately F in its real nature unless it presents itself as F invariably; the phenomenon of variability ensures that this will not be so; and the 'no more F than not-F' locution is designed to convey this state of affairs.

Fourthly, it looks as if early Pyrrhonism—including, very possibly, Pyrrho himself—and Aenesidemus adopted the strategy of relying on the appearances of things as a basis for choice and action. And the 'appearances' of things, I have argued, are best understood as being simply the ways in which things present themselves in specific sets of circumstances. Given the phenomenon of variability, things do not present themselves uniformly in the same ways; and this point, together with the invariability condition, ensures that *none* of these appearances can be identical with how the things are in their true natures. Once this is understood, however, there is no difficulty in allowing oneself to be guided by the appearances. The ways in which things present themselves may vary from situation to situation; but that is no reason not to allow one's behaviour to be shaped, in any *particular* situation, by the way a thing presents itself in *that* situation. Here again, Pyrrho and Aenesidemus are in agreement with one another, but at odds with *Outlines of Pyrrhonism*. As we mentioned in passing in an earlier section, Sextus' distinction between the 'appearances' and the real, or underlying, nature of an object is quite unrelated to any distinction between variable and invariable features. And, though Sextus too insists that the sceptic can live and act by following appearances, his conception of the appearances is not such that *none* of the appearances can *possibly* capture the true nature of the things in question; the problem, for him, is rather that there is no reliable way of telling *which* (if any) of the appearances—that is, our conflicting impressions of a thing—reflects that true nature.

On all of these four points, Pyrrho and Aenesidemus are following to some degree in the footsteps of Plato. The nature of the contrast between appearance and reality in *Republic* V is much the same as the one I have just recalled—or so I argued in Chapter 3, Section 3. Then again, Plato is impressed with the phenomenon of variability in sensible things; because of this variability, he has Socrates consign sensible things to a status below that of genuine or full-grade being; and one of the ways in which this inferior status is expressed is by means of 'no more F than not-F' locutions applied to sensible things. I suggested in Chapter 3 that the points of similarity between Plato and Pyrrho were best explained by the assumption that Pyrrho either read Plato or became acquainted with Plato's ideas through some other channels. But now, if Aenesidemus was anticipated in these respects by Plato as well as by Pyrrho, we are again faced with our central question. Why does Aenesidemus appeal to Pyrrho, and to him exclusively, as a philosophical ancestor? We know that Aenesidemus not only had some acquaintance with

Plato, but also that he was interested, specifically, in the extent to which Plato anticipated Pyrrhonist thinking; Sextus tells us (*PH* 1.222) that he took a position on the question whether Plato was a sceptic.[57] In any case, some acquaintance with Plato would surely be expected if, as seems to be the case, Aenesidemus began his philosophical life as a member of the Academy.

The answer, I think, is twofold. Let us assume that Aenesidemus did know Plato's dialogues, and did notice the similarities between these aspects of Plato's thinking and his own thinking;[58] both assumptions are plausible enough, though the second is by no means incontestable. Even so, he would have had a strong motivation, quite apart from strictly philosophical considerations, to suppress any reference to Plato as an influence; on this point, at least, the desire to distance himself from the Academy would surely have been decisive. But, more importantly, even if Aenesidemus was struck by these elements in Plato's thinking, the example of Pyrrho must in any case have been a far more potent one for him. Though Plato does seem to take a dim view of sensible things—and this leads him to a number of philosophical moves that may have inspired Pyrrho—sensible things are not, for Plato, all that there is. There are also the Forms, which are fully real, fully determinate, and (under the right conditions) fully intelligible; and the importance

---

[57] *What* position Aenesidemus took on this question is difficult to say; the text is corrupt at a crucial point. Sextus is arguing that anyone who takes a dogmatic position on just one issue is not a sceptic, and that on these terms it is easy to see that Plato is not a sceptic. Introducing this, the text says 'Here, in outline form, we say *katapermēdoton* and Aenesidemus (for these especially put forward this position), that when Plato makes assertions about Forms', etc. As the word 'these' makes clear, the corrupt *katapermēdoton* is supposed to include a second name to go alongside that of Aenesidemus; most scholars have taken this name to be Menodotus, an Empiricist doctor and Pyrrhonist. The difficult question is what the 'position' concerning Plato's scepticism was, and whether Sextus is speaking against it or in support of it; different reconstructions of the corrupt portion of the text yield different answers to these questions. A recent discussion, with full references to previous discussions, is Spinelli (2000). Spinelli argues persuasively for the emendation *kathaper <hoi peri> Mē<no>doton*, and more generally for the view that Sextus is *agreeing* with Menodotus and Aenesidemus, whose 'position' was therefore that Plato was *not* a sceptic. For our purposes, though, it is not important to settle this question. Whether or not Aenesidemus took Plato himself to be a sceptic, there is no inconsistency in holding that Aenesidemus' form of scepticism contains numerous elements whose ultimate origin is in Plato—or even that Aenesidemus was aware of the Platonic character of these elements.

[58] It has been observed that Sextus frequently uses the adverb *eilikrinōs*, 'purely', in contexts where Aenesidemus is likely to have been his source—seven times in the Ten Modes of Aenesidemus (*PH* 1.92, 93, 124, 126, 127, 134, 140), and also in *PH* 1.222, the passage referred to just above; *eilikrinōs* and the related adjective *eilikrinēs* are favourite terms of Plato (and recur a number of times, incidentally, in the passage of *Republic* V that I pointed to in the previous chapter as an important antecedent of Pyrrho's position—see e.g. 477a7, 478d6, e2–3 (on which see Ch. 3 n. 42), 479d5). It is tempting to infer that Aenesidemus borrowed this usage from Plato; see Woodruff (1988: 168 (drawing on Tarrant (1985: 75)), and Ioppolo (1995: n. 63). However, the matter is not as clear as it looks; as Decleva Caizzi points out (1992*b*: n. 81), *eilikrinēs* is also common in the medical tradition—a tradition with which the Pyrrhonist tradition had many ties.

accorded to the Forms by Plato obviously means that his philosophy as a whole looks very different from either Pyrrho's or Aenesidemus'. Despite a similarity between *Republic* V's conception of the appearances and that of early Pyrrhonism and Aenesidemus, Plato certainly does not suggest a practical strategy of *following* the appearances; despite his employment of phrases of the form 'no more *F* than not-*F*', he does not suggest that *everything* is to be described by means of such phrases—with the Forms it is quite the opposite; the list of such divergences could easily be extended. So, although Plato may have influenced Pyrrho, it makes sense—and not only for political reasons—that Aenesidemus should have referred to Pyrrho, and not to Plato, as his main inspiration, whatever the extent of his interest in or understanding of Plato.

Besides, there is one more crucial point of contact between Aenesidemus and Pyrrho for which there is no analogue in Plato—or, for that matter, in any other of Aenesidemus' predecessors. Both claim that, as a *result* of their mistrust of either everyday impressions or the theorizing of philosophers as revelatory of how things really are, they have achieved a trouble-free existence—whereas philosophers who adopt other persuasions and procedures are perpetually troubled. As we saw in Chapter 2, the evidence on Pyrrho includes frequent reference to both poles of this contrast. Pyrrho calls the trouble-free existence *ataraxia*; the word itself is not attested in the evidence concerning Aenesidemus, but it looks as if his conception of the emotional outcome of Pyrrhonist reflections is very much the same. The Photius passage makes clear that Aenesidemus conceived of the dogmatists—that is, anyone who, in his terminology, 'makes determinations' of things—as emotionally disturbed as a result of their dogmatism, and of the Pyrrhonists as free from such disturbances as a result of their Pyrrhonism. And on this point Sextus, too, has a closely analogous attitude;[59] for Sextus, *ataraxia* is a direct consequence of

---

[59] This is not to retract anything said in Ch. 2, Sect. 7, on the differences between Pyrrho's and Sextus' practical attitudes. As we saw, there are numerous differences of detail between the two, having to do with the precise character of the *ataraxia* strived for and the precise manner in which it is supposed to be generated. But, to recall, these differences were themselves largely a function of Pyrrho's acceptance of the indeterminacy thesis, which to Sextus would have counted as a piece of dogmatism. What the two have in common is that *ataraxia* is said to be the result of the appropriate attitude of mistrust or withdrawal, whatever exactly that consists of in each case. Here again, Aenesidemus (and Sextus' own *Against the Ethicists*) seems to occupy an intermediate position, philosophically as well as historically (and this too was occasionally referred to in Ch. 2, Sect. 7). He does not propose any indeterminacy thesis; yet, as we saw in the first few sections of this chapter, he is willing to issue various types of assertions that to Sextus would count as dogmatic. His conception of the 'attitude of mistrust or withdrawal' that can be expected to yield *ataraxia* is therefore closer to Pyrrho's than is Sextus' conception; indeed, to say this is really just to reiterate the discussion of the previous few pages, concerning the common ground shared by Aenesidemus and Pyrrho as against Sextus. Thus, if it is understandable that, on this score at least, Pyrrho might have looked to Sextus like a forerunner, it is all the more understandable why (again on this score in particular) he might have looked like one to Aenesidemus.

epochē, and those who are unfortunate enough to hold positive beliefs about the nature of things—in particular, beliefs to the effect that certain things are by nature good and others by nature bad—are subject to severe disturbance (see e.g. *PH* 1.8, 25–30).

Indeed, this is perhaps the thread running most consistently through the entire history of Pyrrhonism. But it is also a point that sets the Pyrrhonists apart from all other Greek philosophers, and certainly from Plato. The goal of a trouble-free existence, of one form or another, is far from uncommon in Greek philosophy—especially in the Hellenistic period, but not only then. Equally, it is by no means unusual to find Greek philosophers expressing an attitude towards our prospects for understanding that can be broadly described as sceptical—even if it is not precisely the same as the attitude of any member of the Pyrrhonist tradition. We saw plenty of examples of both these types of phenomena in the previous chapter; and, if the focus there had not been limited to the period up to and including Pyrrho himself, both lists could obviously have been continued. What is unique about the Pyrrhonists, however, is the *connection* they draw between these two elements.[60] Others who adopt the goal of *ataraxia*, or some related form of tranquillity, typically aspire to achieve this goal as a result of coming to understand the nature of things through painstaking enquiry, and being able to ascribe to them some set of definite characteristics[61]—not through a renunciation of any attempt at such understanding; indeed, this is precisely what Sextus refers to (*PH* 1.12, 26) as the initial ambition of those who eventually become sceptics. And none of the others who express some form of sceptical attitude towards our prospects for understanding see *ataraxia*, or anything like it, as the result (nor trouble and torment as the result of continuing to strive for such understanding).[62] The idea that one is *better off*, in practical or emotional terms, adopt-

---

[60] The only possible exception, as we saw in Ch. 3, was Pyrrho's teacher Anaxarchus; in his case we have evidence both of a goal resembling *ataraxia* and of a claim that, at least on one interpretation, looks like a forerunner of Pyrrho's indeterminacy thesis. But, as I pointed out, there is no evidence that Anaxarchus attempted to connect the two elements in anything like the manner of Pyrrho or the later Pyrrhonists; see especially Ch. 3 n. 120 and accompanying text.

[61] Pyrrho, unlike any of the later Pyrrhonists, does of course claim to understand how things really are, according to the interpretation offered in Ch. 1. But the *type* of understanding he claims to have is very different from that of most philosophers. He does not claim to be able to ascribe definite characteristics to things—since they are in his view *in*definite, no such description is available—nor does he imagine that *enquiry*, of the type engaged in by physical thinkers and others, is going to make possible any progress towards pinning down their features (for again, they have *no* determinate features). Cf. Ch. 1 n. 23 and accompanying text.

[62] The Academics Arcesilaus and Carneades are both concerned to show that a human life, even a happy human life, is just as *possible* for a sceptic as for anyone else; on this see Bett (1989a, 1990). But neither suggests that it is *preferable* to live as a sceptic, nor that the 'happiness' that the sceptic is, according to them, capable of achieving takes the specific form of *ataraxia*. In fact, there is no evidence that their motivations for maintaining a sceptical attitude had anything to do with the desirability of the life that results.

ing an attitude of mistrust or withdrawal than if one persists with a conventional, optimistic attitude towards enquiry belongs to the Pyrrhonists and to them alone.

It is hard to say, in the abstract, what some philosopher *A* may reasonably consider sufficient common ground in the thought of some earlier philosopher *B* in order for *B* to qualify as having *anticipated A*'s philosophy. I have emphasized the distinctiveness of the Pyrrhonist connection between, on the one hand, an attitude of mistrust or withdrawal concerning our ordinary impressions of things and, on the other hand, a trouble-free life. And this by itself could perhaps have been regarded by any later Pyrrhonist as sufficient justification for appealing to Pyrrho as the starting point of their tradition. However, since both the attitude of mistrust or withdrawal and the trouble-free life seem to take considerably different specific forms in the hands of different members of the Pyrrhonist tradition, one might instead think that this alone would not be enough, and that a greater degree of philosophical kinship would be required. In particular, one might well think that the Pyrrhonism of Sextus' *Outlines of Pyrrhonism* is too far removed from the ideas of Pyrrho himself to make the figure of Pyrrho altogether suitable as founding father. Possibly Sextus' vagueness, in that very work, about why Pyrrhonism is so called (*PH* 1.7) reflects an unease along these lines.[63] In any case, whether or not this is correct, there is substantially less difficulty in seeing why Pyrrho might have been appropriated in this way by Aenesidemus. As we have seen, Aenesidemus' variety of Pyrrhonism is in numerous respects closer to that of Pyrrho himself than is the variety represented by *Outlines of Pyrrhonism*; in Aenesidemus' case, the connection with Pyrrho does not rest solely, or even mainly, on the point discussed in the previous two paragraphs—significant as that point undoubtedly is—but on several more detailed points of correspondence as well. And, once this has been attended to, Aenesidemus' adoption of Pyrrho, and no one else, as a figurehead for his new movement need not seem mysterious or unmotivated.

It remains to say a little more about the central difference between Aenesidemus and Pyrrho to which I referred at the beginning of the section. As a result of considerations concerning variability, or relativity to circumstances, Pyrrho holds that reality is indeterminate; but, though variability is also the starting point for Aenesidemus' thinking, he refuses any attempt to specify the nature of things. This difference, I think, is not hard to account for. In Aenesidemus' day, as opposed to Pyrrho's, it would have seemed thoroughly irresponsible to derive from the phenomenon of variability any positive characterization of the nature of reality, such as that it was indefinite. The Stoics and the Academics had been engaged in a couple of centuries of debate on epistemological issues, in which the legitimacy of claiming to be able to

---

[63] On this, see again the penultimate paragraph of Ch. 1, Sect. 7.

specify how things really are, on the basis of how they strike one—and the difficulty of trying to do so when they strike one in *conflicting* ways—was central throughout. Anyone familiar with the history of those debates—and the Photius passage shows that Aenesidemus *was* familiar with them, whether or not he was himself ever a member of the Academy—would naturally be very cautious about any pretensions to specify the real nature of things. Because of his acceptance of the invariability condition, Aenesidemus is prepared to make certain types of definite assertions; but the whole point about these is that, given the invariability condition, they do *not* count as specifications of the nature of things. Though doubts about our ability to say how things really are had certainly been broached by Pyrrho's time—we saw several examples in Chapter 3—they had nowhere near the centrality in philosophical discourse that they were to acquire in the Hellenistic period.[64] And so, given the different eras in which they lived, it is not surprising that the same kinds of observations about the variability in how things strike us might have led Pyrrho to a bold thesis to the effect that reality is inherently indeterminate, and Aenesidemus to a withdrawal from any attempts to 'determine'—that is, to specify—the nature of things. Plato, too, boldly draws metaphysical consequences from certain types of variability; and, as I argued, it is plausible to see Pyrrho as having been affected by this. But once the question of the 'criterion of truth' became a question of primary importance, in the Hellenistic period,[65] such bold moves would naturally have begun to seem suspect; by Aenesidemus' time, they would surely have seemed foolhardy or worse. We have no way of telling what exactly was Aenesidemus' reaction to Pyrrho's indeterminacy thesis. But, however precisely he understood it, and whether or not he found it embarrassing, it is easy to picture him, given the philosophical constraints of his own time, simply detaching it from the many other, highly congenial ideas and attitudes that he saw in Pyrrho's philosophy, and treating the remainder as an inspiration for his own philosophy.

---

[64] Plato and Aristotle, it has been well said, 'had little patience with doubts about the possibility of knowledge'. See Striker (1990: 143). Not everyone would agree that Aristotle is unconcerned with sceptical worries. For example, Irwin (1988) argues that much of Aristotle's philosophical strategy is dictated by the need to ward off challenges from certain forms of sceptic. But, even if this is correct, it is at least clear that Aristotle does not *talk about* the question 'Is knowledge even possible?' in any sustained or systematic way; on the difficulty of finding where such a topic is even broached in Aristotle's vast corpus, see the opening section of Taylor (1990). For a recent defence, against Irwin and others, of the view that scepticism about knowledge does not figure among Aristotle's serious concerns (either overt or hidden), see Vasiliou (1996).

[65] On the criterion and its importance in Hellenistic philosophy, see Striker (1974, 1990).

5. The 'Heracliteanism' of Aenesidemus

It may be felt that the above account has neglected a crucial aspect of the evidence relating to Aenesidemus. A number of passages in Sextus appear to associate Aenesidemus with the philosophy of Heraclitus. Now, we saw in Chapter 3 that a certain connection, albeit a rather indirect one, appeared to obtain between Heraclitean ideas and the ideas of Pyrrho; it was Plato's examination (and, as it turned out, dismissal) of Heraclitean ideas in the *Theaetetus* that seemed to furnish one of the most suggestive antecedents for Pyrrho's central philosophical attitudes. And, if this is so, a connection between Aenesidemus and Heraclitus might well be expected to be relevant to our understanding of Aenesidemus' relations with Pyrrho.[66]

The question of Aenesidemus' 'Heraclitean' tendencies has received scrutiny from many scholars over a period of more than a century.[67] Inevitably, therefore, much of what I have to offer on the subject has been anticipated to some degree by others. What may, however, shed a partially new light on the problem, and help to make it look less intractable, is the divergence that I have emphasized between Aenesidemus' variety of Pyrrhonism and the variety espoused (with the exception, as always, of *Against the Ethicists*) by Sextus himself. As we shall see, Sextus is thoroughly hostile to the idea of a connection between scepticism and Heracliteanism; and his apparent willingness to claim that Aenesidemus adopted Heraclitean ideas may well be associated with his discomfort at the position represented by Aenesidemus as the Pyrrhonist position.

Several passages in Sextus' *Against the Logicians* and *Against the Physicists* attribute views to *Ainēsidēmos kata Hērakleiton*.[68] The views in

---

[66] See e.g. Conche (1994: ch. XV); Conche reads Aenesidemus' 'Heracliteanism' as constituting one of the most significant philosophical connections between him and Pyrrho.

[67] Debate on this topic stretches back at least to Diels, Zeller, and von Arnim. See Diels (1879: 209–12); von Arnim (1888: 79–85); Zeller (1903, 36–46).

[68] *M* 7.349, 9.337, 10.216 (which adds *ton* before *Hērakleiton*). There is also *M* 8.8, where, as noted above (n. 17), the manuscripts read *hoi de peri ton Ainēsidēmon kai Hērakleiton*, but *kai* has been altered by editors to *kath'*. However, *hoi de peri ton Ainēsidēmon kath'Hērakleiton*—literally, 'those around Aenesidemus in accordance with [or, "in relation to"] Heraclitus'—is extremely awkward and extremely hard to accept. Though the expression '*hoi peri X*', 'those around *X*', is regularly used in a non-literal way, as a periphrasis for '*X*', the term '*X*'—referring to the figure 'around' whom followers are imagined as clustering—is always, as one might expect, a simple name or sequence of names, not a more complicated phrase, designating an *aspect* of someone's views or writings, such as *Ainēsidēmos kath'Hērakleiton*. (One might suggest that *kath'Hērakleiton* should instead be understood as qualifying the whole phrase *hoi de peri ton Ainēsidēmon*: 'those around Aenesidemus, in accordance with Heraclitus', as opposed to 'those around Aenesidemus-in-accordance-with-Heraclitus'. However, the *hoi peri* phrase also includes *kai ton Epikouron* immediately after the words we have been considering; the complete phrase is 'those around Aenesidemus . . . and Epicurus'. If *kath'Hērakleiton* was read in the manner suggested, *kai ton Epikouron* could not also be

question are not all obviously Heraclitean in character; one of them, for example, is that time is corporeal (*M* 10.216), which does not seem to correspond with anything in the surviving fragments of Heraclitus. However, since the very same view is attributed in the subsequent discussion to 'the Heracliteans' (*M* 10.230), it seems clear that it, and the other views attributed to *Ainēsidēmos kata Hērakleiton*, are indeed supposed to have been held by Heraclitus or his followers. The question then is what is Aenesidemus' relation to these views—or, in other words, what this puzzling phrase means. The most straightforward way to translate it would be 'Aenesidemus according to Heraclitus', but this is clearly impossible. But a more feasible option might be 'Aenesidemus in accordance with Heraclitus', where this in turn was taken to mean 'Aenesidemus *in agreement with* Heraclitus'; and, if this was correct, then we would have evidence that Aenesidemus was in some sense an *adherent* of Heraclitus' philosophy. We shall return to this issue in a little while. But first, we need to concentrate on another passage, which has widely been taken as the most important evidence of Aenesidemus' having adopted Heraclitean views.

The passage in question occurs towards the end of book I of *Outlines of Pyrrhonism*; Sextus embarks (*PH* 1.209) on his final main topic for that book—the ways in which Pyrrhonism differs from other philosophies that might, for various reasons, be thought akin to it—and says that he will first treat the philosophy of Heraclitus. He begins (1.210) by saying that Heraclitus clearly differs from the Pyrrhonist, since he makes dogmatic assertions on many subjects; he then reports what is clearly meant to be a contrary view held by Aenesidemus, as follows. 'But those around Aenesidemus used to say that the sceptical method is a route [*hodon*] to the Heraclitean philosophy, because the notion that opposites appear to hold of the same thing precedes [*proēgeitai*] the notion that opposites actually do hold of the same thing, and whereas the sceptics say that opposites appear to hold of the same thing, the Heracliteans move on [*meterchontai*] from this point to their actually holding.' Sextus then gives various reasons against this suggestion,

---

attached to *hoi de peri*—as it has to be, in order to have any function in the sentence; the same occurrence of *hoi de peri* cannot be both part of a sequence of words qualified by *kath'Hērakleiton* and part of a sequence of words unconnected with it.) The main reason why editors have changed *kai* to *kath'* is presumably that the view under discussion is attributed immediately afterwards to *hoi . . . peri ton Ainēsidēmon*, with no further mention of Heraclitus. But this can easily be explained without our having to manufacture the intolerable *hoi de peri ton Ainēsidēmon kath'Hērakleiton*. Maybe Sextus is being careless in his attributions. Or, if this is too much to believe, given that the two seemingly conflicting attributions occur in adjacent sentences—and I think it probably is—we may suppose that *kai Hērakleiton* (or *kath'Hērakleiton*) is a gloss inserted by a scholiast who has noticed a similarity between the view here attributed to Aenesidemus and ideas elsewhere attributed to Heraclitus (e.g. *M* 7.131). I shall, therefore, not treat this passage as exemplifying the phrase that concerns us (though it will continue to be of interest in this section for another reason).

ending with the claim that it is absurd (*atopon* (1.212)) to call scepticism a route to Heracliteanism.

What exactly is Aenesidemus' suggestion? The majority of scholars who have discussed the question have read this passage as indicating that Aenesidemus personally underwent or endorsed some kind of philosophical progression from scepticism to Heracliteanism.[69] In fact the text indicates no such thing. To say that philosophy *A* is a route to philosophy *B* is to say that one possible way in which one might come to accept philosophy *B* is by previously embracing philosophy *A*; it is *not* to say that anyone who at some time embraces philosophy *A* is required, logically or otherwise, to end up accepting philosophy *B*. Thus Aenesidemus' point is that one may become a Heraclitean via the adoption of some kind of sceptical outlook; it is not that the adoption of a sceptical outlook *inevitably* results in one's becoming a Heraclitean. (Routes, as a rule, facilitate travel; they do not compel it.) The claim is strengthened slightly in the explanation that follows. In saying that 'the notion that opposites appear to hold of the same thing *precedes* the notion that opposites actually do hold of the same thing', Aenesidemus appears to be claiming that the sceptical attitude (at least, on this particular point) is logically presupposed by, or is a necessary condition of coming to hold, the Heraclitean view; if so, the sceptical attitude is not just *a* route to Heracliteanism, but the *only* route to it. But this is still not to say anything at all to suggest that adoption of the sceptical attitude of itself creates some kind of *obligation* to take the further step of adopting a Heraclitean position.[70] And, in fact, it is quite unclear *why* acceptance of the claim that opposites appear to hold of the same thing should be thought to compel acceptance of the claim that opposites actually do hold of the same thing; a Pyrrhonist, of all people (and here I speak indiscriminately of *every* phase of Pyrrhonism, from Pyrrho to Sextus), would be expected to insist, precisely, that nothing compels us to advance from the former to the latter claim—in fact, that we

---

[69] Most recently Hankinson (1995: 130). See also Brochard (1923: 272–89); Capone Braga (1931); Rist (1970); Dal Pra (1989: 392–411); Conche (1994: ch. XV).

[70] The word *proēgeisthai*, here translated 'precedes', has as its most literal sense 'go first' or 'lead the way'; see e.g. Xenophon, *Cyropaideia* 2.1.1, 4.2.27. In philosophical usage it often refers, as here, to something that is a *precondition* for some further event; in Sextus, see e.g. *M* 7.263—'a conception precedes every apprehension' (*pasēs katalēpseōs epinoia proēgeitai*)—or *M* 8.60—'experience through sensation must precede [*proēgeisthai*] every conception'—and, for an example outside Sextus, see Epictetus, *Diss.* 3.7, 6. In such cases the thing 'preceding' is *necessary* for the occurrence of the further event, but it is no part of the author's purpose to suggest, by the word *proēgeisthai* or by any other means, that it is *sufficient* for the occurrence of this further event. Whether or not the word ever has this stronger implication—and I have not seen anything to persuade me that it does—parallels such as those just cited show that we do not *need* to read the present passage as containing any suggestion to that effect.

had *better not* do so.[71] It is a plausible suggestion that the latter, Heraclitean claim could not very well be adopted *without* first accepting that opposites at least *appear* to hold of the same thing; but that suggestion in no way entails *advocacy* of the progression of thought that the Heracliteans are being said to undergo.[72]

What, then, of the puzzling phrase *Ainēsidēmos kata Hērakleiton*? If this does indeed mean 'Aenesidemus in agreement with Heraclitus', then, despite the argument of the previous paragraph, we do have evidence of a phase of Aenesidemus' thought in which he accepted Heraclitean positions. However, this is not the only possibility. *Kata* can also be translated 'in relation to' or 'concerning'.[73] If this is how the word is meant here, then the phrase presumably refers to *discussions of* Heraclitus by Aenesidemus—discussions of whose existence the passage from *Outlines of Pyrrhonism* already gave us good evidence; but one may, of course, discuss someone's views without agreeing with them.[74] Another possibility, the outcome of which would be the same, is that the words *kata Hērakleiton* were commonly used by

---

[71] Against this, it might be objected that, according to my own interpretation of Aenesidemus' view, this move would be quite legitimate. Did I not suggest that Aenesidemus may have been willing to issue statements of the form '*X is F* in circumstances *C*', regarding them, because of the restriction to specific circumstances, as species of appearance-statements, rather than statements of the true nature of the things in question? However, the kind of move envisaged in the present passage cannot be of this (from Aenesidemus' point of view) innocuous sort. First, the word *meterchontai*, 'move on', clearly suggests that what is at issue here is a transition between two different orders of statements; if Aenesidemus was willing to say '*X is F* in circumstances *C*', it was precisely because, in his view, this involved no such transition—'*X is F* in circumstances *C*' was legitimate, if it was, for the very reason that it did *not* require him to 'move on' from the realm of appearance-statements, but kept him squarely *within* that realm. Secondly, Heraclitean pronouncements about opposites are clearly meant to apply to the real nature of things, and not merely to the 'appearances', however broadly construed (in fact, he is arguably the first thinker to articulate a version of this distinction itself—on this see below, n. 88); and Aenesidemus must surely have been aware of this. So, although a Pyrrhonist of Aenesidemus' stripe may indeed have been willing to use the word *huparchei*, 'actually is', if appropriate restrictions were in place (for a case of this in Sextus' *Against the Ethicists*, see above, n. 23), we are dealing, in the present situation, with the kind of claim that Aenesidemus would have regarded as unacceptably dogmatic.

[72] This reading of the passage accords in all essentials with that of Burkhard (1973: 34–47) and, much earlier, that of von Arnim (1888: 79–85); Burkhard's interpretation receives further endorsement from Cortassa (1977) and from Viano (1989). No one, to my knowledge, has offered any adequate reason for rejecting this interpretation. Of those cited earlier (see n. 69) as holding the contrary view, Hankinson does not discuss it at all; and Capone Braga (1931: 34–5) and Dal Pra (1989: 399–400), merely say (against von Arnim) that this interpretation contradicts what Sextus says—as does Janáček (1977: 679). But this is simply false, for the reasons given in the main text.

[73] See LSJ s.v. *kata*, B.IV.2.

[74] This understanding of the phrase is proposed by Barnes (1988: n. 75). Barnes also flirts with the idea that the phrase means 'Aenesidemus in the *Heraclitus*', i.e. in a work (expounding Heraclitus' ideas) called *Heraclitus*. But, as he admits, this does not seem to fit all the occurrences of the phrase. (A similar idea is proposed by Tarrant (1985: 81).)

Aenesidemus in discussions of Heraclitus, in the straightforward sense 'according to Heraclitus', but subsequently became detached from their natural grammatical context. Perhaps 'according to Heraclitus' became something of a catchphrase in these discussions, or in reports of them by others; if 'Aenesidemus said "According to Heraclitus, . . ." ' was a standard refrain in such contexts, then it might have seemed natural to distinguish between Aenesidemus in his guise as the advocate of Pyrrhonism, and Aenesidemus in his guise as expositor of Heraclitus—and to employ the words 'Aenesidemus "according to Heraclitus" ' as a shorthand label for the latter. Again, this would give us an Aenesidemus who was interested in Heraclitus, and talked about him a lot, but not (or not necessarily) an Aenesidemus who was a devotee of Heraclitean positions.[75]

Several pieces of evidence have been offered, or might be offered, in favour of readings of this type. Unfortunately, none of them does the work required. One of the views attributed to *Ainēsidēmos kata Hērakleiton* is accompanied by a view attributed to 'some people *kata* Democritus' (*M* 7.349), and it has been suggested that this latter phrase, which is clearly parallel with the one with which we are concerned, must refer to people *expounding* the ideas of Democritus, not to people promoting them.[76] But there is no reason to accept this; *kata Dēmokriton* may just as well be read 'in agreement with Democritus' as 'in relation to Democritus'[77]—either way, these unnamed people laid out a certain Democritean view, and that is all that matters in the context. Then again, it has been observed that Sextus does tell us that Aenesidemus *said that* 'according to Heraclitus [*kata ton Hērakleiton*], what is is air' (*M* 10.233). But, however tempting it may be to suppose that attributions of this kind are the origin of the phrase *Ainēsidēmos kata Hērakleiton*,[78] nothing whatever forces us to do so; the latter phrase might be of an entirely different origin and significance. Another point that might be thought relevant and helpful is that two different and incompatible views are attributed in the same context to *Ainēsidē mos kata Hērakleiton* and to Aenesidemus *tout court* (*M* 7.349–50).[79] But it does not follow that the phrase refers to Aenesidemus' exposition of

[75] I take it that something like this is what Burkhard has in mind (1973: ch. VII). Burkhard insists on the importance of *M* 10.233, in which Aenesidemus is represented as saying that, 'according to Heraclitus', what is is air (see esp. p. 171), and regards *Ainēsidēmos kata Hērakleiton* as a contraction of expressions of this type; but he does not really explain how the contraction came about.

[76] See Burkhard (1973: 174); Barnes (1988: n. 75).

[77] As observed by Hankinson (1995: 337 n. 27).

[78] As supposed by Burkhard (see above, n. 75). Here Cortassa (1977: 69) is too ready to accept Burkhard's reasoning; his observations against Burkhard's other arguments concerning the phrase are, however, telling.

[79] *Ainēsidēmos kata Hērakleiton* is said to hold that thought (*dianoia*) is outside the body, while Aenesidemus is said to hold that it is the senses and 'peeps out' (*prokuptousan*) through the sense organs. Hankinson (1995: 337 n. 28) claims that there is no conflict here; the first point

Heraclitus' views *rather than* to his own acceptance of them; Aenesidemus might have accepted Heraclitean ideas at just one stage of his career, in which case these ideas could very easily be incompatible with those adopted by him at another stage. Finally, a view attributed to *Ainēsidēmos kata ton Hē rakleiton* (*M* 10.216) is referred to shortly afterwards (*M* 10.230) as the view of the 'Heracliteans', with no mention of Aenesidemus. But this too is indecisive; Aenesidemus *might* have been merely expounding Heraclitus, but he might just as well have been agreeing with him (and in the latter case he would himself be one of these 'Heracliteans').

There is, then, no way to demonstrate that *Ainēsidēmos kata Hērakleiton* does *not* mean 'Aenesidemus in agreement with Heraclitus'. On the other hand, we have not yet seen anything to compel us to conclude that it *does* mean this—nor anything else to suggest that Aenesidemus was personally attracted to Heraclitean positions. For all that has been said so far, it is entirely possible that Aenesidemus simply saw a certain genuine similarity between Pyrrhonism and Heracliteanism, and was therefore interested enough in Heraclitus' ideas to write about them. There is, however, one further piece of evidence bearing on the question.[80] Though, as mentioned earlier, the view that time is corporeal is attributed in *Against the Physicists* (*M* 10.216) to

refers to Heraclitus' divine *logos*, the second to 'our poor apology for it'. But the thought that is referred to in the first point as 'outside the body' must surely be the thought *of beings in possession of bodies*—that is, of human beings. Or at any rate, if this is not so, the phrase 'outside the body' is highly misleading.

Quite apart from the question of a conflict, the second view may well seem troubling in itself. Is not the view that thought is identical with the senses a dogmatic theory of the nature of things, with which Aenesidemus ought to have been reluctant to associate himself? It would certainly seem so. But Sextus' report is in one respect curious. He says that Strato of Lampsacus and Aenesidemus 'began' (*ērxe*) this view, i.e. were the first to hold it. Now, Strato of Lampsacus succeeded Theophrastus as head of the Peripatetic school; he died around 268 BC. It seems very odd to refer to Strato and Aenesidemus collectively—men who lived at least two centuries apart and belonged to quite different philosophical traditions—as having 'begun' a certain view. So I suspect that, whatever Sextus or his source originally said, it has become somehow garbled in transmission. In this case we need not suppose that Aenesidemus actually did subscribe to this dogmatic theory. Perhaps he gave a summary of it, alongside a summary of Heraclitus' contrasting view; or perhaps 'and Aenesidemus' has crept into the manuscripts in some more random (and now unaccountable) way.

[80] Yet another fact that has often been thought relevant to this issue is that Tertullian three times attributes to Aenesidemus himself (twice in conjunction with Heraclitus, once without him) views that Sextus attributes to Aenesidemus *kata Hērakleiton*; see *De anima* 9.5, 14.5, 25.2. But this is of no help to us. Even if the phrase is in fact meant to indicate Aenesidemus' *treatment* of Heraclitus' ideas, not his acceptance of them, Tertullian, his probable source Soranus, or someone else could very easily have misunderstood it (as it occurred in Sextus or in some other sceptic source) as indicating his acceptance of them; neither Tertullian nor Soranus had any reason to concern themselves with achieving a deep understanding of Aenesidemus' thought. That someone has misunderstood something is in any case clear from the fact that one of these passages (14.5) attributes the same view to Aenesidemus, Heraclitus, and Strato. The passage is evidently connected in some way with *M* 7.349–50 (most probably,

Ainēsidēmos kata ton Hērakleiton, the same view is attributed in the parallel passage of *Outlines of Pyrrhonism* (*PH* 3.138) to Aenesidemus
himself,[81] with no mention of Heraclitus. Now, if the phrase *Ainēsidēmos
kata ton Hērakleiton* referred to Aenesidemus in his role as *interpreter* (but
not adherent) of Heraclitus' philosophy, then one would expect that Sextus
would be very concerned to distinguish between Aenesidemus' pronouncements in this vein and the sceptical pronouncements that he delivered in his
own person. The fact that he considers 'Aenesidemus' to be an acceptable
shorthand for *Ainēsidēmos kata ton Hērakleiton* strongly suggests, on the
contrary, that the Heraclitean ideas Aenesidemus wrote about were, after
all, ideas that Sextus took him to be endorsing.[82] The alternative would be
to accuse him of extreme carelessness on a point about which one would
expect him to be most vigilant; this is not, I admit, impossible, but it looks
highly unattractive. But now, from the fact, if it is a fact, that *Sextus* thought
that Aenesidemus endorsed Heraclitean ideas, it does not follow that *we*
should think so too.[83]

We have seen that, according to Sextus' testimony, Aenesidemus considers
there to be a certain significant point of contact between Pyrrhonism and
Heracliteanism. We have also seen that Sextus himself is utterly opposed to
this suggestion;[84] according to him, the notion that scepticism shares anything
with the philosophy of Heraclitus is simply absurd. Now, since Sextus found
Aenesidemus' *rapprochement* with Heracliteanism so objectionable, it would

they both derive ultimately from the same source); but in *M* 7.349–50, as we have seen, the
views attributed to Aenesidemus *kata Hērakleiton* and to Strato (and Aenesidemus) are far from
identical. On these passages of Tertullian, see Waszink (1947: commentary *ad loc*).

[81] Or, strictly speaking, to 'those around Aenesidemus'; but see above, n. 68.

[82] This point is independent of the question which of the two works came first. My own view
(see above, n. 47) is that the physical portion of *PH* 3 is a condensed version of *Against the
Physicists*. But the present argument works just as well either way. Whichever work came first,
Sextus' sources talked of a certain view discussed by Aenesidemus in the course of his consideration of Heraclitean ideas, and Sextus saw fit, in the more concise work, to abbreviate this to
a simple reference to Aenesidemus. (One might, I suppose, claim that the two works are
independent of one another at this point, and are drawing on *distinct* sources—one of which
mentions the Heraclitean connection and one of which does not. But this, of course—quite apart
from the startlingly low level of initiative that it attributes to Sextus—simply reproduces the
same problem at an earlier stage; even if it was not Sextus himself, *someone* thought that
'Aenesidemus' was an acceptable shorthand for the longer phrase, and *that* person presumably
took Aenesidemus to be in agreement with the Heraclitean ideas he discussed.)

[83] The view that it is Sextus who has misrepresented Aenesidemus was already proposed by
Diels (1879: 209–12)—but not by way of the arguments that I am about to develop. (In Diels'
case, indeed, there is some justice in Capone Braga's objection (1931: 35–6, and cf. above, n.
72) that Sextus' testimony is not taken seriously enough.)

[84] This is in keeping with Sextus' general desire to differentiate Pyrrhonism sharply from all
the philosophies that might be thought to be akin to it. On this see Spinelli (2000); also Spinelli
(1997), who specifically suggests (though the idea is not developed in detail) that this tendency
may have influenced Sextus' treatment of Aenesidemus' relations with Heraclitus.

not be in any way surprising if he also felt that there was something suspect about Aenesidemus' scepticism itself; anyone who claimed an affinity between his own ideas and those of Heraclitus could not, Sextus might think, be a true adherent of Pyrrhonism. And from here it would be an easy step to the thought that the Heraclitean positions that Aenesidemus discussed were positions to which he, Aenesidemus, was himself attached; from the idea that Aenesidemus claimed, wrongly, that scepticism was related to Heracliteanism, and the idea that this claim itself reveals Aenesidemus' supposed scepticism to have been no true scepticism, it would be very natural to conclude that Aenesidemus' true philosophical sympathies were Heraclitean *rather than* sceptical. And in this way it could very well have happened that Sextus came to think of Aenesidemus, when he wrote about Heraclitus, as being 'in agreement with Heraclitus'—even if in fact Aenesidemus was writing *not* as an adherent of Heraclitus' ideas, but from the perspective of an interested outsider.

It is clear in any case that Sextus is ambivalent about Aenesidemus' status as a sceptic. Some of his references to Aenesidemus are unproblematic in this regard, as when Aenesidemus is named as the author of various groups of Modes (*M* 7.345; *PH* 1.180),[85] or is described as raising 'difficulties' (*aporiai*) for various dogmatic concepts or theories (*M* 8.40, 9.218, cf. *M* 8.215–16, 234), or as emphasizing the amount of disagreement that exists on some topic (*M* 11.42). But at other times, quite apart from the Heraclitus question, he appears happy to attribute dogmatic positions to Aenesidemus. Aenesidemus is listed among the holders of dogmatic theories of truth (*M* 8.8), and at least implicitly among the holders of dogmatic theories of motion (*M* 10.38); he is also said to hold the view that the intellect is identical with the senses, alongside the Peripatetic physical thinker Strato (*M* 7.350). In all these cases, there is room for doubt about whether Aenesidemus really did hold dogmatic views.[86] But the fact that Sextus is willing to make these attributions at all indicates that he does not consider Aenesidemus a whole-hearted sceptic. Nor is this surprising, given the considerable differences that we observed earlier in this chapter between Aenesidemus' outlook and that of Sextus himself; from Sextus' point of view, as we saw, Aenesidemus' outlook *would* count as dogmatic, at least in several important respects. The form and the level of the dogmatism Sextus attributes to him may be partly the result of exaggeration or misunderstanding; but, if Sextus anyway regarded Aenesidemus' philosophy as alien and non-sceptical, such exaggerations or misunderstandings would be all too likely to arise. And, if this tendency to interpret Aenesidemus as dogmatic was lodged in Sextus' mind quite independently of the question

---

[85] Even here, however, the picture is not entirely straightforward. On Sextus' somewhat stand-offish attitude towards Aenesidemus' Eight Modes against causal explanations (*PH* 1.180), see Decleva Caizzi (1992*b*: 289–90).

[86] See above, nn. 17, 79.

of Aenesidemus' treatment of Heraclitus, this would only reinforce his inclination to interpret this latter side of Aenesidemus' work, too, as revealing
dogmatic commitments.

Finally, this inclination would receive still further encouragement from the
specific *way* in which Aenesidemus' form of Pyrrhonism differs from Sextus'
own. Aenesidemus, as we have seen, is willing to make assertions that include
certain kinds of relativizing qualifications; and, to judge especially from the
Photius passage, he had a particular penchant for paired *opposing* assertions
of the form '*X* is *F* in some circumstances, but not-*F* in other circumstances'.
But Sextus, except in the special case of *Against the Ethicists*,[87] would have
seen all such assertions as contravening the Pyrrhonist attitude. Moreover,
such assertions, at least on a superficial inspection, look very like some of
Heraclitus' remarks about the coexistence of opposites—for example, 'Sea is
purest and foulest water: drinkable and life-saving for fish, but undrinkable
and deadly for humans' (DK 22B61). Aenesidemus is surely right to say what
Sextus reports him as saying (*PH* 1.210)—that Heraclitus' attributions of
opposites to things are meant to apply at the level of the things' real nature;[88]
Aenesidemus' own relativized assertions, on the other hand, are designed
precisely to *avoid* any commitments concerning the real nature of things. But
this contrast would have been ignored, or dismissed as illusory, by Sextus, for
whom relativized assertions are just as much a violation of the Pyrrhonist
outlook—that is, Sextus' own Pyrrhonist outlook—as are the utterances of
Heraclitus. So one of the central ways in which Aenesidemus' form of
Pyrrhonism differs from that of Sextus is precisely such as to give impetus to
the idea, on Sextus' part, that Aenesidemus was really a Heraclitean.

---

[87] *Against the Ethicists* clearly presents a problem for my interpretation. If Sextus himself
subscribed to an Aenesidemean position when he composed *Against the Ethicists*, why would
he consistently misrepresent Aenesidemus in other books—indeed, in other books of the very
same work (for, as we saw, the references to *Ainēsidēmos kata Hērakleiton* all occur in *Against
the Logicians* and *Against the Physicists*)? However, this is really just one species of a problem
that we are bound to face in any case: the fact that *Against the Ethicists* presents a variety of
Pyrrhonism different from and incompatible with that of the rest of the work to which it belongs.
One possible explanation is simply that Sextus used sources from different phases of the
Pyrrhonist tradition in different parts of this work, and failed to fashion them into a consistent
whole. This, of course, would represent Sextus as a naïve and incompetent thinker (at this stage
in his life, at any rate); but it cannot be conclusively ruled out. For another possibility, which
depends upon a perceived difference, on the part of Sextus or his sources, between the situations
in ethics and in other areas of philosophy, see Bett (1997: introduction, sect. V).

[88] It is not anachronistic to apply a distinction between the real nature of things and the
appearances to Heraclitus (even if his was not a distinction identical to one employed by any
Pyrrhonist). The contrast between the 'private understanding' (*idian phronēsin*) relied on by
most people, and what is 'common' or 'public' (*xunon*), on which one needs to rely if one is to
reach genuine understanding, is the explicit subject of one fragment (Sextus, *M* 7.133 (=DK
22B2)), and is fundamental in many others; Heraclitus quite self-consciously sees himself as
penetrating to how things are, as opposed to how they seem to most people—and the fragments
attributing opposites to things are clearly no exception.

The situation, then, is as follows. There is no good reason to think that Aenesidemus, at any stage of his career, personally subscribed to Heraclitean positions. He clearly took an interest in Heraclitus, and he did claim that Heraclitus' ideas had something noteworthy in common with the Pyrrhonists' ideas; but that is all that the evidence forces us to accept. If it is true—and it probably is—that Sextus *thinks* that Aenesidemus subscribed to Heraclitean positions, this may easily be explained by the particular characteristics of Sextus' own form of Pyrrhonism, and the ways in which it differs from that of Aenesidemus; given the differences, it is quite understandable that Sextus would have arrived (intermittently, at least) at this reading, even if it is inaccurate. And, if the evidence does not *require* us to conclude that Aenesidemus was at some point a Heraclitean, we should *not* do so; for this supposition would be extremely hard to reconcile with the rest of the evidence relating to Aenesidemus (which is why this issue has always been considered one of the thorniest in the study of Pyrrhonism). Hence—to return to the main theme of this chapter—as far as Aenesidemus' position in the history of Pyrrhonism is concerned, his interest in and discussion of Heraclitus is a red herring; it does not shed light on the reasons why he chose Pyrrho as his forerunner. On that question, the conclusions of the previous section may stand.

6. From the initial to the terminal phases of later Pyrrhonism

We have seen how it made sense for Aenesidemus to call his new movement Pyrrhonism, despite the differences between Pyrrho's thought and his own; and we have seen that an adequate explanation for this depends largely upon recognizing the extent to which Aenesidemus' variety of Pyrrhonism itself differed from that represented by most of the writings of Sextus. In addition, we saw just now that Sextus' uneasiness about the Pyrrhonist, or sceptical, credentials of Aenesidemus is plausibly accounted for by reference to these latter differences. But, if Aenesidemus' outlook was not the same as the outlook expressed in *Outlines of Pyrrhonism*, further questions arise concerning how or why Pyrrhonism underwent this additional change. We need, therefore, to try to account for the transition between these two distinct phases of the later Pyrrhonist tradition. It will be convenient to begin with a brief review of the central differences between the initial and the terminal phases of later Pyrrhonism; with this in place, we can then try to understand how the shift from the former to the latter might naturally have occurred.

Let us return to the sequence of points raised in Section 4, when we were discussing the differing levels of agreement among Pyrrho, Aenesidemus, and Sextus; and let us now leave Pyrrho aside. Sextus and Aenesidemus, then, are both (1) preoccupied with versions of what I have been calling the phenomenon of variability; as a response to this variability, both (2) adopt a certain kind of mistrust of our everyday impressions of things—and, one might add, a parallel mistrust of dogmatic theories of the nature of things; as a way of expressing this mistrust, both (3) employ locutions containing the term 'no more'; in order to be consistent in maintaining this mistrust, both (4) adopt a strategy of relying, in their daily lives, on the *appearances* of things; and, finally, both (5) claim that the *result* of this mistrust is *ataraxia*, whereas the result of dogmatic commitments is a tormented existence. The crucial difference between the two views has to do with the precise character of the 'mistrust' in each case (2); and this in turn leads to a different understanding of the term 'no more' (3), and a different conception of the 'appearances' on which the Pyrrhonist is to rely (4).

Aenesidemus reacts to the phenomenon of variability by restricting his positive assertions about things to qualified or relativized assertions; instead of saying unequivocally that some object is *F*, he is willing to refer to it as *F* only in some specific set of circumstances (and will characteristically add that it is not-*F* in other circumstances). From the fact that the object presents itself as *F* in some specific set of circumstances, it cannot be inferred that the object is *F* in its true nature. We can describe it as *F* only *in those circumstances*, where the qualification 'in those circumstances' makes clear that *no* claim is thereby being made about the nature of the object. But we can also say something else. Since the object is *F* only in some circumstances, and is not-*F* in other circumstances, that shows (given the invariability condition) that the object is *not* in its true nature *F* (nor, for that matter, is it in its true nature not-*F*). In order for the object to be *F* in its true nature, it would have to be *F* invariably; but the phenomenon of variability rules that out. Variability thus does allow us to reach some negative conclusions concerning the nature of the thing. What it does not allow us to do is to arrive at any positive specifications of the thing's nature; for (again in virtue of the invariability condition) from the fact that something is not by nature *F*, it does not follow that the thing is by nature not-*F*. Aenesidemus' mistrust of everyday impressions and of dogmatic theories—his refusal to 'determine' anything—thus takes the form of a refusal of any attempt to specify the nature of anything. Neither his relativized assertions nor his negative conclusions concerning the natures of things constitute attempts of this kind; if someone asked Aenesidemus 'What is the nature of things?', he could quite consistently reply 'We are in no position to answer that question'.

Sextus, on the other hand, permits himself neither relativized assertions nor negative conclusions concerning the natures of things. For him, the phenomenon of variability creates a puzzle as to *which*, if any, of the variable ways in which a thing strikes us shows us the way the thing is in its real nature; it is possible that none of them do so—but any one of them *might* do so. There is thus no question of our being able to *rule out* certain features as being parts of something's nature; the fact that an object strikes us sometimes as F, sometimes as not-F means not that the object is *neither* by nature F *nor* by nature not-F, but that we are not in a position to *tell* whether it is F or not-F or neither. And, equally, there is no question of our having special licence to refer to the object as 'F in certain circumstances'; the qualification 'in certain circumstances' does nothing to reduce the level of a statement's commitment concerning the actual character of the object to which it refers.[89] For Sextus, therefore, the appropriate form of mistrust of our everyday impressions and of dogmatic theories is *simply* to suspend judgement as to which, if any, of those impressions or theories reflects things as they really are—where this does not permit either of the types of assertions to which Aenesidemus helped himself.

Accompanying this difference are at least two others. First, the 'no more' locution has a rather different function in the two cases. For Aenesidemus, 'X is no more F than not-F' is either a way of characterizing the object, X, as alternately F and not-F, depending on the circumstances—in other words, a way of asserting that the object's F-ness (and not-F-ness) is subject to relativizing qualifications—or it is a way of saying that the object is not *by nature* either F or not-F. In either case, 'no more' has its natural sense of 'to no greater extent than'. For Sextus, however, 'X is no more F than not-F' cannot mean either of these things, since in his way of thinking both would be illegitimate excursions beyond strict suspension of judgement. For him, rather, 'X is no more F than not-F' is, precisely, a way of expressing suspension of judgement as to whether or not the thing is in reality F or not-F; and it can only have this function, of course, if the words 'no more' themselves do *not* have their straightforward sense—as Sextus admits that they do not. Secondly, the 'appearances' that serve as a guide for decision and action are significantly different in the two cases. For Aenesidemus, relativized statements of the form 'X is F in circumstances C (and not-F in some other set of circumstances $C*$)' qualify as appearance-statements. Such statements count as statements about the 'appearances', in Aenesidemus' understanding of that notion, because they speak about the object *only* as it presents itself in certain limited sets of circumstances; they are appearance-statements as opposed to statements purporting to specify the *real nature* of the object. Hence, as we

---

[89] Sextus could, of course, say that the object *appears* F in certain circumstances. But then, he could also say that the object appears F *without* the restriction 'in certain circumstances'; this restriction, in other words, does nothing to make any assertions more acceptable to Sextus than they would be without it. In this connection, it is interesting that Sextus' general observation that 'is' can sometimes be used to mean 'appears' occurs at the beginning of his discussion of the Mode from Relativity (*PH* 1.135). This perhaps indicates that it was particularly in the context of relativized statements that Sextus' sources used 'is' where he himself would have been more comfortable with 'appears'; given that, in the initial phase of later Pyrrhonism, relativizing one's statements is a way of preserving sceptical caution, whereas in the terminal phase it has no such effect, this would be quite understandable.

saw, it looks as if it is the qualification 'in circumstances C', more than the occurrence of the actual word 'appears' as opposed to 'is', that locates such statements within the realm of the 'appearances'. For Sextus, on the other hand, to speak of the appearances is *not* to speak of the character of objects in some specific set of circumstances. To speak of the appearances is to speak, in some sense, of how things strike us, as opposed to how they really are; but, whatever exactly this amounts to,[90] there is absolutely no indication in Sextus' account of 'following the appearances' that this distinction revolves around a contrast between those features of things that present themselves in specific and limited sets of circumstances and those features that hold without regard to circumstances.

There is a clear sense in which the terminal phase of Pyrrhonism, the phase represented by Sextus' *Outlines of Pyrrhonism*, is more sceptical than the initial phase represented by Aenesidemus. There are certain classes of statements permitted by Aenesidemus but not by Sextus (and no cases in which the reverse situation obtains). To put it another way, the doubts entertained by Sextus seem to go deeper than those entertained by Aenesidemus. Most noteworthy, perhaps, is that Aenesidemus does not seem disposed towards any kind of global doubt about the accuracy of relativized statements.[91] He is willing to assert that an object is F in some particular set of circumstances. For the reasons we have discussed, this does not count as a statement concerning the true nature of the object, and so is consistent with his variety of scepticism; but nor is it itself subject to any sceptical questioning. The thought that, in reporting such relativized states of affairs, we might quite generally be deceived is not one that seems to occur to him.[92] We are deceived if we take the way the object presents itself in some given set of circumstances as a guide to its true nature (and hence relativity poses an obstacle to knowledge of its true nature); but we are not in general deceived if we take our experience of an object, in some given set of circumstances, as a guide to its (temporary and contingent) character *in those circumstances*. For Sextus, though, to relativize a statement about the character of an object does nothing to make

---

[90] As was noted at the end of Ch. 3, Sect. 1, this is the subject of considerable dispute; to attempt to resolve the matter would take us much too far afield. Hence in this context I restrict myself to a single, uncontroversial point that marks the central difference between Sextus and Aenesidemus. I also leave aside the occasional relics of Aenesidemus' conception of the appearances that appear in Sextus' account of the Ten Modes; for, as we saw earlier (Sect. 3), these are clearly inconsistent with Sextus' own main conception.

[91] As we saw earlier (Sect. 4, also n. 22), this is part of the legacy of Pyrrho (and Plato).

[92] If I was right to suggest earlier that Aenesidemus was willing to allow that we can have *knowledge*, of a mundane and untheoretical sort designated by the non-technical word *eidenai*, this lack of susceptibility to global doubts about relativized statements should come as no surprise. In Aenesidemus' conception, relativized states of affairs are the stuff of ordinary experience; so if he allows for a mundane sort of knowledge, these will surely be central among the kinds of things he considers knowable. In fact, as we saw in Sect. 2, the Photius passage appears to include a mention of this very point (169b29–30).

that statement less hazardous; just because the statement applies only to some specific set of circumstances, it in no way follows that it belongs among the types of statement to which the sceptic may consistently assent.

Precisely when, or in whose hands, the shift to this final, more stringent variety of Pyrrhonism took place is very hard to say. It is perhaps tempting to link it with the figure of Agrippa. As we saw, the Five Modes of Agrippa seem to be associated with the terminal phase rather than the initial phase of Pyrrhonism; at several points in Sextus' version of Aenesidemus' Ten Modes, arguments drawn from the Five Modes seem to be tacked on in order to render the material from the Ten Modes more congenial to the variety of Pyrrhonism adhered to by Sextus himself. But to suggest that Agrippa was involved in this transformation is quite unhelpful, since *all* we know about Agrippa is that he devised the Five Modes (DL 9.88).[93] However, if the historical circumstances of the transformation are obscure, there is one philosophical point about it that is relatively clear. The differences that we just observed between the two phases are all bound up, in one way or another, with Aenesidemus' acceptance, and Sextus' non-acceptance, of the invariability condition. If one abandons the invariability condition, the position adhered to by Aenesidemus becomes unsustainable—and the rather different position represented by *Outlines of Pyrrhonism* will naturally tend to take its place.

I shall illustrate this in a moment. But first, it needs to be emphasized—if it is not clear already—that the invariability condition, as a criterion for something's being by nature a certain way, looks like a surprisingly unsceptical item for anyone to accept who claimed to be embarking on a radical new anti-dogmatic path. Aenesidemus might argue that the invariability condition does not itself constitute a specification of how things are by nature—and that refraining from such specifications is what his policy of 'determining nothing' consists in.[94] But, even if this is accepted, there is still a clear sense in which the invariability condition seems to qualify as a doctrine, or as a philosophical commitment; on this score (just as on the other matter just mentioned, his attitude towards relativized statements), his diatribe against his Academic contemporaries for their lack of intellectual caution would seem to invite a *tu quoque* response. It is, of course, quite possible that, despite his criticism of the Academics for being dogmatic, Aenesidemus himself was not immune from the generally less sceptical ethos of the early first century BC, as compared with the heyday of the Academy under Arcesilaus and Carneades. But we can hardly hope to say anything informative on this matter; Aenesidemus is too shadowy a figure for us, and his acceptance of the invariability condition too central to his outlook to be

---

93 The only other occurrence of his name is as the title of a book by the (also otherwise unknown) sceptic Apellas (DL 9.106).

94 On this, cf. above, n. 19.

satisfactorily explained by reference to other, more basic philosophical attitudes. As was emphasized in Section 4, Aenesidemus does not take on board that part of Pyrrho's outlook that clearly constitutes a specification of how things are in reality—that is, his indeterminacy thesis; but, whatever the explanation, he has no comparable qualms about adopting a certain specific conception of *what it is* for some feature of an object to be part of that object's nature. However, though Aenesidemus may have found no difficulty in this, it looks as if, at some point in the Pyrrhonist tradition, the invariability condition did come to seem problematic; for, in the terminal phase of Pyrrhonism, it ceases to play any role at all. But now, given its seemingly unsceptical character, this is not particularly surprising; the surprise, if anything, is that Aenesidemus, with his self-presentation as the hard-line anti-dogmatist, was prepared to accept it in the first place.

The main point, though, is simply this: the invariability condition is the key to the differences between the two phases of later Pyrrhonism. If one makes the single supposition that the invariability condition came to seem problematic—a supposition that, as we have just seen, appears easy enough to grant— then the shift from the initial phase to the terminal phase becomes readily explicable. Let us imagine some successor of Aenesidemus who begins as an adherent of Aenesidemus' variety of Pyrrhonism, but who then comes to feel (or is pressed by charges of inconsistency into feeling) that the invariability condition is unacceptable; if this successor wants to retain a policy of 'determining nothing', but now wishes to do so *without* any reliance on the invariability condition, he is liable to find this one change altering his whole outlook—and altering it precisely in the direction of Sextus' *Outlines of Pyrrhonism*.

For suppose that one no longer takes it that, in order for something to be by nature *F*, that thing must be *F* in all circumstances. Then, first, the various types of assertions permitted by Aenesidemus, but excluded by Sextus, will immediately come to seem suspect. Relativized assertions will no longer be innocuous; for, in the absence of the invariability condition, qualifications of the form 'in circumstances *C*' no longer automatically exclude an assertion from counting as an attempted specification of the nature of things. By the same token, negative assertions having to do with a thing's nature also cease to be immune from sceptical doubts. The fact that the thing strikes us in some circumstances as *F* and in others as not-*F* no longer has any tendency to suggest that the thing is not by nature *either F or* not-*F*; without the invariability condition in place, there is no particular reason to assume that either one of these ways it strikes one is *not* the way it really is. But nor, of course, is there any particular reason to assume that either one *is* the way the thing really is. If one assumes the Law of Non-Contradiction (and this continues to be assumed throughout the Pyrrhonist tradition), the object cannot be in reality *both F and* not-*F*; and there is no reason to favour one possibility over the other (this point, too, is common ground throughout the history of Pyrrhonism). Thus there will be no particular reason to be for or against either one of the possibilities F or not-F; either one might in reality obtain, or it might not obtain. And so, if one abandons the invariability condition, but retains an emphasis on the variability with which things strike one, one will be forced to throw into question the distinctive kinds of assertion allowed under Aenesidemus' position, and will tend to arrive, instead, at a position according to which each of the various ways in which things strike us is of 'equal strength' as an indicator of how the thing really is—which means that none of them can be safely admitted or excluded.

So the posture of suspension of judgement now becomes a posture of refusing to commit oneself one way or the other as to whether some given object is in reality F. One is no longer entitled to *deny* that the object is in reality F; for, without the invariability condition, such denials can no longer be distinguished from specifications of how things are by nature. If 'in reality F' is no longer assumed to entail 'invariably F', then there is nothing to prevent 'X is not in reality F' from being taken to entail 'X *is* in reality *other* than F'. And nor, as we said, does the qualification 'in circumstances C' do the job that it used to do, of removing a statement from the domain of candidate specifications of how things really are. Hence, suspension of judgement can now consist only in a refusal to say whether or not any particular object is either F or not-F by nature; this is the only posture consistent with there being two or more possibilities of 'equal strength'.

In addition, the term 'no more' has to assume a new function, if it is to continue in use. 'No more F than not-F' cannot be used, as it was by Aenesidemus, as a way of *asserting* the relativity of things' features to circumstances, and *denying* that these features hold of the things by nature; for neither of these types of utterance is consistent with the new variety of suspension of judgement. Rather, 'no more F than not-F' now has to be used, if at all, as a way of characterizing that new suspension of judgement—that is, as characterizing the 'equal strength' enjoyed by the various possibilities. Hence, as Sextus says in *Outlines of Pyrrhonism* (1.191), although the term 'no more' 'exhibits the character of assent and denial'—although it sounds as if it is to be used for asserting or denying things—he is going to use it in a way that is at odds with this natural usage. And finally, of course, there is no room for a conception of the 'appearances' such as Aenesidemus seems to have adopted, according to which relativized assertions qualify as assertions having to do with appearances—by *contrast* with assertions purporting to specify the nature of things; for, without the invariability condition, this particular contrast is no longer in force. And so the realm of appearance-statements—those statements that a sceptic may safely use—now excludes relativized assertions. Whatever precisely it means, in the terminal phase of later Pyrrhonism, to speak of how things appear as opposed to how they really are, the qualification 'in circumstances C' does not in the least serve to protect a statement from the stigma of dogmatism.

The lapse of the invariability condition, then, would by itself be enough to explain the shift from Aenesidemus' position to that of *Outlines of Pyrrhonism*. This lapse would entail that none of the distinctive elements of the earlier position were any longer sustainable; and, for someone actually faced with this philosophical crisis, the later position would be the obvious one that would recommend itself as a substitute. As I said, it is not hard to imagine that the invariability condition would indeed have come to seem dubious to a Pyrrhonist. If so, we have at least the outline of an explanation—though not, of course, any of the historical detail we might have wished for—of how the terminal phase of Pyrrhonism came to replace the initial phase.

7. *Conclusion*

The general conclusion of this chapter, then, is that both the transition between Pyrrho's position and Aenesidemus', and the transition between Aenesidemus' position and that of *Outlines of Pyrrhonism*, may be explained without too much difficulty. It is understandable that Aenesidemus adopted Pyrrho as a figurehead for his new movement; though the differences between the two men's philosophies, as I have interpreted them, are by no means negligible, the common ground between them—both its amount and its specific nature—gives more than enough point to Aenesidemus' decision. And it is also understandable that Aenesidemus' own position, the position for which 'Pyrrhonism' could quite plausibly have seemed a suitable name, was transformed into the somewhat different position that we find in most of Sextus, where the link to Pyrrho, though still not non-existent, is much more tenuous. To return to a point from the Introduction, it would have been surprising if Pyrrhonism had stayed essentially unchanged over some 500 years; that shifts, even important ones, took place over such a long period is only to be expected. (Nobody is surprised, for example, when this turns out to be true of Platonism.) So long as the shifts can be made historically and philosophically comprehensible—and this is what I have attempted to do in this chapter—there is no reason to resist the notion that Pyrrhonism encompassed several different views over its long and discontinuous lifespan.

In particular, there is no reason to resist the notion that Pyrrho's own philosophy was so different from that of Pyrrhonism's terminal phase that Sextus would not even have recognized Pyrrho as a sceptic at all. That, as I tried to show in Chapters 1 and 2, is the conclusion recommended by an inspection of the evidence relating to Pyrrho himself. We saw that this evidence needed careful handling, and that there was much less of it (the evidence, that is) than we might have liked; and for these reasons I have throughout been careful to couch my conclusions in a tentative and conditional manner. What we have seen by now is that, if my interpretation of Pyrrho's philosophy in the first two chapters was on the right lines, then his place in the history of Greek philosophy is an eminently comprehensible one; and this, I submit, should make our attitude to this interpretation somewhat less tentative and conditional. In the previous chapter we saw that there were ample parallels and precedents for various aspects of his philosophy, so understood. And in the present chapter we have seen that, despite the important differences between Pyrrho's philosophy (so understood) and that of the terminal phase of later Pyrrhonism, both fit naturally into an account of the history of Pyrrhonism as a whole that includes the intermediate outlook of Aenesidemus. In fact, one might even claim that, once the distinctness of Aenesidemus' outlook and that of most of Sextus is understood, it becomes considerably *more* plausible to suppose what I have argued that the evidence in any case indicates—that Pyrrho's philosophy was importantly different from that of *Outlines of Pyrrhonism*, rather than that they were essentially the same. If they had been essentially the same, it would have been Aenesidemus who was the odd man out in the history of Pyrrhonism; and this would itself be odd, given that he was the one who seems to have appropriated Pyrrho as a figurehead, and thus to have given rise to the very phenomenon of a Pyrrhonist tradition. At any rate, given the significant differences *within* later Pyrrhonism, between its initial and its terminal phases—differences for which the evidence is patchy, but a good deal more substantial than the evidence on Pyrrho himself—there is clearly no firm basis for assuming that Pyrrho's philosophy resembled the terminal phase particularly closely.

I do not claim that any of this settles the matter beyond question. What I do claim is that the evidence on Pyrrho, severely limited as it is, points in the direction discussed in Chapters 1 and 2, and that Pyrrho's place in the history of Greek philosophy is accounted for at least as well on this interpretation of his philosophy as on others. And all of this, I maintain, adds up to a picture of Pyrrho, as well as of his antecedents and his legacy, that is more probable than the alternatives—which, to hark back once more to the Introduction, is as much as we can hope for in the circumstances. Again, the fact that our conclusions cannot realistically be accorded a status any more secure than that should not be thought to diminish the importance of the topic. For we surely do not have a proper understanding of Pyrrhonism until we have some sense of how it started, where it came from, and how it got from its starting point to the final state in which it is best known to us. I hope that this book has made some worthwhile contribution to this goal.

REFERENCES

[This list of references does not include the works cited in the list of abbreviations.]

I. Ancient Sources: Editions, Translations, Commentaries

Annas, J., and Barnes, J. (1994), *Sextus Empiricus: Outlines of Scepticism* (Cambridge: Cambridge University Press).

Bastianini, G., and Sedley, D. (1995), *Commentarium in Platonis 'Theaetetum'*, in *Corpus dei papiri filosofici greci e latini*, iii (Florence: Leo S. Olschki), 227–562.

Bett, R. (1997), *Sextus Empiricus: Against the Ethicists*, Translated with an Introduction and Commentary (Oxford: Clarendon Press).

Blank, D. (1998), *Sextus Empiricus: Against the Grammarians*, Translated with an Introduction and Commentary (Oxford: Clarendon Press).

Burnyeat, M. (1990), *The Theaetetus of Plato* (Indianapolis, Ind.: Hackett).

Diels, H. (1879), *Doxographi Graeci* (Berlin: G. Reimer).

di Marco, M. (1989), *Timone di Fliunte: Silli* (Rome: Edizioni dell'Ateneo).

Döring, K. (1972), *Die Megariker: Kommentierte Sammlung der Testimonien* (Amsterdam: B. R. Grüner).

Giannantoni, G. (1990), *Socratis et Socraticorum Reliquiae* (4 vols.; Naples: Bibliopolis).

Giannini, A. (1966), *Paradoxographicorum Graecorum Reliquiae* (Milan: Istituto Editoriale Italiano).

Heiland, H. (1925), *Aristoclis Messenii reliquiae* (Giessen: O. Meyer).

Indelli, G. (1978), *Polistrato: Sul disprezzo irrazionale delle opinioni popolari*, edition with Italian translation and commentary (Naples: Bibliopolis).

Kahn, C. (1979), *The Art and Thought of Heraclitus*, an edition of the fragments with translation and commentary (Cambridge: Cambridge University Press).

Kidd, I. G. (1988–9), *Posidonius*, Fragments (2nd edn.) and Commentary (3 vols.; Cambridge: Cambridge University Press).

Lesher, J. (1992), *Xenophanes of Colophon: Fragments*, a Text and Translation with a Commentary (Toronto: University of Toronto Press).

Muller, R. (1985), *Les Mégariques: Fragments et témoignages* (Paris: Vrin).

Pellegrin, P. (1997), *Sextus Empiricus: Esquisses pyrrhoniennes*, Introduction, traduction et commentaires (Paris: Éditions du Seuil).

Ross, W. D. (1924), *Aristotle: Metaphysics*, a Revised Text with Introduction and Commentary (2 vols.; Oxford: Clarendon Press).

Rhys Davids, T. (1890), *The Questions of King Milinda*, translated (Max Muller (ed.), *Sacred Books of the East*, vol. 35; Oxford: Clarendon Press).

—— (1899). *Dialogues of the Buddha*, translated (Max Muller (ed.), *Sacred Books of the Buddhists*, vol. 2; London: H. Frowde).

Rhys Davids, T., and Rhys Davids, C. (1921), *Dialogues of the Buddha*, part 3, translated (T. Rhys Davids (ed.), *Sacred Books of the Buddhists*, vol. 4; Oxford: Clarendon Press).

Warren, H. C. (1896). *Buddhism in Translations* (Harvard Oriental Series, vol. 3; Cambridge, Mass.: Harvard University Press).

Waszink, J. (1947), *Quinti Septimi Florentis Tertulliani De Anima*, ed. with introduction and commentary (Amsterdam: J. M. Meullenhoff).

Wehrli, F. (1967–78), *Die Schule des Aristoteles: Texte und Kommentar* (2nd edn.; Basle/Stuttgart: Schwabe & Co.).

Woodruff, P. (1982), *Plato: Hippias Major*, Translation and Commentary (Indianapolis, Ind.: Hackett).

II. Secondary Literature

Annas, J. (1981), *An Introduction to Plato's* Republic (Oxford: Clarendon Press).

—— (1993), *The Morality of Happiness* (New York: Oxford University Press).

—— and Barnes, J. (1985), *The Modes of Scepticism* (Cambridge: Cambridge University Press).

Ausland, H. (1989), 'On the Moral Origin of the Pyrrhonian Philosophy', *Elenchos*, 10: 359–434.

Barnes, J. (1982a), 'The Beliefs of a Pyrrhonist', *Proceedings of the Cambridge Philological Society*, NS 28: 1–29. Reprinted in Burnyeat and Frede (1997: 58–91).

—— (1982b), *The Presocratic Philosophers* (rev. edn.; London: Routledge).

—— (1988), 'Bits and Pieces', in J. Barnes and M. Mignucci (eds.), *Matter and Metaphysics* (Naples: Bibliopolis), 225–94.

—— (1989), 'Antiochus of Ascalon', in M. Griffin and J. Barnes (eds.), *Philosophia Togata* (Oxford: Clarendon Press), 51–96.

—— (1992), 'Diogenes Laertius IX 61–116: The Philosophy of Pyrrhonism', *Aufstieg und Niedergang der Römischen Welt*, II.36.6: 4241–301.

—— (1996), Review of J. Brunschwig, *Papers in Hellenistic Philosophy*, in *Philosophical Review*, 105: 108–9.

Barua, B (1921) *A History of Pre-Buddhist Indian Philosophy* (Calcutta).

Berti, E. (1981). 'La critica allo scetticismo nel libro IV della "Metafisica" ', in G. Giannantoni (ed.), *Lo scetticismo antico* (Naples: Bibliopolis), 63–79.

Bett, R. (1989a), 'Carneades' Pithanon: A Reappraisal of its Role and Status', *Oxford Studies in Ancient Philosophy*, 7: 59–94.

—— (1989b), 'The Sophists and Relativism', *Phronesis*, 34: 139–69.

—— (1990), 'Carneades' Distinction between Assent and Approval', *The Monist*, 73: 3–20.

—— (1993), 'Scepticism and Everyday Attitudes in Ancient and Modern Philosophy', *Metaphilosophy*, 24: 363–81.

—— (1994a), 'Aristocles on Timon on Pyrrho: The Text, its Logic and its Credibility', *Oxford Studies in Ancient Philosophy*, 12: 137–81.

—— (1994b), 'Sextus' *Against the Ethicists*: Scepticism, Relativism or both?', *Apeiron*, 27: 123–61.

—— (1994c), 'What did Pyrrho Think about 'The Nature of the Divine and the Good'?', *Phronesis*, 39: 303–37.

—— (1996), 'Hellenistic Essays Translated', *Apeiron*, 29: 75–97.

Birke, O. (1897), *De particularum mē et ou usu Polybiano Dionysiaco Diodoreo Straboniano* (Leipzig: O. Schmidt).

Brancacci, A. (1981), 'La filosofia di Pirrone e le sue relazioni con il cinismo', in G. Giannantoni (ed.), *Lo scetticismo antico* (Naples: Bibliopolis), 213–42.

Brennan, T. (1994), 'Criterion and Appearance in Sextus Empiricus: The Scope of Sceptical Doubt, the Status of Sceptical Belief', *Bulletin of the Institute of Classical Studies*, 39: 151–69.

Brochard, V. (1923), *Les Sceptiques grecs* (2nd edn.; Paris: Vrin).

Brunschwig, J. (1984), 'Démocrite et Xéniade', in *Proceedings of the First International Congress on Democritus* (no editor) (Xanthi: International Democritus Foundation), ii. 109–24.

—— (1992), 'Pyrrhon et Philista', in M.-O. Goulet-Cazé, G. Madec, and D. O'Brien (eds.), *'Chercheurs de sagesse': Hommage à Jean Pépin* (Paris: Institut d'Études Augustiniennes), 133–46.

—— (1993), 'The Anaxarchus Case: An Essay on Survival', *Proceedings of the British Academy*, 82: 59–88.

—— (1994a), 'Once again on Eusebius on Aristocles on Timon on Pyrrho', in J. Brunschwig, *Papers in Hellenistic Philosophy* (Cambridge: Cambridge University Press), 190–211.

—— (1994b), 'The title of Timon's *Indalmoi*: From Odysseus to Pyrrho', in J. Brunschwig, *Papers in Hellenistic Philosophy* (Cambridge: Cambridge University Press), 212–23.

—— (1997), 'L'Aphasie pyrrhonienne', in C. Lévy and L. Pernot (eds.), *Dire l'évidence (philosophie et rhétorique antiques)* (Paris: L'Harmattan), 297–320.

Burkhard, U. (1973), *Die angebliche Heraklit-Nachfolge des Skeptikers Aenesidem* (Bonn: R. Habelt).

Burnyeat, M. (1976), 'Protagoras and Self-Refutation in Later Greek Philosophy', *Philosophical Review*, 85: 44–69.

—— (1980a), 'Can the Sceptic Live his Scepticism?', in M. Schofield, M. Burnyeat, and J. Barnes (eds.), *Doubt and Dogmatism* (Oxford: Clarendon Press), 20–53. Reprinted in Burnyeat and Frede (1997: 25–57).

—— (1980b), 'Tranquillity Without a Stop: Timon, Frag. 68', *Classical Quarterly*, NS 30: 86–93.

—— (1982), 'Idealism and Greek Philosophy: What Descartes Saw and Berkeley Missed', *Philosophical Review*, 91: 3–40.

—— and Frede, M. (1997), *The Original Sceptics* (Indianapolis, Ind.: Hackett).

Capone Braga, G. (1931), 'L'Eraclitismo di Enesidemo', *Rivista di Filosofia*, 22: 33–47.

Cherniss, H. (1936), 'The Philosophical Economy of the Theory of Ideas', *American Journal of Philology*, 57: 445–56.

—— (1957), 'The Relation of the *Timaeus* to Plato's Later Dialogues', *American Journal of Philology*, 78: 225–66.

Conche, M. (1994), *Pyrrhon ou l'apparence* (2nd edn.; Paris: Presses universitaires de France).

Cornford, F. M. (1935), *Plato's Theory of Knowledge* (London: Routledge).

Cortassa, G. (1977), Review of Burkhard (1973), in *Rivista di filologia e di istruzione classica*, ser. 3, 105: 64–70.

Crystal, I. (1996), 'Parmenidean Allusions in *Republic* V', *Ancient Philosophy*, 16: 351–63.

Curd, P. (1998), *The Legacy of Parmenides: Eleatic Monism and Later Presocratic Thought* (Princeton, NJ: Princeton University Press).

Dal Pra, M. (1989), *Lo scetticismo greco* (3rd edn.; Rome/Bari: Laterza).

Day, J. (1997), 'The Theory of Perception in Plato's *Theaetetus* 152–183', *Oxford Studies in Ancient Philosophy*, 15: 51–80.

Decleva Caizzi, F. (1980), '*Tuphos*: contributo alla storia di una concetto', *Sandalion*, 3: 53–66.

—— (1981), 'Prolegomeni ad una raccolta delle fonti relative a Pirrone di Elide', in G. Giannantoni (ed.), *Lo scetticismo antico* (Naples: Bibliopolis), 93–128.

—— (1984*a*), 'Démocrite, l'école d'Abdère et le premier pyrrhonisme', in *Proceedings of the First International Congress on Democritus* (no editor) (Xanthi: International Democritus Foundation), ii. 139–57. Translated into Italian as 'Pirrone e Democrito—gli atomi: un "mito"?', *Elenchos*, 5: 5–23.

—— (1984*b*), 'Timon di Fliunte: I frammenti 74, 75, 76 Diels', in *La storia della filosofia come sapere critico: Studi offerti a Mario Dal Pra* (no editor) (Milan: Franco Angeli Editore), 92–105.

—— (1986), 'Pirroniani ed Accademici nel III secolo A. C.', in H. Flashar and O. Gigon (eds.), *Aspects de la philosophie hellénistique* (Geneva: Fondation Hardt), xxxii. 147–83.

—— (1992*a*), 'Aenesidemus and the Academy', *Classical Quarterly*, 42: 176–89.

—— (1992*b*), 'Sesto e gli scettici', *Elenchos*, 13: 279–327.

—— (1995), 'Aenesidemus versus Pyrrho: Il fuoco scalda "per natura" (Sextus *M.* VIII 215 e XI 69)', in L. Ayres (ed.), *The Passionate Intellect: Essays on the Transformation of Classical Traditions* (Rutgers University Studies in Classical Humanities VII; New Brunswick, NJ: Transaction Publishers), 145–59. Reprinted in *Elenchos*, 17 (1996): 37–54.

DeLacy, P. (1958), '*Ou mallon* and the Antecedents of Ancient Scepticism', *Phronesis*, 3: 59–71.

—— (1991), 'Galen's Response to Skepticism', *Illinois Classical Studies*, 16: 283–306.

Denniston, J. D. (1950), *The Greek Particles* (2nd edn.; Oxford: Oxford University Press).

Denyer, N. (1991), *Language, Thought and Falsehood in Ancient Greek Philosophy* (London: Routledge).

Dorandi, T. (1991), *Ricerche sulla cronologia dei filosofi ellenistici* (Stuttgart: Teubner).

Farrar, C. (1988), *The Origins of Democratic Thinking: The Invention of Politics in Classical Athens* (Cambridge: Cambridge University Press).

Ferrari, G. (1968), 'Due fonti sullo scetticismo antico', *Studi Italiani di filologia classica*, 40: 200–24.

—— (1981), 'L'immagine dell'equilibrio', in G. Giannantoni (ed.), *Lo scetticismo antico* (Naples: Bibliopolis), 339–70.

Fine, G. (1990), 'Knowledge and Belief in *Republic* V–VII', in S. Everson (ed.), *Epistemology* (Cambridge: Cambridge University Press), 85–115.

—— (1993), *On Ideas: Aristotle's Criticism of Plato's Theory of Forms* (Oxford: Clarendon Press).

—— (1994), 'Protagorean Relativisms', *Proceedings of the Boston Area Colloquium in Ancient Philosophy*, 10: 211–43.

—— (1996), 'Conflicting Appearances', in C. Gill and M. McCabe (eds.), *Form and Argument in Late Plato* (Oxford: Clarendon Press), 105–33.

Flintoff, E. (1980), 'Pyrrho and India', *Phronesis*, 25: 88–108.

Frede, M. (1973), Review of Stough (1969), in *Journal of Philosophy*, 70: 805–10.

—— (1979), 'Des Skeptikers Meinungen', *Neue Hefte für Philosophie*, 15/16: 102–29. Translated as 'The Skeptic's Beliefs', in M. Frede, *Essays in Ancient Philosophy* (Minneapolis: University of Minnesota Press, 1987), 179–200. English version reprinted in Burnyeat and Frede (1997: 1–24).

Frenkian, A. (1957), 'Sextus Empiricus and Indian Logic', *Philosophical Quarterly* (India), 30: 115–26.

—— (1958), 'Der griechische Skeptizismus und die indische Philosophie', *Bibliotheca Classica Orientalis*, 4: 211–50.

Furley, D. (1993), 'Democritus and Epicurus on Sensible Qualities', in J. Brunschwig and M. Nussbaum (eds.), *Passions and Perceptions: Studies in Hellenistic Philosophy of Mind* (Cambridge: Cambridge University Press), 72–94.

Giannantoni, G. (1981), 'Pirrone, la scuola scettica e il sistema delle "successioni" ', in G. Giannantoni (ed.), *Lo scetticismo antico* (Naples: Bibliopolis), 13–34.

Gildersleeve, B. (1880), 'Encroachments of *mē* on *ou* in Later Greek', *American Journal of Philology*, 1: 45–57.

Gill, M. L. (1987), 'Matter and Flux in Plato's *Timaeus*', *Phronesis*, 32: 34–53.

Glidden, D. (1996), 'Philo of Larissa and Platonism', in R. Popkin (ed.), *Scepticism in the History of Philosophy: A Pan-American Dialogue* (Dordrecht: Kluwer), 219–34.

Glucker, J. (1978), *Antiochus and the Late Academy* (Göttingen: Vandenhoeck & Ruprecht).

Görler, W. (1994), 'Älterer Pyrrhonismus. Jüngere Akademie. Antiochos aus Askalon', in H. Flashar (ed.), *Die Philosophie der Antike*, iv. *Die Hellenistische Philosophie* (Basle: Schwabe & Co.), 719–989.

Görannson, T. (1995), *Albinus, Alcinous, Arius Didymus* (Göteborg: Ekblads, Västervik).

Graham, D. (1997), 'Heraclitus' Criticism of Ionian Philosophy', *Oxford Studies in Ancient Philosophy*, 15: 1–50.

Green, E. (1902), '*Mē* for *ou* before Lucian', in *Studies in Honor of Basil L. Gildersleeve* (no editor) (Baltimore: Johns Hopkins University Press), 471–9.

Guthrie, W. (1971), *The Sophists* (Cambridge: Cambridge University Press).

Hadot, P. (1995), *Qu'est-ce que la philosophie antique?* (Paris: Gallimard).

Hankinson, R. J. (1995), *The Sceptics* (London: Routledge).

—— (1997), 'Natural Criteria and the Transparency of Judgement: Antiochus, Philo and Galen on Epistemological Justification', in B. Inwood and J. Mansfeld (eds.), *Assent and Argument: Studies in Cicero's Academic Books* (Leiden: Brill), 161–216.

House, D. (1980), 'The Life of Sextus Empiricus', *Classical Quarterly*, 30: 227–38.

Ioppolo, A. M. (1980a), 'Anassarco e il cinismo', in F. Romano (ed.), *Democrito e l'atomismo antico* (Catania: Università di Catania).

—— (1980b), *Aristone di Chio e lo stoicismo antico* (Naples: Bibliopolis).

—— (1995), 'Socrate nelle tradizioni Accademico-scettica e pirroniana', in *La tradizione socratica* (no editor) (Naples: Bibliopolis), 89–123.

Irwin, T. (1977), 'Plato's Heracliteanism', *Philosophical Quarterly*, 27: 1–13.

—— (1988), *Aristotle's First Principles* (Oxford: Clarendon Press).

Janáček, K. (1972), *Sextus Empiricus' Sceptical Methods* (Prague: Universita Karlova)

—— (1976), 'Zur Interpretation des Photios-Abschnittes über Aenesidemos', *Eirene*, 14: 93–100.

—— (1977), Review of Burkhard (1973), in *Gnomon*, 49: 676–81.

Jannaris, A. (1897), *An Historical Greek Grammar* (London: MacMillan).

Jayatilleke, K. (1963), *Early Buddhist Theory of Knowledge* (London: Allen & Unwin).

Kerferd, G. (1981), *The Sophistic Movement* (Cambridge: Cambridge University Press).

Kirk, G., Raven, J., and Schofield, M. (1983), *The Presocratic Philosophers* (2nd edn.; Cambridge: Cambridge University Press).

Lesher, J. (1978), 'Xenophanes' Scepticism', *Phronesis*, 23: 1–21.

Lévy, C. (1992), *Cicero Academicus: recherches sur les Académiques et sur la philosophie cicéronienne* (Rome: École française de Rome).

—— (1997), 'Lucrèce avait-il lu Enésidème?', in K. Algra, M. Koenen, and P. Schrijvers (eds.), *Lucretius and his Intellectual Background* (Amsterdam: Publications of the Royal Netherlands Academy of Arts), 115–24.

Long, A. A. (1978), 'Timon of Phlius: Pyrrhonist and Satirist', *Proceedings of the Cambridge Philological Society*, NS 24: 68–91.

—— (1981), 'Aristotle and the History of Greek Scepticism', in D. O'Meara (ed.), *Studies in Aristotle* (Washington: Catholic University of America Press), 79–106.

—— (1986), *Hellenistic Philosophy* (2nd edn.; Berkeley and Los Angeles: University of California Press).

—— (1988), 'Socrates in Hellenistic Philosophy', *Classical Quarterly*, 38: 150–71.

Luibhéid, C. (1995), Review of Conche (1994), in *Classical Review*, NS 45: 293–5.

McKirahan, R. (1994), *Philosophy before Socrates* (Indianapolis, Ind.: Hackett).

Maier, H. (1900), *Die Syllogistik des Aristoteles* (2 vols.; Tübingen: Laupp).

Makin, S. (1993), *Indifference Arguments* (Oxford: Blackwell).

Mansfeld, J. (1987), 'Theophrastus and the Xenophanes Doxography', *Mnemosyne*, 40: 286–312.

—— (1995), 'Aenesidemus and the Academics', in L. Ayres (ed.), *The Passionate Intellect: Essays on the Transformation of Classical Traditions* (Rutgers University Studies in Classical Humanities, 7; New Brunswick, NJ: Transaction Publishers), 235–48.

Moraux, P. (1984), *Der Aristotelismus bei den Griechen*, ii (Berlin/New York: Walter de Gruyter).

Muller, R. (1988), *Introduction à la pensée des Mégariques* (Paris: Vrin).

Murti, T. (1955), *The Central Philosophy of Buddhism* (London: Allen & Unwin).

Organ, T. (1975), *Western Approaches to Eastern Philosophy* (Athens, Oh.: Ohio University Press).

Owen, G. (1953), 'The Place of the *Timaeus* in Plato's Dialogues', *Classical Quarterly*, 3: 79–95.

Patrick, M. M. (1929), *The Greek Sceptics* (New York: Columbia University Press).

Piantelli, M. (1978), 'Possibili elementi Indiani nella formazione del pensiero di Pirrone d'Elide', *Filosofia*, 29: 135–64.

Reale, G. (1981), 'Ipotesi per una rilettura della filosofia di Pirrone di Elide', in G. Giannantoni (ed.), *Lo scetticismo antico* (Naples: Bibliopolis), 245–336.

Rist, J. (1970), 'The Heracliteanism of Aenesidemus', *Phoenix*, 24: 309–19.

Sakezles, P. (1993), 'Pyrrhonian Indeterminacy: A Pragmatic Interpretation', *Apeiron*, 26: 77–95.

Salem, J. (1996), *Démocrite: Grains de poussière dans un rayon de soleil* (Paris: Vrin).

Schwyzer, E. (1950), *Griechische Grammatik*, ii, ed. Albert Debrunner (Munich: C. H. Beck.)

Sedley, D. (1977), 'Diodorus Cronus and Hellenistic Philosophy', *Proceedings of the Cambridge Philological Society*, 23: 74–120.

—— (1981), 'The End of the Academy', *Phronesis*, 26: 67–75.

—— (1983*a*), 'The Motivation of Greek Skepticism', in M. Burnyeat (ed.), *The Skeptical Tradition* (Berkeley and Los Angeles: University of California Press), 9–29.

—— (1983*b*), Review of Indelli (1978), in *Classical Review*, 33: 335–6.

—— (1992), 'Sextus Empiricus and the Atomist Criteria of Truth', *Elenchos*, 13: 21–56.

—— (1997), 'Plato's *Auctoritas* and the Rebirth of the Commentary Tradition', in J. Barnes and M. Griffin (eds.), *Philosophia Togata II* (Oxford: Clarendon Press), 110–29.

Sharples, R. (1996), *Stoics, Epicureans and Sceptics: An Introduction to Hellenistic Philosophy* (London: Routledge).

Smart, N. (1967*a*), 'Buddhism', in P. Edwards (ed.), *The Encyclopedia of Philosophy* (8 vols.; New York: MacMillan), i. 416–20.

—— (1967*b*), 'Indian Philosophy', in P. Edwards (ed.), *The Encyclopedia of Philosophy* (8 vols.; New York: MacMillan), iv. 155–69.

Smyth, H. (1956), *Greek Grammar,* rev. G. Messing (Cambridge, Mass.: Harvard University Press.)

Spinelli, E. (1997), 'La corporeità del tempo. Ancora su Enesidemo e il suo eraclitismo', in G. Casertano (ed.), *Il concetto di tempo* (Naples: Loffredo), 159–71.

—— (2000), 'Sextus Empiricus, the Neighboring Philosophies and the Sceptical Tradition (again on *PH* I 220–225)', in J. Sihvola (ed.), *Ancient Skepticism and the Skeptical Tradition*: *Acta Philosophica Fennica*, 64.

Stoneman, R. (1994), 'Who are the Brahmans? Indian Lore and Cynic Doctrines in Palladius' *De Bragmanibus* and its Models', *Classical Quarterly*, 44: 500–10.

—— (1995), 'Naked Philosophers: The Brahmans in the Alexander Historians and the Alexander Romance', *Journal of Hellenic Studies*, 115: 99–114.

Stopper, M. R. (1983), 'Schizzi Pirroniani', *Phronesis*, 28. 265–97.

Stough, C. (1969), *Greek Skepticism* (Berkeley and Los Angeles: University of California Press).

Striker, G. (1974), '*Kritērion tēs alētheias*', *Nachrichten der Akademie der Wissenshcaften zu Göttingen*, I. Phil.-hist. Klasse, 2: 49–110. In English translation in G. Striker, *Essays on Hellenistic Epistemology and Ethics* (Cambridge: Cambridge University Press, 1996), 22–76.

—— (1983), 'The Ten Tropes of Aenesidemus', in M. Burnyeat (ed.), *The Skeptical Tradition* (Berkeley and Los Angeles: University of California Press), 95–115.

—— (1990), 'The Problem of the Criterion', in S. Everson (ed.), *Epistemology* (Cambridge: Cambridge University Press), 143–60.

—— (1991), 'Following Nature: A Study in Stoic Ethics', *Oxford Studies in Ancient Philosophy*, 9: 1–73.

—— (1996), 'Methods of Sophistry', in G. Striker, *Essays on Hellenistic Epistemology and Ethics* (Cambridge: Cambridge University Press), 3–21.

—— (1997), 'Academics Fighting Academics', in B. Inwood and J. Mansfeld (eds.), *Assent and Argument: Studies in Cicero's Academic Books* (Leiden: Brill), 257–76.

Tarn, W. (1985), *The Greeks in Bactria and India* (3rd edn., ed. F. L. Holt), (Chicago: Ares).

Tarrant, H. (1983), 'The Date of the Anon. *In Theaetetum*', *Classical Quarterly*, 33: 161–87.

—— (1985), *Scepticism or Platonism? The Philosophy of the Fourth Academy* (Cambridge: Cambridge University Press).

Taylor, C. C. W. (1990), 'Aristotle's Epistemology', in S. Everson (ed.), *Epistemology* (Cambridge: Cambridge University Press), 116–42.

Vasiliou, I. (1996), 'Perception, Knowledge, and the Sceptic in Aristotle', *Oxford Studies in Ancient Philosophy*, 14: 83–131.

Viano, C. (1989), ' "*Ainēsidēmos kata ton Hērakleiton*": Les Phénomènes et le *koinos*', in K. J. Boudouris (ed.), *Ionian Philosophy* (Athens: Kardamitsa Pub. Co.), 403–11.

von Arnim, H. (1888), *Quellenstudien zu Philo von Alexandria*, vol. xi of A. Kiessling and U. von Wilamowitz-Moellendorff (eds.), *Philologische Untersuchungen* (Berlin: Weidmann).

von Fritz, K. (1963), 'Pyrrhon', in *Paulys Realencyclopädie der Classischen Altertumswissenschaft*, xxiv (Stuttgart: A. Druckenmüller), 89–106.

Wilamowitz-Moellendorff, U. von (1881), *Antigonos von Karystos*, vol. iv of A. Kiessling and U. von Wilamowitz-Moellendorff (eds.), *Philologische Untersuchungen* (Berlin: Weidmann).

White, N. (1976), *Plato on Knowledge and Reality* (Indianapolis, Ind.: Hackett).

Woodruff, P. (1988), 'Aporetic Pyrrhonism', *Oxford Studies in Ancient Philosophy*, 6: 139–68.

Zeller, E. (1903), *Die Philosophie der Griechen in ihrer geschichtlichen Entwicklung*, pt. 3, vol. 2 (4th edn.) (Leipzig: O. R. Reisland).

—— (1909), *Die Philosophie der Griechen in ihrer geschichtlichen Entwicklung*, pt. 3, vol. 1 (4th edn., ed. E. Wellmann) (Leipzig: O. R. Reisland).

INDEX OF NAMES

INDEX LOCORUM

SUBJECT INDEX